COLLECTOR'S VALUE GUIDE™

by ENESCO

Secondary Market Price Guide & Collector Handbook

SECOND EDITION

by ENESCO

This publication is *not* affiliated with PRECIOUS MOMENTS, Inc., Enesco Corporation or any of their affiliates, subsidiaries, distributors or representatives. Any opinions expressed are solely those of the authors, and do not necessarily reflect those of PRECIOUS MOMENTS, Inc. or Enesco Corporation. The market values listed in this guide are based on compilations of current market trends, but the publisher assumes no liability or responsibility for any loss incurred by users of this guide due to variable market conditions. All PRECIOUS MOMENTS artwork is the copyrighted property of PRECIOUS MOMENTS, Inc. "PRECIOUS MOMENTS®" is a registered trademark of PRECIOUS MOMENTS, Inc. Licensee, CheckerBee, Inc.
All Rights Reserved Worldwide.

Managing Editor:	Jeff Mahony	Creative Director:	Joe T. Nguyen
Associate Editors:	Melissa A. Bennett	Production Supervisor:	Scott Sierakowski
	Jan Cronan	Senior Graphic Designers:	Lance Doyle
	Gia C. Manalio		Carole Mattia-Slater
	Paula Stuckart		Leanne Peters
Contributing Editor:	Mike Micciulla	Graphic Designers:	Jennifer J. Denis
Editorial Assistants:	Jennifer Filipek		Sean-Ryan Dudley
	Nicole LeGard Lenderking		Peter Dunbar
	Christina Levere		Kimberly Eastman
	Joan C. Wheal		Ryan Falis
Research Assistants:	Timothy R. Affleck		Jason Jasch
	Priscilla Berthiaume		David S. Maloney
	Heather N. Carreiro		David Ten Eyck
	Beth Hackett	Art Interns:	Janice Evert
	Victoria Puorro		Joycelyn R. Parente
	Steven Shinkaruk		
Web Reporters:	Samantha Bouffard		
	Ren Messina		

ISBN 1-888914-44-0

CheckerBee
PUBLISHING

(formerly Collectors' Publishing)
306 Industrial Park Road • Middletown, CT 06457

TABLE OF CONTENTS

*D*ear Collectors,

It's hard to believe that 21 years ago the PRECIOUS MOMENTS collection began. I consider myself privileged to be involved in such a wonderful endeavor with special people like you. PRECIOUS MOMENTS® has been one of the most important and meaningful parts  of my life and I treasure the friendships that I have made with PRECIOUS MOMENTS collectors and club members since the introduction of the collection in 1978.

It has also been an added pleasure to work with two of the most talented and inspired people I know, artist Sam Butcher and master sculptor Yasuhei Fujioka. Together they have created a collection, capturing those special moments in our lives from birthdays to weddings, friendship to love.

Twenty years of loving, caring and sharing seems to have gone by so fast, but I firmly believe that we never could have made it this far without your generous support and friendship. You have made PRECIOUS MOMENTS the phenomenon it is today. PRECIOUS MOMENTS is not only a collection of figurines, but also a way of life.

Thank you, valued collectors, for your continued support of the PRECIOUS MOMENTS collection. It's been an unforgettable 20 years and, as we head into the next 20 years together, I am completely confident that the best is yet to come.

God Bless,

Eugene Freedman
Founding Chairman
Enesco Corporation

*W*elcome to the 1999 edition of the Collector's Value Guide™ to PRECIOUS MOMENTS® featuring the inspirational figurines that are known to spread artist Sam Butcher's message of "loving, caring and sharing." Since its origination over 20 years ago, the PRECIOUS MOMENTS line has grown enormously, and so have the values of each piece. That's why our Collector's Value Guide™ is so useful. It offers the most up-to-date information about the PRECIOUS MOMENTS line, including the current worth of more than 1,500 pieces. You'll also read interesting facts about how the PRECIOUS MOMENTS line began, biographies about the artist and sculptor of these heartwarming teardrop-eyed figurines and descriptions of every piece introduced in 1999.

Within the Value Guide itself, you'll find color pictures of every piece, along with its name, stock number and status (current, suspended or retried). Original and current retail prices are also given, as well as the secondary market value for each production mark of each piece.

There are a lot of new sections in the guide this year, including a special "Year In Review," looking back at the happenings of 1998, the year that coincided with the PRECIOUS MOMENTS 20th Anniversary celebration. You can also learn about the interesting stories and experiences that led to the names of some of the pieces, as well as find out about The PRECIOUS MOMENTS Chapel built by artist Sam Butcher.

This comprehensive 1999 edition is the most convenient way for you, the collector, to keep track of your PRECIOUS MOMENTS collection, as well as learn about one of the most loved collectible lines in the industry today.

*T*he words "loving, caring and sharing" have kept Sam Butcher going throughout his life. In 1978, those words were translated into a new and innovative line of inspirational figurines, and now, 20 years later, they continue to keep the PRECIOUS MOMENTS line alive.

Born in 1939, Butcher loved to draw and as a schoolboy, he dreamt of becoming a professor of fine arts. But the choices he made and the paths he took throughout his earlier years led elsewhere. His religious faith was very strong and deep, and it was through this faith that the PRECIOUS MOMENTS collection was born. In 1975, Butcher began a greeting card business with Bill Biel, a man who almost immediately became one of Sam's closest friends. Together, the two formed "Jonathan And David," a company which would go on to produce greeting cards and posters with pictures of teardrop-eyed children with the best intentions of sending messages of comfort and guidance. At one point, the two men were invited to attend a Christian booksellers convention in California and it was for this convention that they decided on a name for the line: PRECIOUS MOMENTS.

It was in 1978, as a result of another gift show in Los Angeles, California, that Sam Butcher's life took an unforeseen turn. Eugene Freedman, then CEO and Chairman of Enesco Corporation, noticed the artist's cards and immediately saw their potential. But when he approached Butcher about the idea of turning his pictures into porcelain figurines, the artist did not share the sentiment, feeling that his message would not translate well into a line of collectibles. Nonetheless, Freedman took one of the cards to longtime friend and sculptor, Yasuhei Fujioka, and asked him to create a three-dimensional porcelain figurine from the drawing. When the piece now known as "Love One Another" was presented to Butcher, he began to weep, overcome by how his inspirational idea had been so perfectly represented and recreated in porcelain.

Twenty-one figurines made their debut at a trade show in Chicago in the Fall of that same year. Now, more than 20 years later, Sam Butcher, Yasuhei Fujioka and Eugene Freedman still draw, sculpt and produce these "little messengers" of love and hope, making the PRECIOUS MOMENTS line one of the most popular collectibles ever.

Over the years, the PRECIOUS MOMENTS collection has grown to include music boxes, ornaments, bells, plates, hinged boxes . . . even night lights! Founded in 1958, Enesco, based in Itasca, Illinois, has become one of the leading producers of fine collectibles, with a product line made up of more than 12,000 giftware, collectible and home accent items. To date, Enesco Corporation has produced over 1,700 PRECIOUS MOMENTS pieces – efforts that have been noticed and appreciated by more than just collectors. Enesco has won several awards for the PRECIOUS MOMENTS line, including The National Association of Limited Edition Dealers' (NALED) "Collectible Of The Year" in 1992 and the "Figurine Of The Year" in 1994. The company was also honored with the "Ornament Of The Year" in 1994, 1995 and 1996.

Not only is Enesco committed to its customers and to the production of fine products, but also to community affairs. In 1987, the company became a national corporate sponsor of Easter Seals. Each year, two special limited edition figurines are designed – one is the same size as the regular figurines, the second is a special 9-inch version. The company sponsors several other organizations as well, including the Boys And Girls Clubs Of America, St. Jude's Children's Research Hospital and C.A.U.S.E.S., an organization which supports the prevention of child abuse.

PRECIOUS MOMENTS® OVERVIEW

To further add to the excitement of the line, Enesco issues several types of special pieces each year. Limited edition pieces are limited to one year of production or by a specific quantity of pieces. Annuals are available for one year only and are noted as "Dated," as they are marked with the year in which they are available. Both limited and dated pieces are considered "closed" after their production run is complete. General pieces taken out of production are either retired, meaning they will never be produced again, or they are "suspended," leaving the door open for reintroduction at a later date.

In an effort to keep up with collector demand, Enesco is constantly creating new pieces and series, as well as adding on to existing series. LITTLE MOMENTS, a line of smaller versions of the teardrop-eyed figurines, joined the PRECIOUS MOMENTS family in 1996. In 1999, four series made a big hit among these "little" pieces. In 1998, collectors got to take a walk down COUNTRY LANE, a collection featuring a line of figurines based on Butcher's memories of his time spent on his Grandma Ethel's farm. TENDER TAILS, a collection of plush beanbags, was introduced in 1997 and in 1999, three series were introduced among the critters. Also in 1999, The *Four Seasons* series debuted in the general line.

Through the years, Sam Butcher's faith left him wanting to do more for others. In 1984, he began building The PRECIOUS MOMENTS Chapel, hoping to offer a place of worship, comfort and peace. One of the most intriguing parts of The Chapel is Butcher's hand-painted mural

ENESCO AND EASTER SEALS!

In 1987 an association between Enesco Corporation and the Easter Seals Society was formed that would impact the charity organization in ways that no one ever imagined. As a corporate sponsor, Enesco and its far-reaching society of collectors has raised over $28 million. While the money (including proceeds from the three yearly Easter Seals PRECIOUS MOMENTS Commemorative pieces) has had tremendous impact on the organization, so has the time devoted to various fund-raisers by collectors. On numerous occasions, Enesco has been the number one national corporate sponsor. Eugene Freedman says, "We are blessed to have such caring members of the Enesco extended family who made this contribution happen." With a strong network of local clubs, retailers, collectors, vendors and employees; you can be sure that the Enesco and Easter Seals partnership will only grow stronger in the new millennium.

that covers more than 1,400 square feet of the ceiling, featuring images of PRECIOUS MOMENTS art.

Over the years, Sam Butcher has added to The Chapel Complex and the work is still not complete. It now stretches over more than 1,500 acres and includes a wedding chapel, a honeymoon suite, several restaurants and gift shops and a 40-acre lake with seven islands. One of the main attractions at The Chapel is the Fountain Of Angels™. The Chapel itself also houses a gallery full of Butcher's artwork such as cards created during his "Jonathan And David" days, as well as every PRECIOUS MOMENTS figurine produced.

In 1981, collectors were given a new and exciting way to share their love of the PRECIOUS MOMENTS designs . . . a collectors' club. Five-thousand PRECIOUS MOMENTS collectors joined the club in the first six weeks, with nearly 70,000 joining by the end of the year. Members of the Enesco PRECIOUS MOMENTS *Collectors' Club* receive the "GOODNEWSLET-TER" publication to keep them up-to-date on all the PRECIOUS MOMENTS news, such as events, releases and retirements. Those who join also have the opportunity to purchase gifts only available to members. Enesco introduced the Enesco PRECIOUS MOMENTS *Birthday Club*® in 1985, but replaced it at the end of 1998 with another new and exciting way to bring collectors together. The PRECIOUS MOMENTS *Fun Club*ˢᴹ is intended to reach out to families to help them enjoy collecting together. Many PRECIOUS MOMENTS fans are members of local clubs too, allowing them the chance to gather with other collectors.

A big accomplishment for the PRECIOUS MOMENTS line came just last year when the inspirational collection celebrated its 20th anniversary. And through the 20 years, the success of the line has increased ten fold. This celebratory year was full of festivities from special events to a Care-A-Van, or traveling museum, that trekked across the United States, offering limited pieces and lots of fun PRECIOUS MOMENTS products. The trip was such a success that the Care-A-Van will continue travelling through 1999.

Since 1981, pieces have been stamped with production marks to indicate the year the particular figurine was made. How do the marks work? A single piece that's been available for seven years will have seven different marks, one for each year it was produced. Pieces produced prior to 1981 are considered "no marks," while those whose mark was unintentionally left off are considered "unmarked." As the year mark indicates the age of the piece, secondary market value tends to be based on these symbols, with the earliest of the marks commanding a higher value.

Each PRECIOUS MOMENTS figurine begins its existence on Sam Butcher's sketch pad. It then makes its way to the Orient where a mold is made by Master Sculptor Yasuhei Fujioka. After being completely assembled, each piece is individually hand-painted. Though quality control is high, sometimes mistakes are made, leading to variations. A variation occurs when an aspect of a piece differs from what is considered the "standard," such as with a color or phrase on either the actual piece or its understamp. Sometimes these "errors" are considered treasures by collectors, often causing the piece to jump in value on the secondary market.

When Sam Butcher first began creating his PRECIOUS MOMENTS characters, he was looking to offer comfort and love to others. And his following and the popularity of the PRECIOUS MOMENTS line are testimony to the success of his mission.

*C*urrently based in Itasca, Illinois, the Enesco Corporation began in 1958 as a division of the N. Shure Company. Originally conceived to handle the company's gift imports, Enesco's unique name comes from the phonetic pronunciation of its parent company's initials. Since Enesco disbanded from the N. Shure Company, it has grown to become a foremost leader in the giftware and collectible industry. The production of the first PRECIOUS MOMENTS figurines in 1978 has been sited as a reason for the company's quick national growth and, after being bought by Stanhome, Inc. in 1983, Enesco went international.

Eugene Freedman, Enesco's Founding Chairman, is still active in the life of Enesco, and is responsible for many of the collectible industry's standard practices, including the use of store events to help fuel collector interest. In recent years, the company has expanded to over 18 worldwide locations and now distributes to more than 30 countries. In addition to the PRECIOUS MOMENTS collection, Enesco also produces other fine collectibles, including Cherished Teddies®, Mary's Moo Moos, David Winter Cottages® and Lilliput Lane®.

As demand for PRECIOUS MOMENTS products grew, the Butcher family soon realized the need for a way to ensure that only the finest quality products were put on the market. PRECIOUS MOMENTS, Inc. was founded in 1991 and is used to oversee the distribution of licenses to manufacturers who wish to use the PRECIOUS MOMENTS images. Today, PRECIOUS MOMENTS, Inc., commonly known as PMI, is run by Sam Butcher's eldest son Jon and is based in St. Charles, Illinois. Along with its library of over 3,500 images, PRECIOUS MOMENTS, Inc. also has a full-service creative department and provides research and development services for the wide variety of companies that are licensees.

*E*ugene Freedman, Founding Chairman of Enesco, has headed the company since 1958. He has been actively involved with the giftware and collectibles industry for over 45 years.

Although born in Philadelphia, Freedman spent most of his childhood in Milwaukee. Upon graduation from high school, he went on to attend Northwestern University and the California Institute of Technology. During World War II, Freedman served in the South Pacific and, upon his return, received his naval officer's commission at Notre Dame University.

In the early 1950's, Freedman returned to Milwaukee, where he accepted a job as a salesman for a gift and novelty company. Although he enjoyed his job, he was an entrepreneur at heart, and in 1958, Freedman left to open his own plastics and decorative figurine production business. Soon after, he sold his share in order to pursue other ventures.

The adventure he was looking for came by means of Enesco, a newly formed branch of the N. Shure Company, which specialized in importing. Freedman and six men pooled their money to buy the branch, and Freedman was placed in charge of buying giftware from Europe and the Orient. Some twenty years later, on layover for a flight, Mr. Freedman stumbled upon a notable discovery: Sam Butcher's tear-drop eyed children.

Freedman says he is proud to be a part of the PRECIOUS MOMENTS commitment to "loving, caring and sharing." He expects that the next 20 years will bring new and exciting developments, as well as continued hope, joy and happiness to collectors everywhere.

*N*ow known as the owner of the "magical hands" behind each and every piece from the PRECIOUS MOMENTS collection, Yasuhei Fujioka, Enesco's Master Sculptor, was born to become an artist. Fujioka was born in 1921 and grew up in Nagoya, Japan. His family was full of artisans and he quickly grew to appreciate their love of their

craft. In high school, Fujioka became a design major and, upon his graduation, he continued his studies in advanced ceramics. In 1955, after a ten year career in the industry, Fujioka opened his own Design Studio where he has worked ever since.

It was 1960 when Fujioka first came into contact with Eugene Freedman, then CEO of Enesco Corporation, and the two immediately became friends as well as business associates. However, it was nearly 20 years later that their relationship would be cemented by a life changing event. In 1978, upon seeing Sam Butcher's artwork for the first time, Freedman immediately turned to the sculptor to help him convince Butcher to work with Enesco. Knowing that his friend could "breathe life" into the two dimensional art, Freedman asked Fujioka to sculpt the first PRECIOUS MOMENTS prototype.

Soon after, The PRECIOUS MOMENTS Collection debuted with Fujioka at the helm as master sculptor, a position he has held ever since. In recent years, Fujioka has added the creation of Enesco's Coral Kingdom and Heavenly Kingdom lines to his credits. Although he retired as president of the design studio in 1995, handing the title over to his son, Shuhei Fujioka, Yasuhei Fujioka still oversees the studio's 10 to 15 artisans; ensuring that each piece is still crafted with much love and care.

*T*he name Sam Butcher has become one of the most well-known names in the collectibles industry as his creations have become the embodiment of love and good-will in the minds of countless people.  Butcher is recognized wherever he goes, and is welcomed with open arms by collectors who share his vision of hope and salvation. But life was not always easy for the artist of the PRECIOUS MOMENTS figurines.

Born on New Year's Day in 1939 in Jackson, Michigan, Sam Butcher was the third of five children born to an English-Irish mechanic and his young Lebanese-Syrian wife. While the rest of the family was interested in race-car driving, Butcher's passion lay elsewhere: in the art world. This clash of interests left Butcher somewhat isolated from his family, and he often used local garbage dumps as a refuge for his loneliness, finding rolls of paper and other materials to draw on to pass the time. Because he was thought of as different from his family, Butcher turned to the stories he created and the pictures he designed for companionship.

Butcher knew he wanted to be an artist by the time he reached kindergarten. Even at such a young age, Butcher's talent far surpassed the stick figure drawings of his classmates. When Butcher was ten, his family moved to northern California. Although the school was 60 miles away from his home, Butcher attended faithfully and continued to pursue his artwork, despite his father's advice to pursue other fields. But there was no denying this young boy's talent and many of his teachers offered plenty of encouragement. Butcher's hard work paid off in 1957 when he received a scholarship to the College Of Arts And Crafts in Berkeley, California.

SAM BUTCHER BIOGRAPHY

In 1962, Butcher left school in search of full-time work so he could better support his new wife, Katie and their first child, Jon. He accepted a variety of jobs, including working as a short order cook and a dishwasher. One year later, he began attending a local church and as his love of God and study of The Bible became stronger, he accepted a job as a "chalkboard minister," using illustrations to teach children about The Lord. He also saw his drawings as a way to reach adults in the church who had gone through a difficult time, as well as those who felt lost.

Through his friends in the church, Butcher became in contact with the International Child Evangelism Fellowship who offered him a job as a staff artist. His job was very rewarding and provided him the opportunity to showcase his art in a variety of mediums, including the weekly children's show. After 10 years with the fellowship, Butcher and his friend Bill Biel began their own company which designed and sold inspirational greeting cards. They named the company "Jonathan and David" after the Biblical friendship of David and Prince Jonathan. During this time, Butcher's family had grown to seven children and was struggling financially, so he continued to supplement his income with janitorial work. Biel was a good friend, though, and encouraged Butcher to keep drawing through the tough times.

CALLING DR. BUTCHER . . .

That's right! In 1997, PRECIOUS MOMENTS creator Sam Butcher got to add "PhD" after his name. Mr. Butcher was awarded an Honorary Doctorate Degree in Humane Letters from Oral Roberts University on May 3, 1997. In response to receiving the honor, Sam was quoted as saying, "Dr. Butcher . . . Isn't that scary?"

In 1978, Eugene Freedman, the president and chief executive officer of Enesco, spotted Butcher's work on the greeting cards at a Los Angeles trade show and approached him about creating a figurine line. Butcher was hesitant at first because he feared commercialization of the line would take away from its meaning. However, after seeing a rendition of his work created by Freedman's friend, master sculptor Yasuhei Fujioka, Butcher fell to his knees with joy. Realizing that the figurine could convey the same heartfelt message his drawings did, he agreed to license his art to Enesco, and the "Original 21" PRECIOUS MOMENTS characters were born.

Since the release of the first 21 pieces, Butcher has been honored with numerous awards over the years, including being named as the National Association Of Limited Edition Dealers' "Artist of the Year" in both 1992 and 1995. In addition, Jackson, Michigan recently declared June 17, 1998 to be "Sam Butcher Day" in honor of the artist.

Despite his commercial success, Butcher considers himself first and foremost a dedicated father to his children. The artist feels blessed by the love he receives from his family, as well as from the millions of collectors around the world who love to share their personal stories with him of how PRECIOUS MOMENTS designs have affected their lives.

Collectors take great solace in the messages of love and hope that these figurines engender as these pieces have, in fact, performed as messengers, helping many people convey their personal sentiments to others. It is the hope of collectors that Butcher will continue to create for years to come and to deliver the message of "loving, caring and sharing" they have come to love.

*W*hen Sam Butcher began designing PRECIOUS MOMENTS artwork, he was looking to create a reminder of how sweet life can be. He has known since he was a child that he wanted to be artist but what he didn't know was that his love for drawing would lead him to the Lord and eventually to create the inspiring collection. CheckerBee Publishing is honored that Mr. Butcher took time out of his busy schedule to answer some questions about his life, his work and his love of the PRECIOUS MOMENTS collection.

CheckerBee Publishing: Congratulations on the recent 20th Anniversary of PRECIOUS MOMENTS. Can you tell us how it feels to reach this milestone?

Sam Butcher: I believe that everyone has a desire to give something back to the world in which we live, especially if it is something good and touches other lives in a warm and effective way. The very fact that this has been a ministry of precious moments in the past 20 years is rewarding enough for me.

CP: In the last 20 years, what, in regards to the collection, has surprised you? What surprises do you think the future holds?

SB: The continued interest in PRECIOUS MOMENTS. I don't really look for surprises as much as I look for integrity and faithfulness to the vision. That, in itself, will not bring surprises but will bring special accomplishments.

"I believe that everyone has a desire to give something back to the world in which we live, especially if it is something good and touches other lives in a warm and effective way"

CP: What has been the most satisfying aspect of the phenomenal success of The PRECIOUS MOMENTS Collection?

SB: How people are brought together and ministered through the message of PRECIOUS MOMENTS.

CP: What other artistic plans do you have? Are there any products or designs in the works that you can tell us about?

SB: I am continually thinking of new products, such as the COUNTRY LANE collection that [recently] came out and *The Lily Pond* which should be out very soon.

CP: Can you tell us what your favorite PRECIOUS MOMENTS piece is?

SB: My favorite piece is "To God Be The Glory" but there is another figurine that is equally important to me. It is the one with the little angel holding the Ten Commandments with a heart over the tablet. The title of the figurine is "The Greatest Of These Is Love." I believe its message says it all, and has therefore become one that I love to share with others.

PRECIOUS MOMENTS artist Sam Butcher greets his fans at a signing event.

CP: You spend a lot of your time counseling many of your fans who are going through troubled times, and on occasion even producing special figurines to help them through. How does this reflect back to your work with PRECIOUS MOMENTS designs?

SB: Counseling and comforting others is what I love to do and nothing more than that. However, there have been times when I have to do a figurine as a result of taking that time with someone.

CP: Through your childhood, your teachers were extremely supportive. How did this affect your career as an artist?

SB: It gave me confidence, as well as an ability to show the same concern to aspiring artists that my teachers showed me.

CP: Who has been the most influential person(s) in your artistic career?

SB: I believe Mr. Rex Moraveck, my high school art teacher.

CP: As a child, you were always interested in art. When did you think that you might be able to make a living as an artist?

SB: I started selling my artwork at the age of 10, working on many projects for baseball teams, parties and special occasions. At the age of 15, I became a sign painter. Throughout my teenage life I sold many kinds of artwork.

CP: You designed the COUNTRY LANE collection based on your Grandma Ethel's farm. Can you share some memories of your time there?

SB: I think one of the most impressive things that I recall about my grandma's farm was a wonderful cut-out of birds, as well as the dressers and other bedroom accessories that her husband did from simple wooden crates, as well as calico prints for my aunt.

CP: Last year you had the honor of attending "Sam Butcher Day" in Jackson, Michigan, the town in which you were born. What was this experience like?

SB: I was amazed to have seen so many people who were my childhood friends. What meant the most to me was that even though they were somewhat intimidated at first, I was able to put them ease and joke with them like we did in our early childhood.

CP: The names for the PRECIOUS MOMENTS pieces tell a lot about what is going on in the piece. How are the names chosen? Which comes first, the name or the design?

SB: It really depends on the occasion. For example, I may

have heard something that may inspire a title, or I may have seen something that may inspire a design.

CP: According to reports, you were inspired by a trip to the Sistine Chapel to create The PRECIOUS MOMENTS Chapel in Carthage, Missouri. Can you tell us about the Chapel?

SB: Actually, it had been in my heart since I became a Christian to build a Chapel that may direct people's attention to the love of God. And while the Sistine Chapel is more a message of God's wrath and judgement, I was inspired to study the Sistine Chapel on the basis of artistic value alone.

CP: This year marks The Chapel's 10th anniversary. In several reports, you have said that The Chapel is a "work in progress." What do you have planned for its future?

SB: There are so many more things, such as inspirational catacombs, the new memorial gardens and the additions to the PRECIOUS MOMENTS Museum, to name a few.

"I started selling my artwork at the age of 10, working on many projects for baseball teams, parties and many special occasions"

CP: The murals in The Chapel sanctuary are your "vision of Heaven." Can you tell us what they represent to you?

SB: Heaven from a child's point of view. In other words, as Jesus said in Matthew 18:5, "And whoso shall receive one such little child in my name receiveth me."

CP: Through your career, you have been actively involved in various charities such as Second Harvest, the International Child Evangelism Fellowship and various scholarship organizations in the United States and the Philippines. Can you tell us about this?

SB: Most of the projects that I am interested in basically have something to do with endeavors that specifically minister to children.

CP: Please tell us about your relationship with Enesco Founding Chairman Eugene Freedman and PRECIOUS MOMENTS Master Sculptor Yasuhei Fujioka.

SB: Mr. Freedman is the first person I met at Enesco. Since that day, we have become not only business associates, but very good friends as well. Mr. Fujioka was Mr. Freedman's choice to translate my artwork in a tri-dimensional form. Since the first day I met Mr. Fujioka, I agreed that he was the perfect choice to carry out the expression.

CP: Collectors would love to know a little more about your personal life. What hobbies and pastimes do you enjoy? Do you collect anything yourself?

SB: Actually, my art is my life and as long as I am busy producing PRECIOUS MOMENTS or painting in any other medium, my life is completely fulfilled. I love to collect books, especially books about the masters.

CP: What do you see as your biggest challenge as the artist and creator of PRECIOUS MOMENTS?

SB: To continue creating fresh and unusual artworks.

CP: What would you like to tell your fans?

SB: I am keenly aware that no one becomes famous without the ingredients of two things, their personal ability, and the people that appreciate the ability. I am very grateful to everyone who makes PRECIOUS MOMENTS a success because of their appreciation for my work.

*M*any new and exciting pieces have joined the PRE-CIOUS MOMENTS collection for the 1999 Fall and Winter seasons. Thirty figurines and 14 ornaments were announced, along with a new LITTLE MOMENTS series, four new TENDER TAILS series, many new TEN-DER TAILS ornaments and a new line of TENDER TAILS "attachables." In addition, several animals have been added to the already vast collection of general TENDER TAILS plush critters.

> ### CHANGING WITH THE TIMES!
>
> New 1999 pieces will include a new, more intense color. Enesco announced last year that some of the releases will appear on store shelves with a color spectrum reminiscent of some of the original PRECIOUS MOMENTS figurines!

FIGURINES

The Beauty Of God Blooms Forever (Four Seasons Series) . . . This delicate figurine reminds us to enjoy the beauty of each day. One of four pieces in the *Four Seasons Series*, it brings inspiration year-round.

Behold The Lamb Of God . . . A gentle lamb, along with blue birds and rabbits, watches over the manger as Baby Jesus sleeps. This adorable scene will make a nice addition to other *Nativity* pieces.

Beside Still Waters (Four Seasons Series) . . . Keeping watch over her lambs is a job this shepherd takes very seriously. With staff in hand, she searches for fresh water for her thirsty charges.

Dear Jon, I Will Never Leave You – JESUS (COUNTRY LANE) . . . This little boy sitting with his puppy has been reassured that his faith will never be questioned. Similar to last year's musical "Bringing In The Sheaves," this is a must for collectors!

Eat Ham (COUNTRY LANE) . . . This little guy is no turkey when it comes to being serious. "Eat Ham" is his last effort to convince you not to make him your next culinary masterpiece.

He Came As The Gift Of God's Love (set/4, Mini-Mini Nativity) . . . This new set featuring Mary, Joseph and Baby Jesus adds a touch of beauty to any holiday decoration as well as your year-round collection. This inspiring set is one of only a few PRECIOUS MOMENTS pieces to include a creche.

He Covers The Earth With His Glory (Four Seasons Series) . . . Braving the cold weather, this adorable little girl and her faithful companion, an Afghan hound, take a stroll through the freshly fallen snow.

He Graces The Earth With Abundance (Four Seasons Series) . . . This piece is a reminder of just how special the autumn season can be. A little girl holds a basket full of fresh fruit while her duck friend looks on in anticipation of leftovers.

I Couldn't Make It Without You (Boys And Girls Clubs Of America Commemorative Figurine) . . . As in any sport, the trick to winning is to work as a team, and "I Couldn't Make It Without You" is a *true* testament to this rule. This Commemorative Figurine shows a boy and girl helping each other to the finish line.

Jesus Is My Lighthouse (lighted) . . . Joined by her feathered friends, this little girl spends her day reading her Bible at the beach. She knows that the light that shines above from the nearby lighthouse will guide her in the right direction.

Lord, Police Protect Us . . . This policeman's job is to protect and serve, so when he happens upon this mother duck and her babies, there is only one thing to do. Complete with a badge, gold star and whistle, he helps the family cross the street!

May Your Seasons Be Jelly And Bright . . . Who would have thought that jelly beans and glue would make a great combination? However, when it comes to wishing you a happy holiday, there's nothing better. This little girl is getting creative with her wishes as she knows homemade gifts are sometimes the ones that mean the most.

My Life Is A Vacuum Without You . . . Do you ever feel empty inside when a loved one isn't around? If so, let them know just how much they matter with this special message of love.

Purr-fect Friends (Catalog Figurine) . . . What better way way to celebrate friendship than with this adorable little girl embracing her most cherished friend. This piece, which is available through special retailers, is the perfect gift for your "purr-fect friend."

RV Haven' Fun Or What . . . Getting lost during a summer camping trip can certainly dampen your spirits, so this little girl and her pup decide to map out the perfect course.

Sharing Our Time Is So Precious (Century Circle Figurine) . . . This elegant Century Circle piece featuring a young couple out for an afternoon boat ride is the perfect reminder of the importance of speding time with the ones you love.

Sharing Our Winter Wonderland (LE-1999) . . . These skaters are hoping to make a perfect landing in your collection.

Shear Happiness And Hare Cuts (COUNTRY LANE) . . . This little lamb was excited about his first "hare" cut, but he had no idea it would be taken so seriously. He doesn't mind his friend helping though – it brings "shear" happiness to everyone involved.

Slide Into The Next Millennium With Joy (Dated 1999) . . . This little girl is riding full speed ahead through the last year of the millennium. The sled she is riding on has "1999" written across the front, sure to make it an extra special keepsake in years to come.

Snow Man Like My Man . . . Complete with a top hat and black coal eyes, this is undoubtedly the best looking snowman in town. To ensure that her new friend is comfortable in the inclement weather to come, the little girl in this piece is bundling him up with a scarf and a little bit of love.

Take Time To Smell The Roses (Carlton Cards Exclusive) . . . In a world where things often seem rushed, this piece is the perfect reminder that no matter how busy you are, you should always "Take Time To Smell The Roses." This exclusive piece is limited to production during 1999.

Thank You Sew Much . . . Appreciation can be expressed in so many different ways, so why not use this figurine as a creative way to thank that special person who's always been there for you.

Warmest Wishes For The Holidays . . . This is the perfect piece for telling someone that you're "stuck" on them. As this cowboy decorates his favorite cactus for the holiday, all he can think about is becoming a part of your collection.

Wishes For The World (Special Event Figurine) . . . Just in time for the new Millennium comes this endearing figurine. Holding a personal treasure in her hands, this girl is wishing for a world full of peace and happiness, as well as whatever good things can come our way.

Wishing You A Moo-ie Christmas (COUN-TRY LANE) *. . .* Decked out in a holiday wreath and bells, this cow (and his owner) hope your holiday is just "Moo-ie." This adorable piece is the first COUNTRY LANE figurine to feature a Christmas theme.

Wishing You An Old Fashioned Christmas (set/6 , LE-1999, lighted) *. . .* The entire family, including the dog, has come to trim the tree for the holidays! This Christmas tree is extra special because it has shiny gold ornaments, silver tinsel and working lights!

Witch Way Do You Spell Love? *. . .* Your loved one is sure to appreciate "witchever" way you decide to spell it! And with nothing but her good spells to cast, why not make this witch a permanent part of your collection?

You Brighten My Field Of Dreams (COUNTRY LANE) *. . .* This little girl can't imagine her life without you in it . . . and she's not afraid to tell the world. Standing atop a bale of hay and looking out over the land, she'll tell anyone who listens, and right now that seems to be her many feathered and furry friends from the nearby field.

You Color Our World With Loving Caring And Sharing (10th Anniversary Chapel Commemorative Figurine) *. . .*

This piece was created to celebrate the 10th anniversary of The PRECIOUS MOMENTS Chapel in Carthage, Missouri. You can, however, locate this piece at retailers across the country.

You Oughta Be In Pictures (Special Event Figurine) *. . .* Do you have a friend who should be in the movies? If you do, this would be the perfect gift for her. If it escaped your

collection, you have to do some searching as this figurine was only available for one day in May.

ORNAMENTS

12 Days Of Christmas Series . . . Following the Christmas song of the same name, four ornaments have been added to this year-old series. Days five through eight are now available for the 1999 season: "The Golden Rings Of Friendship" for the 5th day, "Hatching The Perfect Holiday" for the 6th day, "Swimming Into Your Heart" for the 7th day and "Eight Mice A Milking" for the 8th day.

Baby's First Christmas (Dated 1999) . . . The 1999 editions of these ornaments feature both a boy and a girl dressed like lambs while holding hearts that say "Baby's 1st Christmas." Appropriately, the heart on the boy's ornament is blue, while the girl's is pink. The date "1999" appears on each hat.

May All Your Christmases Be White (LE-1999) . . . This special ornament is returning from suspension to bring you even more holiday cheer. "May All Your Christmases Be White" was available for five years before being suspended in 1994. Act fast, though, as this ornament is limited to a 1999 production run.

May Your Christmas Be Delightful (LE-1999) . . . Another special ornament returning from suspension, this adorable boy is all wrapped up in Christmas lights. But time is limited to add him to your collection. Originally issued in 1985 and suspended for six years, this piece will only be available during 1999.

May Your Christmas Be Delightful (LE-1999) . . . Even though this little girl had a little bit of trouble decorating her Christmas tree, she promises to hang from yours quite beautifully. In conjunction with the return from suspension of the male version of this ornament, collectors are getting a special opportunity to add this new design to their collections, but only during 1999.

May Your Wishes For Peace Take Wing (Dated 1999) . . . This precious angel sends out wishes that all your dreams come true in the coming holiday season. The angel wears a wreath of flowers in her hair and lovingly holds a small bird in her hands. The date "1999" appears on the folds of her gown.

Merry Giftness (LE-1999. Distinguished Service Retailer Ornament) . . . Offering her own gift for the holidays, this little girl is the perfect way to thank someone special. And even though she's not quite ready to give up her teddy bear, she's more than willing to share her holiday cheer.

Our First Christmas Together (Dated 1999) . . . What better way to trim your tree than with an ornament to signify your first year of marriage. This new couple has decided to head feet first, not only into the new Millennium, but into their new life together as well!

Pretty As A Christmas Princess (LE-1999) . . . After playing dress-up, this little girl is "Pretty As A Christmas Princess" in her new clothes. And she feels like a princess, too, with her crown and her wand with a shiny gold star on the end. This charming piece is limited to production in 1999.

Slide Into The Next Millennium With Joy (Dated 1999) . . . Just like the figurine, this ornament is dated with "1999" on the front of the sled. But don't be misled by its name; this ornament will stay steady on your Christmas tree.

LITTLE MOMENTS

A special LITTLE MOMENTS series debuting in 1999 is sure to win the hearts of collectors of all ages. Each piece in the *Highway To Happiness Series* features an angel holding a traffic sign with messages of inspiration. The six pieces for

1999 are "Cross Walk," "Go For It," "God's Children At Play," "Highway To Happiness," "I'll Never Stop Loving You" and "There's No Wrong With You."

TENDER TAILS BIRTHDAY TRAIN

The TENDER TAILS collection has become quite popular with collectors since it was first introduced in 1997. This year for the collection, a new series is the TENDER TAILS *Birthday Train*. There is a total of nine pieces – ages 1 through 6 – with a different animal representing each age, a "Baby Bear," a "Circus Clown" and a quilted displayer.

GRANDMA ETHEL'S FARM

Artist Sam Butcher's Grandma Ethel's farm was the inspiration for the COUNTRY LANE figurines, and now the farm is also being remembered in this new line of TENDER TAILS. Six animals common to barnyards and farms make up the line. They are a "Chipmunk," "Crow," "Field Mouse" (not pictured), "Skunk," "Squirrel" and "Turkey."

NATIVITY

The new TENDER TAILS *Nativity* offers another way to decorate your home during the Christmas holiday. The series is made up of nine pieces: "Camel," "Nativity Cow," "Donkey," "Gray Lamb," "Mary/Jesus/Joseph" (set/3), "Palm Tree" and "Nativity Quilt Display."

ORNAMENTS

The hanging ornaments, smaller versions of the TENDER TAILS, made their debut last year. Now, there are 23, including ten new ones for the

1999 Fall season: "20th Anniversary Bear" (not pictured), "Flamingo," three versions of a "Monkey," "Owl" (not pictured), "Rhino," "Rosie," "Tippy" and "Unicorn."

General Plush

Several more animals joined the growing TENDER TAILS plush line this season. The "Turkey With Sign" looks much like the figurine and comes holding a sign that says "Eat Ham" in hopes of warding off hunters. Also among the new releases is a group of whales made of up eight different colors, one of which is rainbow-colored. And when Halloween comes this year, the three new TENDER TAILS "Pumpkins" are sure to be a big hit. A "Seal" is also part of the new TENDER TAILS line this year. It joins the line as an *Easter Seal Commemorative* plush, marking the first time a TENDER TAILS piece has represented a charitable organization. Don't forget, once you become a proud parent of a TENDER TAILS plush, you'll receive an adoption certificate and a guide on how to love and care for the newest member of your family.

Attachables

These could be the most transportable of all the TENDER TAILS. The "Attachables" are debuting in the Fall line, and are a fun way to keep your plush pets with you throughout the day. A hook attached to the end of each animal allows you to put them on backpacks, keychains and purses . . . or anywhere else they can latch on to! The first group of six is made up of "Cat," "Elephant," "Hippo," "Monkey," "Panda" and "Unicorn."

*S*everal times a year, Enesco honors PRECIOUS MOMENTS pieces by retiring or suspending them. Below is a list of retirements so far for 1999, 40 of which had their molds broken in front of an audience at the International Collectibles Exposition in Long Beach, California.

FIGURINES

- ❏ Baby's First Meal
  (#524077, 1991)
- ❏ Baby's First Word
  (#527238, 1992)
- ❏ Easter's On It's Way
  (#521892, 1990)
- ❏ Eggspecially For You
  (#520667, 1989)
- ❏ The Fruit Of The Spirit
  Is Love
  (#521213, 1993)
- ❏ God Bless Our Family
  (#100498, 1987)
- ❏ God Bless Our Family
  (#100501, 1987)
- ❏ Good Friends Are For
  Always
  (#524123, 1991)
- ❏ Good News Is So Uplifting
  (#523615, 1991)
- ❏ The Greatest Gift Is
  A Friend
  (#109231, 1987)
- ❏ He's The Healer Of
  Broken Hearts
  (#100080, 1987)
- ❏ Heaven Bless Your
  Togetherness
  (#106755, 1988)
- ❏ Hello World
  (#521175, 1989)
- ❏ I Only Have Ice For You
  (#530956, 1995)

FIGURINES, cont.

- ❏ I Would Be Lost
  Without You
  (#526142, 1992)
- ❏ I'll Never Tire Of You
  (#307068, 1998)
- ❏ It's So Uplifting To Have
  A Friend Like You
  (#524905, 1992)
- ❏ Just A Line To Say
  You're Special
  (#522864, 1995)
- ❏ Let's Keep In Touch
  (#102520, 1986)
- ❏ The Light Of The World
  Is Jesus
  (#521507, 1989)
- ❏ The Lord Is With You
  (#526835, 1996)
- ❏ Love Rescued Me
  (#102393, 1986)
- ❏ Luke 2:10-11
  (#532916, 1994)
- ❏ Mom, You're My
  Special-tea
  (#325473, 1999)
- ❏ My Heart Is Exposed
  With Love
  (#520624, 1989)
- ❏ My Universe Is You
  (#487902, 1999)
- ❏ Oinky Birthday
  (#524506, 1994)
- ❏ Perfect Harmony
  (#521914, 1994)

FIGURINES, cont.

- ❏ Precious Memories
  (#E2828, 1984)
- ❏ Press On
  (#E9265, 1983)
- ❏ Puppy Love
  (#520764, 1989)
- ❏ Rejoice O Earth
  (#E5636, 1981)
- ❏ A Reflection Of His Love
  (#522279, 1991)
- ❏ Soot Yourself To A
  Merry Christmas
  (#150096, 1995)
- ❏ The Sun Is Always
  Shining Somewhere
  (#163775, 1996)
- ❏ There Shall Be Showers Of
  Blessings
  (#522090, 1990)
- ❏ To The Apple Of
  God's Eye
  (#522015, 1993)
- ❏ Tubby's First Christmas
  (#525278, 1992)
- ❏ Wishing You A Comfy
  Christmas (#527750, 1992)
- ❏ Wishing You A Very
  Successful Season
  (#522120, 1989)

ORNAMENTS

- ❏ It's So Uplifting To Have A
  Friend Like You
  (#528846, 1993)
- ❏ To My Forever Friend
  (#113956, 1988)

TENDER TAILS

- ❏ Brown Bunny
  (#464422, 1998)
- ❏ Cardinal
  (#471909, 1998)
- ❏ Cat
  (#382256, 1998)
- ❏ Cow
  (#475890, 1998)
- ❏ Harp Seal
  (#382086, 1998)
- ❏ Ladybug
  (#476080, 1999)
- ❏ Lamb
  (#463299, 1998)
- ❏ Pink Bunny
  (#464414, 1998)
- ❏ Tippy
  (#477869, 1999)
- ❏ Whale
  (#577006, 1999)

Enesco Founding Chairman Eugene Freedman watches as a total of 40 PRECIOUS MOMENTS molds were broken on April 24 at the 1999 International Collectibles Exposition in Long Beach, California.

PRECIOUS MOMENTS® Top Ten

he Top Ten most valuable pieces in the PRECIOUS MOMENTS collection are determined by their secondary market values. Qualifying pieces must have top dollar value, and show a significant increase in value from their original prices.

God Loveth A Cheerful Giver

Figurine • #E1378
Issued: 1979 • Retired: 1981
Issue Price: $9.50 • Market Value: NM – $1,000

As one of the "Original 21," this is one of the most sought-after pieces in the line. Known as the "Girl With Puppies," the figurine was retired in 1981, only two years after being issued.

But Love Goes On Forever

Retailer's Dome • #E7350
Issued: 1984 • Closed: 1984
Issue Price: N/A • Market Value: ✝ – $855

This special piece was available as a gift to retailers in 1984. The figurine inside the dome is the regular "But Love Goes On Forever" figurine available since 1980.

Good Friends Are Forever

Special Event Figurine • #525049
Issued: 1990 • Closed: 1990
Issue Price: N/A • Market Value: ✐ – $760

With only one piece given to each Distinguished Service Retailer, this very limited figurine is a hard one for collectors to find. It has a unique rosebud production mark that only appeared on this piece.

COLLECTOR'S
VALUE GUIDE™

Friends Never Drift Apart (LE-1993)

Medallion • #529079
Issued: 1993 • Closed: 1993
Issue Price: N/A • Market Value: UM – $620

A medallion drifts into the fourth most valuable position this year. It was offered to collectors aboard the 15th Anniversary Cruise in 1993.

Nobody's Perfect

Figurine • #E9268
Issued: 1983 • Retired: 1990
Issue Price: $21 • Market Value: Smile Variation – $590

This little boy's smile proved to be quite valuable. Very soon after its release, "Dunce Boy" adopted a more appropriate frown that remained until he retired in 1990.

Tammy (LE-5,000)

Doll • #E7267G
Issued: 1982 • Closed: 1982
Issue Price: $300 • Market Value: UM – $575

This beautiful bride doll was only available for one year, making "Tammy" the sixth most valuable piece in the PRECIOUS MOMENTS line.

Sailabration Cruise (LE-1995)

Figurine • #150061
Issued: 1995 • Closed: 1995
Issue Price: N/A • Market Value: ⌐ – $500

This is the second cruise piece to have a significant secondary market value. It was given to PRECIOUS MOMENTS *Club* members aboard the second Enesco cruise during the Spring of 1995.

PRECIOUS MOMENTS® TOP TEN

Cubby (LE-5,000)

Doll • E7267B
Issued: 1982 • Closed: 1982
Issue Price: $200 • Market Value: UM– $480

Joining his bride "Tammy" in the Top Ten list is "Cubby." Available for only one year, this doll has become the eighth most valuable PRECIOUS MOMENTS piece.

Hello, Lord, It's Me Again

Members Only Figurine • #PM811
Issued 1981: • Closed: 1981
Issue Price: $25 • Market Value: ▲ – $475

This figurine, depicting a love-lorn "Dear Jon," rings in at number nine. "Hello Lord, It's Me Again" was available only to collectors who were *Club* members in 1981.

Jesus Is Born

Figurine • #E2801
Issued: 1980 • Suspended: 1984
Issue Price: $37 • Market Value: NM– 405

Rounding out the Top Ten, this piece was issued as part of the PRECIOUS MOMENTS *Nativity* scene. "Jesus Is Born" was available for four years before being suspended in 1984.

PRODUCTION MARK CHART

*S*ince 1981, each of the porcelain bisque pieces from the Enesco PRECIOUS MOMENTS line has been given a production mark to denote the year the piece was produced. For instance, a piece that was issued in 1990 and retired in 1992 can be found with the following marks: a flame, a vessel and a clef. Often times, pieces can be found with a mark from the year before its release or a year following its retirement or suspension. "Unmarked" pieces, ones missing the production mark, can be found on some pieces produced after 1981.

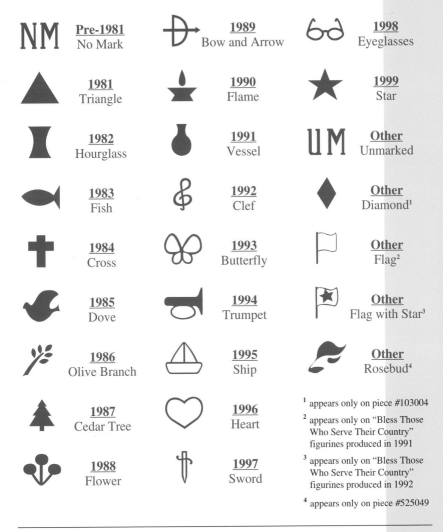

NM — **Pre-1981** No Mark

▲ — **1981** Triangle

1982 Hourglass

1983 Fish

1984 Cross

1985 Dove

1986 Olive Branch

1987 Cedar Tree

1988 Flower

1989 Bow and Arrow

1990 Flame

1991 Vessel

1992 Clef

1993 Butterfly

1994 Trumpet

1995 Ship

1996 Heart

1997 Sword

1998 Eyeglasses

1999 Star

UM — **Other** Unmarked

♦ — **Other** Diamond[1]

Other Flag[2]

Other Flag with Star[3]

Other Rosebud[4]

[1] appears only on piece #103004

[2] appears only on "Bless Those Who Serve Their Country" figurines produced in 1991

[3] appears only on "Bless Those Who Serve Their Country" figurines produced in 1992

[4] appears only on piece #525049

1. Locate your piece in the Value Guide. Figurine series are listed first, followed by general figurines, the COUNTRY LANE COLLECTION and LITTLE MOMENTS. Series and general ornaments are next, then miscellaneous PRECIOUS MOMENTS collectibles (bells, boxes, dolls, musicals, etc.). The Value Guide concludes with TENDER TAILS, *Chapel Exclusives* and *Club* pieces. Within most sections, pieces are listed alphabetically by inspirational title, while in annual groupings, pieces are listed in chronological order. Alphabetical and numerical indexes can be found in the back of the book to help you locate your pieces.

①		Values
		† $45
		➶ $42

Wishing You A Merry
Christmas (Dated 1984)
#E5383
Issued: 1984 • Closed: 1984
Retail Price: $17

2. Find the market value of your piece. First look at the bottom or back of your piece to determine which production mark it has. A handy key is located on the bottom of each page to guide you. Now, find your piece's production mark in the "Values" chart on the right side of the picture box.

ANNUAL CHRISTMAS FIGURINES	
Price Paid	Value Of My Collection
1. **17.00**	**45.00**
2.	
3.	
4.	
5.	
6.	
7.	
45.00	
PENCIL TOTALS	

3. Record the retail price that you paid and the secondary market value in the corresponding boxes at the bottom of the page. In each piece's picture box, the first price in the "Retail Price" line refers to the price at the time of issue, while the second price (where applicable) is the current retail price. For pieces that are no longer available, the second price is the last suggested retail price.

4. Calculate the value for the page by adding all of the boxes in each column. Be sure to use a pencil so you can change the totals as your collection grows!

5. Transfer the totals from each page to the "Total Value Of My Collection" worksheets that begin on page 229.

6. Add all of the totals together to determine the overall value of your collection.

FIGURINE SERIES

So far for 1999, five pieces have been introduced into various PRECIOUS MOMENTS series: one piece in the *Birthday Train Series*, one piece in the *Nativity Series*, one piece in the *Annual Christmas Series*, and two pieces in the *Easter Seals Commemorative Figurine Collection*. This year marks the first time since 1992 that no pieces were added to *Sugar Town* – the collection was retired in 1998.

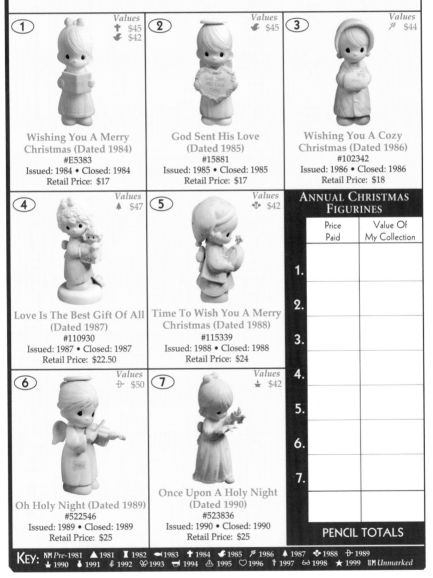

1 — Values † $45 ✔ $42

Wishing You A Merry Christmas (Dated 1984)
#E5383
Issued: 1984 • Closed: 1984
Retail Price: $17

2 — Values ✔ $45

God Sent His Love (Dated 1985)
#15881
Issued: 1985 • Closed: 1985
Retail Price: $17

3 — Values ♪ $44

Wishing You A Cozy Christmas (Dated 1986)
#102342
Issued: 1986 • Closed: 1986
Retail Price: $18

4 — Values ▲ $47

Love Is The Best Gift Of All (Dated 1987)
#110930
Issued: 1987 • Closed: 1987
Retail Price: $22.50

5 — Values ✦ $42

Time To Wish You A Merry Christmas (Dated 1988)
#115339
Issued: 1988 • Closed: 1988
Retail Price: $24

6 — Values Ð $50

Oh Holy Night (Dated 1989)
#522546
Issued: 1989 • Closed: 1989
Retail Price: $25

7 — Values ⚓ $42

Once Upon A Holy Night (Dated 1990)
#523836
Issued: 1990 • Closed: 1990
Retail Price: $25

ANNUAL CHRISTMAS FIGURINES

	Price Paid	Value Of My Collection
1.		
2.		
3.		
4.		
5.		
6.		
7.		
PENCIL TOTALS		

KEY: NM *Pre-1981* ▲ 1981 Ⅱ 1982 ◄1983 † 1984 ✔ 1985 ♪ 1986 ▲ 1987 ✦1988 Ð 1989 ⚓ 1990 ♪ 1991 ♪ 1992 ❀1993 ◄1994 △ 1995 ♡1996 † 1997 ଌ 1998 ★ 1999 UM *Unmarked*

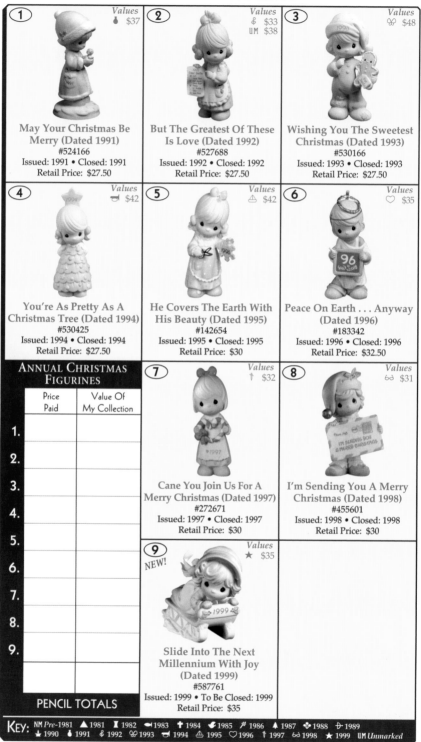

1 — *Values* ♨ $37
May Your Christmas Be Merry (Dated 1991)
#524166
Issued: 1991 • Closed: 1991
Retail Price: $27.50

2 — *Values* ♣ $33 / UM $38
But The Greatest Of These Is Love (Dated 1992)
#527688
Issued: 1992 • Closed: 1992
Retail Price: $27.50

3 — *Values* ⧖ $48
Wishing You The Sweetest Christmas (Dated 1993)
#530166
Issued: 1993 • Closed: 1993
Retail Price: $27.50

4 — *Values* ⊲ $42
You're As Pretty As A Christmas Tree (Dated 1994)
#530425
Issued: 1994 • Closed: 1994
Retail Price: $27.50

5 — *Values* △ $42
He Covers The Earth With His Beauty (Dated 1995)
#142654
Issued: 1995 • Closed: 1995
Retail Price: $30

6 — *Values* ♡ $35
Peace On Earth . . . Anyway (Dated 1996)
#183342
Issued: 1996 • Closed: 1996
Retail Price: $32.50

ANNUAL CHRISTMAS FIGURINES

	Price Paid	Value Of My Collection
1.		
2.		
3.		
4.		
5.		
6.		
7.		
8.		
9.		
PENCIL TOTALS		

7 — *Values* † $32
Cane You Join Us For A Merry Christmas (Dated 1997)
#272671
Issued: 1997 • Closed: 1997
Retail Price: $30

8 — *Values* 6∂ $31
I'm Sending You A Merry Christmas (Dated 1998)
#455601
Issued: 1998 • Closed: 1998
Retail Price: $30

9 NEW! — *Values* ★ $35
Slide Into The Next Millennium With Joy (Dated 1999)
#587761
Issued: 1999 • To Be Closed: 1999
Retail Price: $35

KEY: NM *Pre-1981* ▲ 1981 Ⅱ 1982 ◄1983 † 1984 ✔1985 ♪ 1986 ▲ 1987 ✤1988 ϑ1989 ★ 1990 ♨ 1991 ♣ 1992 ⧖1993 ⊲ 1994 △ 1995 ♡1996 † 1997 6∂ 1998 ★ 1999 UM *Unmarked*

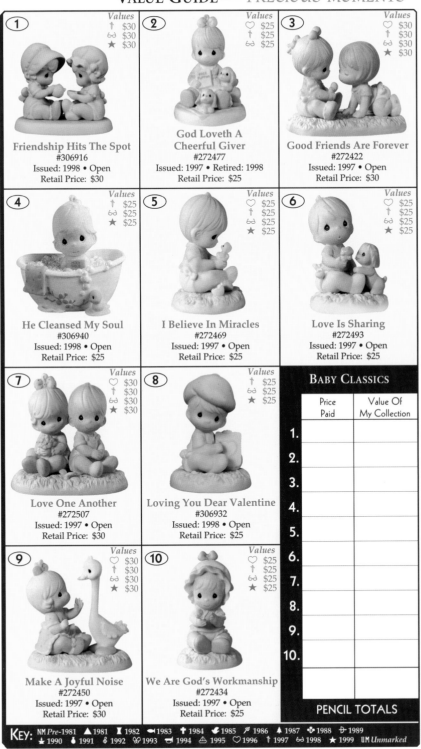

FIGURINE SERIES

1 Values
† $30
6ð $30
★ $30

Friendship Hits The Spot
#306916
Issued: 1998 • Open
Retail Price: $30

2 Values
♡ $25
† $25
6ð $25

God Loveth A Cheerful Giver
#272477
Issued: 1997 • Retired: 1998
Retail Price: $25

3 Values
♡ $30
† $30
6ð $30
★ $30

Good Friends Are Forever
#272422
Issued: 1997 • Open
Retail Price: $30

4 Values
† $25
6ð $25
★ $25

He Cleansed My Soul
#306940
Issued: 1998 • Open
Retail Price: $25

5 Values
♡ $25
† $25
6ð $25
★ $25

I Believe In Miracles
#272469
Issued: 1997 • Open
Retail Price: $25

6 Values
♡ $25
† $25
6ð $25
★ $25

Love Is Sharing
#272493
Issued: 1997 • Open
Retail Price: $25

7 Values
♡ $30
† $30
6ð $30
★ $30

Love One Another
#272507
Issued: 1997 • Open
Retail Price: $30

8 Values
† $25
6ð $25
★ $25

Loving You Dear Valentine
#306932
Issued: 1998 • Open
Retail Price: $25

9 Values
♡ $30
† $30
6ð $30
★ $30

Make A Joyful Noise
#272450
Issued: 1997 • Open
Retail Price: $30

10 Values
♡ $25
† $25
6ð $25
★ $25

We Are God's Workmanship
#272434
Issued: 1997 • Open
Retail Price: $25

BABY CLASSICS

	Price Paid	Value Of My Collection
1.		
2.		
3.		
4.		
5.		
6.		
7.		
8.		
9.		
10.		
PENCIL TOTALS		

KEY: NM *Pre-1981* ▲ 1981 Ⅰ 1982 ◄ 1983 † 1984 ✔ 1985 ♪ 1986 ▲ 1987 ✤ 1988 ৪ 1989 ★ 1990 ● 1991 ৪ 1992 ஐ 1993 ➡ 1994 △ 1995 ♡ 1996 † 1997 6ð 1998 ★ 1999 UM *Unmarked*

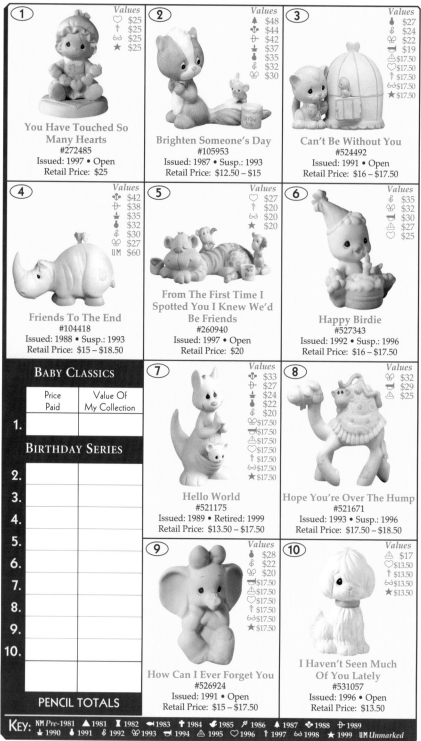

1 — Values
- ♡ $25
- † $25
- 6∂ $25
- ★ $25

You Have Touched So Many Hearts
#272485
Issued: 1997 • Open
Retail Price: $25

2 — Values
- ♠ $48
- ✣ $44
- Ð $42
- ✦ $37
- 🕯 $35
- ₰ $32
- ℅ $30

Brighten Someone's Day
#105953
Issued: 1987 • Susp.: 1993
Retail Price: $12.50 – $15

3 — Values
- 🕯 $27
- ₰ $24
- ℅ $22
- ◥ $19
- △ $17.50
- ♡ $17.50
- † $17.50
- 6∂ $17.50
- ★ $17.50

Can't Be Without You
#524492
Issued: 1991 • Open
Retail Price: $16 – $17.50

4 — Values
- ✣ $42
- Ð $38
- ✦ $35
- 🕯 $32
- ₰ $30
- ℅ $27
- UM $60

Friends To The End
#104418
Issued: 1988 • Susp.: 1993
Retail Price: $15 – $18.50

5 — Values
- ♡ $27
- † $20
- 6∂ $20
- ★ $20

From The First Time I Spotted You I Knew We'd Be Friends
#260940
Issued: 1997 • Open
Retail Price: $20

6 — Values
- ₰ $35
- ℅ $32
- ◥ $30
- △ $27
- ♡ $25

Happy Birdie
#527343
Issued: 1992 • Susp.: 1996
Retail Price: $16 – $17.50

7 — Values
- ✣ $33
- Ð $27
- ✦ $24
- 🕯 $22
- ₰ $20
- ℅ $17.50
- ◥ $17.50
- △ $17.50
- ♡ $17.50
- † $17.50
- 6∂ $17.50
- ★ $17.50

Hello World
#521175
Issued: 1989 • Retired: 1999
Retail Price: $13.50 – $17.50

8 — Values
- ℅ $32
- ◥ $29
- △ $25

Hope You're Over The Hump
#521671
Issued: 1993 • Susp.: 1996
Retail Price: $17.50 – $18.50

9 — Values
- 🕯 $28
- ₰ $22
- ℅ $20
- ◥ $17.50
- △ $17.50
- ♡ $17.50
- † $17.50
- 6∂ $17.50
- ★ $17.50

How Can I Ever Forget You
#526924
Issued: 1991 • Open
Retail Price: $15 – $17.50

10 — Values
- △ $17
- ♡ $13.50
- † $13.50
- 6∂ $13.50
- ★ $13.50

I Haven't Seen Much Of You Lately
#531057
Issued: 1996 • Open
Retail Price: $13.50

BABY CLASSICS

	Price Paid	Value Of My Collection
1.		

BIRTHDAY SERIES

2.		
3.		
4.		
5.		
6.		
7.		
8.		
9.		
10.		

PENCIL TOTALS

KEY: NM *Pre-1981* ▲ 1981 Ⅱ 1982 ◀1983 † 1984 ❀ 1985 ♪ 1986 ♠ 1987 ✣ 1988 Ð 1989 ✦ 1990 🕯 1991 ₰ 1992 ℅ 1993 ◥ 1994 △ 1995 ♡ 1996 † 1997 6∂ 1998 ★ 1999 UM *Unmarked*

1

Values
🕯 $26
❀ $21
🗐 $19
△ $17.50
♡ $17.50
✝ $17.50
👓 $17.50

I Only Have Arms For You
#527769
Issued: 1993 • Retired: 1998
Retail Price: $15 – $17.50

2

Values
🕯 $38
🕯 $34
❀ $30
🗐 $27
△ $25
♡ $24

Let's Be Friends
#527270
Issued: 1992 • Retired: 1996
Retail Price: $15 – $17.50

3

Values
✝ $15
👓 $15
★ $15

My World's Upside Down Without You
#531014
Issued: 1998 • Open
Retail Price: $15

4

Values
★ $37
🕯 $33
❀ $30
🗐 $27
🗐 $25

Not A Creature Was Stirring (set/2)
#524484
Issued: 1990 • Susp.: 1994
Retail Price: $17

5

Values
❀ $20
🗐 $17
△ $15
♡ $15
✝ $15
👓 $15
★ $15

Oinky Birthday
#524506
Issued: 1994 • Open
Retail Price: $13.50 – $15

6

Values
♠ $62
♣ $55
♫ $50
★ $46
🕯 $44
❀ $42
❀ $40

Showers Of Blessings
#105945
Issued: 1987 • Retired: 1993
Retail Price: $16 – $20

7

Values
♫ $53
★ $50
🕯 $48
❀ $44
❀ $42
🗐 $40

To Be With You Is Uplifting
#522260
Issued: 1989 • Retired: 1994
Retail Price: $20 – $22.50

8

Values
♫ $54
★ $40
🕯 $36
🗐 $34
❀ $32

To My Favorite Fan
#521043
Issued: 1990 • Susp.: 1993
Retail Price: $16

9

Values
🗐 $47
△ $42
♡ $38

Wishing You A Happy Bear Hug
#520659
Issued: 1995 • Susp.: 1996
Retail Price: $27.50

BIRTHDAY SERIES

	Price Paid	Value Of My Collection
1.		
2.		
3.		
4.		
5.		
6.		
7.		
8.		
9.		
PENCIL TOTALS		

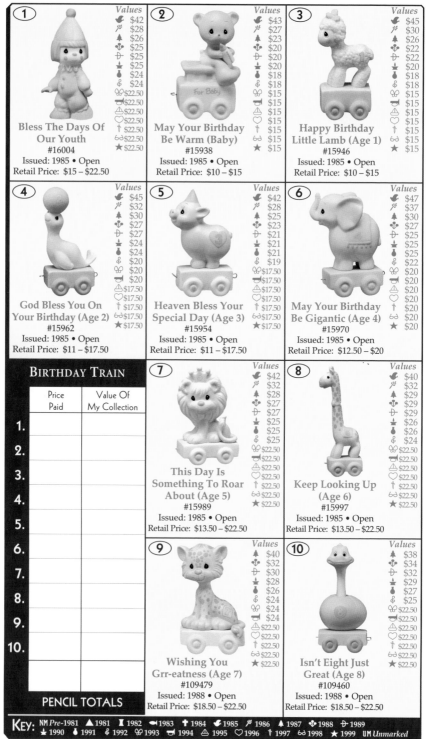

1 — *Values*
🐦 $42
🦋 $28
⚓ $26
⬧ $25
🐟 $25
⚒ $25
🕯 $24
🎗 $24
🎀 $22.50
🛷 $22.50
△ $22.50
♡ $22.50
✝ $22.50
👓 $22.50
★ $22.50

Bless The Days Of Our Youth
#16004
Issued: 1985 • Open
Retail Price: $15 – $22.50

2 — *Values*
🐦 $43
🦋 $27
⚓ $23
⬧ $20
🐟 $20
⚒ $20
🕯 $18
🎗 $18
🎀 $15
🛷 $15
△ $15
♡ $15
✝ $15
👓 $15
★ $15

May Your Birthday Be Warm (Baby)
#15938
Issued: 1985 • Open
Retail Price: $10 – $15

3 — *Values*
🐦 $45
🦋 $30
⚓ $26
⬧ $22
🐟 $22
⚒ $20
🕯 $18
🎗 $18
🎀 $15
🛷 $15
△ $15
♡ $15
✝ $15
👓 $15
★ $15

Happy Birthday Little Lamb (Age 1)
#15946
Issued: 1985 • Open
Retail Price: $10 – $15

4 — *Values*
🐦 $45
🦋 $32
⚓ $30
⬧ $27
🐟 $27
⚒ $24
🕯 $24
🎗 $20
🎀 $20
🛷 $20
△ $17.50
♡ $17.50
✝ $17.50
👓 $17.50
★ $17.50

God Bless You On Your Birthday (Age 2)
#15962
Issued: 1985 • Open
Retail Price: $11 – $17.50

5 — *Values*
🐦 $42
🦋 $28
⚓ $25
⬧ $23
🐟 $21
⚒ $21
🕯 $21
🎗 $19
🎀 $17.50
🛷 $17.50
△ $17.50
♡ $17.50
✝ $17.50
👓 $17.50
★ $17.50

Heaven Bless Your Special Day (Age 3)
#15954
Issued: 1985 • Open
Retail Price: $11 – $17.50

6 — *Values*
🐦 $47
🦋 $37
⚓ $30
⬧ $27
🐟 $25
⚒ $25
🕯 $25
🎗 $22
🎀 $20
🛷 $20
△ $20
♡ $20
✝ $20
👓 $20
★ $20

May Your Birthday Be Gigantic (Age 4)
#15970
Issued: 1985 • Open
Retail Price: $12.50 – $20

BIRTHDAY TRAIN

	Price Paid	Value Of My Collection
1.		
2.		
3.		
4.		
5.		
6.		
7.		
8.		
9.		
10.		

PENCIL TOTALS

7 — *Values*
🐦 $42
🦋 $32
⚓ $28
⬧ $27
🐟 $27
⚒ $25
🕯 $25
🎗 $25
🎀 $22.50
🛷 $22.50
△ $22.50
♡ $22.50
✝ $22.50
👓 $22.50
★ $22.50

This Day Is Something To Roar About (Age 5)
#15989
Issued: 1985 • Open
Retail Price: $13.50 – $22.50

8 — *Values*
🐦 $40
🦋 $32
⚓ $29
⬧ $29
🐟 $29
⚒ $26
🕯 $26
🎗 $24
🎀 $22.50
🛷 $22.50
△ $22.50
♡ $22.50
✝ $22.50
👓 $22.50
★ $22.50

Keep Looking Up (Age 6)
#15997
Issued: 1985 • Open
Retail Price: $13.50 – $22.50

9 — *Values*
⚓ $40
⬧ $32
🐟 $30
⚒ $28
🕯 $26
🎗 $24
🎀 $24
🛷 $24
△ $22.50
♡ $22.50
✝ $22.50
👓 $22.50
★ $22.50

Wishing You Grr-eatness (Age 7)
#109479
Issued: 1988 • Open
Retail Price: $18.50 – $22.50

10 — *Values*
⚓ $38
⬧ $34
🐟 $32
⚒ $29
🕯 $27
🎗 $25
🎀 $22.50
🛷 $22.50
△ $22.50
♡ $22.50
✝ $22.50
👓 $22.50
★ $22.50

Isn't Eight Just Great (Age 8)
#109460
Issued: 1988 • Open
Retail Price: $18.50 – $22.50

KEY: NM *Pre-1981* ▲ 1981 ✗ 1982 ◄ 1983 ✝ 1984 🐦 1985 🦋 1986 ⚓ 1987 ⬧ 1988 🐟 1989 ⚒ 1990 🕯 1991 🎗 1992 🎀 1993 🛷 1994 △ 1995 ♡ 1996 ✝ 1997 👓 1998 ★ 1999 UM *Unmarked*

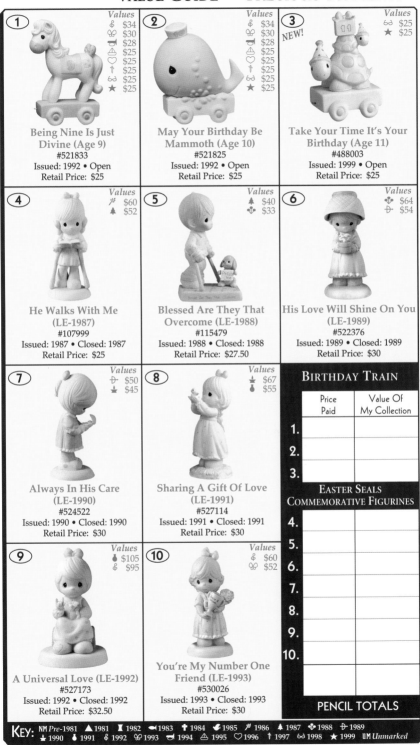

FIGURINE SERIES

1 — *Values*
- ✤ $34
- ♔ $30
- ♡ $28
- △ $25
- ♡ $25
- ✝ $25
- 6∂ $25
- ★ $25

Being Nine Is Just Divine (Age 9)
#521833
Issued: 1992 • Open
Retail Price: $25

2 — *Values*
- ✤ $34
- ♔ $30
- ♡ $28
- △ $25
- ♡ $25
- ✝ $25
- 6∂ $25
- ★ $25

May Your Birthday Be Mammoth (Age 10)
#521825
Issued: 1992 • Open
Retail Price: $25

3 — NEW! — *Values*
- 6∂ $25
- ★ $25

Take Your Time It's Your Birthday (Age 11)
#488003
Issued: 1999 • Open
Retail Price: $25

4 — *Values*
- ✗ $60
- ▲ $52

He Walks With Me (LE-1987)
#107999
Issued: 1987 • Closed: 1987
Retail Price: $25

5 — *Values*
- ▲ $40
- ⚓ $33

Blessed Are They That Overcome (LE-1988)
#115479
Issued: 1988 • Closed: 1988
Retail Price: $27.50

6 — *Values*
- ✤ $64
- Ð $54

His Love Will Shine On You (LE-1989)
#522376
Issued: 1989 • Closed: 1989
Retail Price: $30

7 — *Values*
- Ð $50
- ☀ $45

Always In His Care (LE-1990)
#524522
Issued: 1990 • Closed: 1990
Retail Price: $30

8 — *Values*
- ★ $67
- ♦ $55

Sharing A Gift Of Love (LE-1991)
#527114
Issued: 1991 • Closed: 1991
Retail Price: $30

9 — *Values*
- ♦ $105
- ✤ $95

A Universal Love (LE-1992)
#527173
Issued: 1992 • Closed: 1992
Retail Price: $32.50

10 — *Values*
- ✤ $60
- ♔ $52

You're My Number One Friend (LE-1993)
#530026
Issued: 1993 • Closed: 1993
Retail Price: $30

BIRTHDAY TRAIN

	Price Paid	Value Of My Collection
1.		
2.		
3.		

EASTER SEALS COMMEMORATIVE FIGURINES

4.		
5.		
6.		
7.		
8.		
9.		
10.		

PENCIL TOTALS

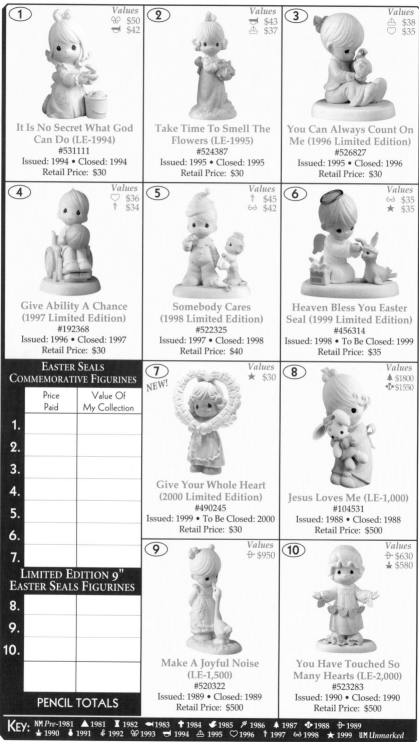

1
Values
🦋 $50
🏺 $42

It Is No Secret What God Can Do (LE-1994)
#531111
Issued: 1994 • Closed: 1994
Retail Price: $30

2
Values
🏺 $43
△ $37

Take Time To Smell The Flowers (LE-1995)
#524387
Issued: 1995 • Closed: 1995
Retail Price: $30

3
Values
△ $38
♡ $35

You Can Always Count On Me (1996 Limited Edition)
#526827
Issued: 1995 • Closed: 1996
Retail Price: $30

4
Values
♡ $36
† $34

Give Ability A Chance (1997 Limited Edition)
#192368
Issued: 1996 • Closed: 1997
Retail Price: $30

5
Values
† $45
6∂ $42

Somebody Cares (1998 Limited Edition)
#522325
Issued: 1997 • Closed: 1998
Retail Price: $40

6
Values
6∂ $35
★ $35

Heaven Bless You Easter Seal (1999 Limited Edition)
#456314
Issued: 1998 • To Be Closed: 1999
Retail Price: $35

EASTER SEALS COMMEMORATIVE FIGURINES

	Price Paid	Value Of My Collection
1.		
2.		
3.		
4.		
5.		
6.		
7.		

LIMITED EDITION 9" EASTER SEALS FIGURINES

8.		
9.		
10.		

PENCIL TOTALS

7
NEW!
Values
★ $30

Give Your Whole Heart (2000 Limited Edition)
#490245
Issued: 1999 • To Be Closed: 2000
Retail Price: $30

8
Values
♠ $1800
⚓ $1550

Jesus Loves Me (LE-1,000)
#104531
Issued: 1988 • Closed: 1988
Retail Price: $500

9
Values
Ð $950

Make A Joyful Noise (LE-1,500)
#520322
Issued: 1989 • Closed: 1989
Retail Price: $500

10
Values
Ð $630
★ $580

You Have Touched So Many Hearts (LE-2,000)
#523283
Issued: 1990 • Closed: 1990
Retail Price: $500

KEY: NM *Pre-1981* ▲1981 ✗ 1982 ◀1983 † 1984 ✦1985 ♪ 1986 ♠ 1987 ⚓1988 Ð 1989 ★ 1990 ♦ 1991 ♒ 1992 🦋1993 🏺 1994 △ 1995 ♡1996 † 1997 6∂ 1998 ★ 1999 UM *Unmarked*

FIGURINE SERIES

1 — *Values*
★ $710
🌡 $675

We Are God's Workmanship (LE-2,000)
#523879
Issued: 1991 • Closed: 1991
Retail Price: $500

2 — *Values*
🌡 $650
ᵬ $600

You Are Such A Purr-fect Friend (LE-2,000)
#526010
Issued: 1992 • Closed: 1992
Retail Price: $500

3 — *Values*
ᵬ $630
♈ $585

Gather Your Dreams (LE-2,000)
#529680
Issued: 1993 • Closed: 1993
Retail Price: $500

4 — *Values*
♈ $550
🝫 $515

You Are The Rose Of His Creation (LE-2,000)
#531243
Issued: 1994 • Closed: 1994
Retail Price: $500

5 — *Values*
🝫 $600
△ $580

He's Got The Whole World In His Hands (LE-2,000)
#526886
Issued: 1995 • Closed: 1995
Retail Price: $500

6 — *Values*
△ $560
♡ $560

HE Loves Me (LE-2,000)
#152277
Issued: 1995 • Closed: 1996
Retail Price: $500

7 — *Values*
♡ $530
† $530

Love Is Universal (LE-2,000)
#192376
Issued: 1996 • Closed: 1997
Retail Price: $500

8 — *Values*
† $520
6ᴣ $520

Love Grows Here (LE-2,000)
#272981
Issued: 1997 • Closed: 1998
Retail Price: $500

9 — *Values*
6ᴣ $500
★ $500

We Are All Precious In His Sight (LE-2,000)
#475068
Issued: 1998 • Open
Retail Price: $500

10 — *Values*
★ $500
NEW!

Jesus Loves Me (LE-1,500)
#634735
Issued: 1999 • Open
Retail Price: $500

LIMITED EDITION 9" EASTER SEALS FIGURINES

	Price Paid	Value Of My Collection
1.		
2.		
3.		
4.		
5.		
6.		
7.		
8.		
9.		
10.		
	PENCIL TOTALS	

KEY: NM *Pre-1981* ▲ 1981 Ⅱ 1982 ◀1983 † 1984 ᵬ 1985 ♪ 1986 ▲ 1987 ♣ 1988 � 1989 ★ 1990 🌡 1991 ᵬ 1992 ♈ 1993 🝫 1994 △ 1995 ♡ 1996 † 1997 6ᴣ 1998 ★ 1999 UM *Unmarked*

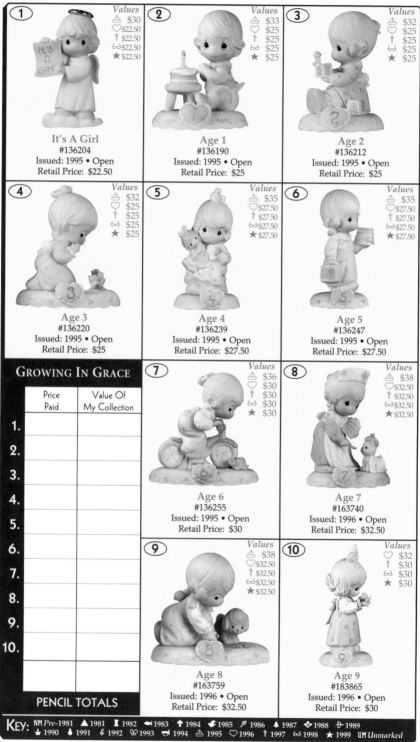

① It's A Girl
#136204
Issued: 1995 • Open
Retail Price: $22.50

Values
⛪ $30
♡ $22.50
✝ $22.50
👓 $22.50
★ $22.50

② Age 1
#136190
Issued: 1995 • Open
Retail Price: $25

Values
⛪ $33
♡ $25
✝ $25
👓 $25
★ $25

③ Age 2
#136212
Issued: 1995 • Open
Retail Price: $25

Values
⛪ $32
♡ $25
✝ $25
👓 $25
★ $25

④ Age 3
#136220
Issued: 1995 • Open
Retail Price: $25

Values
⛪ $32
♡ $25
✝ $25
👓 $25
★ $25

⑤ Age 4
#136239
Issued: 1995 • Open
Retail Price: $27.50

Values
⛪ $35
♡ $27.50
✝ $27.50
👓 $27.50
★ $27.50

⑥ Age 5
#136247
Issued: 1995 • Open
Retail Price: $27.50

Values
⛪ $35
♡ $27.50
✝ $27.50
👓 $27.50
★ $27.50

GROWING IN GRACE

	Price Paid	Value Of My Collection
1.		
2.		
3.		
4.		
5.		
6.		
7.		
8.		
9.		
10.		
PENCIL TOTALS		

⑦ Age 6
#136255
Issued: 1995 • Open
Retail Price: $30

Values
⛪ $36
♡ $30
✝ $30
👓 $30
★ $30

⑧ Age 7
#163740
Issued: 1996 • Open
Retail Price: $32.50

Values
⛪ $38
♡ $32.50
✝ $32.50
👓 $32.50
★ $32.50

⑨ Age 8
#163759
Issued: 1996 • Open
Retail Price: $32.50

Values
⛪ $38
♡ $32.50
✝ $32.50
👓 $32.50
★ $32.50

⑩ Age 9
#183865
Issued: 1996 • Open
Retail Price: $30

Values
♡ $32
✝ $30
👓 $30
★ $30

KEY: NM *Pre-1981* ▲1981 Ⅱ 1982 ◄1983 ✝ 1984 ◀1985 ♫ 1986 ♠ 1987 ♣ 1988 ♦ 1989 ★ 1990 ♦ 1991 ♬ 1992 ♀ 1993 ◄ 1994 ⛪ 1995 ♡ 1996 ✝ 1997 👓 1998 ★ 1999 **UM** *Unmarked*

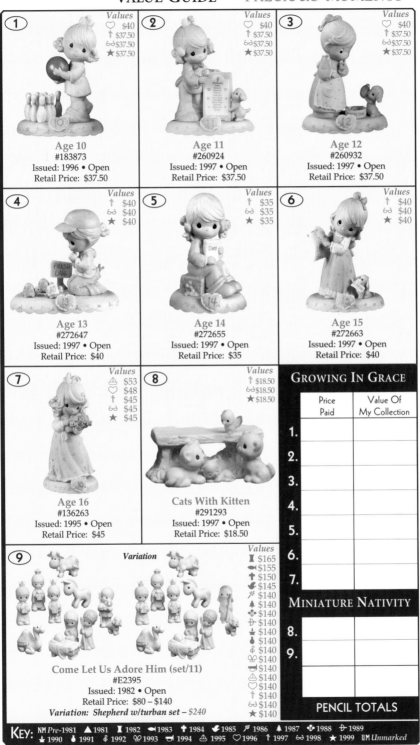

1

Values
♡ $40
✝ $37.50
ᏻ $37.50
★ $37.50

Age 10
#183873
Issued: 1996 • Open
Retail Price: $37.50

2

Values
♡ $40
✝ $37.50
ᏻ $37.50
★ $37.50

Age 11
#260924
Issued: 1997 • Open
Retail Price: $37.50

3

Values
♡ $40
✝ $37.50
ᏻ $37.50
★ $37.50

Age 12
#260932
Issued: 1997 • Open
Retail Price: $37.50

4

Values
✝ $40
ᏻ $40
★ $40

Age 13
#272647
Issued: 1997 • Open
Retail Price: $40

5

Values
✝ $35
ᏻ $35
★ $35

Age 14
#272655
Issued: 1997 • Open
Retail Price: $35

6

Values
✝ $40
ᏻ $40
★ $40

Age 15
#272663
Issued: 1997 • Open
Retail Price: $40

7

Values
⬧ $53
♡ $48
✝ $45
ᏻ $45
★ $45

Age 16
#136263
Issued: 1995 • Open
Retail Price: $45

8

Values
✝ $18.50
ᏻ $18.50
★ $18.50

Cats With Kitten
#291293
Issued: 1997 • Open
Retail Price: $18.50

9

Variation

Values
I $165
◄ $155
✝ $150
✔ $145
♫ $140
♠ $140
⚓ $140
Đ $140
✦ $140
♦ $140
♪ $140
ᏋᏋ $140
━ $140
⬧ $140
♡ $140
✝ $140
ᏻ $140
★ $140

Come Let Us Adore Him (set/11)
#E2395
Issued: 1982 • Open
Retail Price: $80 – $140
Variation: Shepherd w/turban set – $240

GROWING IN GRACE

	Price Paid	Value Of My Collection
1.		
2.		
3.		
4.		
5.		
6.		
7.		

MINIATURE NATIVITY

8.		
9.		
PENCIL TOTALS		

KEY: NM *Pre-1981* ▲ 1981 I 1982 ◄ 1983 ✝ 1984 ✔ 1985 ♫ 1986 ♠ 1987 ✦ 1988 Đ 1989 ♪ 1990 ♦ 1991 Ꮛ 1992 ᏋᏋ 1993 ━ 1994 ⬧ 1995 ♡ 1996 ✝ 1997 ᏻ 1998 ★ 1999 UM *Unmarked*

FIGURINE SERIES

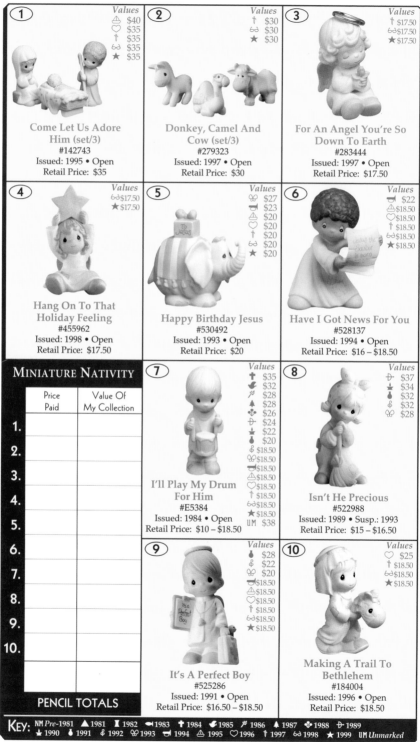

1

Values	
△	$40
♡	$35
†	$35
6ᵍ	$35
★	$35

Come Let Us Adore Him (set/3)
#142743
Issued: 1995 • Open
Retail Price: $35

2

Values	
†	$30
6ᵍ	$30
★	$30

Donkey, Camel And Cow (set/3)
#279323
Issued: 1997 • Open
Retail Price: $30

3

Values	
†	$17.50
6ᵍ	$17.50
★	$17.50

For An Angel You're So Down To Earth
#283444
Issued: 1997 • Open
Retail Price: $17.50

4

Values	
6ᵍ	$17.50
★	$17.50

Hang On To That Holiday Feeling
#455962
Issued: 1998 • Open
Retail Price: $17.50

5

Values	
⅋	$27
⊐	$23
△	$20
♡	$20
†	$20
6ᵍ	$20
★	$20

Happy Birthday Jesus
#530492
Issued: 1993 • Open
Retail Price: $20

6

Values	
⊐	$22
△	$18.50
♡	$18.50
†	$18.50
6ᵍ	$18.50
★	$18.50

Have I Got News For You
#528137
Issued: 1994 • Open
Retail Price: $16 – $18.50

MINIATURE NATIVITY

	Price Paid	Value Of My Collection
1.		
2.		
3.		
4.		
5.		
6.		
7.		
8.		
9.		
10.		
PENCIL TOTALS		

7

Values	
†	$35
⅌	$32
ℐ	$28
♠	$28
⊹	$26
₽	$24
★	$22
▮	$20
⅋	$18.50
⅋	$18.50
⊐	$18.50
△	$18.50
♡	$18.50
†	$18.50
6ᵍ	$18.50
★	$18.50
UM	$38

I'll Play My Drum For Him
#E5384
Issued: 1984 • Open
Retail Price: $10 – $18.50

8

Values	
Ð	$37
★	$34
▮	$32
ℐ	$32
⅋	$28

Isn't He Precious
#522988
Issued: 1989 • Susp.: 1993
Retail Price: $15 – $16.50

9

Values	
▮	$28
ℐ	$22
⅋	$20
⊐	$18.50
△	$18.50
♡	$18.50
†	$18.50
6ᵍ	$18.50
★	$18.50

It's A Perfect Boy
#525286
Issued: 1991 • Open
Retail Price: $16.50 – $18.50

10

Values	
♡	$25
†	$18.50
6ᵍ	$18.50
★	$18.50

Making A Trail To Bethlehem
#184004
Issued: 1996 • Open
Retail Price: $18.50

KEY: NM *Pre-1981* △ 1981 ∐ 1982 ◄ 1983 † 1984 ✇ 1985 ℐ 1986 ♠ 1987 ✤ 1988 Ð 1989 ★ 1990 ▮ 1991 ℰ 1992 ⅋ 1993 ⊐ 1994 △ 1995 ♡ 1996 † 1997 6ᵍ 1998 ★ 1999 UM *Unmarked*

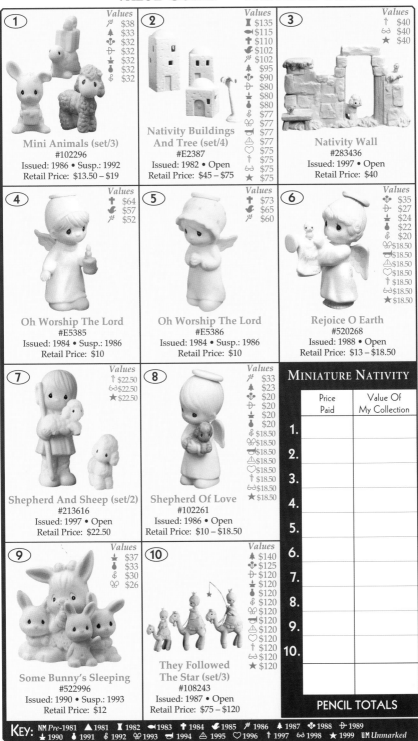

Figurine Series

(1) Values
- ℱ $38
- ▲ $33
- ✿ $32
- ⌐ $32
- ✦ $32
- ● $32
- § $32

Mini Animals (set/3)
#102296
Issued: 1986 • Susp.: 1992
Retail Price: $13.50 – $19

(2) Values
- ▮ $135
- ◀ $115
- ✝ $110
- ✦ $102
- ℱ $102
- ▲ $95
- ✿ $90
- ⌐ $80
- ✦ $80
- ● $80
- § $77
- ♋ $77
- ◅ $77
- ◬ $77
- ♡ $75
- ✝ $75
- ᧖ $75
- ★ $75

Nativity Buildings And Tree (set/4)
#E2387
Issued: 1982 • Open
Retail Price: $45 – $75

(3) Values
- ✝ $40
- ᧖ $40
- ★ $40

Nativity Wall
#283436
Issued: 1997 • Open
Retail Price: $40

(4) Values
- ✝ $64
- ✦ $57
- ℱ $52

Oh Worship The Lord
#E5385
Issued: 1984 • Susp.: 1986
Retail Price: $10

(5) Values
- ✝ $73
- ✿ $65
- ℱ $60

Oh Worship The Lord
#E5386
Issued: 1984 • Susp.: 1986
Retail Price: $10

(6) Values
- ✿ $35
- ⌐ $27
- ✦ $24
- ● $22
- § $20
- ♋ $18.50
- ◅ $18.50
- ◬ $18.50
- ♡ $18.50
- ✝ $18.50
- ᧖ $18.50
- ★ $18.50

Rejoice O Earth
#520268
Issued: 1988 • Open
Retail Price: $13 – $18.50

(7) Values
- ✝ $22.50
- ᧖ $22.50
- ★ $22.50

Shepherd And Sheep (set/2)
#213616
Issued: 1997 • Open
Retail Price: $22.50

(8) Values
- ℱ $33
- ▲ $23
- ✿ $20
- ⌐ $20
- ✦ $20
- ● $20
- § $18.50
- ♋ $18.50
- ◅ $18.50
- ◬ $18.50
- ♡ $18.50
- ✝ $18.50
- ᧖ $18.50
- ★ $18.50

Shepherd Of Love
#102261
Issued: 1986 • Open
Retail Price: $10 – $18.50

Miniature Nativity

	Price Paid	Value Of My Collection
1.		
2.		
3.		
4.		
5.		
6.		
7.		
8.		
9.		
10.		
PENCIL TOTALS		

(9) Values
- ✦ $37
- ● $33
- § $30
- ♋ $26

Some Bunny's Sleeping
#522996
Issued: 1990 • Susp.: 1993
Retail Price: $12

(10) Values
- ▲ $140
- ✿ $125
- ⌐ $120
- ✦ $120
- ● $120
- § $120
- ♋ $120
- ◅ $120
- ◬ $120
- ♡ $120
- ✝ $120
- ᧖ $120
- ★ $120

They Followed The Star (set/3)
#108243
Issued: 1987 • Open
Retail Price: $75 – $120

KEY: NM *Pre-1981* ▲ 1981 ▮ 1982 ◀ 1983 ✝ 1984 ✦ 1985 ℱ 1986 ▲ 1987 ✿ 1988 ⌐ 1989
★ 1990 ● 1991 § 1992 ♋ 1993 ◅ 1994 ◬ 1995 ♡ 1996 ✝ 1997 ᧖ 1998 ★ 1999 UM *Unmarked*

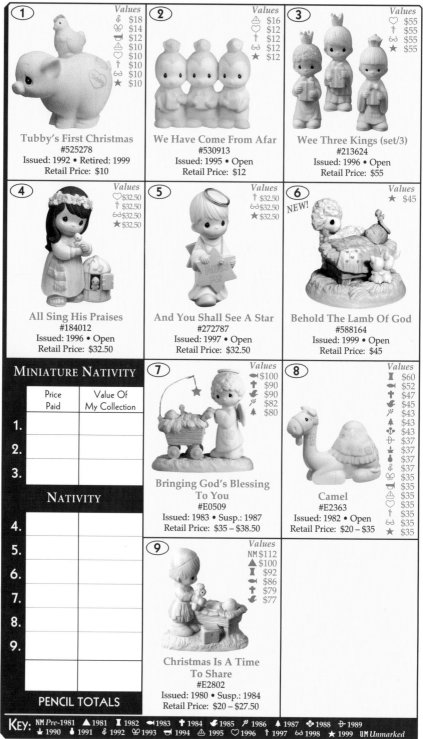

① Tubby's First Christmas

Values	
🎋	$18
🐛	$14
🍞	$12
△	$10
♡	$10
†	$10
👓	$10
★	$10

#525278
Issued: 1992 • Retired: 1999
Retail Price: $10

② We Have Come From Afar

Values	
△	$16
♡	$12
†	$12
👓	$12
★	$12

#530913
Issued: 1995 • Open
Retail Price: $12

③ Wee Three Kings (set/3)

Values	
♡	$55
†	$55
👓	$55
★	$55

#213624
Issued: 1996 • Open
Retail Price: $55

④ All Sing His Praises

Values	
♡	$32.50
†	$32.50
👓	$32.50
★	$32.50

#184012
Issued: 1996 • Open
Retail Price: $32.50

⑤ And You Shall See A Star

Values	
†	$32.50
👓	$32.50
★	$32.50

#272787
Issued: 1997 • Open
Retail Price: $32.50

⑥ Behold The Lamb Of God
NEW!

Values	
★	$45

#588164
Issued: 1999 • Open
Retail Price: $45

MINIATURE NATIVITY

	Price Paid	Value Of My Collection
1.		
2.		
3.		

NATIVITY

	Price Paid	Value Of My Collection
4.		
5.		
6.		
7.		
8.		
9.		

PENCIL TOTALS

⑦ Bringing God's Blessing To You

Values	
◄	$100
†	$90
🐛	$90
🎐	$82
▲	$80

#E0509
Issued: 1983 • Susp.: 1987
Retail Price: $35 – $38.50

⑧ Camel

Values	
✖	$60
◄	$52
†	$47
🐛	$45
🎐	$43
▲	$43
⚓	$43
⊕	$37
★	$37
♦	$37
🎋	$35
🌷	$35
△	$35
♡	$35
†	$35
👓	$35
★	$35

#E2363
Issued: 1982 • Open
Retail Price: $20 – $35

⑨ Christmas Is A Time To Share

Values	
NM	$112
▲	$100
✖	$92
◄	$86
†	$79
🐛	$77

#E2802
Issued: 1980 • Susp.: 1984
Retail Price: $20 – $27.50

KEY: NM *Pre-1981* ▲ 1981 ✖ 1982 ◄ 1983 † 1984 🐛 1985 🎐 1986 ▲ 1987 🌷 1988 ⊕ 1989 ★ 1990 ♦ 1991 🎋 1992 ❀ 1993 🍞 1994 △ 1995 ♡ 1996 † 1997 👓 1998 ★ 1999 **UM** *Unmarked*

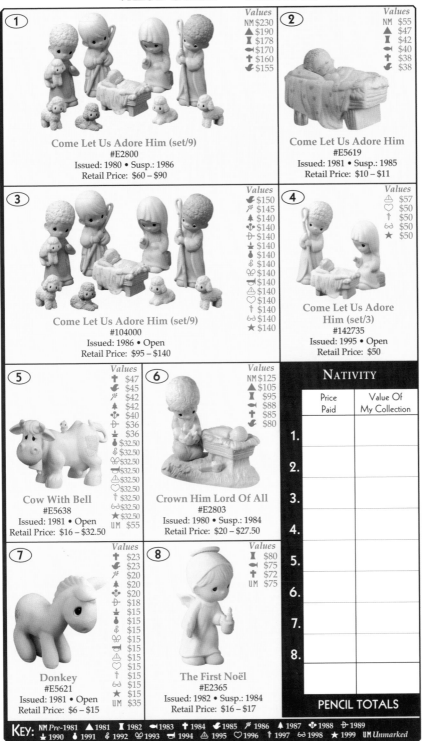

1

Come Let Us Adore Him (set/9)
#E2800
Issued: 1980 • Susp.: 1986
Retail Price: $60 – $90

Values
NM $230
▲ $190
I $178
◀ $170
† $160
◀ $155

2

Come Let Us Adore Him
#E5619
Issued: 1981 • Susp.: 1985
Retail Price: $10 – $11

Values
NM $55
▲ $47
I $42
◀ $40
† $38
◀ $38

3

Come Let Us Adore Him (set/9)
#104000
Issued: 1986 • Open
Retail Price: $95 – $140

Values
◀ $150
♪ $145
▲ $140
✣ $140
Ð $140
★ $140
● $140
✦ $140
ℳ $140
◪ $140
△ $140
♡ $140
† $140
6ð $140
★ $140

4

Come Let Us Adore Him (set/3)
#142735
Issued: 1995 • Open
Retail Price: $50

Values
△ $57
♡ $50
† $50
6ð $50
★ $50

5

Cow With Bell
#E5638
Issued: 1981 • Open
Retail Price: $16 – $32.50

Values
† $47
✦ $45
♪ $42
▲ $42
✣ $40
Ð $36
★ $36
● $32.50
✦ $32.50
ℳ $32.50
◪ $32.50
△ $32.50
♡ $32.50
† $32.50
6ð $32.50
★ $32.50
UM $55

6

Crown Him Lord Of All
#E2803
Issued: 1980 • Susp.: 1984
Retail Price: $20 – $27.50

Values
NM $125
▲ $105
I $95
◀ $88
† $85
◀ $80

7

Donkey
#E5621
Issued: 1981 • Open
Retail Price: $6 – $15

Values
† $23
✦ $23
♪ $20
▲ $20
✣ $20
Ð $18
★ $15
● $15
✦ $15
ℳ $15
◪ $15
△ $15
♡ $15
† $15
6ð $15
★ $15
UM $35

8

The First Noël
#E2365
Issued: 1982 • Susp.: 1984
Retail Price: $16 – $17

Values
I $80
◀ $75
† $72
UM $75

NATIVITY

	Price Paid	Value Of My Collection
1.		
2.		
3.		
4.		
5.		
6.		
7.		
8.		
PENCIL TOTALS		

KEY: NM *Pre-1981* ▲ 1981 I 1982 ◀ 1983 † 1984 ◀ 1985 ♪ 1986 ▲ 1987 ✣ 1988 Ð 1989 ★ 1990 ● 1991 ✦ 1992 ℳ 1993 ◪ 1994 △ 1995 ♡ 1996 † 1997 6ð 1998 ★ 1999 UM *Unmarked*

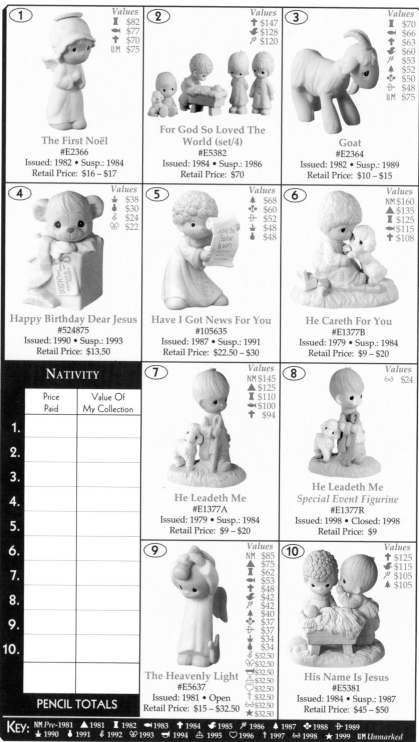

1

Values
- ✠ $82
- ↩ $77
- ✝ $70
- UM $75

The First Noël
#E2366
Issued: 1982 • Susp.: 1984
Retail Price: $16 – $17

2

Values
- ✝ $147
- ✦ $128
- ♫ $120

For God So Loved The World (set/4)
#E5382
Issued: 1984 • Susp.: 1986
Retail Price: $70

3

Values
- ✠ $70
- ↩ $66
- ✝ $63
- ✦ $60
- ♫ $53
- ▲ $52
- ✧ $50
- ֏ $48
- UM $75

Goat
#E2364
Issued: 1982 • Susp.: 1989
Retail Price: $10 – $15

4

Values
- ★ $38
- ◊ $30
- ♒ $24
- ♋ $22

Happy Birthday Dear Jesus
#524875
Issued: 1990 • Susp.: 1993
Retail Price: $13.50

5

Values
- ▲ $68
- ✧ $60
- ֏ $52
- ★ $48
- ◊ $48

Have I Got News For You
#105635
Issued: 1987 • Susp.: 1991
Retail Price: $22.50 – $30

6

Values
- NM $160
- ▲ $135
- ✠ $125
- ↩ $115
- ✝ $108

He Careth For You
#E1377B
Issued: 1979 • Susp.: 1984
Retail Price: $9 – $20

NATIVITY

	Price Paid	Value Of My Collection
1.		
2.		
3.		
4.		
5.		
6.		
7.		
8.		
9.		
10.		
PENCIL TOTALS		

7

Values
- NM $145
- ▲ $125
- ✠ $110
- ↩ $100
- ✝ $94

He Leadeth Me
#E1377A
Issued: 1979 • Susp.: 1984
Retail Price: $9 – $20

8

Values
- ᚼᚼ $24

He Leadeth Me
Special Event Figurine
#E1377R
Issued: 1998 • Closed: 1998
Retail Price: $9

9

Values
- NM $85
- ◊ $75
- ✠ $62
- ✧ $53
- ✝ $48
- ✦ $42
- ♫ $42
- ▲ $40
- ✧ $37
- ֏ $37
- ★ $34
- ◊ $34
- ♒ $32.50
- ♋ $32.50
- ✧ $32.50
- ⚘ $32.50
- ♡ $32.50
- ✝ $32.50
- ★ $32.50

The Heavenly Light
#E5637
Issued: 1981 • Open
Retail Price: $15 – $32.50

10

Values
- ✝ $125
- ✦ $115
- ♫ $105
- ▲ $105

His Name Is Jesus
#E5381
Issued: 1984 • Susp.: 1987
Retail Price: $45 – $50

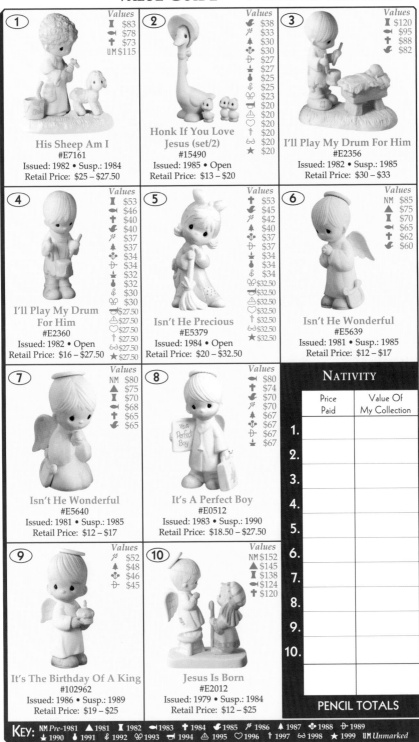

(1) His Sheep Am I
#E7161
Issued: 1982 • Susp.: 1984
Retail Price: $25 – $27.50

Values
I $83
◄ $78
† $73
UM $115

(2) Honk If You Love Jesus (set/2)
#15490
Issued: 1985 • Open
Retail Price: $13 – $20

Values
$38
$33
$30
$30
$27
$27
$25
$25
$23
$20
$20
$20
$20
$20
★ $20

(3) I'll Play My Drum For Him
#E2356
Issued: 1982 • Susp.: 1985
Retail Price: $30 – $33

Values
I $120
◄ $95
† $88
$82

(4) I'll Play My Drum For Him
#E2360
Issued: 1982 • Open
Retail Price: $16 – $27.50

Values
I $53
◄ $46
† $40
$37
$37
$37
$34
$34
$32
$32
$30
$30
$27.50
$27.50
$27.50
$27.50
$27.50
★ $27.50

(5) Isn't He Precious
#E5379
Issued: 1984 • Open
Retail Price: $20 – $32.50

Values
† $53
$45
$42
$40
$37
$37
$34
$34
$34
$32.50
$32.50
$32.50
$32.50
† $32.50
$32.50
★ $32.50

(6) Isn't He Wonderful
#E5639
Issued: 1981 • Susp.: 1985
Retail Price: $12 – $17

Values
NM $85
▲ $75
I $70
◄ $65
† $62
$60

(7) Isn't He Wonderful
#E5640
Issued: 1981 • Susp.: 1985
Retail Price: $12 – $17

Values
NM $80
▲ $75
I $70
◄ $68
† $65
$65

(8) It's A Perfect Boy
#E0512
Issued: 1983 • Susp.: 1990
Retail Price: $18.50 – $27.50

Values
$80
† $74
$70
$70
$67
$67
$67
$67

(9) It's The Birthday Of A King
#102962
Issued: 1986 • Susp.: 1989
Retail Price: $19 – $25

Values
$52
▲ $48
$46
$45

(10) Jesus Is Born
#E2012
Issued: 1979 • Susp.: 1984
Retail Price: $12 – $25

Values
NM $152
▲ $145
I $138
◄ $124
† $120

NATIVITY

	Price Paid	Value Of My Collection
1.		
2.		
3.		
4.		
5.		
6.		
7.		
8.		
9.		
10.		
PENCIL TOTALS		

KEY: NM *Pre-1981* ▲ 1981 I 1982 ◄ 1983 † 1984 1985 1986 ▲ 1987 1988 1989 ★ 1990 1991 1992 1993 1994 1995 ♡ 1996 † 1997 1998 ★ 1999 UM *Unmarked*

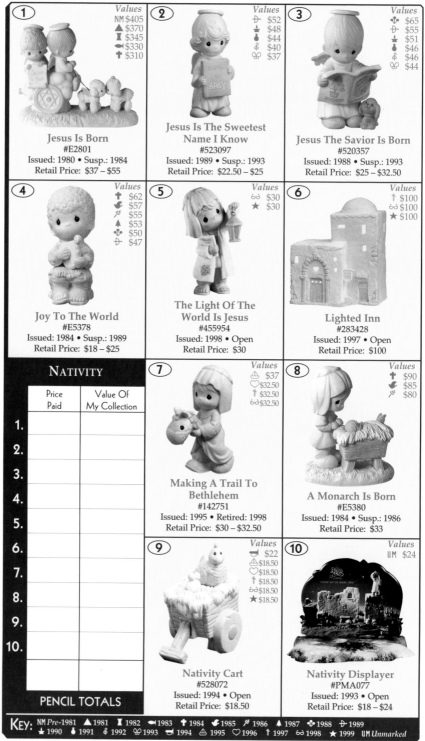

1

Values	
NM	$405
▲	$370
✕	$345
◄	$330
✝	$310

Jesus Is Born
#E2801
Issued: 1980 • Susp.: 1984
Retail Price: $37 – $55

2

Values	
Ð	$52
★	$48
●	$44
⑧	$40
⑨	$37

Jesus Is The Sweetest Name I Know
#523097
Issued: 1989 • Susp.: 1993
Retail Price: $22.50 – $25

3

Values	
✤	$65
Ð	$55
★	$51
●	$46
⑧	$46
⑨	$44

Jesus The Savior Is Born
#520357
Issued: 1988 • Susp.: 1993
Retail Price: $25 – $32.50

4

Values	
✝	$62
❧	$57
♫	$55
▲	$53
✤	$50
Ð	$47

Joy To The World
#E5378
Issued: 1984 • Susp.: 1989
Retail Price: $18 – $25

5

Values	
6ð	$30
★	$30

The Light Of The World Is Jesus
#455954
Issued: 1998 • Open
Retail Price: $30

6

Values	
✝	$100
6ð	$100
★	$100

Lighted Inn
#283428
Issued: 1997 • Open
Retail Price: $100

7

Values	
△	$37
♡	$32.50
✝	$32.50
6ð	$32.50

Making A Trail To Bethlehem
#142751
Issued: 1995 • Retired: 1998
Retail Price: $30 – $32.50

8

Values	
✝	$90
❧	$85
♫	$80

A Monarch Is Born
#E5380
Issued: 1984 • Susp.: 1986
Retail Price: $33

9

Values	
◄	$22
△	$18.50
♡	$18.50
✝	$18.50
6ð	$18.50
★	$18.50

Nativity Cart
#528072
Issued: 1994 • Open
Retail Price: $18.50

10

Values	
UM	$24

Nativity Displayer
#PMA077
Issued: 1993 • Open
Retail Price: $18 – $24

1

Values	
NM	$165
▲	$160
I	$148
◄	$140
†	$135
✿	$132
℔	$130
▲	$130
❖	$125
Ð	$125
♣	$125
★	$125
♨	$120
℘	$120
☟	$120
△	$120
♡	$120
†	$120
6ð	$120
★	$120

Nativity Wall (set/2)
#E5644
Issued: 1981 • Open
Retail Price: $60 – $120

2

Values	
†	$60
6ð	$60
★	$60

Palm Trees, Hay Bale And Baby Food (set/4)
#272582
Issued: 1997 • Open
Retail Price: $60

3

Values	
◄	$170
†	$155
✿	$148
℘	$145

Prepare Ye The Way Of The Lord (set/6)
#E0508
Issued: 1983 • Susp.: 1986
Retail Price: $75

4

Values	
NM	$85
▲	$77
I	$62
◄	$54
†	$50
✿	$45
℘	$42
▲	$42
❖	$37
Ð	$35
♣	$35
★	$32.50
♨	$32.50
℘	$32.50
△	$32.50
♡	$32.50
†	$32.50
6ð	$32.50
★	$32.50

Rejoice O Earth
#E5636
Issued: 1981 • Retired: 1999
Retail Price: $15 – $32.50

5

Values	
♨	$52
☟	$40
△	$32
♡	$32
†	$32

Ring Out The Good News
#529966
Issued: 1993 • Retired: 1997
Retail Price: $27.50 – $30

6

Values	
♡	$40
†	$40
6ð	$40
★	$40

Shepherd With Lambs (set/3)
#183954
Issued: 1996 • Open
Retail Price: $40

7

Values	
†	$40
6ð	$40
★	$40

Shepherd With Two Lambs (set/3)
#183962
Issued: 1997 • Open
Retail Price: $40

8

Values	
❖	$45
Ð	$38
♣	$35
▲	$35
♣	$35
♨	$32
☟	$30
△	$30
♡	$30

Some Bunny's Sleeping
#115274
Issued: 1988 • Susp.: 1996
Retail Price: $15 – $18.50

9

Values	
NM	$345
▲	$300
I	$265
◄	$250
†	$240
✿	$240
℘	$240
▲	$240
❖	$240
Ð	$235
♣	$235
★	$230
♨	$225
℘	$225
△	$225
♡	$225
†	$225
6ð	$225
★	$225

They Followed The Star (set/3)
#E5624
Issued: 1981 • Open
Retail Price: $130 – $225

10

Values	
NM	$260
▲	$250
I	$235
◄	$215
†	$200
✿	$195

They Followed The Star
#E5641
Issued: 1981 • Susp.: 1985
Retail Price: $75 – $100

NATIVITY

	Price Paid	Value Of My Collection
1.		
2.		
3.		
4.		
5.		
6.		
7.		
8.		
9.		
10.		

PENCIL TOTALS

KEY: NM *Pre-1981* ▲ 1981 I 1982 ◄ 1983 † 1984 ✿ 1985 ℘ 1986 ▲ 1987 ❖ 1988 Ð 1989 ★ 1990 ♣ 1991 ♨ 1992 ℘ 1993 ☟ 1994 △ 1995 ♡ 1996 † 1997 6ð 1998 ★ 1999 **UM** *Unmarked*

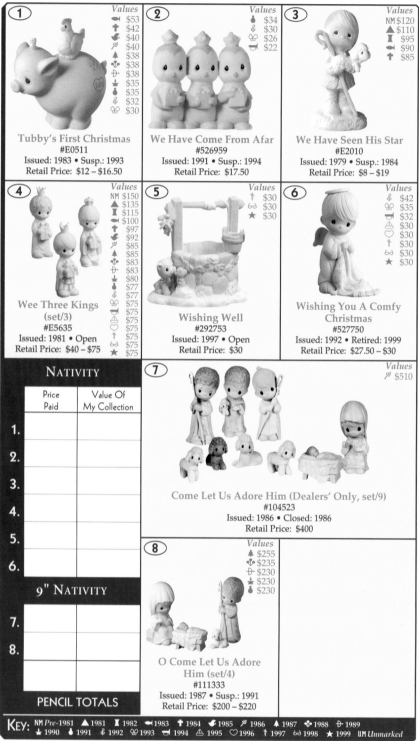

① Values
- 🐟 $53
- ✝ $42
- ✿ $40
- ✹ $40
- ▲ $38
- ⚓ $38
- ⅁ $38
- ✦ $35
- ⚘ $35
- ⅃ $32
- ∞ $30

Tubby's First Christmas
#E0511
Issued: 1983 • Susp.: 1993
Retail Price: $12 – $16.50

② Values
- ⚱ $34
- ♪ $30
- ∞ $26
- ✦ $22

We Have Come From Afar
#526959
Issued: 1991 • Susp.: 1994
Retail Price: $17.50

③ Values
- NM $120
- ▲ $110
- ∎ $95
- ◄ $90
- ✝ $85

We Have Seen His Star
#E2010
Issued: 1979 • Susp.: 1984
Retail Price: $8 – $19

④ Values
- NM $150
- ▲ $135
- ∎ $115
- ◄ $100
- ✝ $97
- ✿ $92
- ✹ $85
- ▲ $85
- ⚓ $83
- ⅁ $83
- ⚘ $80
- ⚘ $77
- ⅃ $77
- ∞ $75
- ∞ $75
- △ $75
- ♡ $75
- ✝ $75
- ⚭ $75
- ★ $75

Wee Three Kings (set/3)
#E5635
Issued: 1981 • Open
Retail Price: $40 – $75

⑤ Values
- ✝ $30
- ⚭ $30
- ★ $30

Wishing Well
#292753
Issued: 1997 • Open
Retail Price: $30

⑥ Values
- ♪ $42
- ∞ $35
- ⚰ $32
- △ $30
- ♡ $30
- ✝ $30
- ⚭ $30
- ★ $30

Wishing You A Comfy Christmas
#527750
Issued: 1992 • Retired: 1999
Retail Price: $27.50 – $30

NATIVITY

	Price Paid	Value Of My Collection
1.		
2.		
3.		
4.		
5.		
6.		

9" NATIVITY

7.		
8.		

PENCIL TOTALS

⑦ Values
- ✹ $510

Come Let Us Adore Him (Dealers' Only, set/9)
#104523
Issued: 1986 • Closed: 1986
Retail Price: $400

⑧ Values
- ▲ $255
- ⚓ $235
- ⅁ $230
- ✦ $230
- ⚱ $230

O Come Let Us Adore Him (set/4)
#111333
Issued: 1987 • Susp.: 1991
Retail Price: $200 – $220

KEY: NM *Pre-1981* ▲1981 ∎1982 ◄1983 ✝1984 ✿1985 ✹1986 ▲1987 ⚓1988 ⅁1989 ✦1990 ⚱1991 ♪1992 ∞1993 ⚰1994 △1995 ♡1996 ✝1997 ⚭1998 ★1999 UM *Unmarked*

58

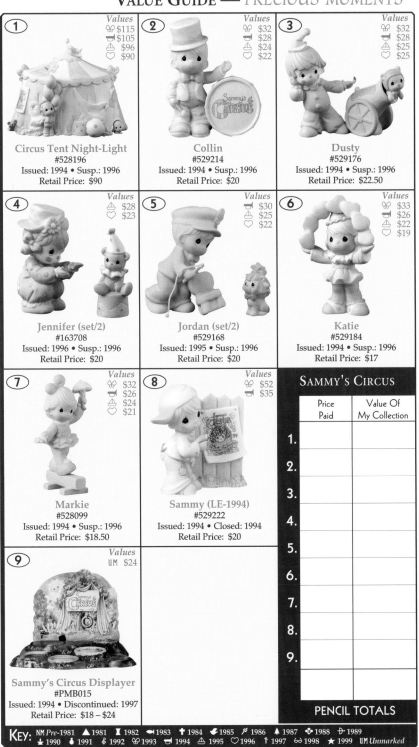

FIGURINE SERIES

1

Values
- 🐛 $115
- ⚄ $105
- △ $96
- ♡ $90

Circus Tent Night-Light
#528196
Issued: 1994 • Susp.: 1996
Retail Price: $90

2

Values
- 🐛 $32
- ⚄ $28
- △ $24
- ♡ $22

Collin
#529214
Issued: 1994 • Susp.: 1996
Retail Price: $20

3

Values
- 🐛 $32
- ⚄ $28
- △ $25
- ♡ $25

Dusty
#529176
Issued: 1994 • Susp.: 1996
Retail Price: $22.50

4

Values
- △ $28
- ♡ $23

Jennifer (set/2)
#163708
Issued: 1996 • Susp.: 1996
Retail Price: $20

5

Values
- ⚄ $30
- △ $25
- ♡ $22

Jordan (set/2)
#529168
Issued: 1995 • Susp.: 1996
Retail Price: $20

6

Values
- 🐛 $33
- ⚄ $26
- △ $22
- ♡ $19

Katie
#529184
Issued: 1994 • Susp.: 1996
Retail Price: $17

7

Values
- 🐛 $32
- ⚄ $26
- △ $24
- ♡ $21

Markie
#528099
Issued: 1994 • Susp.: 1996
Retail Price: $18.50

8

Values
- 🐛 $52
- ⚄ $35

Sammy (LE-1994)
#529222
Issued: 1994 • Closed: 1994
Retail Price: $20

9

Values
- UM $24

Sammy's Circus Displayer
#PMB015
Issued: 1994 • Discontinued: 1997
Retail Price: $18 – $24

SAMMY'S CIRCUS

	Price Paid	Value Of My Collection
1.		
2.		
3.		
4.		
5.		
6.		
7.		
8.		
9.		
PENCIL TOTALS		

KEY: NM *Pre-1981* ▲ 1981 ▌ 1982 ◀ 1983 ✝ 1984 ✦ 1985 ♪ 1986 ▲ 1987 ✤ 1988 ☙ 1989 ★ 1990 ● 1991 ♭ 1992 🐛 1993 ⚄ 1994 △ 1995 ♡ 1996 ✝ 1997 ∞ 1998 ★ 1999 UM *Unmarked*

59

1

Values
🐝 $22
🎀 $19
△ $15
♡ $14

Tippy
#529192
Issued: 1994 • Susp.: 1996
Retail Price: $12

2

Values
🐝 $318
🎀 $267

Sammy's Circus (set/7, *includes* 528099, 528196, 529176, 529184, 529192, 529214 & 529222)
#604070
Issued: 1994 • Closed: 1994
Retail Price: $200

3

Values
UM $22

Accessories (set/8)
#212725
Issued: 1997 • Retired: 1997
Retail Price: $20

4

Values
† $34

Aunt Bulah And Uncle Sam
#272825
Issued: 1997 • Retired: 1997
Retail Price: $22.50

Sammy's Circus

	Price Paid	Value Of My Collection
1.		
2.		

Sugar Town

3.		
4.		
5.		
6.		
7.		
8.		

PENCIL TOTALS

5

Values
† $26

Aunt Cleo
#272817
Issued: 1997 • Retired: 1997
Retail Price: $18.50

6

Values
🍼 $47
🐝 $40
🎀 $35

Aunt Ruth And Aunt Dorothy
#529486
Issued: 1992 • Retired: 1994
Retail Price: $20

7

Values
† $16

Bike Rack
#272906
Issued: 1997 • Retired: 1997
Retail Price: $15

8

Values
△ $16
♡ $10
† $10

Bird Bath
#150223
Issued: 1995 • Retired: 1997
Retail Price: $8.50

Key: NM *Pre-1981* ▲1981 ▮1982 ◀1983 †1984 ✦1985 ✗1986 ▲1987 ✤1988 ✤1989 ★1990 ♦1991 🍼1992 🐝1993 🎀1994 △1995 ♡1996 †1997 👓1998 ★1999 UM *Unmarked*

60

VALUE GUIDE — *PRECIOUS MOMENTS*®

1 Values
♡ $18
✝ $15

Bonfire
#184152
Issued: 1996 • Retired: 1997
Retail Price: $10

2 Values
✝ $12

Bunnies
#531804
Issued: 1997 • Retired: 1997
Retail Price: $10

3 Values
△ $16
♡ $10
✝ $10

Bus Stop
#150207
Issued: 1995 • Retired: 1997
Retail Price: $8.50

4 Values
✝ $33

Chuck (LE-1997)
#272809
Issued: 1997 • Closed: 1997
Retail Price: $22.50

5 Values
◁ $32
△ $24
♡ $24
✝ $22

Cobblestone Bridge
#533203
Issued: 1994 • Retired: 1997
Retail Price: $17

6 Values
♡ $20
✝ $13

Cocoa
#184063
Issued: 1996 • Retired: 1997
Retail Price: $7.50

7 Values
◁ $21
△ $17
♡ $15
✝ $15

Curved Sidewalk
#533149
Issued: 1994 • Retired: 1997
Retail Price: $10

8 Values
◁ $108
△ $100
♡ $95
✝ $95

Doctor's Office Night-Light
#529869
Issued: 1994 • Retired: 1997
Retail Price: $80 – $85

9 Values
△ $37
♡ $33
✝ $29

Donny
#531871
Issued: 1995 • Retired: 1997
Retail Price: $22.50

10 Values
◁ $24
△ $16
♡ $16
✝ $16

Double Tree
#533181
Issued: 1994 • Retired: 1997
Retail Price: $10

SUGAR TOWN

	Price Paid	Value Of My Collection
1.		
2.		
3.		
4.		
5.		
6.		
7.		
8.		
9.		
10.		
	PENCIL TOTALS	

KEY: NM *Pre-1981* ▲1981 ✗1982 ◄1983 ✝1984 ✦1985 ≠1986 ▲1987 ✤1988 ♭1989 ★1990 ♦1991 ♪1992 ℘1993 ◁1994 △1995 ♡1996 ✝1997 ∾1998 ★1999 UM *Unmarked*

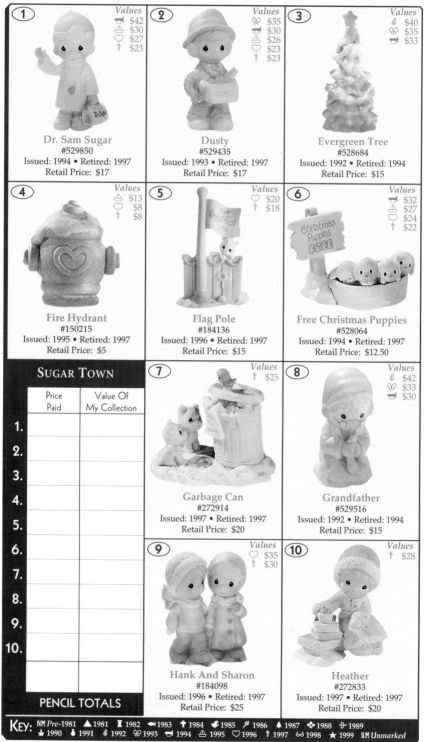

1 Values
🛏 $42
△ $30
♡ $27
✝ $23

Dr. Sam Sugar
#529850
Issued: 1994 • Retired: 1997
Retail Price: $17

2 Values
♀ $35
🛏 $30
△ $26
♡ $23
✝ $23

Dusty
#529435
Issued: 1993 • Retired: 1997
Retail Price: $17

3 Values
🖋 $40
♀ $35
🛏 $33

Evergreen Tree
#528684
Issued: 1992 • Retired: 1994
Retail Price: $15

4 Values
△ $13
♡ $8
✝ $8

Fire Hydrant
#150215
Issued: 1995 • Retired: 1997
Retail Price: $5

5 Values
♡ $20
✝ $18

Flag Pole
#184136
Issued: 1996 • Retired: 1997
Retail Price: $15

6 Values
🛏 $32
△ $27
♡ $24
✝ $22

Free Christmas Puppies
#528064
Issued: 1994 • Retired: 1997
Retail Price: $12.50

SUGAR TOWN

	Price Paid	Value Of My Collection
1.		
2.		
3.		
4.		
5.		
6.		
7.		
8.		
9.		
10.		
PENCIL TOTALS		

7 Values
✝ $25

Garbage Can
#272914
Issued: 1997 • Retired: 1997
Retail Price: $20

8 Values
🖋 $42
♀ $33
🛏 $30

Grandfather
#529516
Issued: 1992 • Retired: 1994
Retail Price: $15

9 Values
♡ $35
✝ $30

Hank And Sharon
#184098
Issued: 1996 • Retired: 1997
Retail Price: $25

10 Values
✝ $28

Heather
#272833
Issued: 1997 • Retired: 1997
Retail Price: $20

KEY: NM *Pre*-1981 ▲ 1981 ✝ 1982 ◄ 1983 ✝ 1984 ✎ 1985 ♪ 1986 ▲ 1987 ✤ 1988 ⊕ 1989 ★ 1990 ♦ 1991 🖋 1992 ♀ 1993 🛏 1994 △ 1995 ♡ 1996 ✝ 1997 6∂ 1998 ★ 1999 UM *Unmarked*

FIGURINE SERIES

1 | Values
♡ $21
✝ $18

Hot Cocoa Stand
#184144
Issued: 1996 • Retired: 1997
Retail Price: $15

2 | Values
🛏 $36
⚠ $30
♡ $25
✝ $21

Jan
#529826
Issued: 1994 • Retired: 1997
Retail Price: $17

3 | Values
❀ $43
🛏 $35
⚠ $32
♡ $28
✝ $25

Katy Lynne
#529524
Issued: 1993 • Retired: 1997
Retail Price: $20

4 | Values
🛏 $17
⚠ $14
♡ $12
✝ $12

Lamp Post
#529559
Issued: 1994 • Retired: 1997
Retail Price: $8

5 | Values
🛏 $37
⚠ $32
♡ $30
✝ $26

Leon And Evelyn Mae
#529818
Issued: 1994 • Retired: 1997
Retail Price: $20

6 | Values
♡ $28
✝ $24

Leroy
#184071
Issued: 1996 • Retired: 1997
Retail Price: $18.50

7 | Values
♡ $58
✝ $50

Lighted Tree
#184039
Issued: 1996 • Retired: 1997
Retail Price: $45

8 | Values
⚠ $23
♡ $18
✝ $16

Luggage Cart
#150185
Issued: 1995 • Retired: 1997
Retail Price: $13

9 | Values
🛏 $14
⚠ $10
♡ $8
✝ $8

Mailbox
#531847
Issued: 1994 • Retired: 1997
Retail Price: $5

10 | Values
♡ $28
✝ $24

Mazie
#184055
Issued: 1996 • Retired: 1997
Retail Price: $18.50

SUGAR TOWN

	Price Paid	Value Of My Collection
1.		
2.		
3.		
4.		
5.		
6.		
7.		
8.		
9.		
10.		
	PENCIL TOTALS	

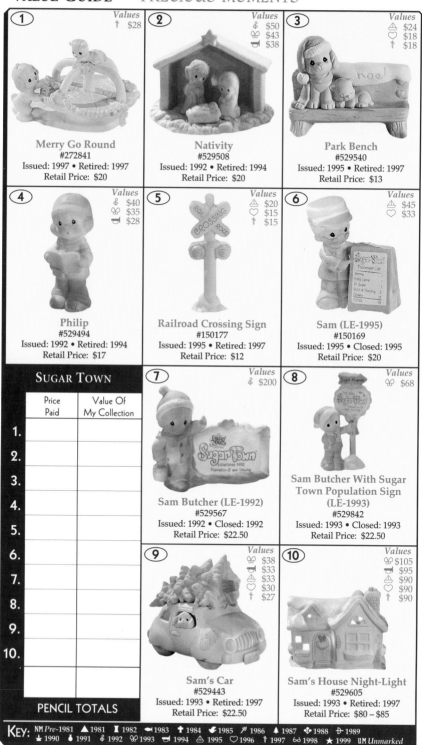

(1) Values † $28

Merry Go Round
#272841
Issued: 1997 • Retired: 1997
Retail Price: $20

(2) Values
♪ $50
◯◯ $43
◁ $38

Nativity
#529508
Issued: 1992 • Retired: 1994
Retail Price: $20

(3) Values
△ $24
♡ $18
† $18

Park Bench
#529540
Issued: 1995 • Retired: 1997
Retail Price: $13

(4) Values
♪ $40
◯◯ $35
◁ $28

Philip
#529494
Issued: 1992 • Retired: 1994
Retail Price: $17

(5) Values
△ $20
♡ $15
† $15

Railroad Crossing Sign
#150177
Issued: 1995 • Retired: 1997
Retail Price: $12

(6) Values
△ $45
♡ $33

Sam (LE-1995)
#150169
Issued: 1995 • Closed: 1995
Retail Price: $20

SUGAR TOWN

	Price Paid	Value Of My Collection
1.		
2.		
3.		
4.		
5.		
6.		
7.		
8.		
9.		
10.		
PENCIL TOTALS		

(7) Values ♪ $200

Sam Butcher (LE-1992)
#529567
Issued: 1992 • Closed: 1992
Retail Price: $22.50

(8) Values ◯◯ $68

Sam Butcher With Sugar Town Population Sign (LE-1993)
#529842
Issued: 1993 • Closed: 1993
Retail Price: $22.50

(9) Values
◯◯ $38
◁ $33
△ $33
♡ $30
† $27

Sam's Car
#529443
Issued: 1993 • Retired: 1997
Retail Price: $22.50

(10) Values
◯◯ $105
◁ $95
△ $90
♡ $90
† $90

Sam's House Night-Light
#529605
Issued: 1993 • Retired: 1997
Retail Price: $80 – $85

KEY: NM *Pre-1981* ▲ 1981 ■ 1982 ◄1983 † 1984 ✦ 1985 ⌐ 1986 ♠ 1987 ✤ 1988 ⊕ 1989 ⭑ 1990 ◉ 1991 ♪ 1992 ◯◯ 1993 ◁ 1994 △ 1995 ♡ 1996 † 1997 ଠଠ 1998 ★ 1999 UM *Unmarked*

64

1

Values	
⚘	$44
◀	$35
△	$28
♡	$26
†	$26

Sammy
#528668
Issued: 1993 • Retired: 1997
Retail Price: $17

2

Values	
†	$100

**School House Night-Light
(also available with
Canadian flag)**
#272795
Issued: 1997 • Retired: 1997
Retail Price: $80

3

Values	
◀	$20
△	$14
♡	$12
†	$12

Single Tree
#533173
Issued: 1994 • Retired: 1997
Retail Price: $10

4

Values	
◀	$53

**Stork With Baby Sam
(LE-1994)**
#529788
Issued: 1994 • Closed: 1994
Retail Price: $22.50

5

Values	
◀	$20
△	$16
♡	$13
†	$13

Straight Sidewalk
#533157
Issued: 1994 • Retired: 1997
Retail Price: $10

6

Values	
△	$21
♡	$15
†	$15

Street Sign
#532185
Issued: 1995 • Retired: 1997
Retail Price: $10

7

Values	
◀	$35
△	$32
♡	$30
†	$27

**Sugar And Her
Doghouse (set/2)**
#533165
Issued: 1994 • Retired: 1997
Retail Price: $20

8

Values	
UM	$30

**Sugar Town Cargo Car
(LE-1997)**
#273007
Issued: 1997 • Closed: 1997
Retail Price: $27.50

9

Values	
₰	$145
⚘	$130
◀	$125

**Sugar Town Chapel
Night-Light**
#529621
Issued: 1992 • Retired: 1994
Retail Price: $85

10

Values	
⚘	$30

**Sugar Town Chapel
Ornament (LE-1993)**
#530484
Issued: 1993 • Closed: 1993
Retail Price: $17.50

SUGAR TOWN

	Price Paid	Value Of My Collection
1.		
2.		
3.		
4.		
5.		
6.		
7.		
8.		
9.		
10.		
PENCIL TOTALS		

KEY: NM *Pre-1981* ▲ 1981 ✗ 1982 ◀ 1983 † 1984 ✦ 1985 ℱ 1986 ▲ 1987 ✤ 1988 ♰ 1989 ★ 1990 ● 1991 ₰ 1992 ⚘ 1993 ◀ 1994 △ 1995 ♡ 1996 † 1997 ໖ 1998 ★ 1999 UM *Unmarked*

1 *Values* UM $24

Sugar Town Displayer
#PMB007
Issued: 1993 • Retired: 1997
Retail Price: $18 – $24

2 *Values* ⚠ $30

Sugar Town Doctor's Office Ornament (LE-1995)
#530441
Issued: 1995 • Closed: 1995
Retail Price: $17.50 – $20

3 *Values* UM $80

Sugar Town Express (set/3)
♪ *Christmas Medley*
#152595
Issued: 1995 • Retired: 1997
Retail Price: $75

4 *Values*
֎ $18
🥄 $14
⚠ $14
♡ $12
† $12

Sugar Town Fence
#529796
Issued: 1993 • Retired: 1997
Retail Price: $10

5 *Values* UM $30

Sugar Town Passenger Car (LE-1996)
#192406
Issued: 1996 • Closed: 1996
Retail Price: $27.50

6 *Values*
🥄 $30
⚠ $22

Sugar Town Sam's House Ornament (LE-1994)
#530468
Issued: 1994 • Closed: 1994
Retail Price: $17.50

SUGAR TOWN

	Price Paid	Value Of My Collection
1.		
2.		
3.		
4.		
5.		
6.		
7.		
8.		
9.		
PENCIL TOTALS		

7 *Values*
♡ $50
† $48

Sugar Town Skating Pond
#184047
Issued: 1996 • Retired: 1997
Retail Price: $40

8 *Values*
♡ $32
† $27

Sugar Town Skating Sign (LE-1996)
#184020
Issued: 1996 • Closed: 1996
Retail Price: $15

9 *Values*
🥄 $110
⚠ $95
♡ $90
† $90

Sugar Town Square Clock
#532908
Issued: 1994 • Retired: 1997
Retail Price: $80 – $85

KEY: NM *Pre-1981* ▲ 1981 ▮ 1982 ◄ 1983 † 1984 ◄ 1985 ♫ 1986 ▲ 1987 ◆ 1988 ♫ 1989 ★ 1990 ♦ 1991 ♪ 1992 ֎ 1993 🥄 1994 ⚠ 1995 ♡ 1996 † 1997 ⌘ 1998 ★ 1999 UM *Unmarked*

66

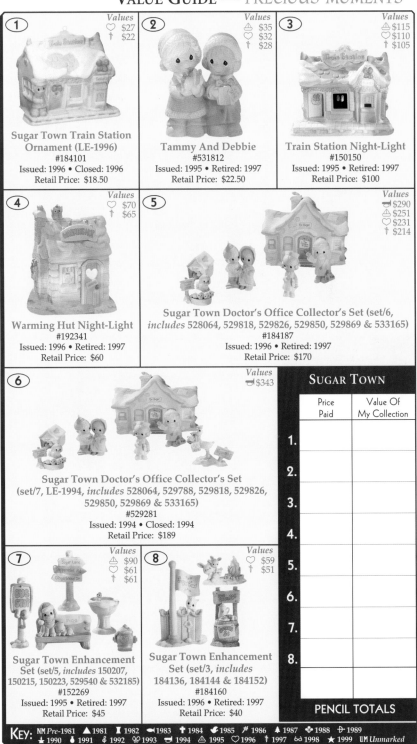

(1)

Values
♡ $27
† $22

Sugar Town Train Station Ornament (LE-1996)
#184101
Issued: 1996 • Closed: 1996
Retail Price: $18.50

(2)

Values
△ $35
♡ $32
† $28

Tammy And Debbie
#531812
Issued: 1995 • Retired: 1997
Retail Price: $22.50

(3)

Values
△ $115
♡ $110
† $105

Train Station Night-Light
#150150
Issued: 1995 • Retired: 1997
Retail Price: $100

(4)

Values
♡ $70
† $65

Warming Hut Night-Light
#192341
Issued: 1996 • Retired: 1997
Retail Price: $60

(5)

Values
🍃 $290
△ $251
♡ $231
† $214

Sugar Town Doctor's Office Collector's Set (set/6, *includes* 528064, 529818, 529826, 529850, 529869 & 533165)
#184187
Issued: 1996 • Retired: 1997
Retail Price: $170

(6)

Values
🍃 $343

Sugar Town Doctor's Office Collector's Set
(set/7, LE-1994, *includes* 528064, 529788, 529818, 529826, 529850, 529869 & 533165)
#529281
Issued: 1994 • Closed: 1994
Retail Price: $189

(7)

Values
△ $90
♡ $61
† $61

Sugar Town Enhancement Set (set/5, *includes* 150207, 150215, 150223, 529540 & 532185)
#152269
Issued: 1995 • Retired: 1997
Retail Price: $45

(8)

Values
♡ $59
† $51

Sugar Town Enhancement Set (set/3, *includes* 184136, 184144 & 184152)
#184160
Issued: 1996 • Retired: 1997
Retail Price: $40

SUGAR TOWN

	Price Paid	Value Of My Collection
1.		
2.		
3.		
4.		
5.		
6.		
7.		
8.		
PENCIL TOTALS		

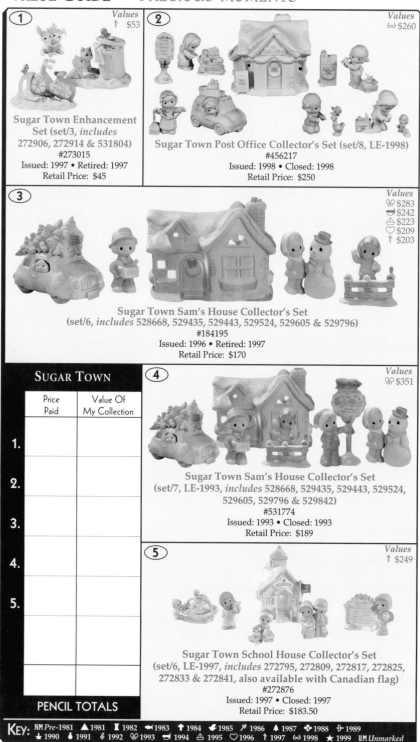

1
Values
† $53

**Sugar Town Enhancement
Set (set/3, *includes*
272906, 272914 & 531804)**
#273015
Issued: 1997 • Retired: 1997
Retail Price: $45

2
Values
6ð $260

Sugar Town Post Office Collector's Set (set/8, LE-1998)
#456217
Issued: 1998 • Closed: 1998
Retail Price: $250

3
Values
ℬ $283
ℑ $242
⬠ $223
♡ $209
† $203

**Sugar Town Sam's House Collector's Set
(set/6, *includes* 528668, 529435, 529443, 529524, 529605 & 529796)**
#184195
Issued: 1996 • Retired: 1997
Retail Price: $170

SUGAR TOWN

	Price Paid	Value Of My Collection
1.		
2.		
3.		
4.		
5.		
PENCIL TOTALS		

4
Values
ℬ $351

**Sugar Town Sam's House Collector's Set
(set/7, LE-1993, *includes* 528668, 529435, 529443, 529524,
529605, 529796 & 529842)**
#531774
Issued: 1993 • Closed: 1993
Retail Price: $189

5
Values
† $249

**Sugar Town School House Collector's Set
(set/6, LE-1997, *includes* 272795, 272809, 272817, 272825,
272833 & 272841, also available with Canadian flag)**
#272876
Issued: 1997 • Closed: 1997
Retail Price: $183.50

KEY: NM *Pre-1981* ▲ 1981 Ⅱ 1982 ◄ 1983 † 1984 ✦ 1985 ♩ 1986 ♠ 1987 ✦ 1988 Ð 1989
★ 1990 ◊ 1991 ♪ 1992 ℬ 1993 ⬛ 1994 ⬠ 1995 ♡ 1996 † 1997 6ð 1998 ★ 1999 UM *Unmarked*

(1)

Values
♡ $263
† $231

Sugar Town Skating Pond Collector's Set
(set/7, LE-1996, *includes* 184020, 184047, 184055, 184063, 184071, 184098 & 192341)
#184128
Issued: 1996 • Closed: 1996
Retail Price: $184.50

(2)

Values
♡ $231
† $204

Sugar Town Skating Pond Collector's Set
(set/6, *includes* 184047, 184055, 184063, 184071, 184098 & 192341)
#272930
Issued: 1997 • Retired: 1997
Retail Price: $169.50

(3)

Values
△ $275
♡ $241

Sugar Town Train Station Collector's Set (set/6, LE-1995, *includes* 150150, 150169, 150177, 150185, 531812 & 531871)
#150193
Issued: 1995 • Closed: 1995
Retail Price: $190

(4)

Values
△ $230
♡ $208
† $193

Sugar Town Train Station Collector's Set
(set/5, *includes* 150150, 150177, 150185, 531812 & 531871)
#184179
Issued: 1996 • Retired: 1997
Retail Price: $170

SUGAR TOWN

	Price Paid	Value Of My Collection
1.		
2.		
3.		
4.		
PENCIL TOTALS		

KEY: NM *Pre*-1981 ▲ 1981 ⧗ 1982 ⟵ 1983 † 1984 ◆ 1985 ✈ 1986 ♠ 1987 ✿ 1988 ✝ 1989 ★ 1990 ● 1991 ✧ 1992 ❀ 1993 ⛵ 1994 △ 1995 ♡ 1996 † 1997 ∞ 1998 ★ 1999 UM *Unmarked*

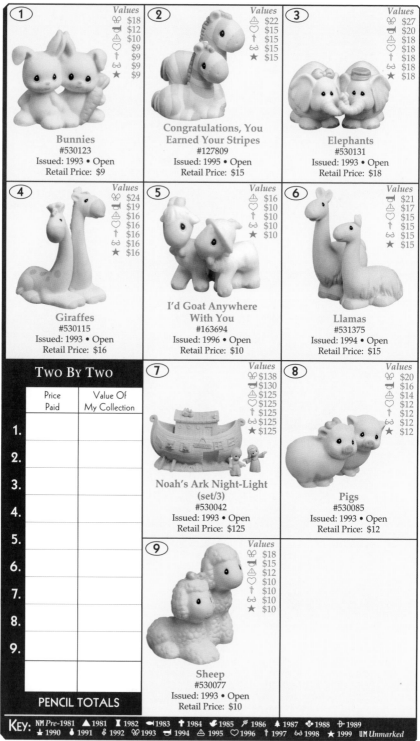

1

Values
- 😲 $18
- 🍥 $12
- ⚠ $10
- ♡ $9
- ✝ $9
- 👓 $9
- ★ $9

Bunnies
#530123
Issued: 1993 • Open
Retail Price: $9

2

Values
- ⚠ $22
- 🍥 $15
- ✝ $15
- 👓 $15
- ★ $15

Congratulations, You Earned Your Stripes
#127809
Issued: 1995 • Open
Retail Price: $15

3

Values
- 😲 $27
- 🍥 $20
- ⚠ $18
- ♡ $18
- ✝ $18
- 👓 $18
- ★ $18

Elephants
#530131
Issued: 1993 • Open
Retail Price: $18

4

Values
- 😲 $24
- 🍥 $19
- ⚠ $16
- ♡ $16
- ✝ $16
- 👓 $16
- ★ $16

Giraffes
#530115
Issued: 1993 • Open
Retail Price: $16

5

Values
- ⚠ $16
- ♡ $10
- ✝ $10
- 👓 $10
- ★ $10

I'd Goat Anywhere With You
#163694
Issued: 1996 • Open
Retail Price: $10

6

Values
- 🍥 $21
- ⚠ $17
- ♡ $15
- ✝ $15
- 👓 $15
- ★ $15

Llamas
#531375
Issued: 1994 • Open
Retail Price: $15

Two By Two

	Price Paid	Value Of My Collection
1.		
2.		
3.		
4.		
5.		
6.		
7.		
8.		
9.		
PENCIL TOTALS		

7

Values
- 😲 $138
- 🍥 $130
- ⚠ $125
- ♡ $125
- ✝ $125
- 👓 $125
- ★ $125

Noah's Ark Night-Light (set/3)
#530042
Issued: 1993 • Open
Retail Price: $125

8

Values
- 😲 $20
- 🍥 $16
- ⚠ $14
- ♡ $12
- ✝ $12
- 👓 $12
- ★ $12

Pigs
#530085
Issued: 1993 • Open
Retail Price: $12

9

Values
- 😲 $18
- 🍥 $15
- ⚠ $12
- ♡ $10
- ✝ $10
- 👓 $10
- ★ $10

Sheep
#530077
Issued: 1993 • Open
Retail Price: $10

KEY: NM *Pre-1981* ▲ 1981 ✕ 1982 ◀ 1983 ✝ 1984 ✓ 1985 ♫ 1986 ▲ 1987 ❀ 1988 ⊕ 1989 ★ 1990 ♦ 1991 ♪ 1992 😲 1993 🍥 1994 ⚠ 1995 ♡ 1996 ✝ 1997 👓 1998 ★ 1999 UM *Unmarked*

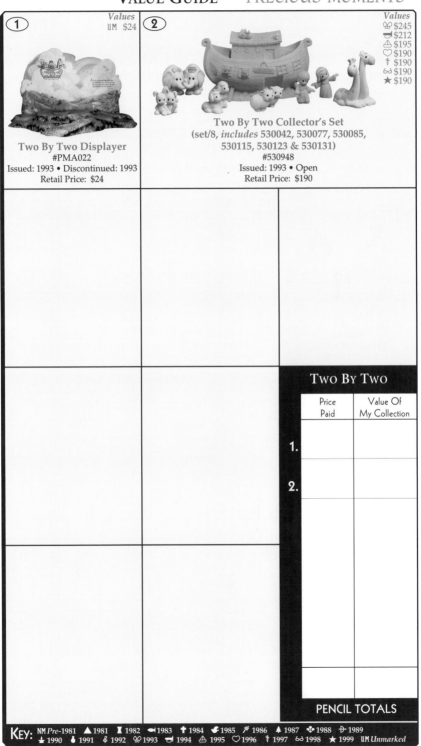

FIGURINE SERIES

① *Values*
UM $24

Two By Two Displayer
#PMA022
Issued: 1993 • Discontinued: 1993
Retail Price: $24

② *Values*
❦ $245
🐚 $212
⚖ $195
♡ $190
† $190
👁 $190
★ $190

Two By Two Collector's Set
(set/8, *includes* 530042, 530077, 530085,
530115, 530123 & 530131)
#530948
Issued: 1993 • Open
Retail Price: $190

TWO BY TWO

	Price Paid	Value Of My Collection
1.		
2.		

PENCIL TOTALS

KEY: NM *Pre*-1981 ▲1981 Ⅱ1982 ◄1983 †1984 🍀1985 ♪1986 ▲1987 ⚜1988 Đ1989
★1990 🔔1991 ♪1992 ❦1993 🐚1994 ⚖1995 ♡1996 †1997 👁1998 ★1999 UM *Unmarked*

71

FIGURINES

Since 1978, the **PRECIOUS MOMENTS** collection has grown to include approximately 1,700 pieces, over 600 of which are general figurines. For 1999, 50 additional pieces have been introduced. To make room for these new pieces, Enesco has suspended, closed or retired over 50 figurines since 1998.

① Values
6ᵭ $35
★ $35

Alaska Once More, How's Yer Christmas?
#455784
Issued: 1998 • Open
Retail Price: $35

② NEW! Values
6ᵭ $60
★ $60

All Girls Are Beautiful (set/5)
Exclusive To Japan
#481661
Issued: 1999 • Open
Retail Price: $60

③ NEW! Values
6ᵭ $25
★ $25

Always Listen To Your Heart
#488356
Issued: 1999 • Open
Retail Price: $25

④ Values
ᵬ $58
ᵠ $52

America You're Beautiful (LE-1993)
National Day Of Prayer Figurine
#528862
Issued: 1993 • Closed: 1993
Retail Price: $35

GENERAL FIGURINES

	Price Paid	Value Of My Collection
1.		
2.		
3.		
4.		
5.		
6.		
7.		
8.		
PENCIL TOTALS		

⑤ Values
♡ $55
✝ $55
6ᵭ $55
★ $55

And A Child Shall Lead Them
#E9287R
Issued: 1997 • Open
Retail Price: $50 – $55

⑥ Values
ᴶ⁄ $51
▲ $43
❖ $40
ᵭ $37
☦ $35
🕯 $35
ᵬ $32.50
ᵠ$32.50
☷$32.50
△$32.50
♡$32.50
✝ $32.50
6ᵭ$32.50
★ $32.50

Angel Of Mercy
#102482
Issued: 1986 • Open
Retail Price: $20 – $32.50

⑦ Values
♡ $45
✝ $45
6ᵭ $45
★ $45

Angels On Earth
#183776
Issued: 1996 • Open
Retail Price: $40 – $45

⑧ Values
🕯 $95
ᵬ $87
ᵠ $83
☷ $80
△ $78
♡ $78

Angels We Have Heard On High
#524921
Issued: 1991 • Retired: 1996
Retail Price: $60 – $70

KEY: NM *Pre-1981* ▲1981 Ⅱ1982 ◂1983 ✝1984 ✔1985 ᴶ⁄1986 ▲1987 ❖1988 ᵭ1989 🕯1990 🕯1991 ᵬ1992 ᵠ1993 ☷1994 △1995 ♡1996 ✝1997 6ᵭ1998 ★1999 UM *Unmarked*

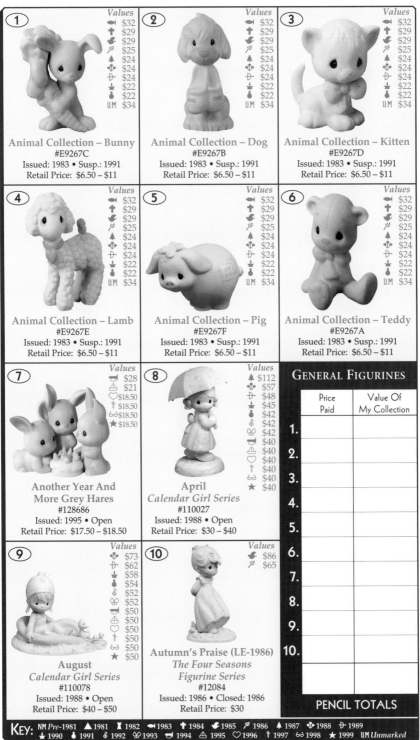

1 Values
🐟 $32
✝ $29
🍂 $29
〃 $25
♠ $24
✠ $24
ⴱ $24
★ $22
🍶 $22
UM $34

Animal Collection – Bunny
#E9267C
Issued: 1983 • Susp.: 1991
Retail Price: $6.50 – $11

2 Values
🐟 $32
✝ $29
🍂 $29
〃 $25
♠ $24
✠ $24
ⴱ $24
★ $22
🍶 $22
UM $34

Animal Collection – Dog
#E9267B
Issued: 1983 • Susp.: 1991
Retail Price: $6.50 – $11

3 Values
🐟 $32
✝ $29
🍂 $29
〃 $25
♠ $24
✠ $24
ⴱ $24
★ $22
🍶 $22
UM $34

Animal Collection – Kitten
#E9267D
Issued: 1983 • Susp.: 1991
Retail Price: $6.50 – $11

4 Values
🐟 $32
✝ $29
🍂 $29
〃 $25
♠ $24
✠ $24
ⴱ $24
★ $22
🍶 $22
UM $34

Animal Collection – Lamb
#E9267E
Issued: 1983 • Susp.: 1991
Retail Price: $6.50 – $11

5 Values
🐟 $32
✝ $29
🍂 $29
〃 $25
♠ $24
✠ $24
ⴱ $24
★ $22
🍶 $22
UM $34

Animal Collection – Pig
#E9267F
Issued: 1983 • Susp.: 1991
Retail Price: $6.50 – $11

6 Values
🐟 $32
✝ $29
🍂 $29
〃 $25
♠ $24
✠ $24
ⴱ $24
★ $22
🍶 $22
UM $34

Animal Collection – Teddy
#E9267A
Issued: 1983 • Susp.: 1991
Retail Price: $6.50 – $11

7 Values
🛷 $28
△ $21
♡ $18.50
✝ $18.50
6ð $18.50
★ $18.50

**Another Year And
More Grey Hares**
#128686
Issued: 1995 • Open
Retail Price: $17.50 – $18.50

8 Values
♠ $112
✠ $57
ⴱ $48
★ $45
🍶 $42
𝄪 $42
♀ $42
🛷 $40
△ $40
♡ $40
✝ $40
6ð $40
★ $40

April
Calendar Girl Series
#110027
Issued: 1988 • Open
Retail Price: $30 – $40

9 Values
✠ $73
ⴱ $62
★ $58
🍶 $54
𝄪 $52
♀ $52
🛷 $50
△ $50
♡ $50
✝ $50
6ð $50
★ $50

August
Calendar Girl Series
#110078
Issued: 1988 • Open
Retail Price: $40 – $50

10 Values
🍂 $86
〃 $65

Autumn's Praise (LE-1986)
*The Four Seasons
Figurine Series*
#12084
Issued: 1986 • Closed: 1986
Retail Price: $30

GENERAL FIGURINES

	Price Paid	Value Of My Collection
1.		
2.		
3.		
4.		
5.		
6.		
7.		
8.		
9.		
10.		

PENCIL TOTALS

FIGURINES

KEY: NM *Pre-1981* ▲ 1981 ✗ 1982 🐟 1983 ✝ 1984 🍂 1985 〃 1986 ♠ 1987 ✠ 1988 ⴱ 1989 ★ 1990 🍶 1991 𝄪 1992 ♀ 1993 🛷 1994 △ 1995 ♡ 1996 ✝ 1997 6ð 1998 ★ 1999 UM *Unmarked*

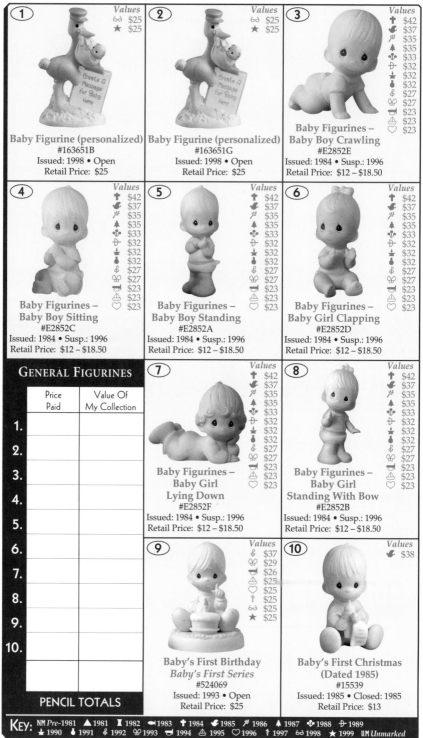

1

Values
6ঠ $25
★ $25

Baby Figurine (personalized)
#163651B
Issued: 1998 • Open
Retail Price: $25

2

Values
6ঠ $25
★ $25

Baby Figurine (personalized)
#163651G
Issued: 1998 • Open
Retail Price: $25

3

Values
✝ $42
✔ $37
♪ $35
▲ $35
⬧ $33
➴ $32
⚖ $32
♠ $32
♗ $27
❀ $27
⌥ $23
△ $23
♡ $23

Baby Figurines –
Baby Boy Crawling
#E2852E
Issued: 1984 • Susp.: 1996
Retail Price: $12 – $18.50

4

Values
✝ $42
✔ $37
♪ $35
▲ $35
⬧ $33
➴ $32
⚖ $32
♠ $32
♗ $27
❀ $27
⌥ $23
△ $23
♡ $23

Baby Figurines –
Baby Boy Sitting
#E2852C
Issued: 1984 • Susp.: 1996
Retail Price: $12 – $18.50

5

Values
✝ $42
✔ $37
♪ $35
▲ $35
⬧ $33
➴ $32
⚖ $32
♠ $32
♗ $27
❀ $27
⌥ $23
♡ $23

Baby Figurines –
Baby Boy Standing
#E2852A
Issued: 1984 • Susp.: 1996
Retail Price: $12 – $18.50

6

Values
✝ $42
✔ $37
♪ $35
▲ $35
⬧ $33
➴ $32
⚖ $32
♠ $32
♗ $27
❀ $27
⌥ $23
△ $23
♡ $23

Baby Figurines –
Baby Girl Clapping
#E2852D
Issued: 1984 • Susp.: 1996
Retail Price: $12 – $18.50

GENERAL FIGURINES

	Price Paid	Value Of My Collection
1.		
2.		
3.		
4.		
5.		
6.		
7.		
8.		
9.		
10.		
PENCIL TOTALS		

7

Values
✝ $42
✔ $37
♪ $35
▲ $35
⬧ $33
➴ $32
⚖ $32
♠ $32
♗ $27
❀ $27
⌥ $23
♡ $23

Baby Figurines –
Baby Girl
Lying Down
#E2852F
Issued: 1984 • Susp.: 1996
Retail Price: $12 – $18.50

8

Values
✝ $42
✔ $37
♪ $35
▲ $35
⬧ $33
➴ $32
⚖ $32
♠ $32
♗ $27
❀ $27
⌥ $23
♡ $23

Baby Figurines –
Baby Girl
Standing With Bow
#E2852B
Issued: 1984 • Susp.: 1996
Retail Price: $12 – $18.50

9

Values
⚖ $37
❀ $29
⌥ $26
△ $25
♡ $25
✝ $25
6ঠ $25
★ $25

Baby's First Birthday
Baby's First Series
#524069
Issued: 1993 • Open
Retail Price: $25

10

Values
✔ $38

Baby's First Christmas
(Dated 1985)
#15539
Issued: 1985 • Closed: 1985
Retail Price: $13

KEY: NM *Pre-1981* ▲ 1981 Ⅱ 1982 ◀1983 ✝ 1984 ✔ 1985 ♪ 1986 ▲ 1987 ⬧ 1988 ➴ 1989 ♠ 1990 ⚖ 1991 ⚖ 1992 ❀ 1993 ⌥ 1994 △ 1995 ♡ 1996 ✝ 1997 6ঠ 1998 ★ 1999 UM *Unmarked*

74

FIGURINES

① *Values*
🐦 $38

Baby's First Christmas
(Dated 1985)
#15547
Issued: 1985 • Closed: 1985
Retail Price: $13

② *Values*
🐦 $183
♬ $172
▲ $165

Baby's First Haircut
Baby's First Series
#12211
Issued: 1985 • Susp.: 1987
Retail Price: $32.50 – $40

③ *Values*
🔔 $55
& $47
❀ $44
🍴 $42
△ $40
▱ $40
† $40
👓 $40
★ $40

Baby's First Meal
Baby's First Series
#524077
Issued: 1991 • Retired: 1999
Retail Price: $35 – $40

④ *Values*
🐦 $90
▽ $82
★ $78
🔔 $72
& $69
❀ $67
🍴 $65

Baby's First Pet
Baby's First Series
#520705
Issued: 1989 • Susp.: 1994
Retail Price: $45 – $50

⑤ *Values*
† $195
🐦 $176
♬ $170

Baby's First Picture
Baby's First Series
#E2841
Issued: 1984 • Retired: 1986
Retail Price: $45

⑥ *Values*
† $106
▲ $102
♬ $100
▲ $95
🐦 $95

Baby's First Step
Baby's First Series
#E2840
Issued: 1984 • Susp.: 1988
Retail Price: $35 – $40

⑦ *Values*
🐦 $320
♬ $315
▲ $300
🐦 $290
▽ $285

Baby's First Trip
Baby's First Series
#16012
Issued: 1986 • Susp.: 1989
Retail Price: $32.50 – $45

⑧ *Values*
& $32
❀ $29
🍴 $27
△ $25
♡ $25
🍴 $25
👓 $25
★ $25

Baby's First Word
Baby's First Series
#527238
Issued: 1992 • Retired: 1999
Retail Price: $25

⑨
Variation
| Be Not Weary And Well Doing |

Values
NM $142
▲ $125
I $110
🍴 $100
† $94
🐦 $88

Be Not Weary In Well Doing
#E3111
Issued: 1980 • Retired: 1985
Retail Price: $14 – $19
Variation: "Be Not Weary And Well Doing" – $220

General Figurines

	Price Paid	Value Of My Collection
1.		
2.		
3.		
4.		
5.		
6.		
7.		
8.		
9.		
PENCIL TOTALS		

KEY: NM *Pre-1981* ▲ 1981 I 1982 ◀ 1983 † 1984 🐦 1985 ♬ 1986 ▲ 1987 🐦 1988 ▽ 1989 ★ 1990 🔔 1991 & 1992 ❀ 1993 🍴 1994 △ 1995 ♡ 1996 † 1997 👓 1998 ★ 1999 UM *Unmarked*

1 | *Values*
NM $122
▲ $105
Ⅱ $96
⚓ $88
✝ $85

**Bear Ye One
Another's Burdens**
#E5200
Issued: 1981 • Susp.: 1984
Retail Price: $20 – $25

2 | NEW! | *Values*
★ N/E

**The Beauty Of God Blooms
Forever**
Four Seasons Series
#129143
Issued: 1999 • Open
Retail Price: N/A

3 | NEW! | *Values*
6ð $35
★ $35

**Believe It Or Knot,
I Luv You**
#487910
Issued: 1999 • Open
Retail Price: $35

4 | *Values*
▲ $107
❖ $88
Đ $80
★ $76
🌡 $72

Believe The Impossible
#109487
Issued: 1988 • Susp.: 1991
Retail Price: $35 – $45

5 | NEW! | *Values*
★ N/E

Beside Still Waters
Four Seasons Series
#129127
Issued: 1999 • Open
Retail Price: N/A

6 | *Values*
✝ $38
✝ $36
♫ $34
▲ $34
❖ $32
Đ $32
🌡 $32
🌡 $29
ᗱ $29
🥄 $27
🥄 $27
🔺 $25
♡ $25
✝ $25
6ð $25
★ $25

Best Man
Bridal Party Series
#E2836
Issued: 1984 • Open
Retail Price: $13.50 – $25

GENERAL FIGURINES

	Price Paid	Value Of My Collection
1.		
2.		
3.		
4.		
5.		
6.		
7.		
8.		
9.		
PENCIL TOTALS		

7 | *Values*
6ð $35
★ $35

**Birthday Figurine
(personalized)**
#163686
Issued: 1998 • Open
Retail Price: $35

8 | *Values*
Ⅱ $260
⚓ $230
✝ $222

Bless This House
#E7164
Issued: 1982 • Susp.: 1984
Retail Price: $45 – $50

9 | *Values*
⊡ $132
⊛ $125

**Bless Those Who Serve
Their Country**
#526568
Issued: 1991 • Susp.: 1992
Retail Price: $32.50

(1) Values
P $54
📷 $50

Bless Those Who Serve
Their Country
#526576
Issued: 1991 • Susp.: 1992
Retail Price: $32.50

(2) Values
P $62
📷 $57

Bless Those Who Serve
Their Country
#526584
Issued: 1991 • Susp.: 1992
Retail Price: $32.50

(3) Values
P $47
📷 $44

Bless Those Who Serve
Their Country
#527289
Issued: 1991 • Susp.: 1992
Retail Price: $32.50

(4) Values
P $45
📷 $43

Bless Those Who Serve
Their Country
#527297
Issued: 1991 • Susp.: 1992
Retail Price: $32.50

(5) Values
P $65
📷 $63

Bless Those Who Serve
Their Country
#527521
Issued: 1991 • Susp.: 1992
Retail Price: $32.50

(6) Values
$58
$54
$53
$50
$50
$50
$48
$48
$47
$47
$47
$45
$45
$45
$45
$45
$45

Bless You Two
#E9255
Issued: 1983 • Open
Retail Price: $21 – $45

(7) Values
$42
$34
$27.50
$27.50
$27.50
$27.50

Bless Your Soul
#531162
Issued: 1995 • Open
Retail Price: $25 – $27.50

(8) Values
NM $128
$112
$96
$86
$81
$75

Blessed Are The
Peacemakers
#E3107
Issued: 1980 • Retired: 1985
Retail Price: $13 – $19

(9) Values
NM $63
$55
$53
$53
$47
$47
$42
$42
$42
$38
$38
$38

Blessed Are
The Pure In Heart
#E3104
Issued: 1980 • Susp.: 1991
Retail Price: $9 – $19

(10) Values
$55
NEW!

Blessed Are They With A
Caring Heart
Century Circle Figurine
#163724
Issued: 1999 • To Be Closed: 1999
Retail Price: $55

FIGURINES

GENERAL FIGURINES

	Price Paid	Value Of My Collection
1.		
2.		
3.		
4.		
5.		
6.		
7.		
8.		
9.		
10.		
PENCIL TOTALS		

KEY: NM *Pre-1981* ▲1981 I 1982 ◀1983 †1984 ✦1985 ♪1986 ♠1987 ✤1988 ✫1989 ✦1990 ♦1991 ♀1992 ♀1993 ☜1994 △1995 ♡1996 †1997 ☌1998 ★1999 UM *Unmarked*

1 NEW!

Values
6ᕽ $175
★ $175

Blessed Art Thou Amongst Women (LE-1999)
#261556
Issued: 1999 • To Be Closed: 1999
Retail Price: $175

2

Values
✝ $90
🕊 $83
🕯 $80
♪ $77

Blessing From My House To Yours
#E0503
Issued: 1983 • Susp.: 1986
Retail Price: $27

3

Values
★ $112
🕯 $102
🔑 $95
◯◯ $90
⊟ $84

Blessings From Above
#523747
Issued: 1990 • Retired: 1994
Retail Price: $45 – $50

4

Values
🔑 $48
◯◯ $44
⊟ $38
△ $38
♡ $35
✝ $35
6ᕽ $35

Bless-Um You
#527335
Issued: 1993 • Retired: 1998
Retail Price: $35

5

Values
ᕽ $144
★ $133
🕯 $125
🔑 $117
◯◯ $109
⊟ $105
△ $105
♡ $100

Bon Voyage
#522201
Issued: 1989 • Susp.: 1996
Retail Price: $75 – $90

6

Values
♡ $40
✝ $40
6ᕽ $40
★ $40

A Bouquet From God's Garden Of Love
Growing In God's Garden Of Love Series
#184268
Issued: 1997 • Open
Retail Price: $37.50 – $40

GENERAL FIGURINES

	Price Paid	Value Of My Collection
1.		
2.		
3.		
4.		
5.		
6.		
7.		
8.		
9.		
10.		
PENCIL TOTALS		

7

Values
▲ $38
🐟 $35
ᕽ $32
△ $32
🕯 $30
🔑 $28
◯◯ $28
⊟ $27.50
△ $27.50
♡ $27.50
✝ $27.50
6ᕽ $27.50
★ $27.50

Bride
Bridal Party Series
#E2846
Issued: 1987 • Open
Retail Price: $18 – $27.50

8

Values
✝ $42
🐟 $35
🔆 $34
▲ $33
🐟 $31
ᕽ $31
★ $29
🕯 $29
🔑 $27
◯◯ $27
△ $25
♡ $25
✝ $25
6ᕽ $25
★ $25

Bridesmaid
Bridal Party Series
#E2831
Issued: 1984 • Open
Retail Price: $13.50 – $25

9

Values
🕯 $113
🔑 $105
◯◯ $98
⊟ $95
△ $92
♡ $90
✝ $90
6ᕽ $90
★ $90

Bring The Little Ones To Jesus
Child Evangelism Fellowship Figurine
#527556
Issued: 1992 • Open
Retail Price: $90

10

Values
◯◯ $92
△ $85
⊟ $80

Bringing You A Merry Christmas
#527599
Issued: 1993 • Retired: 1995
Retail Price: $45

KEY: NM *Pre-1981* ▲ 1981 ✕ 1982 ◀ 1983 ✝ 1984 🐟 1985 ♪ 1986 ▲ 1987 🔆 1988 ᕽ 1989
★ 1990 🕯 1991 🔑 1992 ◯◯ 1993 ⊟ 1994 △ 1995 ♡ 1996 ✝ 1997 6ᕽ 1998 ★ 1999 **UM** *Unmarked*

78

VALUE GUIDE — *PRECIOUS MOMENTS*®

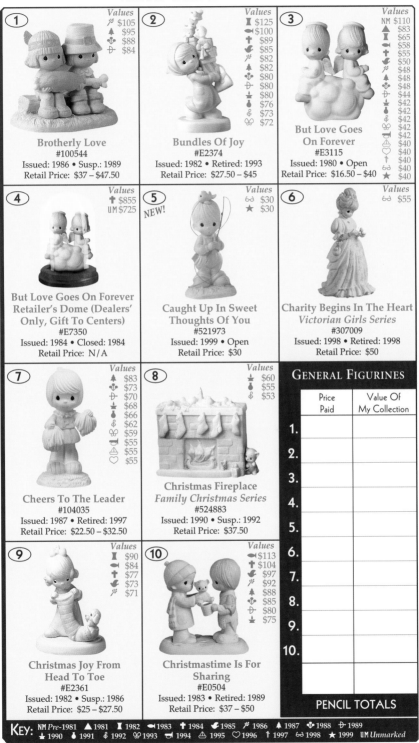

1 Values
- 🎿 $105
- ▲ $95
- ⬧ $88
- ⅁ $84

Brotherly Love
#100544
Issued: 1986 • Susp.: 1989
Retail Price: $37 – $47.50

2 Values
- ✖ $125
- ◄ $100
- ✝ $89
- 🌿 $85
- ✿ $82
- ▲ $82
- ⬧ $80
- ⅁ $80
- ★ $80
- 🔔 $76
- 𝄢 $73
- ஐ $72

Bundles Of Joy
#E2374
Issued: 1982 • Retired: 1993
Retail Price: $27.50 – $45

3 Values
- NM $110
- ✖ $83
- ✖ $65
- ✝ $58
- ✝ $55
- 🌿 $50
- 🎿 $48
- ▲ $48
- ⬧ $48
- ⅁ $44
- ★ $42
- 🔔 $42
- ⅁ $42
- ஐ $42
- ◄ $42
- ♡ $40
- ✝ $40
- 6ठ $40
- ★ $40

**But Love Goes
On Forever**
#E3115
Issued: 1980 • Open
Retail Price: $16.50 – $40

4 Values
- ✝ $855
- UM $725

**But Love Goes On Forever
Retailer's Dome (Dealers'
Only, Gift To Centers)**
#E7350
Issued: 1984 • Closed: 1984
Retail Price: N/A

5 *NEW!* Values
- 6ठ $30
- ★ $30

**Caught Up In Sweet
Thoughts Of You**
#521973
Issued: 1999 • Open
Retail Price: $30

6 Values
- 6ठ $55

Charity Begins In The Heart
Victorian Girls Series
#307009
Issued: 1998 • Retired: 1998
Retail Price: $50

7 Values
- ▲ $83
- ⬧ $73
- ⅁ $70
- ★ $68
- 🔔 $66
- ⅁ $62
- ஐ $59
- ◄ $55
- △ $55
- ♡ $55

Cheers To The Leader
#104035
Issued: 1987 • Retired: 1997
Retail Price: $22.50 – $32.50

8 Values
- ★ $60
- 🔔 $55
- ⅁ $53

Christmas Fireplace
Family Christmas Series
#524883
Issued: 1990 • Susp.: 1992
Retail Price: $37.50

9 Values
- ✖ $90
- ◄ $84
- ✝ $77
- 🌿 $73
- 🎿 $71

**Christmas Joy From
Head To Toe**
#E2361
Issued: 1982 • Susp.: 1986
Retail Price: $25 – $27.50

10 Values
- ◄ $113
- ✝ $104
- 🌿 $97
- 🎿 $92
- ▲ $88
- ⬧ $85
- ⅁ $80
- ★ $75

**Christmastime Is For
Sharing**
#E0504
Issued: 1983 • Retired: 1989
Retail Price: $37 – $50

GENERAL FIGURINES

	Price Paid	Value Of My Collection
1.		
2.		
3.		
4.		
5.		
6.		
7.		
8.		
9.		
10.		
PENCIL TOTALS		

FIGURINES

KEY: NM *Pre-1981* ▲ 1981 ✖ 1982 ◄ 1983 ✝ 1984 🌿 1985 🎿 1986 ▲ 1987 ⬧ 1988 ⅁ 1989 ★ 1990 🔔 1991 ⅁ 1992 ஐ 1993 ◄ 1994 △ 1995 ♡ 1996 ✝ 1997 6ठ 1998 ★ 1999 UM *Unmarked*

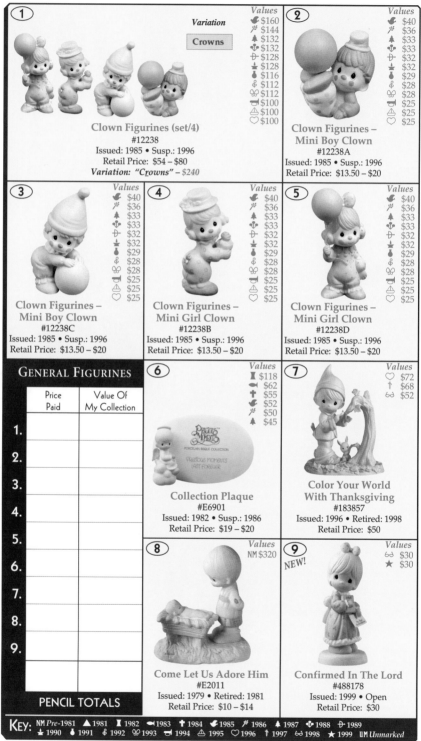

①

Variation

| Crowns |

Values
🦋 $160
❦ $144
⚓ $132
🔱 $132
ϑ $128
✴ $128
🍶 $116
ℰ $112
❀ $112
◁ $100
△ $100
♡ $100

Clown Figurines (set/4)
#12238
Issued: 1985 • Susp.: 1996
Retail Price: $54 – $80
Variation: "Crowns" – $240

②

Values
🦋 $40
❦ $36
⚓ $33
🔱 $33
ϑ $32
✴ $32
🍶 $29
ℰ $28
❀ $28
◁ $25
△ $25
♡ $25

Clown Figurines –
Mini Boy Clown
#12238A
Issued: 1985 • Susp.: 1996
Retail Price: $13.50 – $20

③

Values
🦋 $40
❦ $36
⚓ $33
🔱 $33
ϑ $32
✴ $32
🍶 $29
ℰ $28
❀ $28
◁ $25
△ $25
♡ $25

Clown Figurines –
Mini Boy Clown
#12238C
Issued: 1985 • Susp.: 1996
Retail Price: $13.50 – $20

④

Values
🦋 $40
❦ $36
⚓ $33
🔱 $33
ϑ $32
✴ $32
🍶 $29
ℰ $28
❀ $28
◁ $25
△ $25
♡ $25

Clown Figurines –
Mini Girl Clown
#12238B
Issued: 1985 • Susp.: 1996
Retail Price: $13.50 – $20

⑤

Values
🦋 $40
❦ $36
⚓ $33
🔱 $33
ϑ $32
✴ $32
🍶 $29
ℰ $28
❀ $28
◁ $25
△ $25
♡ $25

Clown Figurines –
Mini Girl Clown
#12238D
Issued: 1985 • Susp.: 1996
Retail Price: $13.50 – $20

GENERAL FIGURINES

	Price Paid	Value Of My Collection
1.		
2.		
3.		
4.		
5.		
6.		
7.		
8.		
9.		

PENCIL TOTALS

⑥

Values
▯ $118
🐟 $62
✝ $55
✴ $52
❦ $50
⚓ $45

Collection Plaque
#E6901
Issued: 1982 • Susp.: 1986
Retail Price: $19 – $20

⑦

Values
♡ $72
✝ $68
6∂ $52

Color Your World
With Thanksgiving
#183857
Issued: 1996 • Retired: 1998
Retail Price: $50

⑧

Values
NM $320

Come Let Us Adore Him
#E2011
Issued: 1979 • Retired: 1981
Retail Price: $10 – $14

⑨

NEW!

Values
6∂ $30
★ $30

Confirmed In The Lord
#488178
Issued: 1999 • Open
Retail Price: $30

KEY: NM *Pre-1981* ▲1981 ▯1982 ◀1983 ✝1984 🦋1985 ❦1986 ⚓1987 🔱1988 ϑ1989 ✴1990 🍶1991 ℰ1992 ❀1993 ◁1994 △1995 ♡1996 ✝1997 6∂1998 ★1999 UM *Unmarked*

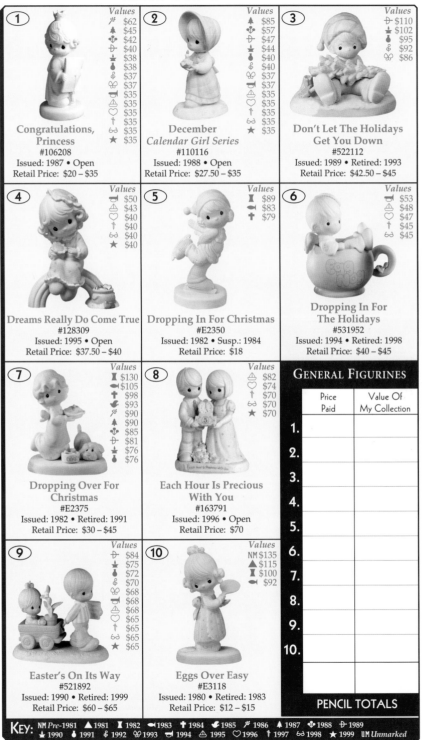

1 Congratulations, Princess
#106208
Issued: 1987 • Open
Retail Price: $20 – $35

Values
🪰 $62
🔺 $45
🔶 $42
🔱 $40
⭐ $38
🍶 $38
🔔 $37
🔁 $37
🥢 $35
♡ $35
✝ $35
🔗 $35
🔗 $35
★ $35

2 December
Calendar Girl Series
#110116
Issued: 1988 • Open
Retail Price: $27.50 – $35

Values
🔺 $85
🔶 $57
🔱 $47
⭐ $44
🍶 $40
🔔 $40
🔁 $37
🔗 $37
🔺 $35
♡ $35
✝ $35
🔗 $35
★ $35

3 Don't Let The Holidays Get You Down
#522112
Issued: 1989 • Retired: 1993
Retail Price: $42.50 – $45

Values
🔱 $110
⭐ $102
🔁 $95
🔔 $92
🔗 $86

4 Dreams Really Do Come True
#128309
Issued: 1995 • Open
Retail Price: $37.50 – $40

Values
🥢 $50
🔺 $43
♡ $40
✝ $40
🔗 $40
★ $40

5 Dropping In For Christmas
#E2350
Issued: 1982 • Susp.: 1984
Retail Price: $18

Values
I $89
◀ $83
✝ $79

6 Dropping In For The Holidays
#531952
Issued: 1994 • Retired: 1998
Retail Price: $40 – $45

Values
🥢 $53
🔺 $48
♡ $47
✝ $45
🔗 $45

7 Dropping Over For Christmas
#E2375
Issued: 1982 • Retired: 1991
Retail Price: $30 – $45

Values
I $130
◀ $105
✝ $98
🔶 $93
🪰 $90
🔺 $90
🔱 $85
🔱 $81
⭐ $76
🍶 $76

8 Each Hour Is Precious With You
#163791
Issued: 1996 • Open
Retail Price: $70

Values
🔺 $82
♡ $74
✝ $70
🔗 $70
★ $70

9 Easter's On Its Way
#521892
Issued: 1990 • Retired: 1999
Retail Price: $60 – $65

Values
🔱 $84
⭐ $75
🍶 $72
🔔 $70
🔗 $68
🥢 $68
🔺 $68
♡ $65
✝ $65
🔗 $65
★ $65

10 Eggs Over Easy
#E3118
Issued: 1980 • Retired: 1983
Retail Price: $12 – $15

Values
NM $135
🔺 $115
I $100
◀ $92

GENERAL FIGURINES

	Price Paid	Value Of My Collection
1.		
2.		
3.		
4.		
5.		
6.		
7.		
8.		
9.		
10.		
PENCIL TOTALS		

FIGURINES

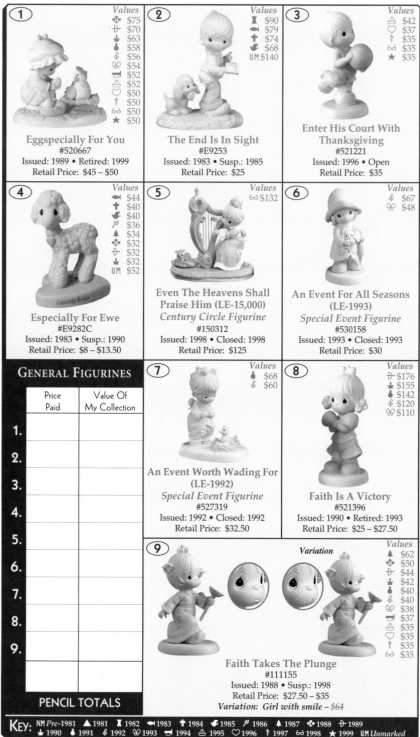

1

Values	
✤	$75
Đ	$70
⊁	$63
▮	$58
&	$56
❦	$54
⊸	$52
⬠	$52
♡	$50
✝	$50
6∂	$50
★	$50

Eggspecially For You
#520667
Issued: 1989 • Retired: 1999
Retail Price: $45 – $50

2

Values	
▮	$90
⊁	$79
✝	$74
❦	$68
UM	$140

The End Is In Sight
#E9253
Issued: 1983 • Susp.: 1985
Retail Price: $25

3

Values	
△	$42
♡	$37
✝	$35
6∂	$35
★	$35

Enter His Court With Thanksgiving
#521221
Issued: 1996 • Open
Retail Price: $35

4

Values	
◀	$44
✝	$40
❦	$40
⅍	$36
▲	$34
✤	$32
Đ	$32
⊁	$32
UM	$52

Especially For Ewe
#E9282C
Issued: 1983 • Susp.: 1990
Retail Price: $8 – $13.50

5

Values	
6∂	$132

Even The Heavens Shall Praise Him (LE-15,000)
Century Circle Figurine
#150312
Issued: 1998 • Closed: 1998
Retail Price: $125

6

Values	
&	$67
ৡ	$48

An Event For All Seasons
(LE-1993)
Special Event Figurine
#530158
Issued: 1993 • Closed: 1993
Retail Price: $30

GENERAL FIGURINES

	Price Paid	Value Of My Collection
1.		
2.		
3.		
4.		
5.		
6.		
7.		
8.		
9.		

PENCIL TOTALS

7

Values	
▮	$68
&	$60

An Event Worth Wading For
(LE-1992)
Special Event Figurine
#527319
Issued: 1992 • Closed: 1992
Retail Price: $32.50

8

Values	
Đ	$176
⊁	$155
▮	$142
&	$120
ৡ	$110

Faith Is A Victory
#521396
Issued: 1990 • Retired: 1993
Retail Price: $25 – $27.50

9

Variation

Values	
▲	$62
✤	$50
Đ	$44
⊁	$42
▮	$40
&	$40
ৡ	$38
⊸	$37
△	$35
♡	$35
✝	$35
6∂	$35

Faith Takes The Plunge
#111155
Issued: 1988 • Susp.: 1998
Retail Price: $27.50 – $35
Variation: Girl with smile – $64

KEY: NM *Pre-1981* ▲ 1981 ▮ 1982 ◀ 1983 ✝ 1984 ❦ 1985 ⅍ 1986 ▲ 1987 ✤ 1988 Đ 1989 ⊁ 1990 ▮ 1991 & 1992 ৡ 1993 ⊸ 1994 △ 1995 ♡ 1996 ✝ 1997 6∂ 1998 ★ 1999 UM *Unmarked*

82

FIGURINES

1

Values
- ♠ $60
- ♣ $49
- ♫ $45
- ★ $42
- ♦ $42
- ♪ $42
- ♫ $40
- ♒ $40
- △ $37.50
- ♡ $37.50
- † $37.50
- 6♂ $37.50
- ★ $37.50

February
Calendar Girl Series
#109991
Issued: 1988 • Open
Retail Price: $27.50 – $37.50

2

Values
- † $55

A Festival Of Precious Moments (LE-1997)
Regional Conference Figurine
#270741
Issued: 1997 • Closed: 1997
Retail Price: $30

3

Values
- ♪ $170
- ♒ $138

Fifteen Happy Years Together, What A Tweet (LE-1993)
15th Anniversary Commemorative Figurine
#530786
Issued: 1993 • Closed: 1993
Retail Price: $100

4

Values
- 6♂ $80

Flight Into Egypt (LE-1998)
#455970
Issued: 1998 • Closed: 1998
Retail Price: $75

5

Values
- ♫ $37
- ♪ $32
- ♠ $30
- ♫ $25
- ♫ $25
- ★ $22
- ♦ $22
- ♪ $20
- ♒ $20
- ♫ $18.50
- △ $18.50
- ♡ $18.50
- † $18.50
- 6♂ $18.50
- ★ $18.50

Flower Girl
Bridal Party Series
#E2835
Issued: 1985 • Open
Retail Price: $11 – $18.50

6

Values
- ♫ $57
- △ $47

Follow Your Heart (LE-1995)
Special Event Figurine
#528080
Issued: 1995 • Closed: 1995
Retail Price: $30

7

Values
- † $32.50
- 6♂ $32.50
- ★ $32.50

For The Sweetest Tu-Lips In Town
#306959
Issued: 1998 • Open
Retail Price: $30 – $32.50

8

Values
- ♫ $95
- † $88
- ♫ $86
- ♪ $84
- ♠ $79
- ♫ $74
- ♫ $70

Forgiving Is Forgetting
#E9252
Issued: 1983 • Susp.: 1989
Retail Price: $37.50 – $47.50

GENERAL FIGURINES

	Price Paid	Value Of My Collection
1.		
2.		
3.		
4.		
5.		
6.		
7.		
8.		
9.		
10.		
PENCIL TOTALS		

9

Values
- ♫ $92
- ♫ $77
- ★ $70
- ♦ $65
- ♪ $63
- ♒ $60
- ♫ $60
- △ $60

A Friend Is Someone Who Cares
#520632
Issued: 1989 • Retired: 1995
Retail Price: $30 – $35

10

Values
- 6♂ $60
- ★ $60

Friends Are Forever, Sew Bee It
#455903
Issued: 1998 • Open
Retail Price: $60

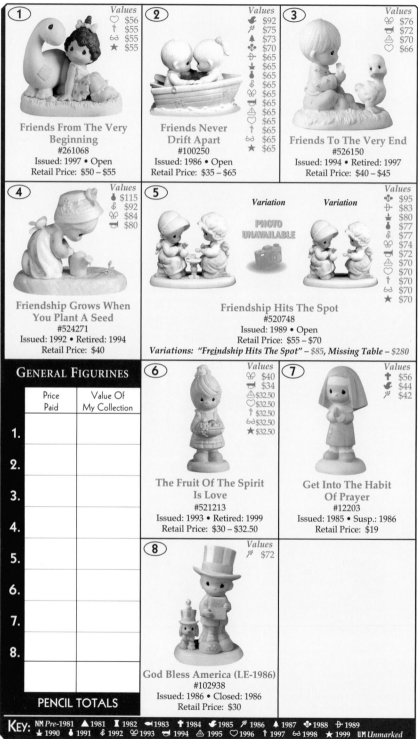

1

Values
♡ $56
♦ $55
⚭ $55
★ $55

Friends From The Very Beginning
#261068
Issued: 1997 • Open
Retail Price: $50 – $55

2

Values
🍃 $92
🌹 $75
♣ $73
⚓ $70
⚕ $65
⚖ $65
♬ $65
🎵 $65
⚭ $65
⚒ $65
♡ $65
† $65
⚬ $65
★ $65

Friends Never Drift Apart
#100250
Issued: 1986 • Open
Retail Price: $35 – $65

3

Values
⚭ $76
⚒ $72
⚠ $70
♡ $66

Friends To The Very End
#526150
Issued: 1994 • Retired: 1997
Retail Price: $40 – $45

4

Values
🌹 $115
♬ $92
⚭ $84
⚒ $80

Friendship Grows When You Plant A Seed
#524271
Issued: 1992 • Retired: 1994
Retail Price: $40

5

Variation   *Variation*

PHOTO UNAVAILABLE

Values
⚕ $95
⚓ $83
★ $80
🌹 $77
♬ $77
⚭ $74
⚒ $72
⚠ $70
♡ $70
† $70
⚬ $70
★ $70

Friendship Hits The Spot
#520748
Issued: 1989 • Open
Retail Price: $55 – $70
Variations: "Freindship Hits The Spot" – $85, Missing Table – $280

GENERAL FIGURINES

	Price Paid	Value Of My Collection
1.		
2.		
3.		
4.		
5.		
6.		
7.		
8.		
PENCIL TOTALS		

6

Values
⚭ $40
⚒ $34
⚠ $32.50
♡ $32.50
† $32.50
⚬ $32.50
★ $32.50

The Fruit Of The Spirit Is Love
#521213
Issued: 1993 • Retired: 1999
Retail Price: $30 – $32.50

7

Values
† $56
🍃 $44
🎵 $42

Get Into The Habit Of Prayer
#12203
Issued: 1985 • Susp.: 1986
Retail Price: $19

8

Values
🎵 $72

God Bless America (LE-1986)
#102938
Issued: 1986 • Closed: 1986
Retail Price: $30

KEY: NM *Pre*-1981 ▲1981 Ⅰ1982 ◀1983 †1984 🍃1985 🎵1986 ♣1987 ⚕1988 ⚓1989 ★1990 🌹1991 ♬1992 ⚭1993 ⚒1994 ⚠1995 ♡1996 †1997 ⚬1998 ★1999 **UM** *Unmarked*

1 God Bless Our Family
#100498
Issued: 1987 • Retired: 1999
Retail Price: $35 – $50

Values
- ♠ $68
- ⬧ $63
- ◌ $60
- ⭑ $57
- ▮ $57
- ⬨ $55
- ∞ $53
- ⊐ $52
- △ $50
- ♡ $50
- † $50
- ∽ $50
- ★ $50

2 God Bless Our Family
#100501
Issued: 1987 • Retired: 1999
Retail Price: $35 – $50

Values
- ♠ $65
- ⬧ $60
- ◌ $58
- ⭑ $56
- ▮ $56
- ⬨ $54
- ∞ $52
- ⊐ $52
- △ $50
- ♡ $50
- † $50
- ∽ $50
- ★ $50

3 God Bless Our Home
#12319
Issued: 1985 • Retired: 1998
Retail Price: $40 – $65

Values
- ⬨ $87
- ⅍ $81
- ♠ $77
- ⬧ $77
- ◌ $74
- ⭑ $72
- ▮ $72
- ⬨ $67
- ∞ $67
- ⊐ $67
- △ $65
- ♡ $65
- † $65
- ∽ $65

4 God Bless The Bride
#E2832
Issued: 1984 • Open
Retail Price: $35 – $50

Values
- † $64
- ⬨ $62
- ⅍ $60
- ♠ $60
- ⬧ $58
- ◌ $57
- ⭑ $57
- ▮ $55
- ⬨ $55
- ∞ $52
- ⊐ $52
- ♡ $50
- † $50
- ∽ $50
- ★ $50

5 God Bless The Day We Found You
#100145
Issued: 1986 • Susp.: 1990
Retail Price: $40 – $55

Values
- ⅍ $124
- ♠ $118
- ⬧ $115
- ◌ $110
- ⭑ $105

6 God Bless The Day We Found You
#100145R
Issued: 1995 • Open
Retail Price: $60

Values
- ⊐ $70
- ∞ $65
- ♡ $60
- † $60
- ∽ $60
- ★ $60

7 God Bless The Day We Found You
#100153
Issued: 1986 • Susp.: 1990
Retail Price: $40 – $55

Values
- ⅍ $120
- ♠ $112
- ⬧ $103
- ◌ $97
- ⭑ $94

8 God Bless The Day We Found You
#100153R
Issued: 1995 • Open
Retail Price: $60

Values
- ⊐ $67
- △ $62
- ♡ $60
- † $60
- ∽ $60
- ★ $60

9 God Bless The U.S.A.
(LE-1992)
National Day Of Prayer Figurine
#527564
Issued: 1992 • Closed: 1992
Retail Price: $32.50

Values
- ▮ $44
- ⬨ $40

10 God Bless You Graduate
#106194
Issued: 1987 • Open
Retail Price: $20 – $35

Values
- ⅍ $53
- ♠ $42
- ⬧ $39
- ◌ $39
- ⭑ $37
- ▮ $37
- ⬨ $37
- ∞ $35
- ⊐ $35
- △ $35
- ♡ $35
- † $35
- ∽ $35
- ★ $35

GENERAL FIGURINES

	Price Paid	Value Of My Collection
1.		
2.		
3.		
4.		
5.		
6.		
7.		
8.		
9.		
10.		
PENCIL TOTALS		

FIGURINES

KEY: NM *Pre-1981* ▲1981 ▮1982 ◄1983 †1984 ⬨1985 ⅍1986 ♠1987 ⬧1988 ◌1989 ⭑1990 ▮1991 ⬨1992 ∞1993 ⊐1994 △1995 ♡1996 †1997 ∽1998 ★1999 UM *Unmarked*

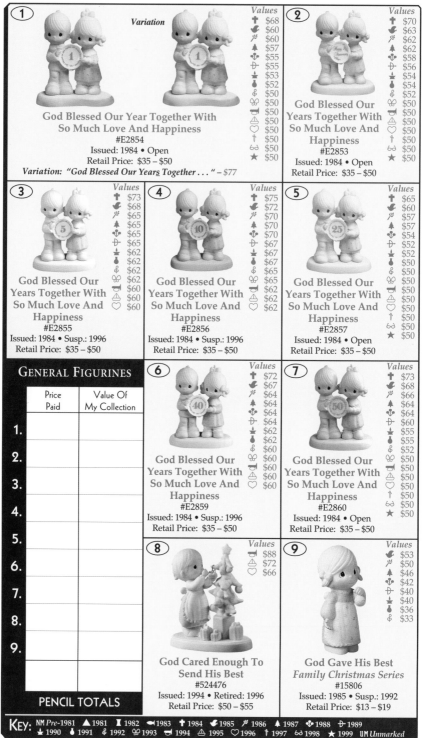

1

Variation

	Values
✝	$68
🐦	$60
⚜	$60
♠	$57
⚓	$55
☦	$55
⚒	$53
🔔	$52
ℰ	$50
👣	$50
△	$50
♡	$50
†	$50
6⋈	$50
★	$50

**God Blessed Our Year Together With
So Much Love And Happiness**
#E2854
Issued: 1984 • Open
Retail Price: $35 – $50
Variation: "God Blessed Our Years Together . . . " – $77

2

	Values
✝	$70
🐦	$63
⚜	$62
♠	$62
⚓	$58
☦	$56
⚒	$54
🔔	$54
ℰ	$52
👣	$50
△	$50
♡	$50
†	$50
6⋈	$50
★	$50

**God Blessed Our
Years Together With
So Much Love And
Happiness**
#E2853
Issued: 1984 • Open
Retail Price: $35 – $50

3

	Values
✝	$73
🐦	$68
⚜	$65
♠	$65
⚓	$65
☦	$65
⚒	$62
🔔	$62
ℰ	$62
👣	$60
△	$60
♡	$60

**God Blessed Our
Years Together With
So Much Love And
Happiness**
#E2855
Issued: 1984 • Susp.: 1996
Retail Price: $35 – $50

4

	Values
✝	$75
🐦	$72
⚜	$70
♠	$70
⚓	$70
☦	$67
⚒	$67
🔔	$67
ℰ	$65
👣	$65
△	$62
♡	$62

**God Blessed Our
Years Together With
So Much Love And
Happiness**
#E2856
Issued: 1984 • Susp.: 1996
Retail Price: $35 – $50

5

	Values
✝	$65
🐦	$60
⚜	$57
♠	$57
⚓	$54
☦	$52
⚒	$52
🔔	$50
ℰ	$50
👣	$50
△	$50
♡	$50
†	$50
6⋈	$50
★	$50

**God Blessed Our
Years Together With
So Much Love And
Happiness**
#E2857
Issued: 1984 • Open
Retail Price: $35 – $50

GENERAL FIGURINES

	Price Paid	Value Of My Collection
1.		
2.		
3.		
4.		
5.		
6.		
7.		
8.		
9.		
PENCIL TOTALS		

6

	Values
✝	$72
🐦	$67
⚜	$64
♠	$64
⚓	$64
☦	$64
⚒	$62
🔔	$62
ℰ	$60
👣	$60
△	$60
♡	$60

**God Blessed Our
Years Together With
So Much Love And
Happiness**
#E2859
Issued: 1984 • Susp.: 1996
Retail Price: $35 – $50

7

	Values
✝	$73
🐦	$68
⚜	$66
♠	$64
⚓	$64
⚒	$60
🔔	$55
ℰ	$55
👣	$52
△	$50
♡	$50
†	$50
6⋈	$50
★	$50

**God Blessed Our
Years Together With
So Much Love And
Happiness**
#E2860
Issued: 1984 • Open
Retail Price: $35 – $50

8

	Values
⊴	$88
△	$72
♡	$66

**God Cared Enough To
Send His Best**
#524476
Issued: 1994 • Retired: 1996
Retail Price: $50 – $55

9

	Values
🐦	$53
⚜	$50
♠	$46
⚓	$42
☦	$40
⚒	$40
🔔	$36
ℰ	$33

God Gave His Best
Family Christmas Series
#15806
Issued: 1985 • Susp.: 1992
Retail Price: $13 – $19

KEY: NM *Pre-1981* ▲ 1981 ✗ 1982 ◄ 1983 ✝ 1984 ✔ 1985 ⚜ 1986 ♠ 1987 ⚓ 1988 ☦ 1989 ⚒ 1990 🔔 1991 ℰ 1992 👣 1993 ⊴ 1994 △ 1995 ♡ 1996 † 1997 6⋈ 1998 ★ 1999 UM *Unmarked*

1 | Values
NM $130
▲ $94
✠ $85
⚓ $80
✝ $72
☙ $70
♫ $68
⚓ $65
✤ $65
ↁ $65

God Is Love
#E5213
Issued: 1981 • Susp.: 1989
Retail Price: $17 – $30

2 | Values
▲ $58
✠ $44
☙ $40
✝ $35
♫ $35
ↁ $32

God Is Love, Dear Valentine
#E7153
Issued: 1982 • Susp.: 1986
Retail Price: $16 – $17

3 | Values
▲ $60
✠ $50
☙ $40
✝ $40
♫ $35
ↁ $35

God Is Love, Dear Valentine
#E7154
Issued: 1982 • Susp.: 1986
Retail Price: $16 – $17

4 | Values
ↁ $44
✤ $38
🕯 $37
ℰ $37
❀ $34
◪ $32
△ $30
♡ $30
✝ $30
👓 $30
★ $30

God Is Love, Dear Valentine
#523518
Issued: 1990 • Open
Retail Price: $27.50 – $30

5 | Values
✠ $110
☙ $102
✝ $93

God Is Watching Over You
#E7163
Issued: 1982 • Susp.: 1984
Retail Price: $27.50 – $30

6 | Values
NM $1000

**God Loveth
A Cheerful Giver**
#E1378
Issued: 1979 • Retired: 1981
Retail Price: $9.50 – $15

7 | Values
👓 N/E

**God Loveth A
Cheerful Giver (LE-20)**
#456225
Issued: 1998 • Closed: 1998
Retail Price: N/A

8 | Values
☙ $88
✝ $72
☙ $66
♫ $63
🔺 $60

**God Sends The Gift
Of His Love**
#E6613
Issued: 1984 • Susp.: 1987
Retail Price: $22.50 – $25

9 | Values
☙ $105
✝ $96
☙ $92
♫ $88
🔺 $80

God Sent His Son
#E0507
Issued: 1983 • Susp.: 1987
Retail Price: $32.50 – $37

10 | Values
NM $148
▲ $112
✠ $107
☙ $97
✝ $94

God Understands
#E1379B
Issued: 1979 • Susp.: 1984
Retail Price: $8 – $19

GENERAL FIGURINES

	Price Paid	Value Of My Collection
1.		
2.		
3.		
4.		
5.		
6.		
7.		
8.		
9.		
10.		
PENCIL TOTALS		

FIGURINES

KEY: NM *Pre-1981* ▲ 1981 ✠ 1982 ☙ 1983 ✝ 1984 ☙ 1985 ♫ 1986 🔺 1987 ✤ 1988 ↁ 1989
★ 1990 🕯 1991 ℰ 1992 ❀ 1993 ◪ 1994 △ 1995 ♡ 1996 ✝ 1997 👓 1998 ★ 1999 UM *Unmarked*

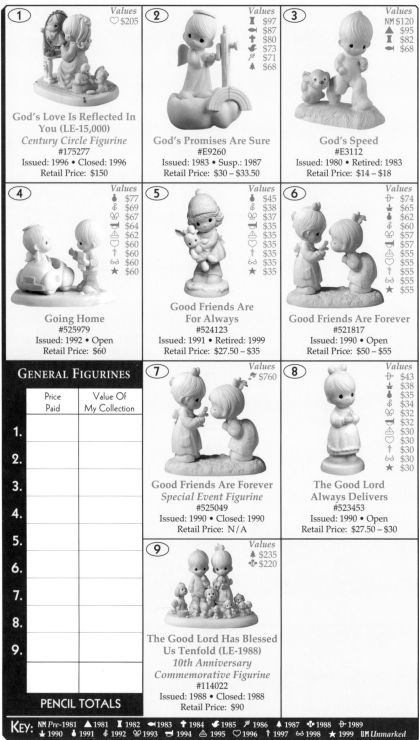

(1)

Values
♡ $205

God's Love Is Reflected In You (LE-15,000)
Century Circle Figurine
#175277
Issued: 1996 • Closed: 1996
Retail Price: $150

(2)

Values
Ⅰ $97
▲ $87
✝ $80
🐦 $73
♫ $71
♠ $68

God's Promises Are Sure
#E9260
Issued: 1983 • Susp.: 1987
Retail Price: $30 – $33.50

(3)

Values
NM $120
▲ $95
Ⅰ $82
🐦 $68

God's Speed
#E3112
Issued: 1980 • Retired: 1983
Retail Price: $14 – $18

(4)

Values
⚬ $77
ℰ $69
⚘ $67
🖂 $64
⚖ $62
♡ $60
✝ $60
ᏮᏮ $60
★ $60

Going Home
#525979
Issued: 1992 • Open
Retail Price: $60

(5)

Values
⚬ $45
ℰ $38
⚘ $37
🖂 $35
⚖ $35
♡ $35
✝ $35
ᏮᏮ $35
★ $35

Good Friends Are For Always
#524123
Issued: 1991 • Retired: 1999
Retail Price: $27.50 – $35

(6)

Values
Ꮭ $74
★ $65
⚬ $62
ℰ $60
⚘ $57
🖂 $57
⚖ $55
♡ $55
✝ $55
ᏮᏮ $55
★ $55

Good Friends Are Forever
#521817
Issued: 1990 • Open
Retail Price: $50 – $55

GENERAL FIGURINES

	Price Paid	Value Of My Collection
1.		
2.		
3.		
4.		
5.		
6.		
7.		
8.		
9.		

PENCIL TOTALS

(7)

Values
🖊 $760

Good Friends Are Forever
Special Event Figurine
#525049
Issued: 1990 • Closed: 1990
Retail Price: N/A

(8)

Values
Ꮭ $43
★ $38
⚬ $35
ℰ $34
⚘ $32
🖂 $32
⚖ $30
♡ $30
✝ $30
ᏮᏮ $30
★ $30

The Good Lord Always Delivers
#523453
Issued: 1990 • Open
Retail Price: $27.50 – $30

(9)

Values
▲ $235
⚓ $220

The Good Lord Has Blessed Us Tenfold (LE-1988)
10th Anniversary Commemorative Figurine
#114022
Issued: 1988 • Closed: 1988
Retail Price: $90

KEY: NM *Pre-1981* ▲ 1981 Ⅰ 1982 🐦1983 ✝ 1984 🖂1985 ♫ 1986 ▲ 1987 ⚓1988 Ꮭ 1989 ★ 1990 ⚬ 1991 ℰ 1992 ⚘1993 🖂 1994 ⚖ 1995 ♡ 1996 ✝ 1997 ᏮᏮ 1998 ★ 1999 ⅡM *Unmarked*

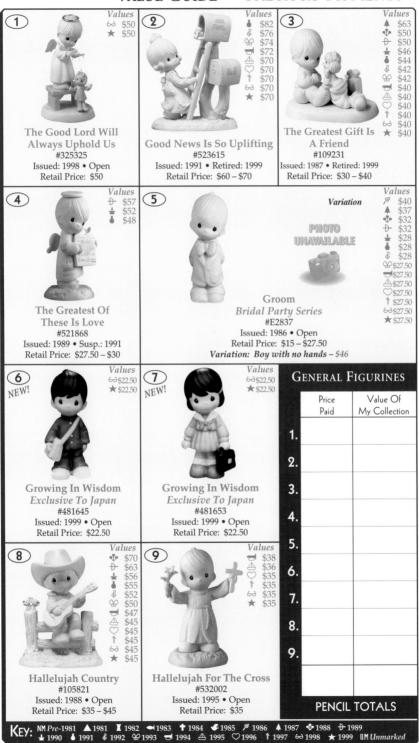

FIGURINES

1

Values	
6ᗺ	$50
★	$50

The Good Lord Will
Always Uphold Us
#325325
Issued: 1998 • Open
Retail Price: $50

2

Values	
🔔	$82
⅋	$76
⅋	$74
⊟	$72
△	$70
♡	$70
†	$70
🔔	$70
6ᗺ	$70
★	$70

Good News Is So Uplifting
#523615
Issued: 1991 • Retired: 1999
Retail Price: $60 – $70

3

Values	
♣	$63
✤	$50
ᗺ	$50
★	$46
🔔	$44
⅋	$42
🖤	$42
⊟	$40
△	$40
♡	$40
†	$40
6ᗺ	$40
★	$40

The Greatest Gift Is
A Friend
#109231
Issued: 1987 • Retired: 1999
Retail Price: $30 – $40

4

Values	
ᗺ	$57
★	$52
🔔	$48

The Greatest Of
These Is Love
#521868
Issued: 1989 • Susp.: 1991
Retail Price: $27.50 – $30

5

Variation

PHOTO
UNAVAILABLE

Values	
ℐ	$40
♣	$37
✤	$32
ᗺ	$32
★	$28
🔔	$28
⅋	$28
🖤	$27.50
⊟	$27.50
△	$27.50
♡	$27.50
†	$27.50
6ᗺ	$27.50
★	$27.50

Groom
Bridal Party Series
#E2837
Issued: 1986 • Open
Retail Price: $15 – $27.50
Variation: Boy with no hands – $46

6

NEW!

Values	
6ᗺ	$22.50
★	$22.50

Growing In Wisdom
Exclusive To Japan
#481645
Issued: 1999 • Open
Retail Price: $22.50

7

NEW!

Values	
6ᗺ	$22.50
★	$22.50

Growing In Wisdom
Exclusive To Japan
#481653
Issued: 1999 • Open
Retail Price: $22.50

8

Values	
✤	$70
ᗺ	$63
★	$56
🔔	$55
⅋	$52
🖤	$50
⊟	$47
△	$45
♡	$45
†	$45
6ᗺ	$45
★	$45

Hallelujah Country
#105821
Issued: 1988 • Open
Retail Price: $35 – $45

9

Values	
⊟	$38
△	$36
♡	$35
†	$35
6ᗺ	$35
★	$35

Hallelujah For The Cross
#532002
Issued: 1995 • Open
Retail Price: $35

GENERAL FIGURINES

	Price Paid	Value Of My Collection
1.		
2.		
3.		
4.		
5.		
6.		
7.		
8.		
9.		

PENCIL TOTALS

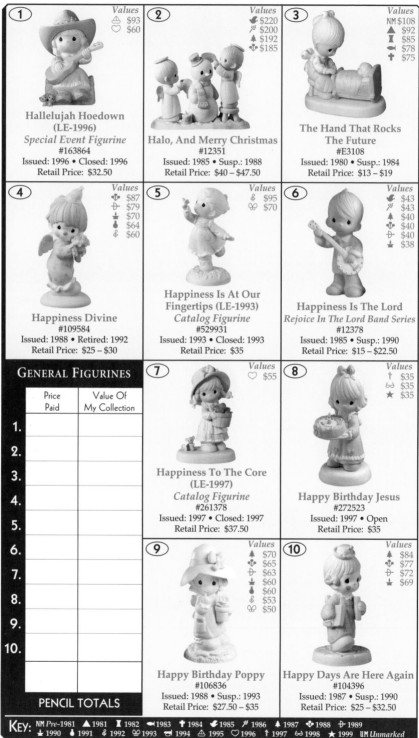

1

Values
🔺 $93
♡ $60

Hallelujah Hoedown
(LE-1996)
Special Event Figurine
#163864
Issued: 1996 • Closed: 1996
Retail Price: $32.50

2

Values
🍂 $220
🕊 $200
♣ $192
❦ $185

Halo, And Merry Christmas
#12351
Issued: 1985 • Susp.: 1988
Retail Price: $40 – $47.50

3

Values
NM $108
▲ $92
✖ $85
⚓ $78
✝ $75

The Hand That Rocks
The Future
#E3108
Issued: 1980 • Susp.: 1984
Retail Price: $13 – $19

4

Values
❦ $87
Ð $79
⚖ $70
🔥 $64
✎ $60

Happiness Divine
#109584
Issued: 1988 • Retired: 1992
Retail Price: $25 – $30

5

Values
✎ $95
❀ $70

Happiness Is At Our
Fingertips (LE-1993)
Catalog Figurine
#529931
Issued: 1993 • Closed: 1993
Retail Price: $35

6

Values
🍂 $43
🕊 $43
▲ $40
❦ $40
Ð $40
⚖ $38

Happiness Is The Lord
Rejoice In The Lord Band Series
#12378
Issued: 1985 • Susp.: 1990
Retail Price: $15 – $22.50

GENERAL FIGURINES

	Price Paid	Value Of My Collection
1.		
2.		
3.		
4.		
5.		
6.		
7.		
8.		
9.		
10.		
PENCIL TOTALS		

7

Values
♡ $55

Happiness To The Core
(LE-1997)
Catalog Figurine
#261378
Issued: 1997 • Closed: 1997
Retail Price: $37.50

8

Values
✝ $35
6∂ $35
★ $35

Happy Birthday Jesus
#272523
Issued: 1997 • Open
Retail Price: $35

9

Values
▲ $70
❦ $65
Ð $63
⚖ $60
🔥 $60
✎ $53
❀ $50

Happy Birthday Poppy
#106836
Issued: 1988 • Susp.: 1993
Retail Price: $27.50 – $35

10

Values
▲ $84
❦ $77
Ð $72
⚖ $69

Happy Days Are Here Again
#104396
Issued: 1987 • Susp.: 1990
Retail Price: $25 – $32.50

KEY: NM *Pre-1981* ▲ 1981 ✖ 1982 ◀ 1983 ✝ 1984 🍂 1985 🕊 1986 ▲ 1987 ❦ 1988 Ð 1989 ★ 1990 🔥 1991 ✎ 1992 ❀ 1993 🍃 1994 🔺 1995 ♡ 1996 ✝ 1997 6∂ 1998 ★ 1999 **UM** *Unmarked*

FIGURINES

1 — Happy Hula Days

Values
- △ $39
- ♡ $35
- † $32.50
- 6ᵭ $32.50
- ★ $32.50

Happy Hula Days
#128694
Issued: 1995 • Open
Retail Price: $30 – $32.50

2 — Happy Trip

Values
- ⅁ $97
- ★ $63
- $59
- ᵭ $56
- ✿ $53
- $50

Happy Trip
#521280
Issued: 1990 • Susp.: 1994
Retail Price: $35

3 — Have A Beary Merry Christmas

Values
- ⅁ $44
- ★ $40
- $38
- ᵭ $34

**Have A Beary
Merry Christmas**
Family Christmas Series
#522856
Issued: 1989 • Susp.: 1992
Retail Price: $15 – $16.50

4 — Have A Cozy Country Christmas

Values
- 6ᵭ $50
- ★ $50

**Have A Cozy
Country Christmas**
#455873
Issued: 1998 • Open
Retail Price: $50

5 — Have A Heavenly Journey

Values
- 6ᵭ $25
- ★ $25

Have A Heavenly Journey
Care-A-Van Exclusive
#12416R
Issued: 1998 • Open
Retail Price: $25

6 — Have I Toad You Lately

Values
- ♡ $45

**Have I Toad You Lately
That I Love You? (LE-1996)**
Catalog Figurine
#521329
Issued: 1996 • Closed: 1996
Retail Price: $30

7 — Have You Any Room For Jesus

Values
- ♡ $38
- † $35
- 6ᵭ $35
- ★ $35

**Have You Any Room
For Jesus**
#261130
Issued: 1997 • Open
Retail Price: $35

8 — NEW! He Came As The Gift Of God's Love

Values
- ★ $30

**He Came As The Gift Of
God's Love (set/4)**
Mini-Mini Nativity
#528128
Issued: 1999 • Open
Retail Price: $30

9 — He Cleansed My Soul

Values
- ✿ $62
- ⅁ $50
- ▲ $47
- ⚓ $45
- ✝ $44
- ★ $44
- $42
- ᵭ $42
- ✿ $40
- $40
- △ $40
- ♡ $40
- † $40
- 6ᵭ $40
- ★ $40

**He Cleansed
My Soul**
#100277
Issued: 1986 • Open
Retail Price: $24 – $40

10 — NEW! He Covers The Earth With His Glory

Values
- ★ $50

**He Covers The Earth With
His Glory**
Four Seasons Series
#129135
Issued: 1999 • Open
Retail Price: $50

GENERAL FIGURINES

	Price Paid	Value Of My Collection
1.		
2.		
3.		
4.		
5.		
6.		
7.		
8.		
9.		
10.		
PENCIL TOTALS		

KEY: NM *Pre-1981* ▲ 1981 ▮ 1982 ◄ 1983 † 1984 ✿ 1985 ✻ 1986 ▲ 1987 ✤ 1988 ⅁ 1989 ★ 1990 ᵭ 1991 ᵭ 1992 ✿ 1993 ◄ 1994 △ 1995 ♡ 1996 † 1997 6ᵭ 1998 ★ 1999 UM *Unmarked*

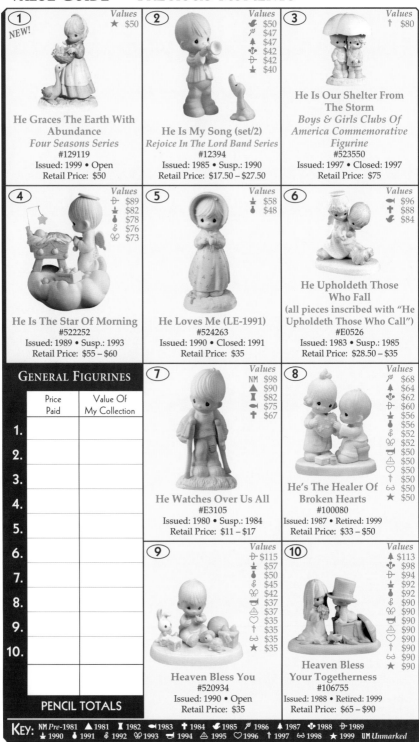

① NEW!

Values
★ $50

He Graces The Earth With Abundance
Four Seasons Series
#129119
Issued: 1999 • Open
Retail Price: $50

②

Values
🕊 $50
♫ $47
♣ $47
⚓ $42
🕊 $42
★ $40

He Is My Song (set/2)
Rejoice In The Lord Band Series
#12394
Issued: 1985 • Susp.: 1990
Retail Price: $17.50 – $27.50

③

Values
✝ $80

He Is Our Shelter From The Storm
Boys & Girls Clubs Of America Commemorative Figurine
#523550
Issued: 1997 • Closed: 1997
Retail Price: $75

④

Values
✝ $89
★ $82
🌡 $78
🎵 $76
🐝 $73

He Is The Star Of Morning
#522252
Issued: 1989 • Susp.: 1993
Retail Price: $55 – $60

⑤

Values
★ $58
🌡 $48

He Loves Me (LE-1991)
#524263
Issued: 1990 • Closed: 1991
Retail Price: $35

⑥

Values
◀ $96
🌡 $88
✿ $84

He Upholdeth Those Who Fall
(all pieces inscribed with "He Upholdeth Those Who Call")
#E0526
Issued: 1983 • Susp.: 1985
Retail Price: $28.50 – $35

General Figurines

	Price Paid	Value Of My Collection
1.		
2.		
3.		
4.		
5.		
6.		
7.		
8.		
9.		
10.		
PENCIL TOTALS		

⑦

Values
NM $98
▲ $90
✖ $82
◀ $75
✝ $67

He Watches Over Us All
#E3105
Issued: 1980 • Susp.: 1984
Retail Price: $11 – $17

⑧

Values
♫ $68
▲ $64
⚓ $62
✝ $60
★ $56
🌡 $56
🎵 $52
🐝 $52
🎺 $50
△ $50
♡ $50
✝ $50
👓 $50
★ $50

He's The Healer Of Broken Hearts
#100080
Issued: 1987 • Retired: 1999
Retail Price: $33 – $50

⑨

Values
✝ $115
★ $57
🌡 $50
🎵 $45
🐝 $42
🎺 $37
△ $37
♡ $35
✝ $35
👓 $35
★ $35

Heaven Bless You
#520934
Issued: 1990 • Open
Retail Price: $35

⑩

Values
▲ $113
⚓ $98
✝ $94
★ $92
🌡 $90
🎵 $90
🐝 $90
🎺 $90
△ $90
♡ $90
✝ $90
👓 $90
★ $90

Heaven Bless Your Togetherness
#106755
Issued: 1988 • Retired: 1999
Retail Price: $65 – $90

KEY: NM *Pre-1981* ▲ 1981 ✖ 1982 ◀ 1983 ✝ 1984 ✿ 1985 ♫ 1986 ▲ 1987 ⚓ 1988 ✝ 1989 ★ 1990 🌡 1991 🎵 1992 🐝 1993 🎺 1994 △ 1995 ♡ 1996 ✝ 1997 👓 1998 ★ 1999 UM *Unmarked*

92

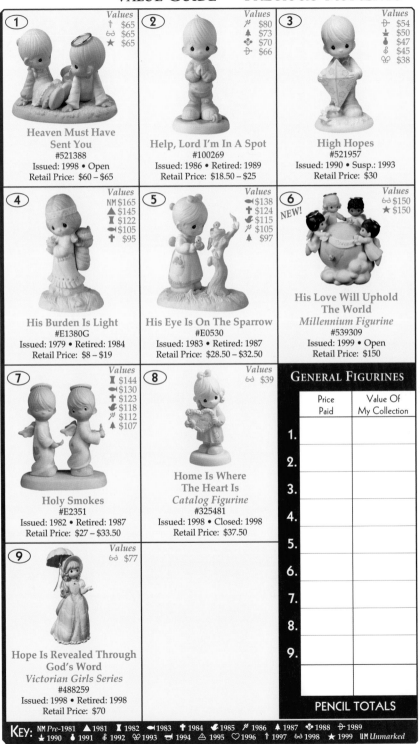

FIGURINES

1

Values	
✝	$65
63	$65
★	$65

Heaven Must Have Sent You
#521388
Issued: 1998 • Open
Retail Price: $60 – $65

2

Values	
ℋ	$80
▲	$73
✿	$70
⅁	$66

Help, Lord I'm In A Spot
#100269
Issued: 1986 • Retired: 1989
Retail Price: $18.50 – $25

3

Values	
⅁	$54
✦	$50
⚬	$47
ℰ	$45
♋	$38

High Hopes
#521957
Issued: 1990 • Susp.: 1993
Retail Price: $30

4

Values	
NM	$165
▲	$145
✠	$122
◀	$105
✝	$95

His Burden Is Light
#E1380G
Issued: 1979 • Retired: 1984
Retail Price: $8 – $19

5

Values	
✝	$138
✝	$124
✿	$115
ℋ	$105
▲	$97

His Eye Is On The Sparrow
#E0530
Issued: 1983 • Retired: 1987
Retail Price: $28.50 – $32.50

6 NEW!

Values	
63	$150
★	$150

His Love Will Uphold The World
Millennium Figurine
#539309
Issued: 1999 • Open
Retail Price: $150

7

Values	
✠	$144
◀	$130
✝	$123
✿	$118
ℋ	$112
▲	$107

Holy Smokes
#E2351
Issued: 1982 • Retired: 1987
Retail Price: $27 – $33.50

8

Values	
63	$39

Home Is Where The Heart Is
Catalog Figurine
#325481
Issued: 1998 • Closed: 1998
Retail Price: $37.50

9

Values	
63	$77

Hope Is Revealed Through God's Word
Victorian Girls Series
#488259
Issued: 1998 • Retired: 1998
Retail Price: $70

GENERAL FIGURINES

	Price Paid	Value Of My Collection
1.		
2.		
3.		
4.		
5.		
6.		
7.		
8.		
9.		
PENCIL TOTALS		

KEY: NM *Pre-1981* ▲ 1981 ✠ 1982 ◀ 1983 ✝ 1984 ✿ 1985 ℋ 1986 ▲ 1987 ✿ 1988 ⅁ 1989 ✦ 1990 ⚬ 1991 ℰ 1992 ♋ 1993 ◀ 1994 △ 1995 ♡ 1996 ✝ 1997 63 1998 ★ 1999 ∥M *Unmarked*

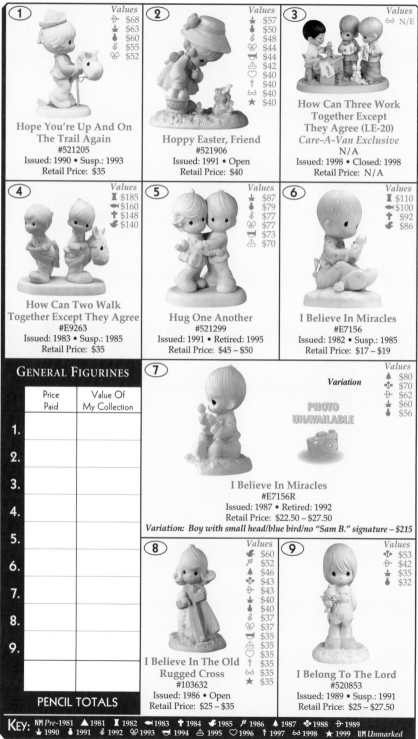

(1)

Values	
Đ	$68
★	$63
♦	$60
ℰ	$55
♀	$52

Hope You're Up And On The Trail Again
#521205
Issued: 1990 • Susp.: 1993
Retail Price: $35

(2)

Values	
★	$57
♦	$50
ℰ	$48
♀	$44
⊟	$44
△	$42
♡	$40
†	$40
6Ə	$40
★	$40

Hoppy Easter, Friend
#521906
Issued: 1991 • Open
Retail Price: $40

(3)

Values	
6Ə	N/E

How Can Three Work Together Except They Agree (LE-20)
Care-A-Van Exclusive
N/A
Issued: 1998 • Closed: 1998
Retail Price: N/A

(4)

Values	
Ⅱ	$185
◄	$160
†	$148
✔	$140

How Can Two Walk Together Except They Agree
#E9263
Issued: 1983 • Susp.: 1985
Retail Price: $35

(5)

Values	
★	$87
♦	$79
ℰ	$77
♀	$77
⊟	$73
△	$70

Hug One Another
#521299
Issued: 1991 • Retired: 1995
Retail Price: $45 – $50

(6)

Values	
Ⅱ	$110
◄	$100
†	$92
✔	$86

I Believe In Miracles
#E7156
Issued: 1982 • Susp.: 1985
Retail Price: $17 – $19

GENERAL FIGURINES

	Price Paid	Value Of My Collection
1.		
2.		
3.		
4.		
5.		
6.		
7.		
8.		
9.		

PENCIL TOTALS

(7)

Values	
▲	$80
✠	$70
Đ	$62
★	$60
♦	$56

Variation

PHOTO UNAVAILABLE

I Believe In Miracles
#E7156R
Issued: 1987 • Retired: 1992
Retail Price: $22.50 – $27.50
Variation: Boy with small head/blue bird/no "Sam B." signature – $215

(8)

Values	
✔	$60
♪	$52
▲	$46
✠	$43
Đ	$43
★	$40
♦	$40
ℰ	$37
♀	$37
⊟	$35
△	$35
♡	$35
†	$35
6Ə	$35
★	$35

I Believe In The Old Rugged Cross
#103632
Issued: 1986 • Open
Retail Price: $25 – $35

(9)

Values	
✠	$53
Đ	$42
★	$35
♦	$32

I Belong To The Lord
#520853
Issued: 1989 • Susp.: 1991
Retail Price: $25 – $27.50

KEY: NM *Pre-1981* ▲1981 Ⅱ1982 ◄1983 †1984 ✔1985 ♪1986 ▲1987 ✠1988 Đ1989
★1990 ♦1991 ℰ1992 ♀1993 ⊟1994 △1995 ♡1996 †1997 6Ə1998 ★1999 ⅠⅠM *Unmarked*

1

Values	
🍴	$62
🔺	$54
⚓	$52
✝	$50
👓	$50
⭐	$50

I Can't Bear To Let You Go
#532037
Issued: 1995 • Open
Retail Price: $50

2

Values	
⭐	$105
👓	$83
💰	$70
🌀	$70
🍴	$66

**I Can't Spell Success
Without You**
#523763
Issued: 1991 • Susp.: 1994
Retail Price: $40 – $45

3 NEW!

Values	
⭐	$60

**I Couldn't Make It
Without You**
*Boys & Girls Clubs Of
America Commemorative
Figurine*
#635030
Issued: 1999 • Open
Retail Price: $60

4

Values	
🎵	$88
🏵	$82
⚓	$75
⚓	$75
⚓	$70
⚓	$67
💰	$67
💰	$64
🌀	$64
🍴	$62
⚠	$62
♡	$62

**I Get A Bang
Out Of You**
The Clown Series
#12262
Issued: 1985 • Retired: 1997
Retail Price: $30 – $45

5

Values	
🍴	$235
✝	$215
🍃	$200
🎵	$195

I Get A Kick Out Of You
#E2827
Issued: 1984 • Susp.: 1986
Retail Price: $50

6

Values	
🍴	$86
🏵	$76
♡	$73
✝	$70
👓	$70
⭐	$70

**I Give You My Love
Forever True**
#129100
Issued: 1995 • Open
Retail Price: $70

7

Values	
👓	$30
⭐	$30

**I Now Pronounce You
Man And Wife**
#455938
Issued: 1998 • Open
Retail Price: $30

8

Values	
⚠	$59
♡	$55
✝	$55
👓	$55
⭐	$55

I Only Have Ice For You
#530956
Issued: 1995 • Retired: 1999
Retail Price: $55

9

Values	
🎵	$90
⚓	$82

**I Picked A Very Special
Mom (LE-1987)**
#100536
Issued: 1987 • Closed: 1987
Retail Price: $40

10

Values	
👓	$65
⭐	$65

**I Saw Mommy Kissing
Santa Claus**
#455822
Issued: 1998 • Open
Retail Price: $65

FIGURINES

GENERAL FIGURINES

	Price Paid	Value Of My Collection
1.		
2.		
3.		
4.		
5.		
6.		
7.		
8.		
9.		
10.		
PENCIL TOTALS		

KEY: NM *Pre-1981* ▲1981 ▮1982 ◀1983 ✝1984 🍃1985 🎵1986 ▲1987 🏵1988 ᚦ1989 ⚓1990 💰1991 💲1992 🌀1993 🍴1994 ⚠1995 ♡1996 ✝1997 👓1998 ⭐1999 UM *Unmarked*

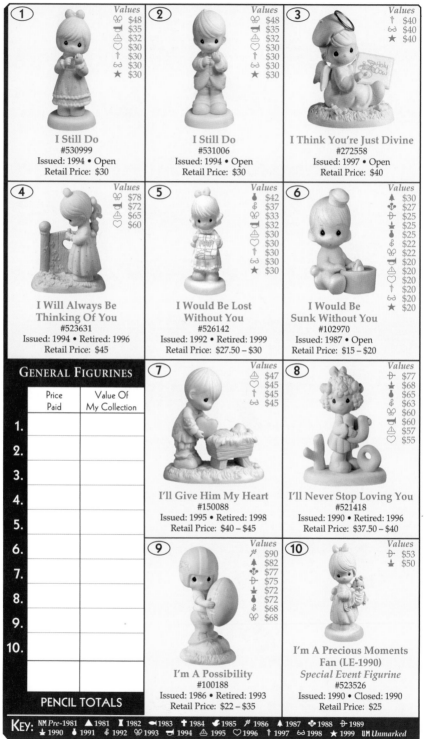

1

Values	
✿	$48
⊐	$35
△	$32
♡	$30
†	$30
6ᴓ	$30
★	$30

I Still Do
#530999
Issued: 1994 • Open
Retail Price: $30

2

Values	
✿	$48
⊐	$35
△	$32
♡	$30
†	$30
6ᴓ	$30
★	$30

I Still Do
#531006
Issued: 1994 • Open
Retail Price: $30

3

Values	
†	$40
6ᴓ	$40
★	$40

I Think You're Just Divine
#272558
Issued: 1997 • Open
Retail Price: $40

4

Values	
✿	$78
⊐	$72
△	$65
♡	$60

I Will Always Be Thinking Of You
#523631
Issued: 1994 • Retired: 1996
Retail Price: $45

5

Values	
◑	$42
∫	$37
✿	$33
⊐	$32
△	$30
♡	$30
†	$30
6ᴓ	$30
★	$30

I Would Be Lost Without You
#526142
Issued: 1992 • Retired: 1999
Retail Price: $27.50 – $30

6

Values	
▲	$30
⚓	$27
⊅	$25
★	$25
◑	$25
∫	$22
✿	$22
⊐	$20
△	$20
♡	$20
†	$20
6ᴓ	$20
★	$20

I Would Be Sunk Without You
#102970
Issued: 1987 • Open
Retail Price: $15 – $20

GENERAL FIGURINES

	Price Paid	Value Of My Collection
1.		
2.		
3.		
4.		
5.		
6.		
7.		
8.		
9.		
10.		

PENCIL TOTALS

7

Values	
△	$47
♡	$45
†	$45
6ᴓ	$45

I'll Give Him My Heart
#150088
Issued: 1995 • Retired: 1998
Retail Price: $40 – $45

8

Values	
⊅	$77
★	$68
◑	$65
∫	$63
✿	$60
⊐	$60
△	$57
♡	$55

I'll Never Stop Loving You
#521418
Issued: 1990 • Retired: 1996
Retail Price: $37.50 – $40

9

Values	
⌀	$90
▲	$82
⚓	$77
⊅	$75
★	$72
◑	$72
∫	$68
✿	$68

I'm A Possibility
#100188
Issued: 1986 • Retired: 1993
Retail Price: $22 – $35

10

Values	
⊅	$53
★	$50

I'm A Precious Moments Fan (LE-1990)
Special Event Figurine
#523526
Issued: 1990 • Closed: 1990
Retail Price: $25

KEY: NM *Pre-1981* ▲ 1981 ✗ 1982 ◄1983 † 1984 ✦ 1985 ⌀ 1986 ▲ 1987 ⚓ 1988 ⊅ 1989 ★ 1990 ◑ 1991 ∫ 1992 ✿ 1993 ⊐ 1994 △ 1995 ♡ 1996 † 1997 6ᴓ 1998 ★ 1999 UM *Unmarked*

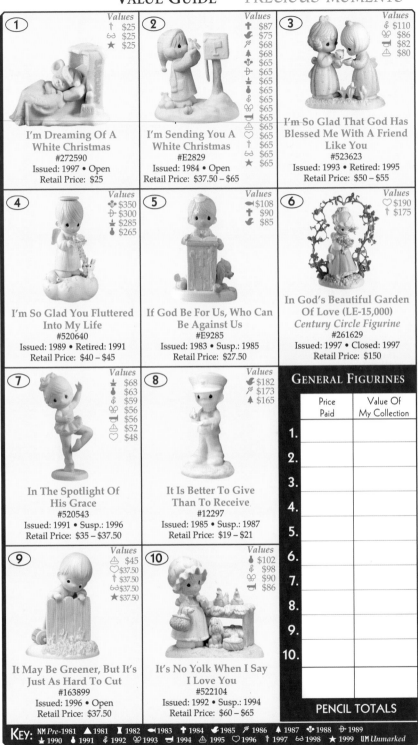

1

Values
† $25
੬ð $25
★ $25

**I'm Dreaming Of A
White Christmas**
#272590
Issued: 1997 • Open
Retail Price: $25

2

Values
† $87
✿ $75
∦ $68
▲ $68
✤ $65
♫ $65
�’ $65
⚓ $65
♒ $65
⚖ $65
♡ $65
੬ð $65
★ $65

**I'm Sending You A
White Christmas**
#E2829
Issued: 1984 • Open
Retail Price: $37.50 – $65

3

Values
∮ $110
✿ $86
⚓ $82
⚖ $80

**I'm So Glad That God Has
Blessed Me With A Friend
Like You**
#523623
Issued: 1993 • Retired: 1995
Retail Price: $50 – $55

4

Values
✤ $350
੭ $300
★ $285
♦ $265

**I'm So Glad You Fluttered
Into My Life**
#520640
Issued: 1989 • Retired: 1991
Retail Price: $40 – $45

5

Values
◥ $108
♦ $90
✦ $85

**If God Be For Us, Who Can
Be Against Us**
#E9285
Issued: 1983 • Susp.: 1985
Retail Price: $27.50

6

Values
♡ $190
† $175

**In God's Beautiful Garden
Of Love (LE-15,000)**
Century Circle Figurine
#261629
Issued: 1997 • Closed: 1997
Retail Price: $150

7

Values
★ $68
♦ $63
∮ $59
♒ $56
⚓ $56
⚖ $52
♡ $48

**In The Spotlight Of
His Grace**
#520543
Issued: 1991 • Susp.: 1996
Retail Price: $35 – $37.50

8

Values
✦ $182
∦ $173
▲ $165

**It Is Better To Give
Than To Receive**
#12297
Issued: 1985 • Susp.: 1987
Retail Price: $19 – $21

9

Values
⚖ $45
♡ $37.50
† $37.50
੬ð $37.50
★ $37.50

**It May Be Greener, But It's
Just As Hard To Cut**
#163899
Issued: 1996 • Open
Retail Price: $37.50

10

Values
♦ $102
∮ $98
♒ $90
⚓ $86

**It's No Yolk When I Say
I Love You**
#522104
Issued: 1992 • Susp.: 1994
Retail Price: $60 – $65

FIGURINES

GENERAL FIGURINES

	Price Paid	Value Of My Collection
1.		
2.		
3.		
4.		
5.		
6.		
7.		
8.		
9.		
10.		
PENCIL TOTALS		

KEY: NM *Pre-1981* ▲ 1981 ▌ 1982 ◀ 1983 † 1984 ✦ 1985 ∦ 1986 ▲ 1987 ✤ 1988 ੭ 1989
★ 1990 ♦ 1991 ∮ 1992 ♒ 1993 ⚓ 1994 ⚖ 1995 ♡ 1996 † 1997 ੬ð 1998 ★ 1999 UM *Unmarked*

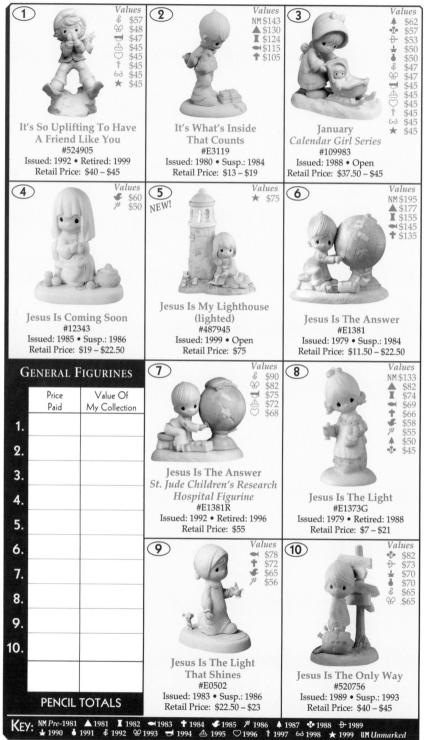

1 Values
- ₰ $57
- ℗ $48
- ☜ $47
- ⊿ $45
- ♡ $45
- ✝ $45
- ꙮ $45
- ★ $45

It's So Uplifting To Have
A Friend Like You
#524905
Issued: 1992 • Retired: 1999
Retail Price: $40 – $45

2 Values
- NM $143
- ▲ $130
- Ⅱ $124
- ◀ $115
- ✝ $105

It's What's Inside
That Counts
#E3119
Issued: 1980 • Susp.: 1984
Retail Price: $13 – $19

3 Values
- ▲ $62
- ✛ $57
- ꝗ $53
- ⤓ $50
- ♦ $50
- ₰ $47
- ℗ $47
- ꙭ $45
- ⊿ $45
- ♡ $45
- ✝ $45
- ꙮ $45
- ★ $45

January
Calendar Girl Series
#109983
Issued: 1988 • Open
Retail Price: $37.50 – $45

4 Values
- ꝉ $60
- ℐ $50

Jesus Is Coming Soon
#12343
Issued: 1985 • Susp.: 1986
Retail Price: $19 – $22.50

5 Values
- ★ $75

NEW!

Jesus Is My Lighthouse
(lighted)
#487945
Issued: 1999 • Open
Retail Price: $75

6 Values
- NM $195
- ▲ $177
- Ⅱ $155
- ◀ $145
- ✝ $135

Jesus Is The Answer
#E1381
Issued: 1979 • Susp.: 1984
Retail Price: $11.50 – $22.50

General Figurines

	Price Paid	Value Of My Collection
1.		
2.		
3.		
4.		
5.		
6.		
7.		
8.		
9.		
10.		

PENCIL TOTALS

7 Values
- ₰ $90
- ℗ $82
- ꙭ $75
- ꝗ $72
- ♡ $68

Jesus Is The Answer
*St. Jude Children's Research
Hospital Figurine*
#E1381R
Issued: 1992 • Retired: 1996
Retail Price: $55

8 Values
- NM $133
- ▲ $82
- Ⅱ $74
- ꝗ $69
- ✝ $66
- ✛ $58
- ℐ $55
- ▲ $50
- ⚓ $45

Jesus Is The Light
#E1373G
Issued: 1979 • Retired: 1988
Retail Price: $7 – $21

9 Values
- ◀ $78
- ✝ $72
- ꝗ $65
- ℐ $56

Jesus Is The Light
That Shines
#E0502
Issued: 1983 • Susp.: 1986
Retail Price: $22.50 – $23

10 Values
- ✛ $82
- ꝗ $73
- ⤓ $70
- ♦ $70
- ₰ $65
- ℗ $65

Jesus Is The Only Way
#520756
Issued: 1989 • Susp.: 1993
Retail Price: $40 – $45

KEY: NM *Pre-1981* ▲1981 Ⅱ1982 ◀1983 ✝1984 ꝉ1985 ℐ1986 ▲1987 ✛1988 ꝗ1989 ⤓1990 ♦1991 ₰1992 ℗1993 ꙭ1994 ⊿1995 ♡1996 ✝1997 ꙮ1998 ★1999 UM *Unmarked*

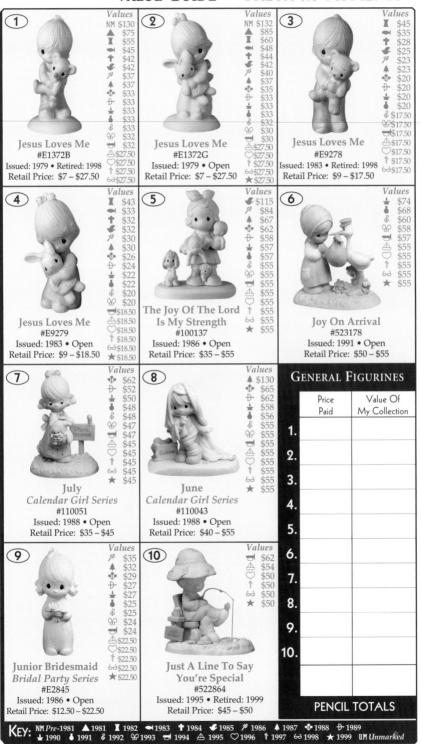

FIGURINES

1

Values	
NM	$130
▲	$75
Ⅰ	$55
◄	$45
✝	$42
✿	$42
♫	$37
▲	$37
✤	$33
Ð	$33
☆	$33
♨	$33
₰	$33
☆	$32
♚	$32
△	$27.50
♡	$27.50
✝	$27.50
63	$27.50
★	$27.50

Jesus Loves Me
#E1372B
Issued: 1979 • Retired: 1998
Retail Price: $7 – $27.50

2

Values	
NM	$132
▲	$85
Ⅰ	$60
◄	$48
✝	$44
♫	$42
✿	$40
▲	$37
✤	$35
Ð	$33
☆	$33
♚	$33
₰	$32
♨	$30
☆	$30
△	$27.50
♡	$27.50
✝	$27.50
63	$27.50
★	$27.50

Jesus Loves Me
#E1372G
Issued: 1979 • Open
Retail Price: $7 – $27.50

3

Values	
Ⅰ	$45
◄	$35
✝	$28
✿	$25
♫	$23
▲	$23
✤	$20
Ð	$20
☆	$20
♨	$20
₰	$17.50
♨	$17.50
♚	$17.50
△	$17.50
♡	$17.50
✝	$17.50
63	$17.50

Jesus Loves Me
#E9278
Issued: 1983 • Retired: 1998
Retail Price: $9 – $17.50

4

Values	
Ⅰ	$43
◄	$33
✝	$32
✿	$32
♫	$30
▲	$30
✤	$26
Ð	$24
☆	$22
♨	$22
₰	$20
♨	$20
♚	$18.50
△	$18.50
♡	$18.50
✝	$18.50
63	$18.50
★	$18.50

Jesus Loves Me
#E9279
Issued: 1983 • Open
Retail Price: $9 – $18.50

5

Values	
✿	$115
◄	$84
▲	$67
✤	$62
Ð	$58
☆	$57
♨	$57
₰	$57
♚	$55
♨	$55
♨	$55
△	$55
♡	$55
✝	$55
63	$55
★	$55

**The Joy Of The Lord
Is My Strength**
#100137
Issued: 1986 • Open
Retail Price: $35 – $55

6

Values	
▲	$74
₰	$68
₰	$60
✤	$58
♨	$57
△	$55
♡	$55
✝	$55
63	$55
★	$55

Joy On Arrival
#523178
Issued: 1991 • Open
Retail Price: $50 – $55

7

Values	
✤	$62
Ð	$52
♚	$50
♨	$48
₰	$48
♨	$47
♨	$47
△	$45
♡	$45
✝	$45
63	$45
★	$45

July
Calendar Girl Series
#110051
Issued: 1988 • Open
Retail Price: $35 – $45

8

Values	
▲	$130
✤	$65
Ð	$62
♨	$58
♨	$56
₰	$55
♨	$55
♨	$55
△	$55
♡	$55
✝	$55
63	$55
★	$55

June
Calendar Girl Series
#110043
Issued: 1988 • Open
Retail Price: $40 – $55

9

Values	
♫	$35
▲	$32
✤	$29
Ð	$27
♚	$27
♨	$25
₰	$25
♨	$24
♨	$24
△	$22.50
♡	$22.50
✝	$22.50
63	$22.50
★	$22.50

Junior Bridesmaid
Bridal Party Series
#E2845
Issued: 1986 • Open
Retail Price: $12.50 – $22.50

10

Values	
♨	$62
△	$54
♡	$50
✝	$50
63	$50
★	$50

**Just A Line To Say
You're Special**
#522864
Issued: 1995 • Retired: 1999
Retail Price: $45 – $50

GENERAL FIGURINES

	Price Paid	Value Of My Collection
1.		
2.		
3.		
4.		
5.		
6.		
7.		
8.		
9.		
10.		
PENCIL TOTALS		

KEY: NM *Pre-1981* ▲ 1981 Ⅰ 1982 ◄ 1983 ✝ 1984 ✿ 1985 ♫ 1986 ▲ 1987 ✤ 1988 Ð 1989 ♚ 1990 ₰ 1991 ♨ 1992 ♨ 1993 ♨ 1994 △ 1995 ♡ 1996 ✝ 1997 63 1998 ★ 1999 ⅡM *Unmarked*

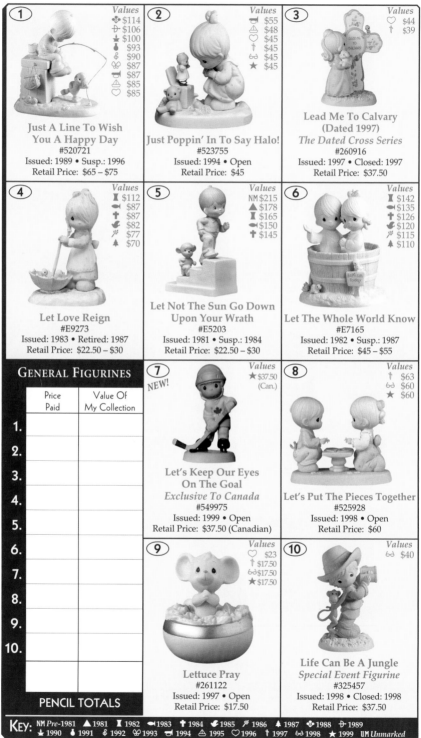

1 *Values*
🐟 $114
👕 $106
💉 $100
🕯️ $93
🐝 $90
🎀 $87
🍞 $87
🔺 $85
♡ $85

**Just A Line To Wish
You A Happy Day**
#520721
Issued: 1989 • Susp.: 1996
Retail Price: $65 – $75

2 *Values*
🍞 $55
🔺 $48
♡ $45
🕯️ $45
👓 $45
★ $45

Just Poppin' In To Say Halo!
#523755
Issued: 1994 • Open
Retail Price: $45

3 *Values*
♡ $44
🕯️ $39

**Lead Me To Calvary
(Dated 1997)**
The Dated Cross Series
#260916
Issued: 1997 • Closed: 1997
Retail Price: $37.50

4 *Values*
𝕀 $112
🐟 $87
🕯️ $87
💉 $82
🎀 $77
🔺 $70

Let Love Reign
#E9273
Issued: 1983 • Retired: 1987
Retail Price: $22.50 – $30

5 *Values*
NM $215
▲ $178
𝕀 $165
◀ $150
🕯️ $145

**Let Not The Sun Go Down
Upon Your Wrath**
#E5203
Issued: 1981 • Susp.: 1984
Retail Price: $22.50 – $30

6 *Values*
𝕀 $142
◀ $135
🕯️ $126
🎀 $120
🎀 $115
🔺 $110

Let The Whole World Know
#E7165
Issued: 1982 • Susp.: 1987
Retail Price: $45 – $55

GENERAL FIGURINES

	Price Paid	Value Of My Collection
1.		
2.		
3.		
4.		
5.		
6.		
7.		
8.		
9.		
10.		

PENCIL TOTALS

7 NEW! *Values*
★ $37.50
(Can.)

**Let's Keep Our Eyes
On The Goal**
Exclusive To Canada
#549975
Issued: 1999 • Open
Retail Price: $37.50 (Canadian)

8 *Values*
🕯️ $63
👓 $60
★ $60

Let's Put The Pieces Together
#525928
Issued: 1998 • Open
Retail Price: $60

9 *Values*
♡ $23
🕯️ $17.50
👓 $17.50
★ $17.50

Lettuce Pray
#261122
Issued: 1997 • Open
Retail Price: $17.50

10 *Values*
👓 $40

Life Can Be A Jungle
Special Event Figurine
#325457
Issued: 1998 • Closed: 1998
Retail Price: $37.50

KEY: NM *Pre-1981* ▲ 1981 𝕀 1982 ◀ 1983 🕯️ 1984 ✦ 1985 🎀 1986 🔺 1987 🐟 1988 👕 1989
★ 1990 💉 1991 🐝 1992 ❀ 1993 🍞 1994 🔺 1995 ♡ 1996 🕯️ 1997 👓 1998 ★ 1999 UM *Unmarked*

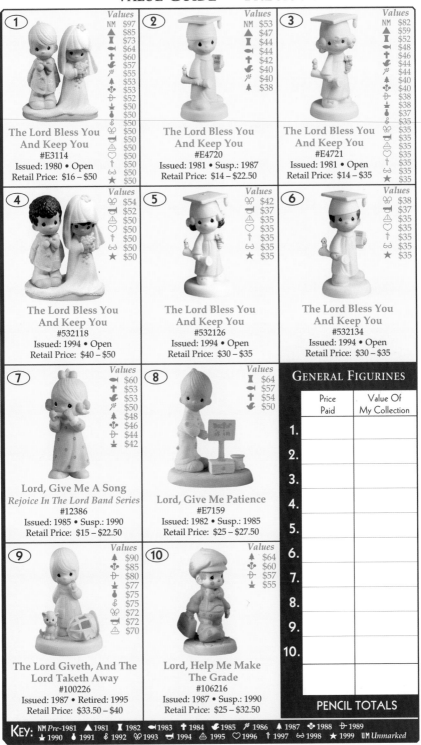

1 Values
NM $97
▲ $85
▌ $73
◀ $64
◆ $60
✦ $57
♪ $55
✿ $53
✤ $53
♦ $52
★ $50
♨ $50
⚘ $50
♡ $50
✝ $50
63 $50
★ $50

**The Lord Bless You
And Keep You**
#E3114
Issued: 1980 • Open
Retail Price: $16 – $50

2 Values
NM $53
▲ $47
▌ $44
◀ $44
✝ $42
✦ $40
♪ $40
▲ $38

**The Lord Bless You
And Keep You**
#E4720
Issued: 1981 • Susp.: 1987
Retail Price: $14 – $22.50

3 Values
NM $82
▲ $59
▌ $52
◀ $48
✝ $46
✦ $44
♪ $44
▲ $40
✤ $40
♦ $38
♨ $38
⚘ $37
♡ $35
✝ $35
63 $35
★ $35

**The Lord Bless You
And Keep You**
#E4721
Issued: 1981 • Open
Retail Price: $14 – $35

4 Values
♧ $54
✤ $52
♡ $50
✝ $50
63 $50
★ $50

**The Lord Bless You
And Keep You**
#532118
Issued: 1994 • Open
Retail Price: $40 – $50

5 Values
♧ $42
✤ $37
△ $35
♡ $35
✝ $35
63 $35
★ $35

**The Lord Bless You
And Keep You**
#532126
Issued: 1994 • Open
Retail Price: $30 – $35

6 Values
♧ $38
✤ $37
△ $35
✝ $35
♡ $35
63 $35
★ $35

**The Lord Bless You
And Keep You**
#532134
Issued: 1994 • Open
Retail Price: $30 – $35

7 Values
◀ $60
✝ $53
✦ $53
♪ $50
▲ $48
✤ $46
♦ $44
★ $42

Lord, Give Me A Song
Rejoice In The Lord Band Series
#12386
Issued: 1985 • Susp.: 1990
Retail Price: $15 – $22.50

8 Values
▌ $64
◀ $57
✝ $54
✦ $50

Lord, Give Me Patience
#E7159
Issued: 1982 • Susp.: 1985
Retail Price: $25 – $27.50

9 Values
▲ $90
✤ $85
♦ $80
★ $77
♦ $75
♨ $75
♧ $72
⚘ $72
△ $70

**The Lord Giveth, And The
Lord Taketh Away**
#100226
Issued: 1987 • Retired: 1995
Retail Price: $33.50 – $40

10 Values
▲ $64
✤ $60
♦ $57
★ $55

**Lord, Help Me Make
The Grade**
#106216
Issued: 1987 • Susp.: 1990
Retail Price: $25 – $32.50

GENERAL FIGURINES

	Price Paid	Value Of My Collection
1.		
2.		
3.		
4.		
5.		
6.		
7.		
8.		
9.		
10.		

PENCIL TOTALS

FIGURINES

KEY: NM *Pre-1981* ▲ 1981 ▌ 1982 ◀ 1983 ✝ 1984 ✦ 1985 ♪ 1986 ▲ 1987 ✤ 1988 ♦ 1989 ★ 1990 ♦ 1991 ♨ 1992 ♧ 1993 ⚘ 1994 △ 1995 ♡ 1996 ✝ 1997 63 1998 ★ 1999 UM *Unmarked*

(1)

Values	
⅌	$78
★	$73
♨	$67
⚯	$65
⚶	$65
⬎	$62
△	$59
♡	$59

Lord, Help Me Stick To My Job
#521450
Issued: 1990 • Retired: 1997
Retail Price: $30 – $35

(2)

Values	
△	$42
♡	$40
†	$35
ᬑ	$35
★	$35

Lord Help Me To Stay On Course
#532096
Issued: 1995 • Open
Retail Price: $35

(3)

Values	
⅍	$122
▲	$115
⚜	$110
⅌	$110
★	$105
♨	$100

Lord, Help Us Keep Our Act Together
#101850
Issued: 1987 • Retired: 1992
Retail Price: $35 – $50

(4)

Values	
⚶	$90
⅍	$60
▲	$53
⚜	$46
⅌	$46
★	$43
♨	$43
⚯	$43
♔	$40
⬎	$38
△	$37
♡	$35
†	$35
ᬑ	$35
★	$35

Lord, I'm Coming Home
#100110
Issued: 1986 • Open
Retail Price: $22.50 – $35

(5)

Values	
⬎	$43
△	$38
♡	$35
†	$35
ᬑ	$35
★	$35

The Lord Is Counting On You
#531707
Issued: 1994 • Open
Retail Price: $32.50 – $35

(6)

Values	
♡	$46
†	$40
ᬑ	$40
★	$40

The Lord Is The Hope Of Our Future
#261564
Issued: 1997 • Open
Retail Price: $40

GENERAL FIGURINES

	Price Paid	Value Of My Collection
1.		
2.		
3.		
4.		
5.		
6.		
7.		
8.		
9.		
10.		

PENCIL TOTALS

(7)

Values	
△	$34
♡	$29
†	$27.50
ᬑ	$27.50
★	$27.50

The Lord Is With You
#526835
Issued: 1996 • Retired: 1999
Retail Price: $27.50

(8)

Values	
⚜	$77
⅌	$73
★	$70
♨	$70
⚶	$67
♔	$67
⬎	$65
△	$65
♡	$65
†	$65
ᬑ	$65
★	$65

The Lord Is Your Light To Happiness
#520837
Issued: 1989 • Open
Retail Price: $50 – $65

(9)

Values	
⚶	$117
⅍	$95
▲	$87
⚜	$82

Lord, Keep Me On My Toes
#100129
Issued: 1986 • Retired: 1988
Retail Price: $22.50 – $27

(10)

Values	
⅍	$72
▲	$62
⚜	$59
⅌	$59
★	$56
♨	$56
⚶	$54
⚯	$50
⬎	$48
△	$45
♡	$45
†	$45
ᬑ	$45

Lord, Keep Me On The Ball
The Clown Series
#12270
Issued: 1986 • Susp.: 1998
Retail Price: $30 – $45

KEY: NM *Pre-1981* ▲ 1981 ✕ 1982 ◄1983 † 1984 ✔1985 ⅍ 1986 ▲ 1987 ⚜ 1988 ⅌ 1989 ★ 1990 ♨ 1991 ⚶ 1992 ♔ 1993 ⬎ 1994 △ 1995 ♡ 1996 † 1997 ᬑ 1998 ★ 1999 UM *Unmarked*

FIGURINES

1 NEW!
Values
★ $45

Lord, Police Protect Us
#539953
Issued: 1999 • Open
Retail Price: $45

2
Values
♡ $40
† $40
6ð $40
★ $40

Lord, Spare Me
#521191
Issued: 1997 • Open
Retail Price: $37.50 – $40

3 NEW!
Values
6ð $45
★ $45

Lord Speak To Me
#531987
Issued: 1999 • Open
Retail Price: $45

4
Values
🝚 $47

Lord Teach Us To Pray
(LE-1994)
National Day Of Prayer Figurine
#524158
Issued: 1994 • Closed: 1994
Retail Price: $35

5
Values
Ð $70
🕯 $64
🔔 $60
𝄐 $60
⅋ $56
△ $56
♡ $52
$46

Lord, Turn My Life Around
#520551
Issued: 1990 • Susp.: 1996
Retail Price: $35 – $37.50

6
Values
⅋ $57
⅋ $55
🝚 $55
△ $52
♡ $52

The Lord Turned My Life Around
#520535
Issued: 1992 • Susp.: 1996
Retail Price: $35.50 – $37.50

7
Values
🎈 $93
🎵 $90
♠ $84
🔱 $80

The Lord Will Carry You Through
The Clown Series
#12467
Issued: 1986 • Retired: 1988
Retail Price: $30 – $35

8
Values
⅋ $70
⅋ $60

The Lord Will Provide
(LE-1993)
#523593
Issued: 1993 • Closed: 1993
Retail Price: $40

9
Values
𝕀 $76
🐚 $56
† $54
🔱 $54
🎵 $52
♠ $50
🔱 $50
Ð $48
🕯 $48
⅋ $47
⅋ $47
🝚 $45
△ $45
♡ $45
† $45
6ð $45
★ $45

Love Beareth All Things
#E7158
Issued: 1982 • Open
Retail Price: $25 – $45

10
Values
🝚 $46
△ $40

Love Blooms Eternal
(Dated 1995)
The Dated Cross Series
#127019
Issued: 1995 • Closed: 1995
Retail Price: $35

GENERAL FIGURINES

	Price Paid	Value Of My Collection
1.		
2.		
3.		
4.		
5.		
6.		
7.		
8.		
9.		
10.		
PENCIL TOTALS		

KEY: NM *Pre-1981* ▲ 1981 𝕀 1982 ◀ 1983 † 1984 🍃 1985 🎵 1986 ♠ 1987 🔱 1988 Ð 1989
🔱 1990 🕯 1991 ⅋ 1992 ⅋ 1993 🝚 1994 △ 1995 ♡ 1996 † 1997 6ð 1998 ★ 1999 **UM** *Unmarked*

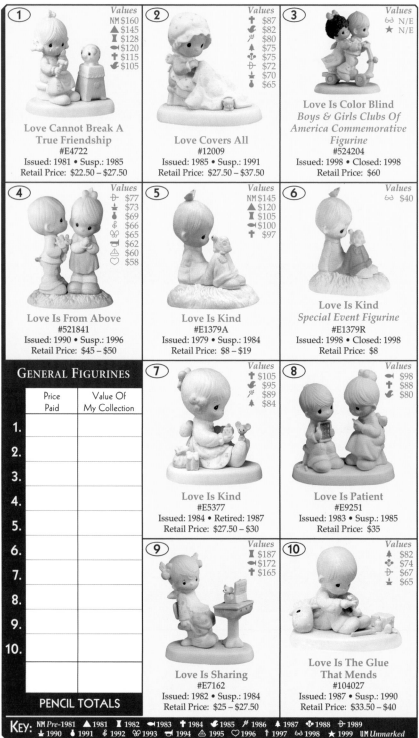

(1)

Values
NM $160
▲ $145
Ⅱ $128
◄ $120
✝ $115
✔ $105

**Love Cannot Break A
True Friendship**
#E4722
Issued: 1981 • Susp.: 1985
Retail Price: $22.50 – $27.50

(2)

Values
✝ $87
✔ $82
♫ $80
▲ $75
✤ $75
Ð $72
✦ $70
● $65

Love Covers All
#12009
Issued: 1985 • Susp.: 1991
Retail Price: $27.50 – $37.50

(3)

Values
◖ N/E
★ N/E

Love Is Color Blind
*Boys & Girls Clubs Of
America Commemorative
Figurine*
#524204
Issued: 1998 • Closed: 1998
Retail Price: $60

(4)

Values
Ð $77
✦ $73
● $69
♪ $66
♧ $65
✇ $62
△ $60
♡ $58

Love Is From Above
#521841
Issued: 1990 • Susp.: 1996
Retail Price: $45 – $50

(5)

Values
NM $145
▲ $120
Ⅱ $105
◄ $100
✝ $97

Love Is Kind
#E1379A
Issued: 1979 • Susp.: 1984
Retail Price: $8 – $19

(6)

Values
◖ $40

Love Is Kind
Special Event Figurine
#E1379R
Issued: 1998 • Closed: 1998
Retail Price: $8

GENERAL FIGURINES

	Price Paid	Value Of My Collection
1.		
2.		
3.		
4.		
5.		
6.		
7.		
8.		
9.		
10.		

PENCIL TOTALS

(7)

Values
✝ $105
✔ $95
♫ $89
▲ $84

Love Is Kind
#E5377
Issued: 1984 • Retired: 1987
Retail Price: $27.50 – $30

(8)

Values
◄ $98
✝ $88
✔ $80

Love Is Patient
#E9251
Issued: 1983 • Susp.: 1985
Retail Price: $35

(9)

Values
Ⅱ $187
◄ $172
✝ $165

Love Is Sharing
#E7162
Issued: 1982 • Susp.: 1984
Retail Price: $25 – $27.50

(10)

Values
▲ $82
✤ $74
Ð $67
✦ $65

**Love Is The Glue
That Mends**
#104027
Issued: 1987 • Susp.: 1990
Retail Price: $33.50 – $40

KEY: NM *Pre-1981* ▲ 1981 Ⅱ 1982 ◄ 1983 ✝ 1984 ✔ 1985 ♫ 1986 ▲ 1987 ✤ 1988 Ð 1989
★ 1990 ● 1991 ♪ 1992 ✇ 1993 ◄ 1994 △ 1995 ♡ 1996 ✝ 1997 ◖ 1998 ★ 1999 UM *Unmarked*

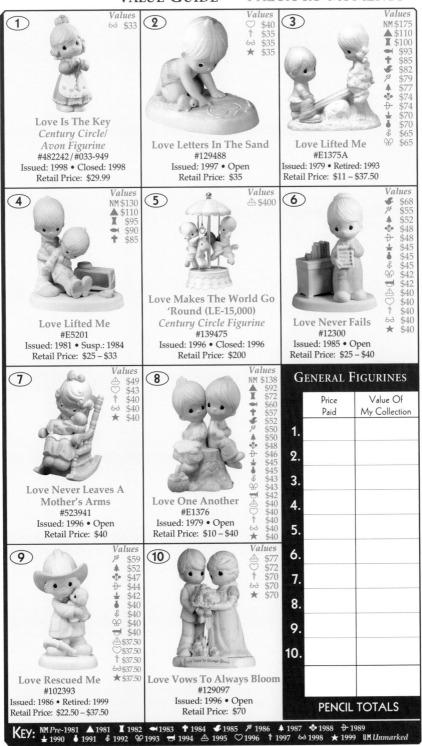

(1) **Values**
6ə $33

Love Is The Key
*Century Circle/
Avon Figurine*
#482242 / #033-949
Issued: 1998 • Closed: 1998
Retail Price: $29.99

(2) **Values**
♡ $40
† $35
6ə $35
★ $35

Love Letters In The Sand
#129488
Issued: 1997 • Open
Retail Price: $35

(3) **Values**
NM $175
▲ $110
✕ $100
◄ $93
† $85
❡ $82
ℱ $79
▲ $77
✧ $74
Ð $74
♦ $70
♦ $70
⅋ $65
ೲ $65

Love Lifted Me
#E1375A
Issued: 1979 • Retired: 1993
Retail Price: $11 – $37.50

(4) **Values**
NM $130
▲ $110
✕ $95
◄ $90
† $85

Love Lifted Me
#E5201
Issued: 1981 • Susp.: 1984
Retail Price: $25 – $33

(5) **Values**
△ $400

**Love Makes The World Go
'Round (LE-15,000)**
Century Circle Figurine
#139475
Issued: 1996 • Closed: 1996
Retail Price: $200

(6) **Values**
❡ $68
ℱ $55
▲ $52
✧ $48
Ð $48
✦ $45
♦ $45
⅋ $45
ೲ $42
✐ $42
△ $40
♡ $40
† $40
6ə $40
★ $40

Love Never Fails
#12300
Issued: 1985 • Open
Retail Price: $25 – $40

(7) **Values**
△ $49
♡ $43
† $40
6ə $40
★ $40

**Love Never Leaves A
Mother's Arms**
#523941
Issued: 1996 • Open
Retail Price: $40

(8) **Values**
NM $138
▲ $92
✕ $72
◄ $60
† $57
❡ $52
ℱ $50
✦ $50
▲ $48
✧ $46
♦ $45
✐ $45
⅋ $43
ೲ $43
✐ $42
△ $40
♡ $40
† $40
6ə $40
★ $40

Love One Another
#E1376
Issued: 1979 • Open
Retail Price: $10 – $40

(9) **Values**
ℱ $59
▲ $52
✧ $47
Ð $44
✦ $42
♦ $40
⅋ $40
ೲ $40
✐ $40
△ $37.50
♡ $37.50
† $37.50
6ə $37.50
★ $37.50

Love Rescued Me
#102393
Issued: 1986 • Retired: 1999
Retail Price: $22.50 – $37.50

(10) **Values**
△ $77
✕ $72
† $70
6ə $70
★ $70

Love Vows To Always Bloom
#129097
Issued: 1996 • Open
Retail Price: $70

FIGURINES

GENERAL FIGURINES

	Price Paid	Value Of My Collection
1.		
2.		
3.		
4.		
5.		
6.		
7.		
8.		
9.		
10.		

PENCIL TOTALS

KEY: NM *Pre-1981* ▲ 1982 ✕ 1982 ◄ 1983 † 1984 ❡ 1985 ℱ 1986 ▲ 1987 ✧ 1988 Ð 1989 ✦ 1990 ♦ 1991 ⅋ 1992 ೲ 1993 ✐ 1994 △ 1995 ♡ 1996 † 1997 6ə 1998 ★ 1999 ∥M *Unmarked*

1

Values	
NM	$146
▲	$118
Ⅱ	$105
◄	$88
✝	$85
◄	$85
♫	$83
▲	$80
✛	$80
Ð	$80
▲	$75
◊	$75
◊	$72
∞	$72

Loving Is Sharing
#E3110B
Issued: 1980 • Retired: 1993
Retail Price: $13 – $30

2

Values	
NM	$112
Ⅱ	$80
▲	$68
✝	$50
✝	$45
◄	$42
▲	$40
◊	$40
Ð	$38
✛	$38
◊	$35
◊	$35
◊	$35
◊	$35
✝	$35
♀	$35
★	$35

Loving Is Sharing
#E3110G
Issued: 1980 • Open
Retail Price: $13 – $35

3

Values	
◄	$39
◊	$37.50
♡	$37.50
✝	$37.50
♀	$37.50
★	$37.50

Luke 2:10-11
#532916
Issued: 1994 • Retired: 1999
Retail Price: $35 – $37.50

4

Values	
NM	$135
▲	$87
Ⅱ	$56
◄	$44
✝	$42
◄	$40
♫	$40
▲	$40
◊	$37
Ð	$37
▲	$35
◊	$35
◊	$35
∞	$32.50
◊	$32.50
♡	$32.50
✝	$32.50
♀	$32.50
★	$32.50

Make A Joyful Noise
#E1374G
Issued: 1979 • Open
Retail Price: $8 – $32.50

5

Values	
♫	$130
▲	$95
◊	$90
Ð	$83
⚐	$77

Make Me A Blessing
#100102
Issued: 1987 • Retired: 1990
Retail Price: $35 – $50

6 NEW!

Values	
♀	$60
★	$60

Make Me Strong (set/4)
Exclusive To Japan
#481688
Issued: 1999 • Open
Retail Price: $60

General Figurines

	Price Paid	Value Of My Collection
1.		
2.		
3.		
4.		
5.		
6.		
7.		
8.		
9.		
10.		
PENCIL TOTALS		

7

Values	
◊	$42
♡	$39
✝	$37.50
♀	$37.50

Making Spirits Bright
#150118
Issued: 1995 • Retired: 1998
Retail Price: $37.50

8

Values	
◊	$358
Ð	$325
⚐	$320

Many Moons In Same Canoe, Blessum You
#520772
Issued: 1989 • Retired: 1990
Retail Price: $50 – $55

9

Values	
♀	$63

Many Years Of Blessing You (LE-1998)
#384887
Issued: 1998 • Closed: 1998
Retail Price: $60

10

Values	
▲	$64
◊	$48
Ð	$47
⚐	$43
▲	$42
◊	$40
♀	$40
◄	$40
◊	$40
♡	$40
✝	$40
♀	$40
★	$40

March
Calendar Girl Series
#110019
Issued: 1988 • Open
Retail Price: $27.50 – $40

KEY: NM *Pre-1981* ▲ 1981 Ⅱ 1982 ◄ 1983 ✝ 1984 ◄ 1985 ♫ 1986 ▲ 1987 ◊ 1988 Ð 1989 ▲ 1990 ◊ 1991 ◊ 1992 ∞ 1993 ◄ 1994 ◊ 1995 ♡ 1996 ✝ 1997 ♀ 1998 ★ 1999 UM *Unmarked*

106

1 Values
△ $44
♡ $38
† $35
6∂ $35
★ $35

Marching To The Beat Of Freedom's Drum
#521981
Issued: 1996 • Open
Retail Price: $35

2 Values
6∂ $52

Marvelous Grace (LE-1998)
Century Circle Figurine
#325503
Issued: 1998 • Closed: 1998
Retail Price: $50

3 Values
▲ $120
❖ $50
Ð $44
⚓ $42
♦ $40
❀ $40
☀ $37
⏾ $37
△ $35
♡ $35
† $35
6∂ $35
★ $35

May
Calendar Girl Series
#110035
Issued: 1988 • Open
Retail Price: $25 – $35

4 Values
⚓ $65
♦ $50
❀ $45
☀ $42
⏾ $40
△ $37.50
♡ $37.50
† $37.50
6∂ $37.50

May Only Good Things Come Your Way
#524425
Issued: 1991 • Retired: 1998
Retail Price: $30 – $37.50

5 Values
♡ $70

May The Sun Always Shine On You (LE-1996)
Century Circle Figurine
#184217
Issued: 1996 • Closed: 1996
Retail Price: $37.50

6 Values
❖ $55
∱ $50
▲ $47
❖ $47
Ð $45
⚓ $42
♦ $42
❀ $40

May You Have The Sweetest Christmas
Family Christmas Series
#15776
Issued: 1985 • Susp.: 1992
Retail Price: $17 – $25

7 Values
⌐ $130
✝ $105
✔ $100
∱ $95

May Your Birthday Be A Blessing
#E2826
Issued: 1984 • Susp.: 1986
Retail Price: $37.50

8 Values
⚓ $55
♦ $47
❀ $42
☀ $40
⏾ $38
△ $37
♡ $35
† $35
6∂ $35
★ $35

May Your Birthday Be A Blessing
#524301
Issued: 1991 • Open
Retail Price: $30 – $35

GENERAL FIGURINES

	Price Paid	Value Of My Collection
1.		
2.		
3.		
4.		
5.		
6.		
7.		
8.		
9.		
10.		
PENCIL TOTALS		

9 Values
† $85
✔ $76
∱ $72

May Your Christmas Be Blessed
#E5376
Issued: 1984 • Susp.: 1986
Retail Price: $37.50

10 Values
Ⅱ $94
⌐ $83
† $78

May Your Christmas Be Cozy
#E2345
Issued: 1982 • Susp.: 1984
Retail Price: $23 – $25

KEY: NM *Pre-1981* ▲ 1981 Ⅱ 1982 ⌐ 1983 † 1984 ✔ 1985 ∱ 1986 ▲ 1987 ❖ 1988 Ð 1989 ⚓ 1990 ♦ 1991 ❀ 1992 ❀ 1993 ⏾ 1994 △ 1995 ♡ 1996 † 1997 6∂ 1998 ★ 1999 UM *Unmarked*

FIGURINES

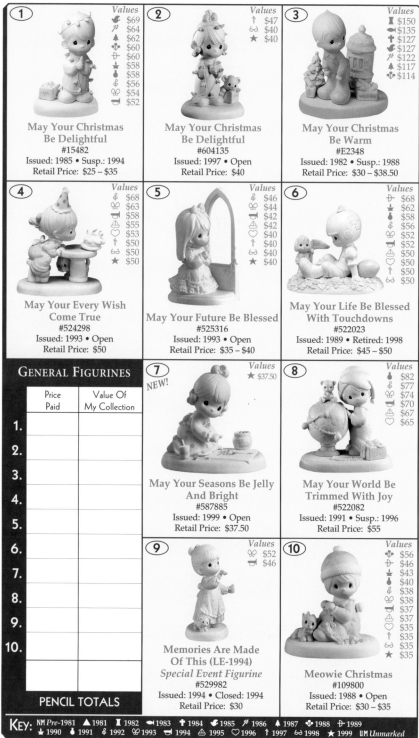

1

Values	
🕊	$69
🎋	$64
♣	$62
✤	$60
⊕	$60
⚱	$58
🔔	$58
⅋	$56
☯	$54
⊟	$52

May Your Christmas Be Delightful
#15482
Issued: 1985 • Susp.: 1994
Retail Price: $25 – $35

2

Values	
†	$47
6∂	$40
★	$40

May Your Christmas Be Delightful
#604135
Issued: 1997 • Open
Retail Price: $40

3

Values	
Ⅱ	$150
◄	$135
†	$127
✔	$127
🎋	$122
♣	$117
✤	$114

May Your Christmas Be Warm
#E2348
Issued: 1982 • Susp.: 1988
Retail Price: $30 – $38.50

4

Values	
⅋	$68
☯	$63
🔔	$58
△	$55
♡	$53
†	$50
6∂	$50
★	$50

May Your Every Wish Come True
#524298
Issued: 1993 • Open
Retail Price: $50

5

Values	
⅋	$46
☯	$44
⊟	$42
🔔	$42
♡	$40
†	$40
6∂	$40
★	$40

May Your Future Be Blessed
#525316
Issued: 1993 • Open
Retail Price: $35 – $40

6

Values	
⊕	$68
♣	$62
⚱	$58
⅋	$56
☯	$52
⊟	$52
△	$50
♡	$50
†	$50
6∂	$50

May Your Life Be Blessed With Touchdowns
#522023
Issued: 1989 • Retired: 1998
Retail Price: $45 – $50

GENERAL FIGURINES

	Price Paid	Value Of My Collection
1.		
2.		
3.		
4.		
5.		
6.		
7.		
8.		
9.		
10.		

PENCIL TOTALS

7
NEW!

Values	
★	$37.50

May Your Seasons Be Jelly And Bright
#587885
Issued: 1999 • Open
Retail Price: $37.50

8

Values	
⚱	$82
⅋	$77
☯	$74
⊟	$70
△	$67
♡	$65

May Your World Be Trimmed With Joy
#522082
Issued: 1991 • Susp.: 1996
Retail Price: $55

9

Values	
☯	$52
⊟	$46

Memories Are Made Of This (LE-1994)
Special Event Figurine
#529982
Issued: 1994 • Closed: 1994
Retail Price: $30

10

Values	
✤	$56
⊕	$46
♣	$43
⚱	$40
⅋	$38
☯	$38
⊟	$37
△	$37
♡	$35
†	$35
6∂	$35
★	$35

Meowie Christmas
#109800
Issued: 1988 • Open
Retail Price: $30 – $35

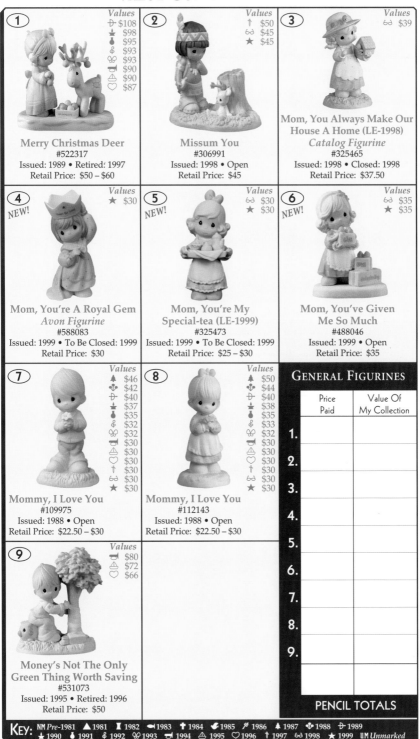

1 — Values
- ♈ $108
- ★ $98
- ♠ $95
- ♣ $93
- ♋ $93
- ♒ $90
- ♎ $90
- ♡ $87

Merry Christmas Deer
#522317
Issued: 1989 • Retired: 1997
Retail Price: $50 – $60

2 — Values
- ✝ $50
- 6♂ $45
- ★ $45

Missum You
#306991
Issued: 1998 • Open
Retail Price: $45

3 — Values
- 6♂ $39

Mom, You Always Make Our House A Home (LE-1998)
Catalog Figurine
#325465
Issued: 1998 • Closed: 1998
Retail Price: $37.50

4 — Values
- ★ $30

NEW!

Mom, You're A Royal Gem
Avon Figurine
#588083
Issued: 1999 • To Be Closed: 1999
Retail Price: $30

5 — Values
- 6♂ $30
- ★ $30

NEW!

Mom, You're My Special-tea (LE-1999)
#325473
Issued: 1999 • To Be Closed: 1999
Retail Price: $25 – $30

6 — Values
- 6♂ $35
- ★ $35

NEW!

Mom, You've Given Me So Much
#488046
Issued: 1999 • Open
Retail Price: $35

7 — Values
- ♠ $46
- ♣ $42
- ♈ $40
- ★ $37
- ♠ $35
- ♣ $32
- ♋ $32
- ♒ $30
- ♎ $30
- ♡ $30
- ✝ $30
- 6♂ $30
- ★ $30

Mommy, I Love You
#109975
Issued: 1988 • Open
Retail Price: $22.50 – $30

8 — Values
- ♠ $50
- ♣ $44
- ♈ $40
- ★ $38
- ♠ $35
- ♣ $33
- ♋ $32
- ♒ $30
- ♎ $30
- ♡ $30
- ✝ $30
- 6♂ $30
- ★ $30

Mommy, I Love You
#112143
Issued: 1988 • Open
Retail Price: $22.50 – $30

9 — Values
- ♒ $80
- ♎ $72
- ♡ $66

Money's Not The Only Green Thing Worth Saving
#531073
Issued: 1995 • Retired: 1996
Retail Price: $50

GENERAL FIGURINES

	Price Paid	Value Of My Collection
1.		
2.		
3.		
4.		
5.		
6.		
7.		
8.		
9.		
PENCIL TOTALS		

FIGURINES

KEY: NM *Pre-1981* ▲ 1981 ✗ 1982 ◄1983 ✝ 1984 ✦ 1985 ♪ 1986 ♠ 1987 ♣ 1988 ♈ 1989 ★ 1990 ♠ 1991 ♣ 1992 ♋ 1993 ♒ 1994 ♎ 1995 ♡ 1996 ✝ 1997 6♂ 1998 ★ 1999 ∪M *Unmarked*

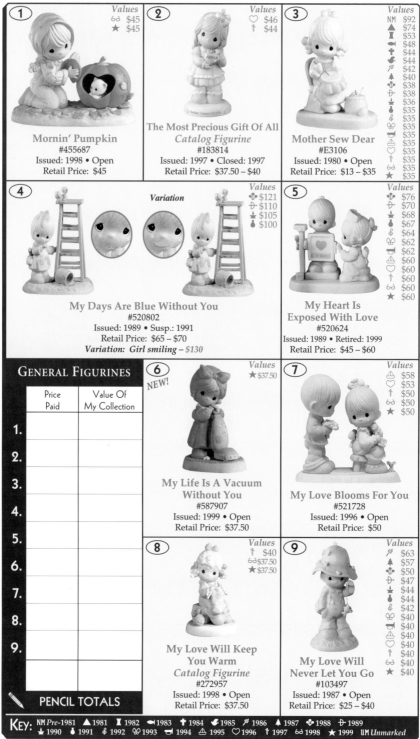

1

Values
6ð $45
★ $45

Mornin' Pumpkin
#455687
Issued: 1998 • Open
Retail Price: $45

2

Values
♡ $46
✝ $44

The Most Precious Gift Of All
Catalog Figurine
#183814
Issued: 1997 • Closed: 1997
Retail Price: $37.50 – $40

3

Values
NM $92
▲ $74
Ⅱ $53
◀ $48
✝ $44
❧ $44
♪ $42
♠ $40
⚓ $38
♠ $38
★ $36
$35
$35
$35
$35
↕ $35
✝ $35
6ð $35
★ $35

Mother Sew Dear
#E3106
Issued: 1980 • Open
Retail Price: $13 – $35

4

Variation

Values
♠ $121
♆ $110
★ $105
♦ $100

My Days Are Blue Without You
#520802
Issued: 1989 • Susp.: 1991
Retail Price: $65 – $70
Variation: Girl smiling – $130

5

Values
♠ $76
♆ $70
★ $68
♦ $67
♣ $64
♘ $62
♘ $62
⚕ $60
♡ $60
✝ $60
6ð $60
6ð $60
★ $60

**My Heart Is
Exposed With Love**
#520624
Issued: 1989 • Retired: 1999
Retail Price: $45 – $60

GENERAL FIGURINES

	Price Paid	Value Of My Collection
1.		
2.		
3.		
4.		
5.		
6.		
7.		
8.		
9.		

✏ **PENCIL TOTALS**

6

NEW!

Values
★ $37.50

**My Life Is A Vacuum
Without You**
#587907
Issued: 1999 • Open
Retail Price: $37.50

7

Values
△ $58
♡ $53
✝ $50
6ð $50
★ $50

My Love Blooms For You
#521728
Issued: 1996 • Open
Retail Price: $50

8

Values
✝ $40
6ð $37.50
★ $37.50

**My Love Will Keep
You Warm**
Catalog Figurine
#272957
Issued: 1998 • Open
Retail Price: $37.50

9

Values
♪ $63
▲ $57
♠ $50
♆ $47
★ $44
♦ $44
⚕ $42
♘ $40
◀ $40
△ $40
♡ $40
✝ $40
6ð $40
★ $40

**My Love Will
Never Let You Go**
#103497
Issued: 1987 • Open
Retail Price: $25 – $40

KEY: NM *Pre-1981* ▲ 1981 Ⅱ 1982 ◀ 1983 ✝ 1984 ❧ 1985 ♪ 1986 ♠ 1987 ♠ 1988 ♆ 1989
★ 1990 ♦ 1991 ♦ 1992 ♘ 1993 ◀ 1994 △ 1995 ♡ 1996 ✝ 1997 6ð 1998 ★ 1999 UM *Unmarked*

110

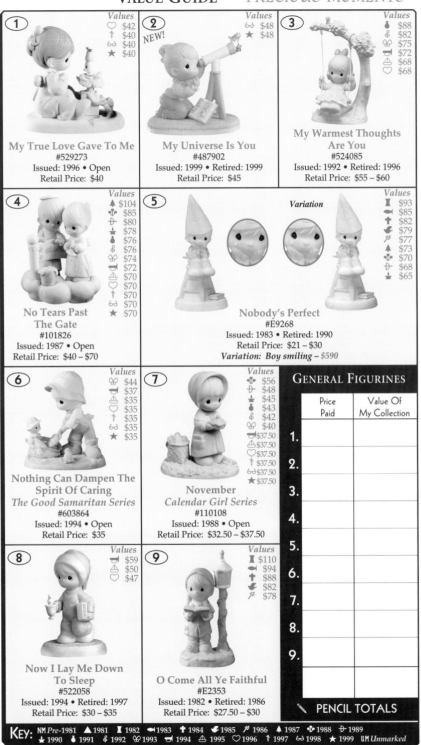

FIGURINES

1

My True Love Gave To Me
#529273
Issued: 1996 • Open
Retail Price: $40

Values	
♡	$42
†	$40
ᛋᚼ	$40
★	$40

2 NEW!

My Universe Is You
#487902
Issued: 1999 • Retired: 1999
Retail Price: $45

Values	
ᛋᚼ	$48
★	$48

3

My Warmest Thoughts Are You
#524085
Issued: 1992 • Retired: 1996
Retail Price: $55 – $60

Values	
♠	$88
♣	$82
♫	$75
ᗧ	$72
△	$68
♡	$68

4

No Tears Past The Gate
#101826
Issued: 1987 • Open
Retail Price: $40 – $70

Values	
▲	$104
♱	$85
Ⴆ	$80
★	$78
♦	$76
♣	$76
♘	$74
ᗧ	$72
△	$70
♡	$70
†	$70
ᛋᚼ	$70
★	$70

5

Variation

Nobody's Perfect
#E9268
Issued: 1983 • Retired: 1990
Retail Price: $21 – $30
Variation: Boy smiling – $590

Values	
Ⅱ	$93
♱	$85
†	$82
♱	$79
♫	$77
▲	$73
♱	$70
Ⴆ	$68
★	$65

6

Nothing Can Dampen The Spirit Of Caring
The Good Samaritan Series
#603864
Issued: 1994 • Open
Retail Price: $35

Values	
♘	$44
ᗧ	$37
△	$35
♡	$35
†	$35
ᛋᚼ	$35
★	$35

7

November
Calendar Girl Series
#110108
Issued: 1988 • Open
Retail Price: $32.50 – $37.50

Values	
♱	$56
Ⴆ	$48
★	$45
♦	$43
♣	$42
★	$40
ᗧ	$37.50
△	$37.50
♡	$37.50
†	$37.50
ᛋᚼ	$37.50
★	$37.50

8

Now I Lay Me Down To Sleep
#522058
Issued: 1994 • Retired: 1997
Retail Price: $30 – $35

Values	
ᗧ	$59
△	$50
♡	$47

9

O Come All Ye Faithful
#E2353
Issued: 1982 • Retired: 1986
Retail Price: $27.50 – $30

Values	
Ⅱ	$110
◀	$94
†	$88
♣	$82
♫	$78

GENERAL FIGURINES

	Price Paid	Value Of My Collection
1.		
2.		
3.		
4.		
5.		
6.		
7.		
8.		
9.		

＼ PENCIL TOTALS

KEY: NM *Pre-1981* ▲ 1981 Ⅱ 1982 ◀ 1983 † 1984 ♣ 1985 ♫ 1986 ▲ 1987 ♱ 1988 Ⴆ 1989 ★ 1990 ♦ 1991 ♣ 1992 ♘ 1993 ᗧ 1994 △ 1995 ♡ 1996 † 1997 ᛋᚼ 1998 ★ 1999 UM *Unmarked*

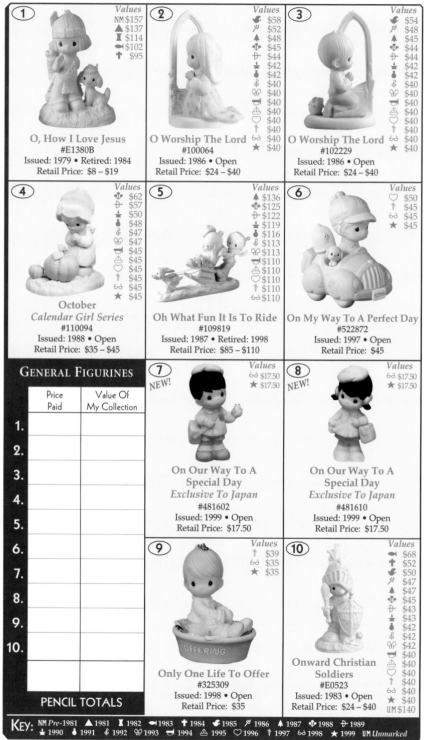

1

Values
NM $157
▲ $137
Ⅱ $114
◀ $102
✝ $95

O, How I Love Jesus
#E1380B
Issued: 1979 • Retired: 1984
Retail Price: $8 – $19

2

Values
🕊 $58
🎋 $52
▲ $48
⚓ $45
✝ $44
★ $42
🌂 $42
💧 $42
𝄞 $40
🐛 $40
🍶 $40
△ $40
♡ $40
✝ $40
👓 $40
★ $40

O Worship The Lord
#100064
Issued: 1986 • Open
Retail Price: $24 – $40

3

Values
🕊 $54
🎋 $48
▲ $45
⚓ $44
✝ $44
★ $42
🌂 $42
💧 $40
𝄞 $40
🐛 $40
🍶 $40
△ $40
♡ $40
✝ $40
👓 $40
★ $40

O Worship The Lord
#102229
Issued: 1986 • Open
Retail Price: $24 – $40

4

Values
⚓ $62
✝ $57
★ $50
💧 $48
𝄞 $47
🐛 $47
△ $45
♡ $45
✝ $45
👓 $45
★ $45

October
Calendar Girl Series
#110094
Issued: 1988 • Open
Retail Price: $35 – $45

5

Values
▲ $136
★ $125
✝ $122
★ $119
💧 $116
𝄞 $113
🐛 $113
△ $110
♡ $110
✝ $110
👓 $110

Oh What Fun It Is To Ride
#109819
Issued: 1987 • Retired: 1998
Retail Price: $85 – $110

6

Values
♡ $50
★ $45
👓 $45
★ $45

On My Way To A Perfect Day
#522872
Issued: 1997 • Open
Retail Price: $45

GENERAL FIGURINES

	Price Paid	Value Of My Collection
1.		
2.		
3.		
4.		
5.		
6.		
7.		
8.		
9.		
10.		
PENCIL TOTALS		

7
NEW!

Values
👓 $17.50
★ $17.50

On Our Way To A Special Day
Exclusive To Japan
#481602
Issued: 1999 • Open
Retail Price: $17.50

8
NEW!

Values
👓 $17.50
★ $17.50

On Our Way To A Special Day
Exclusive To Japan
#481610
Issued: 1999 • Open
Retail Price: $17.50

9

Values
✝ $39
👓 $35
★ $35

Only One Life To Offer
#325309
Issued: 1998 • Open
Retail Price: $35

10

Values
🐟 $68
✝ $52
🕊 $50
🎋 $47
▲ $47
⚓ $45
✝ $43
💧 $43
𝄞 $42
🐛 $42
△ $40
♡ $40
✝ $40
👓 $40
★ $40
UM $140

Onward Christian Soldiers
#E0523
Issued: 1983 • Open
Retail Price: $24 – $40

KEY: NM *Pre-1981* ▲ 1981 Ⅱ 1982 ◀ 1983 ✝ 1984 🕊 1985 🎋 1986 ▲ 1987 ⚓ 1988 ✝ 1989 ★ 1990 💧 1991 𝄞 1992 🐛 1993 △ 1994 △ 1995 ♡ 1996 ✝ 1997 👓 1998 ★ 1999 UM *Unmarked*

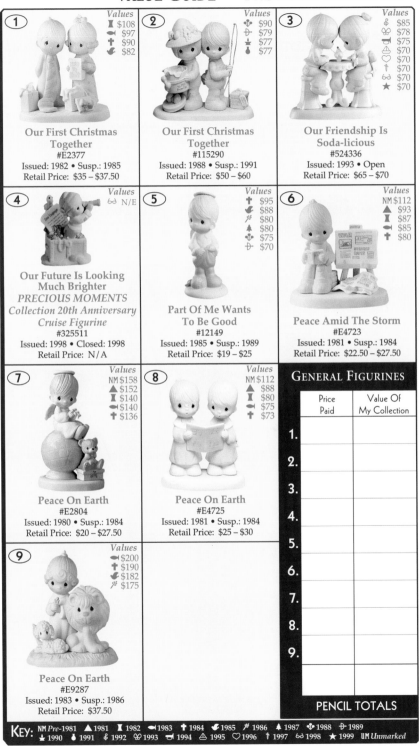

FIGURINES

① *Values*
🎁 $108
✝ $97
🕯 $90
🔔 $82

Our First Christmas Together
#E2377
Issued: 1982 • Susp.: 1985
Retail Price: $35 – $37.50

② *Values*
⚜ $90
🔔 $79
🕯 $77
🔔 $77

Our First Christmas Together
#115290
Issued: 1988 • Susp.: 1991
Retail Price: $50 – $60

③ *Values*
🔔 $85
🎀 $78
🔔 $75
⚠ $70
♡ $70
✝ $70
🔔 $70
★ $70

Our Friendship Is Soda-licious
#524336
Issued: 1993 • Open
Retail Price: $65 – $70

④ *Values*
🔔 N/E

Our Future Is Looking Much Brighter
PRECIOUS MOMENTS Collection 20th Anniversary Cruise Figurine
#325511
Issued: 1998 • Closed: 1998
Retail Price: N/A

⑤ *Values*
✝ $95
🔔 $88
🔔 $80
▲ $80
⚜ $75
🔔 $70

Part Of Me Wants To Be Good
#12149
Issued: 1985 • Susp.: 1989
Retail Price: $19 – $25

⑥ *Values*
NM $112
▲ $93
🎁 $87
🔔 $85
✝ $80

Peace Amid The Storm
#E4723
Issued: 1981 • Susp.: 1984
Retail Price: $22.50 – $27.50

⑦ *Values*
NM $158
▲ $152
🎁 $140
🔔 $140
✝ $136

Peace On Earth
#E2804
Issued: 1980 • Susp.: 1984
Retail Price: $20 – $27.50

⑧ *Values*
NM $112
▲ $88
🎁 $80
🔔 $75
✝ $73

Peace On Earth
#E4725
Issued: 1981 • Susp.: 1984
Retail Price: $25 – $30

⑨ *Values*
🔔 $200
✝ $190
🕯 $182
🔔 $175

Peace On Earth
#E9287
Issued: 1983 • Susp.: 1986
Retail Price: $37.50

GENERAL FIGURINES

	Price Paid	Value Of My Collection
1.		
2.		
3.		
4.		
5.		
6.		
7.		
8.		
9.		

PENCIL TOTALS

KEY: NM *Pre-1981* ▲ 1981 🎁 1982 🔔 1983 ✝ 1984 🔔 1985 🔔 1986 ▲ 1987 ⚜ 1988 🔔 1989 🔔 1990 🔔 1991 🔔 1992 🎀 1993 🔔 1994 ⚠ 1995 ♡ 1996 ✝ 1997 🔔 1998 ★ 1999 UM *Unmarked*

1 Values
† $72

The Pearl Of Great Price
(LE-1997)
Century Circle Figurine
#526061
Issued: 1997 • Closed: 1997
Retail Price: $50

2 Values
6ə $35
★ $35

Peas On Earth
#455768
Issued: 1998 • Open
Retail Price: $35

3 Values
Ⅱ $85
♦ $80
† $72
✿ $66
﹋ $60

The Perfect Grandpa
#E7160
Issued: 1982 • Susp.: 1986
Retail Price: $25 – $27.50

4 Values
⊲ $62
△ $58
♡ $55
† $55
₰ $55
6ə $55
★ $55

Perfect Harmony
#521914
Issued: 1994 • Retired: 1999
Retail Price: $55

5 Values
† $55
6ə $55
★ $55

Pizza On Earth
#521884
Issued: 1997 • Open
Retail Price: $55

6 Values
⊲ $43
△ $38
♡ $37
† $35
6ə $35

A Poppy For You
#604208
Issued: 1995 • Susp.: 1998
Retail Price: $35

GENERAL FIGURINES

	Price Paid	Value Of My Collection
1.		
2.		
3.		
4.		
5.		
6.		
7.		
8.		
9.		
PENCIL TOTALS		

7 Values
♡ $32
† $25
6ə $25
★ $25

Potty Time
#531022
Issued: 1997 • Open
Retail Price: $25

8 Values
6ə $40
★ $40

Praise God From Whom
All Blessings Flow
#455695
Issued: 1998 • Open
Retail Price: $40

9 Values
6ə $50
★ $50

Praise The Lord And
Dosie-Do
#455733
Issued: 1998 • Open
Retail Price: $50

KEY: NM *Pre-1981* ▲ 1981 Ⅱ 1982 ◄ 1983 † 1984 ✿ 1985 ﹋ 1986 ♦ 1987 ✿ 1988 ⅁ 1989 ★ 1990 ● 1991 ₰ 1992 ♀ 1993 ⊲ 1994 △ 1995 ♡ 1996 † 1997 6ə 1998 ★ 1999 **UM** *Unmarked*

114

VALUE GUIDE — *PRECIOUS MOMENTS*®

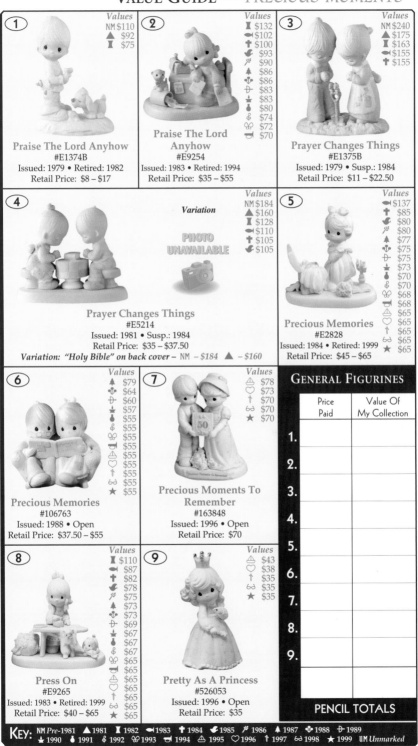

1 Values
NM $110
▲ $92
✖ $75

Praise The Lord Anyhow
#E1374B
Issued: 1979 • Retired: 1982
Retail Price: $8 – $17

2 Values
✖ $132
▲ $102
✝ $100
✔ $93
♫ $90
$86
✤ $86
꠸ $83
✦ $83
♦ $80
§ $74
֍ $72
⇨ $70

Praise The Lord Anyhow
#E9254
Issued: 1983 • Retired: 1994
Retail Price: $35 – $55

3 Values
NM $240
▲ $175
✖ $163
⇦ $155
✝ $155

Prayer Changes Things
#E1375B
Issued: 1979 • Susp.: 1984
Retail Price: $11 – $22.50

4 *Variation* Values
NM $184
▲ $160
✖ $128
⇦ $110
✝ $105
✔ $105

PHOTO UNAVAILABLE

Prayer Changes Things
#E5214
Issued: 1981 • Susp.: 1984
Retail Price: $35 – $37.50
Variation: "Holy Bible" on back cover – NM – $184 ▲ – $160

5 Values
⇦ $137
✔ $85
✦ $80
♫ $80
▲ $77
✤ $75
꠸ $73
♦ $70
§ $70
⇨ $68
⛟ $68
♡ $65
✝ $65
ᦒ $65
★ $65

Precious Memories
#E2828
Issued: 1984 • Retired: 1999
Retail Price: $45 – $65

6 Values
▲ $79
✤ $64
꠸ $60
♦ $57
♦ $55
§ $55
֍ $55
⇨ $55
♡ $55
✝ $55
ᦒ $55
★ $55

Precious Memories
#106763
Issued: 1988 • Open
Retail Price: $37.50 – $55

7 Values
⛟ $78
♡ $73
✝ $70
ᦒ $70
★ $70

Precious Moments To Remember
#163848
Issued: 1996 • Open
Retail Price: $70

8 Values
✖ $110
⇦ $87
✝ $82
✔ $78
♫ $75
▲ $73
✤ $73
꠸ $69
♦ $67
♦ $67
§ $67
֍ $65
⇨ $65
⛟ $65
♡ $65
✝ $65
ᦒ $65
★ $65

Press On
#E9265
Issued: 1983 • Retired: 1999
Retail Price: $40 – $65

9 Values
⛟ $43
♡ $38
✝ $35
ᦒ $35
★ $35

Pretty As A Princess
#526053
Issued: 1996 • Open
Retail Price: $35

GENERAL FIGURINES

	Price Paid	Value Of My Collection
1.		
2.		
3.		
4.		
5.		
6.		
7.		
8.		
9.		
PENCIL TOTALS		

FIGURINES (side tab)

KEY: NM *Pre-1981* ▲ 1981 ✖ 1982 ⇦ 1983 ✝ 1984 ✔ 1985 ♫ 1986 ▲ 1987 ✤ 1988 ꠸ 1989 ♦ 1990 ♦ 1991 § 1992 ֍ 1993 ⇨ 1994 ⛟ 1995 ♡ 1996 ✝ 1997 ᦒ 1998 ★ 1999 UM *Unmarked*

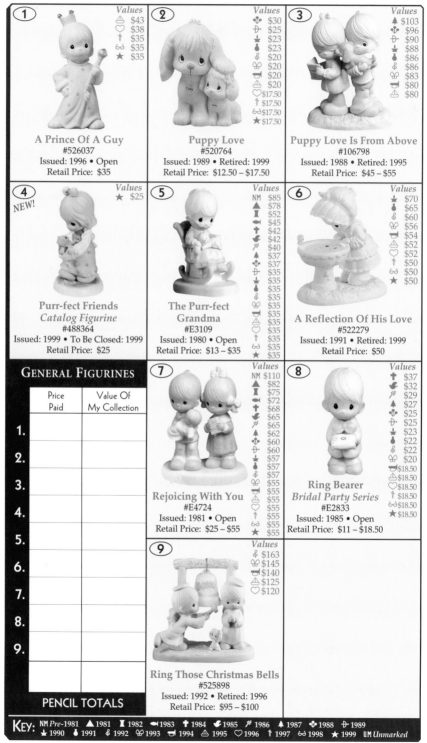

1 A Prince Of A Guy
#526037
Issued: 1996 • Open
Retail Price: $35

Values
♤ $43
♡ $38
† $35
👓 $35
★ $35

2 Puppy Love
#520764
Issued: 1989 • Retired: 1999
Retail Price: $12.50 – $17.50

Values
♧ $30
Ð $25
★ $23
🔔 $23
♪ $20
🐚 $20
🍜 $20
△ $20
♡ $17.50
† $17.50
👓 $17.50
★ $17.50

3 Puppy Love Is From Above
#106798
Issued: 1988 • Retired: 1995
Retail Price: $45 – $55

Values
▲ $103
♪ $96
Ð $90
★ $88
🔔 $86
♪ $86
🐚 $83
△ $80
△ $80

4 NEW! Purr-fect Friends
Catalog Figurine
#488364
Issued: 1999 • To Be Closed: 1999
Retail Price: $25

Values
★ $25

5 The Purr-fect Grandma
#E3109
Issued: 1980 • Open
Retail Price: $13 – $35

Values
NM $85
▲ $78
I $52
★ $45
† $42
🍃 $42
🌿 $40
▲ $37
🔔 $37
Ð $35
🔔 $35
🔔 $35
🐚 $35
🍜 $35
♡ $35
† $35
👓 $35
★ $35

6 A Reflection Of His Love
#522279
Issued: 1991 • Retired: 1999
Retail Price: $50

Values
★ $70
🔔 $65
♪ $60
🐚 $56
🍜 $54
△ $52
△ $52
† $50
👓 $50
★ $50

GENERAL FIGURINES

	Price Paid	Value Of My Collection
1.		
2.		
3.		
4.		
5.		
6.		
7.		
8.		
9.		
PENCIL TOTALS		

7 Rejoicing With You
#E4724
Issued: 1981 • Open
Retail Price: $25 – $55

Values
NM $110
▲ $82
I $75
★ $72
† $68
🔔 $65
🔔 $65
▲ $62
♧ $60
Ð $60
★ $57
🔔 $57
🔔 $57
🐚 $55
🍜 $55
△ $55
† $55
👓 $55
★ $55

8 Ring Bearer
Bridal Party Series
#E2833
Issued: 1985 • Open
Retail Price: $11 – $18.50

Values
† $37
🍃 $32
🌿 $29
▲ $27
⚓ $25
Ð $25
★ $23
🔔 $22
♪ $22
🐚 $20
🍜 $18.50
△ $18.50
♡ $18.50
† $18.50
👓 $18.50
★ $18.50

9 Ring Those Christmas Bells
#525898
Issued: 1992 • Retired: 1996
Retail Price: $95 – $100

Values
♪ $163
🐚 $145
🍜 $140
△ $125
♡ $120

KEY: NM *Pre-1981* ▲ 1981 I 1982 ◄ 1983 † 1984 🍃 1985 🌿 1986 ▲ 1987 ♧ 1988 Ð 1989 ★ 1990 🔔 1991 ♪ 1992 🐚 1993 🍜 1994 △ 1995 ♡ 1996 † 1997 👓 1998 ★ 1999 UM *Unmarked*

VALUE GUIDE — *PRECIOUS MOMENTS*®

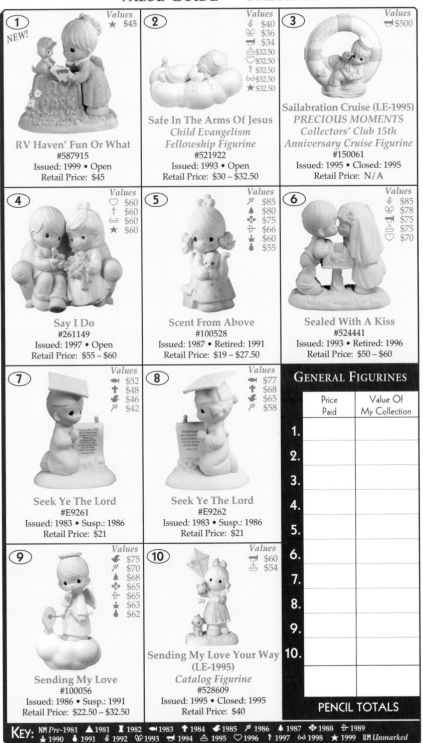

1 NEW!

Values
★ $45

RV Haven' Fun Or What
#587915
Issued: 1999 • Open
Retail Price: $45

2

Values
𝄢 $40
♀ $36
☷ $34
△ $32.50
♡ $32.50
† $32.50
👓 $32.50
★ $32.50

Safe In The Arms Of Jesus
Child Evangelism
Fellowship Figurine
#521922
Issued: 1993 • Open
Retail Price: $30 – $32.50

3

Values
☲ $500

Sailabration Cruise (LE-1995)
PRECIOUS MOMENTS
Collectors' Club 15th
Anniversary Cruise Figurine
#150061
Issued: 1995 • Closed: 1995
Retail Price: N/A

4

Values
♡ $60
† $60
👓 $60
★ $60

Say I Do
#261149
Issued: 1997 • Open
Retail Price: $55 – $60

5

Values
ℐ $85
▲ $80
⚜ $75
Ð $66
☼ $60
⬤ $55

Scent From Above
#100528
Issued: 1987 • Retired: 1991
Retail Price: $19 – $27.50

6

Values
𝄢 $85
♀ $78
☲ $75
⚜ $75
♡ $70

Sealed With A Kiss
#524441
Issued: 1993 • Retired: 1996
Retail Price: $50 – $60

7

Values
☲ $52
† $48
✦ $46
ℐ $42

Seek Ye The Lord
#E9261
Issued: 1983 • Susp.: 1986
Retail Price: $21

8

Values
☲ $77
† $68
✦ $65
ℐ $58

Seek Ye The Lord
#E9262
Issued: 1983 • Susp.: 1986
Retail Price: $21

GENERAL FIGURINES

	Price Paid	Value Of My Collection
1.		
2.		
3.		
4.		
5.		
6.		
7.		
8.		
9.		
10.		
PENCIL TOTALS		

9

Values
✦ $75
ℐ $70
▲ $68
⚜ $65
Ð $65
☼ $63
⬤ $62

Sending My Love
#100056
Issued: 1986 • Susp.: 1991
Retail Price: $22.50 – $32.50

10

Values
☲ $60
△ $54

Sending My Love Your Way
(LE-1995)
Catalog Figurine
#528609
Issued: 1995 • Closed: 1995
Retail Price: $40

FIGURINES

KEY: NM *Pre-1981* ▲ 1981 ✗ 1982 ◄1983 † 1984 ✔1985 ℐ 1986 ▲ 1987 ⚜1988 Ð 1989 ★ 1990 ⬤ 1991 𝄢 1992 ♀1993 ☲ 1994 △ 1995 ♡1996 † 1997 👓 1998 ★ 1999 UM *Unmarked*

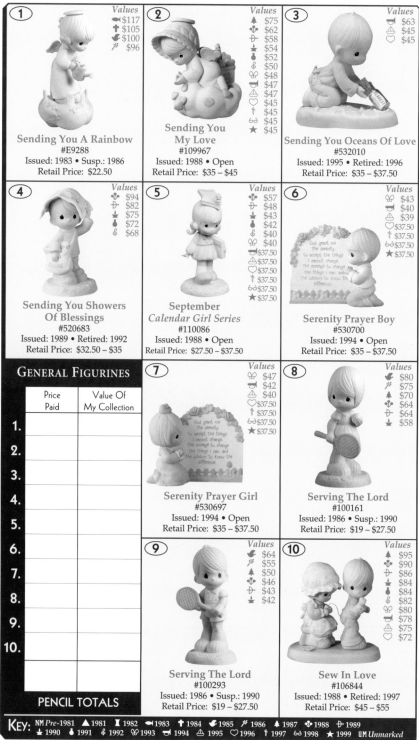

1

Values	
◀	$117
†	$105
✔	$100
ℐ	$96

Sending You A Rainbow
#E9288
Issued: 1983 • Susp.: 1986
Retail Price: $22.50

2

Values	
♠	$75
✿	$62
⌀	$58
⚱	$54
⚘	$52
⚶	$50
◯◯	$48
⌐	$47
△	$47
♡	$45
†	$45
∞	$45
★	$45

Sending You My Love
#109967
Issued: 1988 • Open
Retail Price: $35 – $45

3

Values	
⊒	$63
△	$45
♡	$45

Sending You Oceans Of Love
#532010
Issued: 1995 • Retired: 1996
Retail Price: $35 – $37.50

4

Values	
✿	$94
⌀	$82
⚱	$75
⚶	$72
⚘	$68

Sending You Showers Of Blessings
#520683
Issued: 1989 • Retired: 1992
Retail Price: $32.50 – $35

5

Values	
✿	$57
⌀	$48
⚱	$43
⚶	$42
⚘	$40
◯◯	$40
⌐	$37.50
△	$37.50
♡	$37.50
†	$37.50
∞	$37.50
★	$37.50

September
Calendar Girl Series
#110086
Issued: 1988 • Open
Retail Price: $27.50 – $37.50

6

Values	
◯◯	$43
⌐	$40
△	$39
♡	$37.50
†	$37.50
∞	$37.50
★	$37.50

Serenity Prayer Boy
#530700
Issued: 1994 • Open
Retail Price: $35 – $37.50

GENERAL FIGURINES

	Price Paid	Value Of My Collection
1.		
2.		
3.		
4.		
5.		
6.		
7.		
8.		
9.		
10.		
PENCIL TOTALS		

7

Values	
◯◯	$47
⌐	$42
⚶	$40
♡	$37.50
†	$37.50
∞	$37.50
★	$37.50

Serenity Prayer Girl
#530697
Issued: 1994 • Open
Retail Price: $35 – $37.50

8

Values	
✔	$80
ℐ	$75
♠	$70
✿	$64
⌀	$64
⚱	$58

Serving The Lord
#100161
Issued: 1986 • Susp.: 1990
Retail Price: $19 – $27.50

9

Values	
✔	$64
ℐ	$55
♠	$50
✿	$46
⌀	$43
⚱	$42

Serving The Lord
#100293
Issued: 1986 • Susp.: 1990
Retail Price: $19 – $27.50

10

Values	
♠	$95
✿	$90
⌀	$86
⚱	$84
⚶	$84
⚘	$82
◯◯	$80
ℐ	$78
△	$75
♡	$72

Sew In Love
#106844
Issued: 1988 • Retired: 1997
Retail Price: $45 – $55

KEY: NM *Pre-1981* ▲1981 ⊠1982 ◀1983 †1984 ✔1985 ℐ1986 ♠1987 ✿1988 ⌀1989
⚱1990 ⚶1991 ⚘1992 ◯◯1993 ⌐1994 △1995 ♡1996 †1997 ∞1998 ★1999 UM *Unmarked*

1 Values
✤ $82
Ð $50

Sharing Begins In The Heart (LE-1989)
Special Event Figurine
#520861
Issued: 1989 • Closed: 1989
Retail Price: $25

2 Values
⅊ $95
▲ $88
✤ $82

Sharing Our Christmas Together
#102490
Issued: 1986 • Susp.: 1988
Retail Price: $37 – $45

3 Values
† $35
6∂ $35
★ $35

Sharing Our Christmas Together
#531944
Issued: 1997 • Open
Retail Price: $35

4 Values
⅊ $70
▲ $65
✤ $63
Ð $57
⊥ $55
⊥ $52

Sharing Our Joy Together
#E2834
Issued: 1986 • Susp.: 1991
Retail Price: $31 – $40

5 Values
◀ $165
† $150
✔ $142
⅊ $137

Sharing Our Season Together
#E0501
Issued: 1983 • Susp.: 1986
Retail Price: $50

6 NEW! Values
★ $110

Sharing Our Time Is So Precious (LE-15,000)
Century Circle Figurine
#456349
Issued: 1999 • To Be Closed: 1999
Retail Price: $110

7 NEW! Values
★ $75

Sharing Our Winter Wonderland (LE-1999)
#539988
Issued: 1999 • To Be Closed: 1999
Retail Price: $75

8 Values
♈ $58
⊟ $50
△ $48
⊥ $45
† $45
6∂ $45
★ $45

Sharing Sweet Moments Together
#526487
Issued: 1994 • Open
Retail Price: $45

9 Values
△ $80
♡ $74
† $70
6∂ $70
★ $70

Sharing The Gift Of 40 Precious Years
#163821
Issued: 1996 • Open
Retail Price: $70

10 Values
† $35
6∂ $35
★ $35

Sharing The Light Of Love
#272531
Issued: 1997 • Open
Retail Price: $35

GENERAL FIGURINES

	Price Paid	Value Of My Collection
1.		
2.		
3.		
4.		
5.		
6.		
7.		
8.		
9.		
10.		
PENCIL TOTALS		

FIGURINES

KEY: NM *Pre-1981* ▲ 1981 ✗ 1982 ◀ 1983 † 1984 ✔ 1985 ⅊ 1986 ▲ 1987 ✤ 1988 Ð 1989 ⊥ 1990 ⵊ 1991 ⸋ 1992 ♈ 1993 ⊟ 1994 △ 1995 ♡ 1996 † 1997 6∂ 1998 ★ 1999 UM *Unmarked*

119

1 NEW!

Values	
6ᗆ	$20
★	$20

Shiny New And Ready For School
Exclusive To Japan
#481637
Issued: 1999 • Open
Retail Price: $20

2 NEW!

Values	
6ᗆ	$20
★	$20

Shiny New And Ready For School
Exclusive To Japan
#481629
Issued: 1999 • Open
Retail Price: $20

3

Values	
♡	$67
†	$60
6ᗆ	$60
★	$60

Shoot For The Stars You'll Never Strike Out
Boys & Girls Clubs Of America Commemorative Figurine
#521701
Issued: 1996 • Closed: 1996
Retail Price: $60

4

Values	
△	$78
♡	$74
†	$70
6ᗆ	$70
★	$70

A Silver Celebration To Share
#163813
Issued: 1996 • Open
Retail Price: $70

5

Values	
▲	$66
✛	$60
⋺	$58
▲	$55
▮	$50

Sitting Pretty
#104825
Issued: 1987 • Susp.: 1990
Retail Price: $22.50 – $30

6

Values	
ⅉ	$200
▲	$188
✛	$165
⋺	$152
▲	$140
▮	$135

Smile Along The Way
#101842
Issued: 1987 • Retired: 1991
Retail Price: $30 – $45

GENERAL FIGURINES

	Price Paid	Value Of My Collection
1.		
2.		
3.		
4.		
5.		
6.		
7.		
8.		
9.		
PENCIL TOTALS		

7

Values	
NM	$116
▲	$90
▮	$77
⋺	$74
†	$59

Smile, God Loves You
#E1373B
Issued: 1979 • Retired: 1984
Retail Price: $7 – $17

8 NEW!

Values	
★	$55

Snow Man Like My Man
#587877
Issued: 1999 • Open
Retail Price: $55

9

Values	
♡	$22
†	$18.50
6ᗆ	$18.50
★	$18.50

Snowbunny Loves You Like I Do
#183792
Issued: 1996 • Open
Retail Price: $18.50

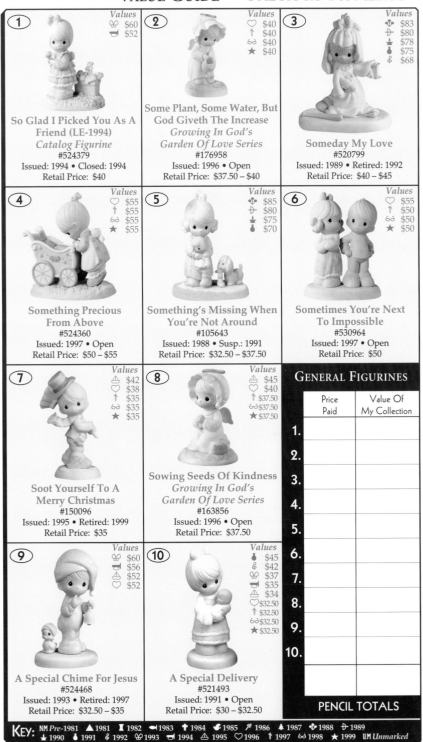

1 So Glad I Picked You As A Friend (LE-1994)
Catalog Figurine
#524379
Issued: 1994 • Closed: 1994
Retail Price: $40

Values
🐝 $60
🥨 $52

2 Some Plant, Some Water, But God Giveth The Increase
Growing In God's Garden Of Love Series
#176958
Issued: 1996 • Open
Retail Price: $37.50 – $40

Values
♡ $40
† $40
👓 $40
★ $40

3 Someday My Love
#520799
Issued: 1989 • Retired: 1992
Retail Price: $40 – $45

Values
❖ $83
Ð $80
🌱 $78
🍶 $75
& $68

4 Something Precious From Above
#524360
Issued: 1997 • Open
Retail Price: $50 – $55

Values
♡ $55
† $55
👓 $55
★ $55

5 Something's Missing When You're Not Around
#105643
Issued: 1988 • Susp.: 1991
Retail Price: $32.50 – $37.50

Values
❖ $85
Ð $80
🌱 $75
🍶 $70

6 Sometimes You're Next To Impossible
#530964
Issued: 1997 • Open
Retail Price: $50

Values
♡ $55
† $50
👓 $50
★ $50

7 Soot Yourself To A Merry Christmas
#150096
Issued: 1995 • Retired: 1999
Retail Price: $35

Values
⚘ $42
♡ $38
† $35
👓 $35
★ $35

8 Sowing Seeds Of Kindness
Growing In God's Garden Of Love Series
#163856
Issued: 1996 • Open
Retail Price: $37.50

Values
⚘ $45
♡ $40
† $37.50
👓 $37.50
★ $37.50

9 A Special Chime For Jesus
#524468
Issued: 1993 • Retired: 1997
Retail Price: $32.50 – $35

Values
🐝 $60
🥨 $56
⚘ $52
♡ $52

10 A Special Delivery
#521493
Issued: 1991 • Open
Retail Price: $30 – $32.50

Values
🍶 $45
& $42
🐝 $37
🥨 $35
⚘ $34
♡ $32.50
† $32.50
👓 $32.50
★ $32.50

GENERAL FIGURINES

	Price Paid	Value Of My Collection
1.		
2.		
3.		
4.		
5.		
6.		
7.		
8.		
9.		
10.		
PENCIL TOTALS		

KEY: NM *Pre-1981* ▲ 1981 Ⅱ 1982 ◄1983 † 1984 ✔ 1985 ⅋ 1986 ♠ 1987 ❖ 1988 Ð 1989 ★ 1990 🍶 1991 & 1992 🐝 1993 🥨 1994 ⚘ 1995 ♡ 1996 † 1997 👓 1998 ★ 1999 UM *Unmarked*

FIGURINES

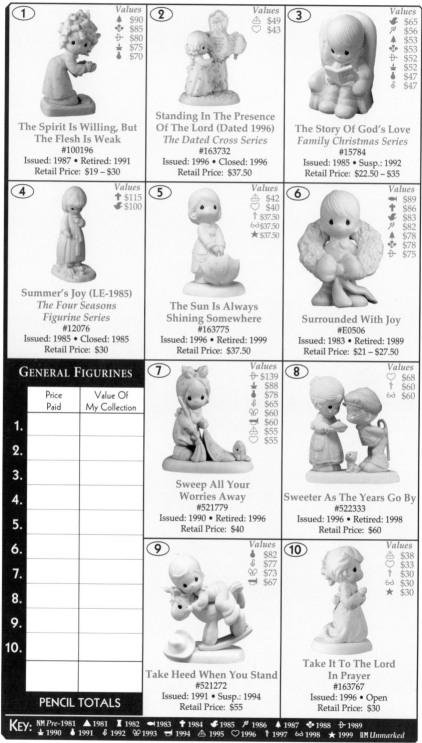

1

Values	
▲	$90
✤	$85
Ð	$80
★	$75
●	$70

**The Spirit Is Willing, But
The Flesh Is Weak**
#100196
Issued: 1987 • Retired: 1991
Retail Price: $19 – $30

2

Values	
△	$49
♡	$43

**Standing In The Presence
Of The Lord (Dated 1996)**
The Dated Cross Series
#163732
Issued: 1996 • Closed: 1996
Retail Price: $37.50

3

Values	
✔	$65
ﭼ	$56
▲	$53
✤	$53
Ð	$52
★	$52
●	$47
ɞ	$47

The Story Of God's Love
Family Christmas Series
#15784
Issued: 1985 • Susp.: 1992
Retail Price: $22.50 – $35

4

Values	
†	$115
✔	$100

Summer's Joy (LE-1985)
*The Four Seasons
Figurine Series*
#12076
Issued: 1985 • Closed: 1985
Retail Price: $30

5

Values	
△	$42
♡	$40
†	$37.50
ɞ	$37.50
★	$37.50

**The Sun Is Always
Shining Somewhere**
#163775
Issued: 1996 • Retired: 1999
Retail Price: $37.50

6

Values	
◄	$89
ﭦ	$86
ﭼ	$83
ﭻ	$82
▲	$78
✤	$78
Ð	$75

Surrounded With Joy
#E0506
Issued: 1983 • Retired: 1989
Retail Price: $21 – $27.50

GENERAL FIGURINES

	Price Paid	Value Of My Collection
1.		
2.		
3.		
4.		
5.		
6.		
7.		
8.		
9.		
10.		

PENCIL TOTALS

7

Values	
Ð	$139
★	$88
●	$78
ɞ	$65
❀	$60
⊟	$60
△	$55
♡	$55

**Sweep All Your
Worries Away**
#521779
Issued: 1990 • Retired: 1996
Retail Price: $40

8

Values	
♡	$68
†	$60
ɞ	$60

Sweeter As The Years Go By
#522333
Issued: 1996 • Retired: 1998
Retail Price: $60

9

Values	
●	$82
ɞ	$77
❀	$73
⊟	$67

Take Heed When You Stand
#521272
Issued: 1991 • Susp.: 1994
Retail Price: $55

10

Values	
△	$38
♡	$33
†	$30
ɞ	$30
★	$30

**Take It To The Lord
In Prayer**
#163767
Issued: 1996 • Open
Retail Price: $30

KEY: NM *Pre-1981* ▲ 1981 I 1982 ◄ 1983 † 1984 ✔ 1985 ﭼ 1986 ▲ 1987 ✤ 1988 Ð 1989 ★ 1990 ● 1991 ɞ 1992 ❀ 1993 ⊟ 1994 △ 1995 ♡ 1996 † 1997 ɞ 1998 ★ 1999 UM *Unmarked*

1 NEW!

Values
★ $35

Take Time To Smell The Roses (LE-1999)
Carlton Cards Exclusive
#634980C
Issued: 1999 • To Be Closed: 1999
Retail Price: $35

2

Values
🐟 $83
✝ $77
🕊 $73
♫ $70

Taste And See That The Lord Is Good
#E9274
Issued: 1983 • Retired: 1986
Retail Price: $22.50

3

Values
ঢ় $63
☆ $50
⚫ $47
⚓ $43
🔵 $42
🎋 $40
△ $40
♡ $40
✝ $40
👓 $40
★ $40

Tell It To Jesus
#521477
Issued: 1989 • Open
Retail Price: $35 – $40

4

Values
🍃 $42
♫ $35
🌲 $35
🌿 $32
ঢ় $30
⚫ $30
⚫ $27
⚓ $25

Tell Me A Story
Family Christmas Series
#15792
Issued: 1985 • Susp.: 1992
Retail Price: $10 – $15

5

Values
I $134
🦆 $117
✝ $110
🍃 $105

Tell Me The Story Of Jesus
#E2349
Issued: 1983 • Susp.: 1985
Retail Price: $30 – $33

6

Values
△ $79
♡ $73
✝ $70
👓 $70
★ $70

Ten Years Heart To Heart
#163805
Issued: 1996 • Open
Retail Price: $70

7

Values
NM $170
▲ $145
I $130
🦆 $122
✝ $118

Thank You For Coming To My Ade
#E5202
Issued: 1981 • Susp.: 1984
Retail Price: $22.50 – $30

8

Values
ঢ় $100
☆ $90
⚫ $87
⚓ $84
🎋 $84

Thank You, Lord, For Everything
#522031
Issued: 1989 • Susp.: 1993
Retail Price: $60

9 NEW!

Values
★ $25

Thank You Sew Much
#587923
Issued: 1999 • Open
Retail Price: $25

10

Values
I $65
🦆 $52
✝ $48

Thanking Him For You
#E7155
Issued: 1982 • Susp.: 1984
Retail Price: $16 – $17

FIGURINES

General Figurines

	Price Paid	Value Of My Collection
1.		
2.		
3.		
4.		
5.		
6.		
7.		
8.		
9.		
10.		

PENCIL TOTALS

KEY: NM *Pre-1981* ▲ 1981 I 1982 🦆 1983 ✝ 1984 🍃 1985 ♫ 1986 ▲ 1987 🌿 1988 ঢ় 1989 ☆ 1990 ⚫ 1991 ⚓ 1992 🎋 1993 ⚫ 1994 △ 1995 ♡ 1996 ✝ 1997 👓 1998 ★ 1999 UM *Unmarked*

123

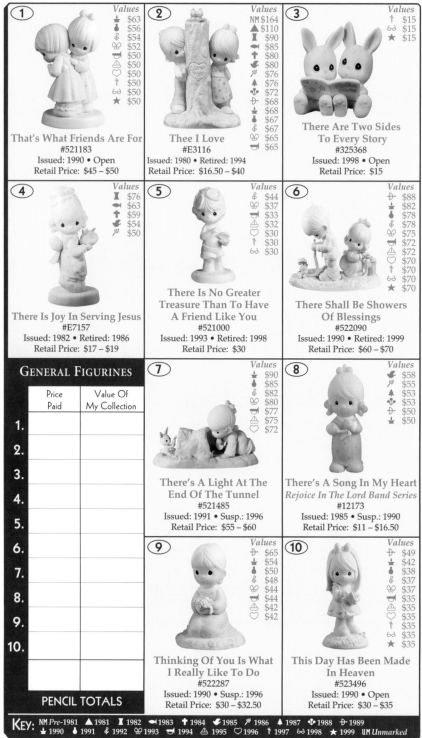

1

Values	
☆	$63
♦	$56
♒	$54
✿	$52
⊟	$50
△	$50
♡	$50
✝	$50
ᵔᴥᵔ	$50
★	$50

That's What Friends Are For
#521183
Issued: 1990 • Open
Retail Price: $45 – $50

2

Values	
NM	$164
▲	$110
Ⅰ	$90
	$85
✝	$80
	$80
ᵞ	$76
▲	$76
✿	$72
ꝺ	$68
	$68
	$67
♒	$67
✿	$65
⊟	$65

Thee I Love
#E3116
Issued: 1980 • Retired: 1994
Retail Price: $16.50 – $40

3

Values	
✝	$15
ᵔᴥᵔ	$15
★	$15

**There Are Two Sides
To Every Story**
#325368
Issued: 1998 • Open
Retail Price: $15

4

Values	
Ⅰ	$76
✿	$63
✝	$59
♒	$54
ᵞ	$50

There Is Joy In Serving Jesus
#E7157
Issued: 1982 • Retired: 1986
Retail Price: $17 – $19

5

Values	
♒	$44
✿	$37
ᵞ	$33
△	$32
☆	$30
✝	$30
ᵔᴥᵔ	$30

**There Is No Greater
Treasure Than To Have
A Friend Like You**
#521000
Issued: 1993 • Retired: 1998
Retail Price: $30

6

Values	
ꝺ	$88
★	$82
♦	$78
✿	$78
✿	$75
⊟	$72
△	$72
♡	$70
✝	$70
ᵔᴥᵔ	$70
★	$70

**There Shall Be Showers
Of Blessings**
#522090
Issued: 1990 • Retired: 1999
Retail Price: $60 – $70

GENERAL FIGURINES

	Price Paid	Value Of My Collection
1.		
2.		
3.		
4.		
5.		
6.		
7.		
8.		
9.		
10.		

PENCIL TOTALS

7

Values	
★	$90
♦	$85
♒	$82
✿	$80
⊟	$77
△	$75
♡	$72

**There's A Light At The
End Of The Tunnel**
#521485
Issued: 1991 • Susp.: 1996
Retail Price: $55 – $60

8

Values	
♒	$58
ᵞ	$55
▲	$53
✿	$53
ꝺ	$50
★	$50

There's A Song In My Heart
Rejoice In The Lord Band Series
#12173
Issued: 1985 • Susp.: 1990
Retail Price: $11 – $16.50

9

Values	
ꝺ	$65
★	$54
♦	$50
♒	$48
✿	$44
⊟	$44
△	$42
♡	$42

**Thinking Of You Is What
I Really Like To Do**
#522287
Issued: 1990 • Susp.: 1996
Retail Price: $30 – $32.50

10

Values	
ꝺ	$49
★	$42
♦	$38
♒	$37
✿	$37
△	$35
♡	$35
✝	$35
ᵔᴥᵔ	$35
★	$35

**This Day Has Been Made
In Heaven**
#523496
Issued: 1990 • Open
Retail Price: $30 – $35

KEY: NM *Pre*-1981 ▲1981 Ⅰ1982 ◂1983 ✝1984 ♒1985 ᵞ1986 ▲1987 ✿1988 ꝺ1989 ★1990 ♦1991 ♒1992 ✿1993 ⊟1994 △1995 ♡1996 ✝1997 ᵔᴥᵔ1998 ★1999 UM *Unmarked*

124

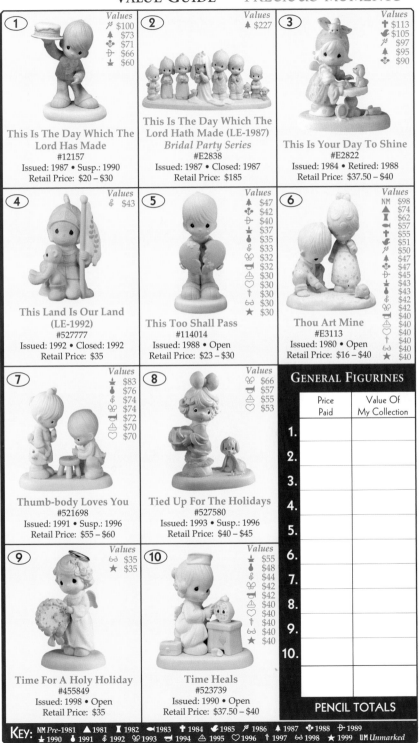

① Values
- ⚜ $100
- ▲ $73
- ✠ $71
- Ð $66
- ★ $60

This Is The Day Which The Lord Has Made
#12157
Issued: 1987 • Susp.: 1990
Retail Price: $20 – $30

② Values
- ▲ $227

This Is The Day Which The Lord Hath Made (LE-1987)
Bridal Party Series
#E2838
Issued: 1987 • Closed: 1987
Retail Price: $185

③ Values
- ✝ $113
- ✦ $105
- ⚜ $97
- ▲ $95
- ✠ $90

This Is Your Day To Shine
#E2822
Issued: 1984 • Retired: 1988
Retail Price: $37.50 – $40

④ Values
- ϟ $43

This Land Is Our Land
(LE-1992)
#527777
Issued: 1992 • Closed: 1992
Retail Price: $35

⑤ Values
- ▲ $47
- ✠ $42
- Ð $40
- ✝ $37
- ★ $35
- ϟ $33
- ⚜ $32
- 🌸 $32
- △ $30
- 🍃 $30
- ✝ $30
- 68 $30
- ★ $30

This Too Shall Pass
#114014
Issued: 1988 • Open
Retail Price: $23 – $30

⑥ Values
- NM $98
- ▲ $74
- I $62
- ✦ $57
- ✝ $55
- ✦ $51
- ⚜ $50
- ▲ $47
- ✠ $47
- Ð $45
- ✝ $43
- 🍃 $43
- ⚜ $42
- 🌸 $42
- △ $40
- ✝ $40
- 68 $40
- ★ $40

Thou Art Mine
#E3113
Issued: 1980 • Open
Retail Price: $16 – $40

⑦ Values
- ★ $83
- 🍶 $76
- ϟ $74
- 🌸 $74
- ✪ $72
- △ $70
- ♡ $70

Thumb-body Loves You
#521698
Issued: 1991 • Susp.: 1996
Retail Price: $55 – $60

⑧ Values
- 🐚 $66
- ✪ $57
- 🐚 $55
- ♡ $53

Tied Up For The Holidays
#527580
Issued: 1993 • Susp.: 1996
Retail Price: $40 – $45

⑨ Values
- 68 $35
- ★ $35

Time For A Holy Holiday
#455849
Issued: 1998 • Open
Retail Price: $35

⑩ Values
- ★ $55
- 🍶 $48
- ϟ $44
- 🐚 $42
- ✪ $42
- △ $40
- ♡ $40
- ✝ $40
- 🌸 $40
- 68 $40
- ★ $40

Time Heals
#523739
Issued: 1990 • Open
Retail Price: $37.50 – $40

GENERAL FIGURINES

	Price Paid	Value Of My Collection
1.		
2.		
3.		
4.		
5.		
6.		
7.		
8.		
9.		
10.		
	PENCIL TOTALS	

FIGURINES

KEY: NM *Pre-1981* ▲1981 I 1982 ◀1983 ✝ 1984 ✦ 1985 ⚜ 1986 ▲ 1987 ✠1988 Ð 1989 ★ 1990 🍶 1991 ϟ 1992 🐚1993 ✪ 1994 △ 1995 ♡1996 ✝ 1997 68 1998 ★ 1999 UM *Unmarked*

125

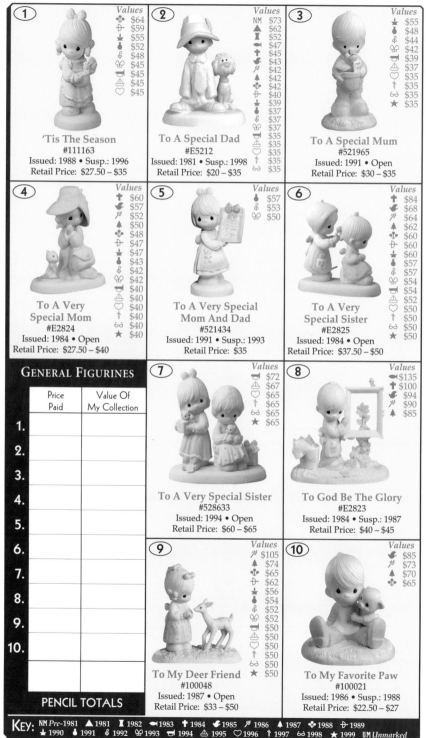

(1)

Values	
🐦	$64
⌁	$59
✦	$55
⚬	$52
✿	$48
✾	$45
⛉	$45
⚗	$45
♡	$45

'Tis The Season
#111163
Issued: 1988 • Susp.: 1996
Retail Price: $27.50 – $35

(2)

Values	
NM	$73
⚬	$62
I	$52
✦	$47
✝	$45
✾	$43
✿	$42
⚓	$42
⛉	$42
⌁	$40
✦	$39
◈	$37
⚬	$37
✾	$37
⛉	$35
♡	$35
✝	$35
⚗	$35

To A Special Dad
#E5212
Issued: 1981 • Susp.: 1998
Retail Price: $20 – $35

(3)

Values	
✦	$55
⚬	$48
✿	$44
✾	$42
⛉	$39
◈	$37
♡	$35
✝	$35
⚗	$35
★	$35

To A Special Mum
#521965
Issued: 1991 • Open
Retail Price: $30 – $35

(4)

Values	
✝	$60
✋	$57
✾	$52
▲	$50
🐦	$48
⌁	$47
✦	$47
⚬	$43
✿	$42
✾	$42
⛉	$40
◈	$40
♡	$40
✝	$40
⚗	$40
★	$40

To A Very Special Mom
#E2824
Issued: 1984 • Open
Retail Price: $27.50 – $40

(5)

Values	
⚬	$57
✿	$53
✾	$50

To A Very Special Mom And Dad
#521434
Issued: 1991 • Susp.: 1993
Retail Price: $35

(6)

Values	
✝	$84
✋	$68
✾	$64
▲	$62
⚬	$60
⌁	$60
✦	$60
⚬	$57
✿	$57
✾	$54
⛉	$54
◈	$52
♡	$50
✝	$50
⚗	$50
★	$50

To A Very Special Sister
#E2825
Issued: 1984 • Open
Retail Price: $37.50 – $50

GENERAL FIGURINES

	Price Paid	Value Of My Collection
1.		
2.		
3.		
4.		
5.		
6.		
7.		
8.		
9.		
10.		
PENCIL TOTALS		

(7)

Values	
⛉	$72
⚗	$67
♡	$65
✝	$65
⚗	$65
★	$65

To A Very Special Sister
#528633
Issued: 1994 • Open
Retail Price: $60 – $65

(8)

Values	
◈	$135
✝	$100
✾	$94
✾	$90
▲	$85

To God Be The Glory
#E2823
Issued: 1984 • Susp.: 1987
Retail Price: $40 – $45

(9)

Values	
✾	$105
▲	$74
🐦	$65
⌁	$62
✦	$56
⚬	$54
✿	$52
✾	$52
⛉	$50
◈	$50
♡	$50
✝	$50
⚗	$50
★	$50

To My Deer Friend
#100048
Issued: 1987 • Open
Retail Price: $33 – $50

(10)

Values	
✋	$85
✾	$73
▲	$70
🐦	$65

To My Favorite Paw
#100021
Issued: 1986 • Susp.: 1988
Retail Price: $22.50 – $27

KEY: NM *Pre*-1981 ▲1981 I 1982 ⛉1983 ✝1984 ✾1985 ✾1986 ▲1987 🐦1988 ⌁1989 ✦1990 ⚬1991 ✿1992 ✾1993 ⛉1994 ⚗1995 ♡1996 ✝1997 ⚗1998 ★1999 ⅡM *Unmarked*

126

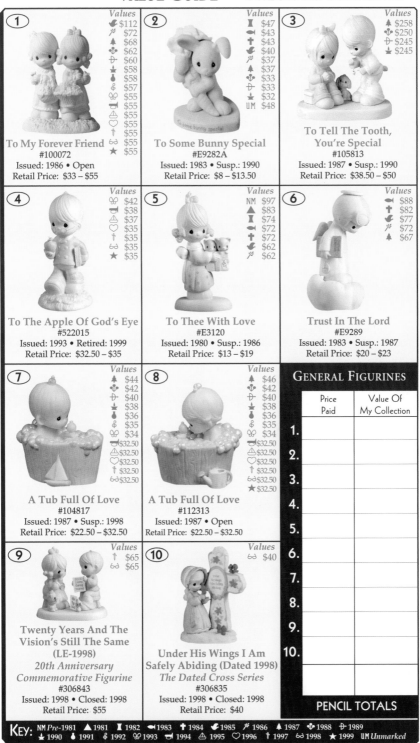

FIGURINES

(1)	Values		(2)	Values		(3)	Values
	🐚 $112			I $47			▲ $258
	♫ $72			➤ $43			✤ $250
	▲ $68			➤ $43			⊕ $245
	✤ $62			♥ $40			⚓ $245
	⊕ $60			♫ $37			
	♠ $58			➤ $37			
	♠ $58			✤ $33			
	♀ $57			⊕ $33			
	⚭ $55			⚓ $32			
	◁ $55			UM $48			
	△ $55						
	♡ $55						
	† $55						
	6♂ $55						

To My Forever Friend 6♂ $55 ★ $55
#100072
Issued: 1986 • Open
Retail Price: $33 – $55

To Some Bunny Special
#E9282A
Issued: 1983 • Susp.: 1990
Retail Price: $8 – $13.50

To Tell The Tooth, You're Special
#105813
Issued: 1987 • Susp.: 1990
Retail Price: $38.50 – $50

(4)	Values		(5)	Values		(6)	Values
	♀♀ $42			NM $97			➤ $88
	◁ $38			▲ $83			➤ $82
	△ $37			I $74			♥ $77
	♡ $35			➤ $72			♫ $72
	† $35			† $72			▲ $67
	6♂ $35			♥ $62			
	★ $35			♫ $62			

To The Apple Of God's Eye
#522015
Issued: 1993 • Retired: 1999
Retail Price: $32.50 – $35

To Thee With Love
#E3120
Issued: 1980 • Susp.: 1986
Retail Price: $13 – $19

Trust In The Lord
#E9289
Issued: 1983 • Susp.: 1987
Retail Price: $20 – $23

(7)	Values		(8)	Values
	▲ $44			▲ $46
	✤ $42			✤ $42
	⊕ $40			⊕ $40
	★ $38			♠ $38
	♠ $36			♠ $36
	♀ $35			♀ $35
	♀♀ $34			♀♀ $34
	◁$32.50			◁$32.50
	△$32.50			△$32.50
	♡$32.50			♡$32.50
	†$32.50			†$32.50
	6♂$32.50			6♂$32.50
				★ $32.50

A Tub Full Of Love
#104817
Issued: 1987 • Susp.: 1998
Retail Price: $22.50 – $32.50

A Tub Full Of Love
#112313
Issued: 1987 • Open
Retail Price: $22.50 – $32.50

GENERAL FIGURINES

	Price Paid	Value Of My Collection
1.		
2.		
3.		
4.		
5.		
6.		
7.		
8.		
9.		
10.		

PENCIL TOTALS

(9)	Values
	† $65
	6♂ $65

Twenty Years And The Vision's Still The Same
(LE-1998)
20th Anniversary Commemorative Figurine
#306843
Issued: 1998 • Closed: 1998
Retail Price: $55

(10)	Values
	6♂ $40

Under His Wings I Am Safely Abiding (Dated 1998)
The Dated Cross Series
#306835
Issued: 1998 • Closed: 1998
Retail Price: $40

KEY: NM *Pre-1981* ▲ 1981 I 1982 ◄ 1983 † 1984 ♥ 1985 ♫ 1986 ▲ 1987 ✤ 1988 ⊕ 1989 ★ 1990 ♦ 1991 ♠ 1992 ♀♀ 1993 ◁ 1994 △ 1995 ♡ 1996 † 1997 6♂ 1998 ★ 1999 UM *Unmarked*

1

Values	
NM	$140
I	$110
◄	$105
†	$100

Unto Us A Child Is Born
#E2013
Issued: 1979 • Susp.: 1984
Retail Price: $12 – $25

2

Values	
▽	$42
△	$37
♡	$35
†	$35
6Ə	$35
★	$35

Vaya Con Dios
#531146
Issued: 1995 • Open
Retail Price: $32.50 – $35

3 NEW!

Values	
6Ə	$70
★	$70

A Very Special Bond
#488240
Issued: 1999 • Open
Retail Price: $70

4

Values	
†	$300
✔	$280

The Voice Of Spring
(LE-1985)
The Four Seasons
Figurine Series
#12068
Issued: 1985 • Closed: 1985
Retail Price: $30

5

Values	
†	$113
✔	$106
ℐ	$102
▲	$99
✤	$93
Ð	$90

Waddle I Do Without You
The Clown Series
#12459
Issued: 1985 • Retired: 1989
Retail Price: $30 – $40

6

Values	
△	$42
♡	$35
†	$35
6Ə	$35
★	$35

Walk In The Sonshine
#524212
Issued: 1995 • Open
Retail Price: $35

GENERAL FIGURINES

	Price Paid	Value Of My Collection
1.		
2.		
3.		
4.		
5.		
6.		
7.		
8.		
9.		
10.		
PENCIL TOTALS		

7

Values	
NM	$136
▲	$112
I	$100
◄	$90
†	$86
ℐ	$84
▲	$84
✤	$84
Ð	$80
●	$80
♣	$80
⚬	$80
9Ə	$80
△	$80
♡	$80
†	$80
6Ə	$80
★	$80

Walking By Faith
#E3117
Issued: 1980 • Open
Retail Price: $35 – $80

8

Values	
★	$50

Warmest Wishes For
The Holidays
#455830
Issued: 1999 • Open
Retail Price: $50

9

Values	
†	$40
6Ə	$35
★	$35

Water-Melancholy Day
Without You
#521515
Issued: 1998 • Open
Retail Price: $35

10

Values	
♡	$38
†	$35
6Ə	$35
★	$35

We All Have Our Bad
Hair Days
#261157
Issued: 1997 • Open
Retail Price: $35

KEY: NM *Pre-1981* ▲ 1981 I 1982 ◄1983 † 1984 ✔1985 ℐ 1986 ▲ 1987 ✤1988 Ð 1989 ★ 1990 ● 1991 ✤ 1992 9Ə1993 ◄ 1994 △ 1995 ♡1996 † 1997 6Ə 1998 ★ 1999 UM *Unmarked*

FIGURINES

1

Values
♠ $80

We Are All Precious In His Sight (LE-1987)
#102903
Issued: 1987 • Closed: 1987
Retail Price: $30

2

Values
I $63
🐟 $46
✝ $44
🐚 $42
♫ $42
♠ $40
⚓ $40
ᚦ $37
🔔 $37
🌻 $37
♣ $35
🐚 $35
△ $35
♡ $35
† $35
₲ $35
★ $35

We Are God's Workmanship
#E9258
Issued: 1983 • Open
Retail Price: $19 – $35

3

Values
♦ $245

We Belong To The Lord
Damien-Dutton Figurine
#103004
Issued: 1986 • Closed: 1986
Retail Price: $50

4

Values
♠ $320
🐟 $270
ᚦ $260
★ $250
🔔 $245
₲ $245
♫ $235
🐚 $235
△ $235

We Gather Together To Ask The Lord's Blessing (set/6)
#109762
Issued: 1987 • Retired: 1995
Retail Price: $130 – $150

5

Values
⚓ $63
ᚦ $58
★ $56
🔔 $52

We Need A Good Friend Through The Ruff Times
#520810
Issued: 1989 • Susp.: 1991
Retail Price: $35 – $37.50

6

Values
★ $74
ᚦ $67
₲ $62
♫ $60
🐚 $60
△ $60
♡ $60
† $60
👓 $60
★ $60

We're Going To Miss You
#524913
Issued: 1990 • Open
Retail Price: $50 – $60

7

Values
I $98
🐟 $89
✝ $85
🔔 $80
♫ $78
♠ $76
⚓ $70
ᚦ $70
★ $66

We're In It Together
#E9259
Issued: 1983 • Susp.: 1990
Retail Price: $24 – $35

8

Values
♠ $80
⚓ $76
ᚦ $72
★ $67
🔔 $65

We're Pulling For You
#106151
Issued: 1987 • Susp.: 1991
Retail Price: $40 – $55

9

Values
♡ $45

We're So Hoppy You're Here (LE-1997)
Special Event Figurine
#261351
Issued: 1997 • Closed: 1997
Retail Price: $32.50

10

Values
♫ $58
♠ $55
⚓ $50
ᚦ $48
★ $46
🔔 $44
₲ $40

Wedding Arch
Bridal Party Series
#102369
Issued: 1987 • Susp.: 1992
Retail Price: $22.50 – $30

GENERAL FIGURINES

	Price Paid	Value Of My Collection
1.		
2.		
3.		
4.		
5.		
6.		
7.		
8.		
9.		
10.		

PENCIL TOTALS

KEY: NM *Pre-1981* ▲1981 I 1982 ◀1983 ✝1984 🐚1985 ♫1986 ♠1987 ⚓1988 ᚦ1989 ★1990 🔔1991 ₲1992 ♫1993 🐚1994 △1995 ♡1996 †1997 👓1998 ★1999 UM *Unmarked*

VALUE GUIDE — PRECIOUS MOMENTS®

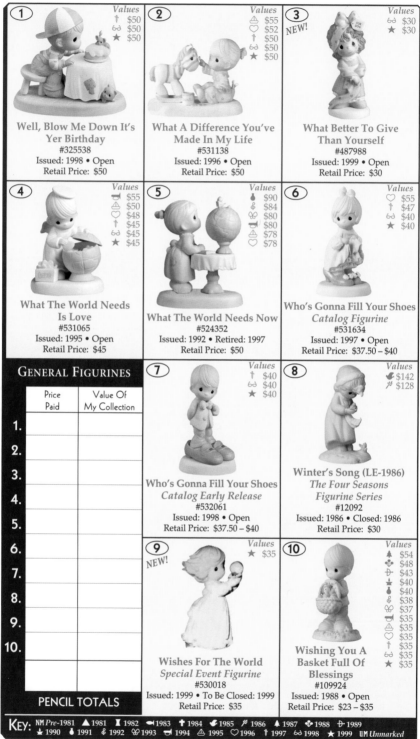

1 Well, Blow Me Down It's Yer Birthday
#325538
Issued: 1998 • Open
Retail Price: $50

Values
† $50
6ð $50
★ $50

2 What A Difference You've Made In My Life
#531138
Issued: 1996 • Open
Retail Price: $50

Values
△ $55
♡ $52
† $50
6ð $50
★ $50

3 NEW! What Better To Give Than Yourself
#487988
Issued: 1999 • Open
Retail Price: $30

Values
6ð $30
★ $30

4 What The World Needs Is Love
#531065
Issued: 1995 • Open
Retail Price: $45

Values
🍲 $55
△ $50
♡ $48
† $45
6ð $45
★ $45

5 What The World Needs Now
#524352
Issued: 1992 • Retired: 1997
Retail Price: $50

Values
🍶 $90
𝒇 $84
🍲 $80
🍶 $80
△ $78
♡ $78

6 Who's Gonna Fill Your Shoes
Catalog Figurine
#531634
Issued: 1997 • Open
Retail Price: $37.50 – $40

Values
♡ $55
† $47
6ð $40
★ $40

GENERAL FIGURINES

	Price Paid	Value Of My Collection
1.		
2.		
3.		
4.		
5.		
6.		
7.		
8.		
9.		
10.		

PENCIL TOTALS

7 Who's Gonna Fill Your Shoes
Catalog Early Release
#532061
Issued: 1998 • Open
Retail Price: $37.50 – $40

Values
† $40
6ð $40
★ $40

8 Winter's Song (LE-1986)
The Four Seasons Figurine Series
#12092
Issued: 1986 • Closed: 1986
Retail Price: $30

Values
🍃 $142
ⁿ $128

9 NEW! Wishes For The World
Special Event Figurine
#530018
Issued: 1999 • To Be Closed: 1999
Retail Price: $35

Values
★ $35

10 Wishing You A Basket Full Of Blessings
#109924
Issued: 1988 • Open
Retail Price: $23 – $35

Values
▲ $54
⚓ $48
🐦 $43
⭐ $40
🍶 $40
𝒇 $38
♋ $37
🍲 $35
△ $35
♡ $35
† $35
6ð $35
★ $35

KEY: NM *Pre-1981* ▲1981 ✗1982 ◀1983 †1984 ✦1985 ⁿ1986 ▲1987 ⚓1988 ᴆ1989 ⭐1990 🍶1991 𝒇1992 ♋1993 🍲1994 △1995 ♡1996 †1997 6ð1998 ★1999 ∪M *Unmarked*

130

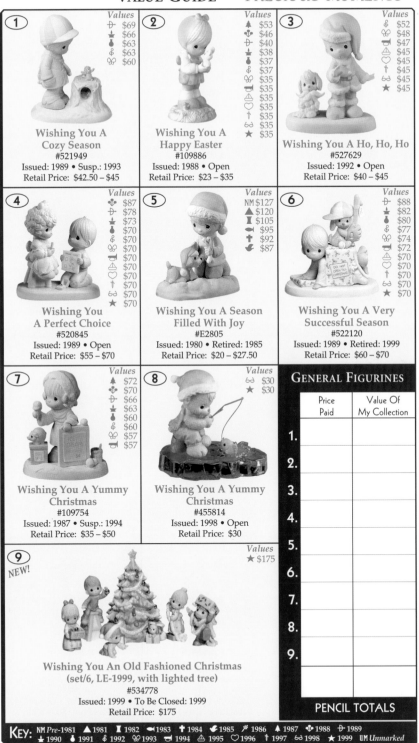

(1)

Values	
♐	$69
⚱	$66
Ð	$63
♒	$63
♈	$60

Wishing You A Cozy Season
#521949
Issued: 1989 • Susp.: 1993
Retail Price: $42.50 – $45

(2)

Values	
♠	$53
✤	$46
Ð	$40
⚱	$38
✝	$37
♒	$37
♈	$35
⊟	$35
△	$35
♡	$35
✝	$35
6ᴓ	$35
★	$35

Wishing You A Happy Easter
#109886
Issued: 1988 • Open
Retail Price: $23 – $35

(3)

Values	
♒	$52
♈	$48
⊟	$47
△	$45
✝	$45
♡	$45
6ᴓ	$45
★	$45

Wishing You A Ho, Ho, Ho
#527629
Issued: 1992 • Open
Retail Price: $40 – $45

(4)

Values	
✤	$87
Ð	$78
⚱	$73
♒	$70
♒	$70
♈	$70
⊟	$70
△	$70
♡	$70
✝	$70
6ᴓ	$70
★	$70

Wishing You A Perfect Choice
#520845
Issued: 1989 • Open
Retail Price: $55 – $70

(5)

Values	
NM	$127
▲	$120
▮	$105
◄	$95
✝	$92
✦	$87

Wishing You A Season Filled With Joy
#E2805
Issued: 1980 • Retired: 1985
Retail Price: $20 – $27.50

(6)

Values	
Ð	$88
⚱	$82
⚱	$80
♒	$77
♈	$74
⊟	$72
△	$70
♡	$70
✝	$70
6ᴓ	$70
★	$70

Wishing You A Very Successful Season
#522120
Issued: 1989 • Retired: 1999
Retail Price: $60 – $70

(7)

Values	
♠	$72
✤	$70
Ð	$66
⚱	$63
⚱	$60
♒	$60
♒	$57
⊟	$57

Wishing You A Yummy Christmas
#109754
Issued: 1987 • Susp.: 1994
Retail Price: $35 – $50

(8)

Values	
6ᴓ	$30
★	$30

Wishing You A Yummy Christmas
#455814
Issued: 1998 • Open
Retail Price: $30

GENERAL FIGURINES

	Price Paid	Value Of My Collection
1.		
2.		
3.		
4.		
5.		
6.		
7.		
8.		
9.		
PENCIL TOTALS		

(9)
NEW!

Values	
★	$175

Wishing You An Old Fashioned Christmas
(set/6, LE-1999, with lighted tree)
#534778
Issued: 1999 • To Be Closed: 1999
Retail Price: $175

FIGURINES

KEY: NM *Pre-1981* ▲1981 ▮1982 ◄1983 ✝1984 ✦1985 ♪1986 ♠1987 ✤1988 Ð1989
⚱1990 ⚱1991 ♒1992 ♈1993 ⊟1994 △1995 ♡1996 ✝1997 6ᴓ1998 ★1999 ⅡM *Unmarked*

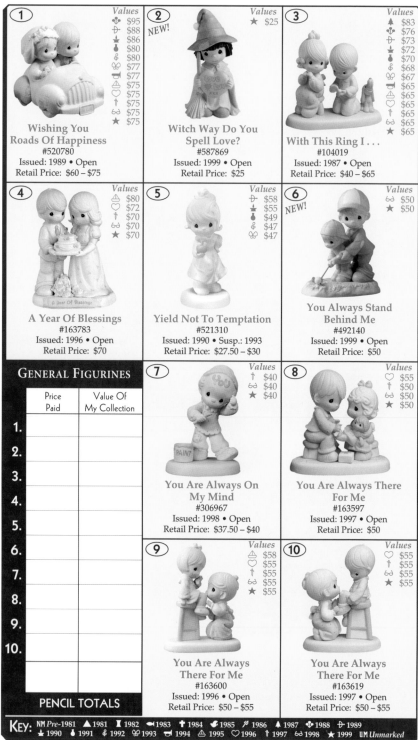

1

Values	
⬥	$95
⌐	$88
⭐	$86
🕯	$80
🐚	$77
⌐	$77
♡	$75
△	$75
†	$75
ᛞ	$75
★	$75

Wishing You
Roads Of Happiness
#520780
Issued: 1989 • Open
Retail Price: $60 – $75

2 NEW!

Values	
★	$25

Witch Way Do You
Spell Love?
#587869
Issued: 1999 • Open
Retail Price: $25

3

Values	
▲	$83
⬥	$76
⌐	$73
⭐	$72
🕯	$70
🐚	$68
🦋	$67
△	$65
♡	$65
†	$65
ᛞ	$65
★	$65

With This Ring I . . .
#104019
Issued: 1987 • Open
Retail Price: $40 – $65

4

Values	
△	$80
♡	$72
†	$70
ᛞ	$70
★	$70

A Year Of Blessings
#163783
Issued: 1996 • Open
Retail Price: $70

5

Values	
⌐	$58
⭐	$55
🕯	$49
🐚	$47
🦋	$47

Yield Not To Temptation
#521310
Issued: 1990 • Susp.: 1993
Retail Price: $27.50 – $30

6 NEW!

Values	
ᛞ	$50
★	$50

You Always Stand
Behind Me
#492140
Issued: 1999 • Open
Retail Price: $50

GENERAL FIGURINES

	Price Paid	Value Of My Collection
1.		
2.		
3.		
4.		
5.		
6.		
7.		
8.		
9.		
10.		
PENCIL TOTALS		

7

Values	
†	$40
ᛞ	$40
★	$40

You Are Always On
My Mind
#306967
Issued: 1998 • Open
Retail Price: $37.50 – $40

8

Values	
♡	$55
†	$50
ᛞ	$50
★	$50

You Are Always There
For Me
#163597
Issued: 1997 • Open
Retail Price: $50

9

Values	
△	$58
♡	$55
†	$55
ᛞ	$55
★	$55

You Are Always
There For Me
#163600
Issued: 1996 • Open
Retail Price: $50 – $55

10

Values	
♡	$55
†	$55
ᛞ	$55
★	$55

You Are Always
There For Me
#163619
Issued: 1997 • Open
Retail Price: $50 – $55

KEY: NM *Pre-1981* ▲ 1981 ✗ 1982 ◄ 1983 † 1984 ✔ 1985 ♯ 1986 ▲ 1987 ⬥ 1988 ⌐ 1989
★ 1990 🕯 1991 🐚 1992 🦋 1993 ⌐ 1994 △ 1995 ♡ 1996 † 1997 ᛞ 1998 ★ 1999 UM *Unmarked*

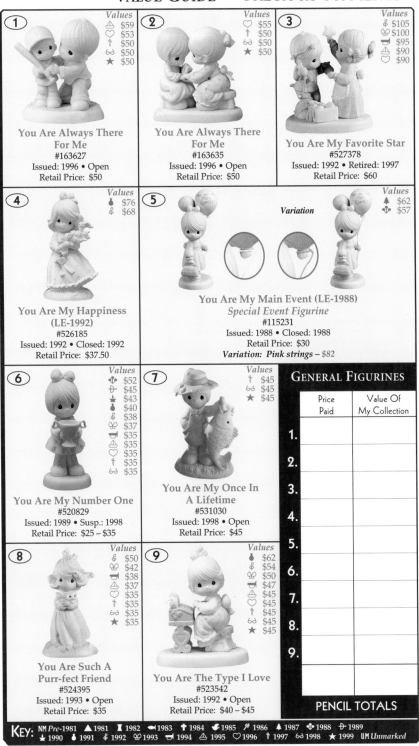

FIGURINES

1

Values
△ $59
♡ $53
✝ $50
δõ $50
★ $50

You Are Always There For Me
#163627
Issued: 1996 • Open
Retail Price: $50

2

Values
♡ $55
✝ $50
✦ $50
★ $50

You Are Always There For Me
#163635
Issued: 1996 • Open
Retail Price: $50

3

Values
δ $105
♋ $100
⊕ $95
△ $90
♡ $90

You Are My Favorite Star
#527378
Issued: 1992 • Retired: 1997
Retail Price: $60

4

Values
δ $76
δ $68

You Are My Happiness (LE-1992)
#526185
Issued: 1992 • Closed: 1992
Retail Price: $37.50

5

Variation

Values
▲ $62
⚓ $57

You Are My Main Event (LE-1988)
Special Event Figurine
#115231
Issued: 1988 • Closed: 1988
Retail Price: $30
Variation: Pink strings – $82

6

Values
✦ $52
✝ $45
✦ $43
δ $40
δ $38
♋ $37
⊿ $35
△ $35
♡ $35
✝ $35
δõ $35

You Are My Number One
#520829
Issued: 1989 • Susp.: 1998
Retail Price: $25 – $35

7

Values
✝ $45
δõ $45
★ $45

You Are My Once In A Lifetime
#531030
Issued: 1998 • Open
Retail Price: $45

8

Values
δ $50
♋ $42
⊿ $38
△ $37
♡ $35
✦ $35
δõ $35
★ $35

You Are Such A Purr-fect Friend
#524395
Issued: 1993 • Open
Retail Price: $35

9

Values
δ $62
δ $54
♋ $50
⊿ $47
△ $45
♡ $45
✝ $45
δõ $45
★ $45

You Are The Type I Love
#523542
Issued: 1992 • Open
Retail Price: $40 – $45

GENERAL FIGURINES

	Price Paid	Value Of My Collection
1.		
2.		
3.		
4.		
5.		
6.		
7.		
8.		
9.		
PENCIL TOTALS		

KEY: NM *Pre-1981* ▲ 1981 ▌ 1982 ◄1983 ✝ 1984 ✦ 1985 δ 1986 ▲ 1987 ✦ 1988 ⊕ 1989 ★ 1990 δ 1991 δ 1992 ♋ 1993 ⊿ 1994 △ 1995 ♡ 1996 ✝ 1997 δõ 1998 ★ 1999 UM *Unmarked*

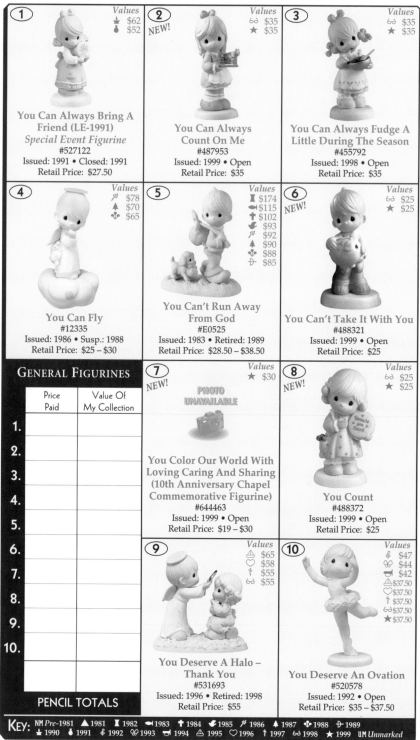

1 Values
⚖ $62
🌡 $52

You Can Always Bring A Friend (LE-1991)
Special Event Figurine
#527122
Issued: 1991 • Closed: 1991
Retail Price: $27.50

2 NEW! Values
6ᴆ $35
★ $35

You Can Always Count On Me
#487953
Issued: 1999 • Open
Retail Price: $35

3 Values
6ᴆ $35
★ $35

You Can Always Fudge A Little During The Season
#455792
Issued: 1998 • Open
Retail Price: $35

4 Values
♪⁵ $78
♠ $70
⚓ $65

You Can Fly
#12335
Issued: 1986 • Susp.: 1988
Retail Price: $25 – $30

5 Values
I $174
◄ $115
† $102
🍂 $93
♪⁵ $92
♠ $90
⬧ $88
Đ $85

You Can't Run Away From God
#E0525
Issued: 1983 • Retired: 1989
Retail Price: $28.50 – $38.50

6 NEW! Values
6ᴆ $25
★ $25

You Can't Take It With You
#488321
Issued: 1999 • Open
Retail Price: $25

GENERAL FIGURINES

	Price Paid	Value Of My Collection
1.		
2.		
3.		
4.		
5.		
6.		
7.		
8.		
9.		
10.		

PENCIL TOTALS

7 NEW! Values
★ $30

PHOTO UNAVAILABLE

You Color Our World With Loving Caring And Sharing (10th Anniversary Chapel Commemorative Figurine)
#644463
Issued: 1999 • Open
Retail Price: $19 – $30

8 NEW! Values
6ᴆ $25
★ $25

You Count
#488372
Issued: 1999 • Open
Retail Price: $25

9 Values
△ $65
♡ $58
† $55
6ᴆ $55

You Deserve A Halo – Thank You
#531693
Issued: 1996 • Retired: 1998
Retail Price: $55

10 Values
♪ $47
99 $44
🍴 $42
△ $37.50
♡ $37.50
† $37.50
6ᴆ $37.50
★ $37.50

You Deserve An Ovation
#520578
Issued: 1992 • Open
Retail Price: $35 – $37.50

KEY: NM *Pre-1981* ▲1981 I 1982 ◄1983 † 1984 🍂1985 ♪⁵ 1986 ♠ 1987 ⬧1988 Đ1989
♪ 1990 🍶 1991 ♪ 1992 99 1993 🍴 1994 △ 1995 ♡1996 † 1997 6ᴆ 1998 ★ 1999 UM *Unmarked*

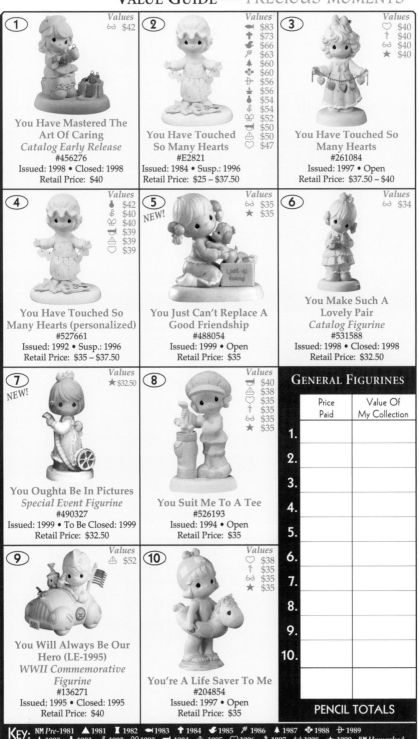

1 Values
🥢 $42

You Have Mastered The Art Of Caring
Catalog Early Release
#456276
Issued: 1998 • Closed: 1998
Retail Price: $40

2 Values
🪶 $83
🌿 $73
♈ $66
♪ $63
▲ $60
⬥ $60
Ð $56
🕯 $56
🍖 $54
🐚 $54
♈ $52
🌂 $50
⚱ $50
♡ $47

You Have Touched So Many Hearts
#E2821
Issued: 1984 • Susp.: 1996
Retail Price: $25 – $37.50

3 Values
♡ $40
† $40
🥢 $40
★ $40

You Have Touched So Many Hearts
#261084
Issued: 1997 • Open
Retail Price: $37.50 – $40

4 Values
🍖 $42
♈ $40
🎀 $40
⬥ $39
🌂 $39
♡ $39

You Have Touched So Many Hearts (personalized)
#527661
Issued: 1992 • Susp.: 1996
Retail Price: $35 – $37.50

5 NEW! Values
🥢 $35
★ $35

You Just Can't Replace A Good Friendship
#488054
Issued: 1999 • Open
Retail Price: $35

6 Values
🥢 $34

You Make Such A Lovely Pair
Catalog Figurine
#531588
Issued: 1998 • Closed: 1998
Retail Price: $32.50

7 NEW! Values
★ $32.50

You Oughta Be In Pictures
Special Event Figurine
#490327
Issued: 1999 • To Be Closed: 1999
Retail Price: $32.50

8 Values
🍴 $40
🌂 $38
♡ $35
† $35
🥢 $35
★ $35

You Suit Me To A Tee
#526193
Issued: 1994 • Open
Retail Price: $35

9 Values
🌂 $52

You Will Always Be Our Hero (LE-1995)
WWII Commemorative Figurine
#136271
Issued: 1995 • Closed: 1995
Retail Price: $40

10 Values
♡ $38
† $35
🥢 $35
★ $35

You're A Life Saver To Me
#204854
Issued: 1997 • Open
Retail Price: $35

GENERAL FIGURINES

	Price Paid	Value Of My Collection
1.		
2.		
3.		
4.		
5.		
6.		
7.		
8.		
9.		
10.		
PENCIL TOTALS		

FIGURINES

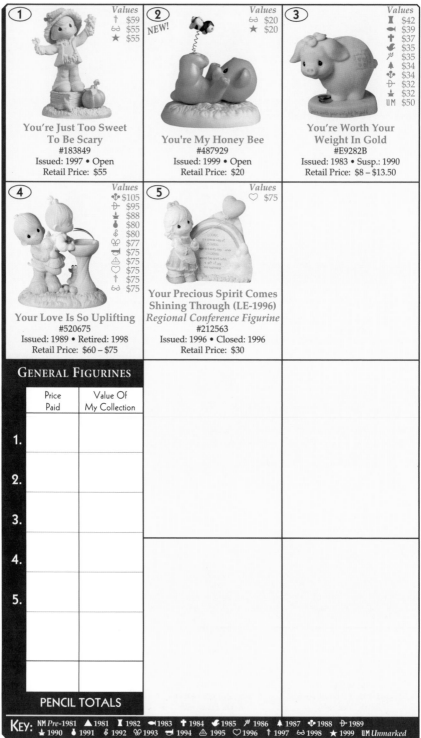

① Values
† $59
68 $55
★ $55

**You're Just Too Sweet
To Be Scary**
#183849
Issued: 1997 • Open
Retail Price: $55

② Values
NEW!
68 $20
★ $20

You're My Honey Bee
#487929
Issued: 1999 • Open
Retail Price: $20

③ Values
I $42
$39
† $37
$35
$35
▲ $34
$34
Đ $32
★ $32
UM $50

**You're Worth Your
Weight In Gold**
#E9282B
Issued: 1983 • Susp.: 1990
Retail Price: $8 – $13.50

④ Values
$105
Đ $95
$88
$80
$80
$77
$75
$75
♡ $75
† $75
68 $75

Your Love Is So Uplifting
#520675
Issued: 1989 • Retired: 1998
Retail Price: $60 – $75

⑤ Values
♡ $75

**Your Precious Spirit Comes
Shining Through (LE-1996)**
Regional Conference Figurine
#212563
Issued: 1996 • Closed: 1996
Retail Price: $30

GENERAL FIGURINES

	Price Paid	Value Of My Collection
1.		
2.		
3.		
4.		
5.		
PENCIL TOTALS		

KEY: NM *Pre*-1981 ▲ 1981 I 1982 ◀1983 † 1984 ✦ 1985 ⌀ 1986 ▲ 1987 ✤ 1988 Đ 1989
↓ 1990 ♦ 1991 ₰ 1992 ✿1993 ⌑ 1994 △ 1995 ♡1996 † 1997 68 1998 ★ 1999 UM *Unmarked*

COUNTRY LANE

Created in 1998, this line is based on PM artist Sam Butcher's memories of his time spent on Grandma Ethel's farm. It began with six figurines and one musical piece, which is dedicated to Jason Eric Wilson, a young man killed by three prowlers on his farm. Seven adorable figurines join this collection of farm-inspired pieces for 1999, bringing the total number of pieces to 14, two of which have have been retired or closed.

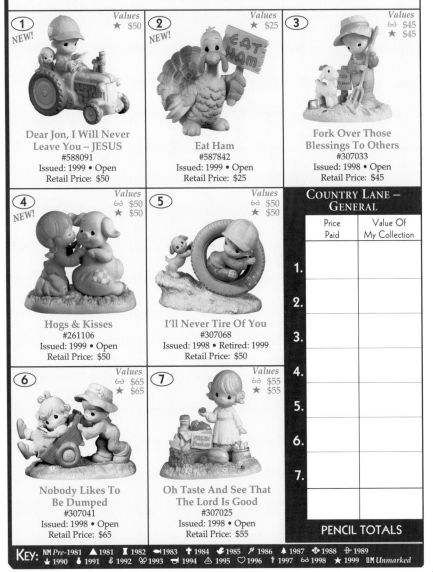

1 NEW!

Values
★ $50

Dear Jon, I Will Never Leave You – JESUS
#588091
Issued: 1999 • Open
Retail Price: $50

2 NEW!

Values
★ $25

Eat Ham
#587842
Issued: 1999 • Open
Retail Price: $25

3

Values
6ð $45
★ $45

Fork Over Those Blessings To Others
#307033
Issued: 1998 • Open
Retail Price: $45

4 NEW!

Values
6ð $50
★ $50

Hogs & Kisses
#261106
Issued: 1999 • Open
Retail Price: $50

5

Values
6ð $50
★ $50

I'll Never Tire Of You
#307068
Issued: 1998 • Retired: 1999
Retail Price: $50

6

Values
6ð $65
★ $65

Nobody Likes To Be Dumped
#307041
Issued: 1998 • Open
Retail Price: $65

7

Values
6ð $55
★ $55

Oh Taste And See That The Lord Is Good
#307025
Issued: 1998 • Open
Retail Price: $55

COUNTRY LANE – GENERAL

	Price Paid	Value Of My Collection
1.		
2.		
3.		
4.		
5.		
6.		
7.		
PENCIL TOTALS		

KEY: NM *Pre-1981* ▲ 1981 ✗ 1982 ◀1983 ✝ 1984 ✦ 1985 ♪ 1986 ▲ 1987 ✤ 1988 ϑ 1989 ✦ 1990 ♦ 1991 ℰ 1992 ♋1993 ◁ 1994 △ 1995 ♡1996 ✝ 1997 6ð 1998 ★ 1999 UM *Unmarked*

1 Values
6ð $35
★ $35

Peas Pass The Carrots
#307076
Issued: 1998 • Open
Retail Price: $35

2 NEW! Values
★ $40

**Shear Happiness And
Hare Cuts**
#539910
Issued: 1999 • Open
Retail Price: $40

3 NEW! Values
★ $60

**Wishing You A Moo-ie
Christmas**
#455865
Issued: 1999 • Open
Retail Price: $60

4 NEW! Values
★ $55

**You Brighten My Field
Of Dreams**
#587850
Issued: 1999 • Open
Retail Price: $55

5 Values
6ð $45
★ $45

You're Just As Sweet As Pie
#307017
Issued: 1998 • Open
Retail Price: $45

6 Values
6ð $175

Bringing In The Sheaves
(LE-12,000)
♪ *"Bringing In The Sheaves"*
#307084
Issued: 1998 • Closed: 1998
Retail Price: $90

COUNTRY LANE – FIGURINES		
	Price Paid	Value Of My Collection
1.		
2.		
3.		
4.		
5.		
COUNTRY LANE – MUSICALS		
6.		
PENCIL TOTALS		

LITTLE MOMENTS

The *Little Moments* line, smaller versions of PRECIOUS MOMENTS figurines, was introduced in 1996 with six pieces, followed by 24 more in 1997. Since 1998, three series have joined the collection. *Bible Stories* includes three pieces, *Highway To Happiness* boasts six and *International Little Moments* adds twelve figurines honoring cultures from across the world. Six *Little Moments Trophies* and one general figurine also join the line in 1999.

1 NEW!	Values UM $25

Daniel And The Lion's Den
#488291
Issued: 1999 • Open
Retail Price: $25

2 NEW!	Values UM $25

Jonah And The Whale
#488283
Issued: 1999 • Open
Retail Price: $25

3 NEW!	Values UM $25

Joseph's Special Coat
#488305
Issued: 1999 • Open
Retail Price: $25

4	Values UM $20

January
#261203
Issued: 1997 • Open
Retail Price: $20

5	Values UM $20

February
#261246
Issued: 1997 • Open
Retail Price: $20

6	Values UM $20

March
#261270
Issued: 1997 • Open
Retail Price: $20

7	Values UM $20

April
#261300
Issued: 1997 • Open
Retail Price: $20

LITTLE MOMENTS – BIBLE STORIES

	Price Paid	Value Of My Collection
1.		
2.		
3.		

LITTLE MOMENTS – BIRTHSTONE COLLECTION

4.		
5.		
6.		
7.		

PENCIL TOTALS

LITTLE MOMENTS

KEY: NM *Pre-1981* ▲1981 ✘1982 ◄1983 ✝1984 ✦1985 ♪1986 ▲1987 ✤1988 ֆ1989
★1990 ♦1991 ⸹1992 ♋1993 ⇌1994 △1995 ♡1996 ✝1997 ଈ1998 ★1999 UM *Unmarked*

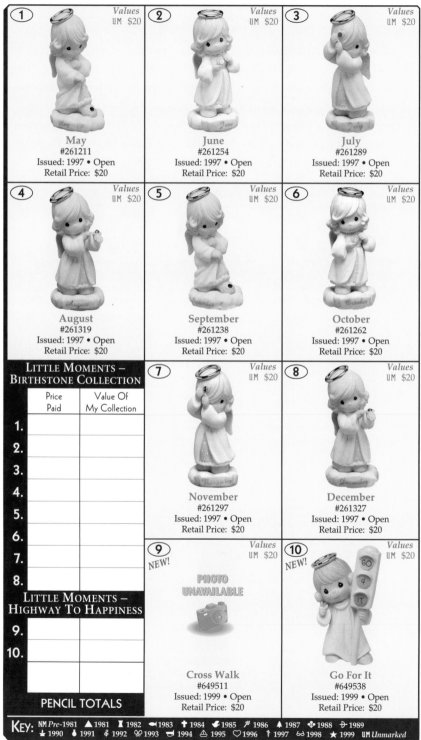

① Values UM $20

May
#261211
Issued: 1997 • Open
Retail Price: $20

② Values UM $20

June
#261254
Issued: 1997 • Open
Retail Price: $20

③ Values UM $20

July
#261289
Issued: 1997 • Open
Retail Price: $20

④ Values UM $20

August
#261319
Issued: 1997 • Open
Retail Price: $20

⑤ Values UM $20

September
#261238
Issued: 1997 • Open
Retail Price: $20

⑥ Values UM $20

October
#261262
Issued: 1997 • Open
Retail Price: $20

⑦ Values UM $20

November
#261297
Issued: 1997 • Open
Retail Price: $20

⑧ Values UM $20

December
#261327
Issued: 1997 • Open
Retail Price: $20

⑨ NEW! Values UM $20

PHOTO UNAVAILABLE

Cross Walk
#649511
Issued: 1999 • Open
Retail Price: $20

⑩ NEW! Values UM $20

Go For It
#649538
Issued: 1999 • Open
Retail Price: $20

LITTLE MOMENTS –
BIRTHSTONE COLLECTION

	Price Paid	Value Of My Collection
1.		
2.		
3.		
4.		
5.		
6.		
7.		
8.		

LITTLE MOMENTS –
HIGHWAY TO HAPPINESS

| 9. | | |
| 10. | | |

PENCIL TOTALS

KEY: NM *Pre*-1981 ▲1981 ▮1982 ◀1983 ✝1984 ✿1985 ♩1986 ♠1987 ✿1988 ⊕1989 ★1990 ♦1991 ♪1992 ♈1993 ☗1994 △1995 ♡1996 ✝1997 ✌1998 ★1999 **UM** *Unmarked*

VALUE GUIDE — *PRECIOUS MOMENTS*®

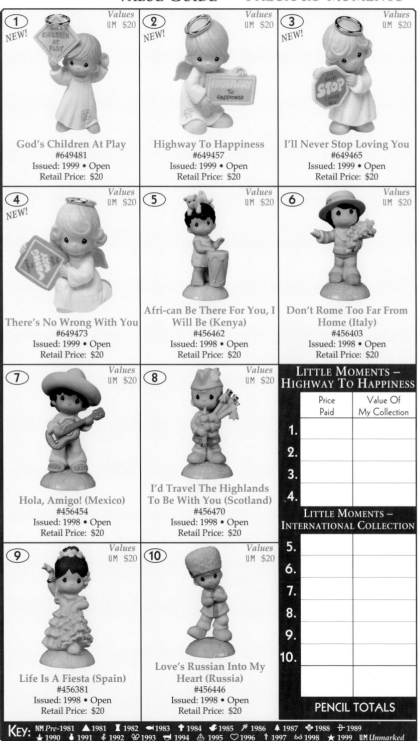

(1) NEW!
Values UM $20
God's Children At Play
#649481
Issued: 1999 • Open
Retail Price: $20

(2) NEW!
Values UM $20
Highway To Happiness
#649457
Issued: 1999 • Open
Retail Price: $20

(3) NEW!
Values UM $20
I'll Never Stop Loving You
#649465
Issued: 1999 • Open
Retail Price: $20

(4) NEW!
Values UM $20
There's No Wrong With You
#649473
Issued: 1999 • Open
Retail Price: $20

(5)
Values UM $20
Afri-can Be There For You, I Will Be (Kenya)
#456462
Issued: 1998 • Open
Retail Price: $20

(6)
Values UM $20
Don't Rome Too Far From Home (Italy)
#456403
Issued: 1998 • Open
Retail Price: $20

(7)
Values UM $20
Hola, Amigo! (Mexico)
#456454
Issued: 1998 • Open
Retail Price: $20

(8)
Values UM $20
I'd Travel The Highlands To Be With You (Scotland)
#456470
Issued: 1998 • Open
Retail Price: $20

(9)
Values UM $20
Life Is A Fiesta (Spain)
#456381
Issued: 1998 • Open
Retail Price: $20

(10)
Values UM $20
Love's Russian Into My Heart (Russia)
#456446
Issued: 1998 • Open
Retail Price: $20

LITTLE MOMENTS – HIGHWAY TO HAPPINESS

	Price Paid	Value Of My Collection
1.		
2.		
3.		
4.		

LITTLE MOMENTS – INTERNATIONAL COLLECTION

5.		
6.		
7.		
8.		
9.		
10.		

PENCIL TOTALS

KEY: NM *Pre-1981* ▲1981 ✗1982 ◄1983 ✝1984 ✦1985 ♫1986 ▲1987 ✤1988 ♫1989 ★1990 ♦1991 ♪1992 ♀1993 ◄1994 △1995 ♡1996 ✝1997 ∞1998 ★1999 UM *Unmarked*

141

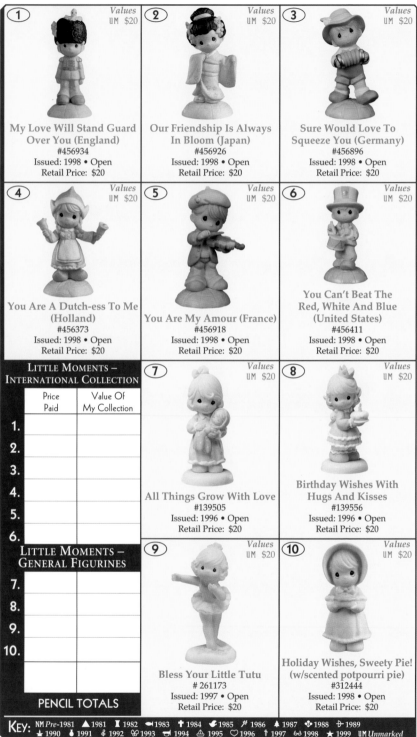

1 Values UM $20
My Love Will Stand Guard
Over You (England)
#456934
Issued: 1998 • Open
Retail Price: $20

2 Values UM $20
Our Friendship Is Always
In Bloom (Japan)
#456926
Issued: 1998 • Open
Retail Price: $20

3 Values UM $20
Sure Would Love To
Squeeze You (Germany)
#456896
Issued: 1998 • Open
Retail Price: $20

4 Values UM $20
You Are A Dutch-ess To Me
(Holland)
#456373
Issued: 1998 • Open
Retail Price: $20

5 Values UM $20
You Are My Amour (France)
#456918
Issued: 1998 • Open
Retail Price: $20

6 Values UM $20
You Can't Beat The
Red, White And Blue
(United States)
#456411
Issued: 1998 • Open
Retail Price: $20

**LITTLE MOMENTS –
INTERNATIONAL COLLECTION**

	Price Paid	Value Of My Collection
1.		
2.		
3.		
4.		
5.		
6.		

7 Values UM $20
All Things Grow With Love
#139505
Issued: 1996 • Open
Retail Price: $20

8 Values UM $20
Birthday Wishes With
Hugs And Kisses
#139556
Issued: 1996 • Open
Retail Price: $20

**LITTLE MOMENTS –
GENERAL FIGURINES**

7.		
8.		
9.		
10.		

PENCIL TOTALS

9 Values UM $20
Bless Your Little Tutu
261173
Issued: 1997 • Open
Retail Price: $20

10 Values UM $20
Holiday Wishes, Sweety Pie!
(w/scented potpourri pie)
#312444
Issued: 1998 • Open
Retail Price: $20

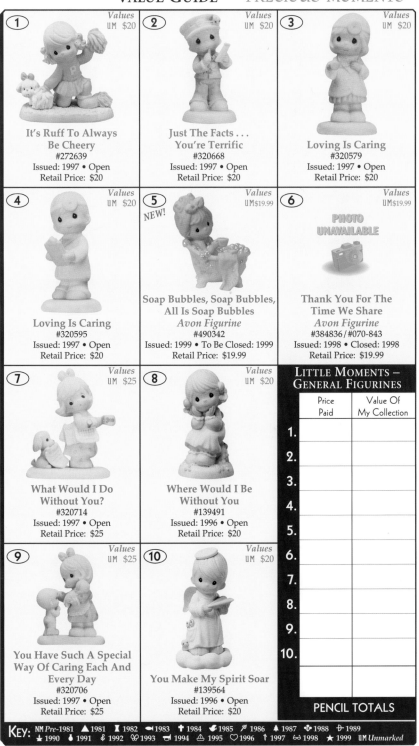

1 | Values UM $20

It's Ruff To Always
Be Cheery
#272639
Issued: 1997 • Open
Retail Price: $20

2 | Values UM $20

Just The Facts . . .
You're Terrific
#320668
Issued: 1997 • Open
Retail Price: $20

3 | Values UM $20

Loving Is Caring
#320579
Issued: 1997 • Open
Retail Price: $20

4 | Values UM $20

Loving Is Caring
#320595
Issued: 1997 • Open
Retail Price: $20

5 NEW! | Values UM $19.99

Soap Bubbles, Soap Bubbles,
All Is Soap Bubbles
Avon Figurine
#490342
Issued: 1999 • To Be Closed: 1999
Retail Price: $19.99

6 | Values UM $19.99

PHOTO UNAVAILABLE

Thank You For The
Time We Share
Avon Figurine
#384836 / #070-843
Issued: 1998 • Closed: 1998
Retail Price: $19.99

7 | Values UM $25

What Would I Do
Without You?
#320714
Issued: 1997 • Open
Retail Price: $25

8 | Values UM $20

Where Would I Be
Without You
#139491
Issued: 1996 • Open
Retail Price: $20

9 | Values UM $25

You Have Such A Special
Way Of Caring Each And
Every Day
#320706
Issued: 1997 • Open
Retail Price: $25

10 | Values UM $20

You Make My Spirit Soar
#139564
Issued: 1996 • Open
Retail Price: $20

LITTLE MOMENTS –
GENERAL FIGURINES

	Price Paid	Value Of My Collection
1.		
2.		
3.		
4.		
5.		
6.		
7.		
8.		
9.		
10.		

PENCIL TOTALS

LITTLE MOMENTS

KEY: NM *Pre-1981* ▲ 1981 ▮ 1982 ◀1983 ✝ 1984 ✦ 1985 ✗ 1986 ▲ 1987 ✛ 1988 ౨ 1989 ★ 1990 ♦ 1991 ♪ 1992 ✿ 1993 ◁ 1994 △ 1995 ♡ 1996 ✝ 1997 ಟ 1998 ★ 1999 UM *Unmarked*

143

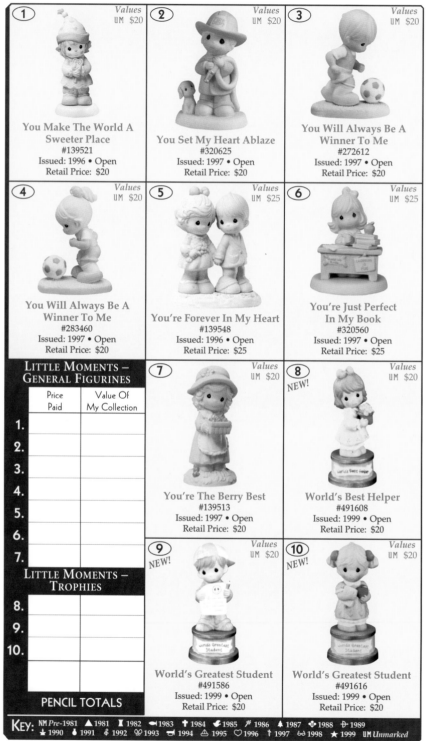

1 — Values UM $20
You Make The World A Sweeter Place
#139521
Issued: 1996 • Open
Retail Price: $20

2 — Values UM $20
You Set My Heart Ablaze
#320625
Issued: 1997 • Open
Retail Price: $20

3 — Values UM $20
You Will Always Be A Winner To Me
#272612
Issued: 1997 • Open
Retail Price: $20

4 — Values UM $20
You Will Always Be A Winner To Me
#283460
Issued: 1997 • Open
Retail Price: $20

5 — Values UM $25
You're Forever In My Heart
#139548
Issued: 1996 • Open
Retail Price: $25

6 — Values UM $25
You're Just Perfect In My Book
#320560
Issued: 1997 • Open
Retail Price: $25

7 — Values UM $20
You're The Berry Best
#139513
Issued: 1997 • Open
Retail Price: $20

8 — Values UM $20 — NEW!
World's Best Helper
#491608
Issued: 1999 • Open
Retail Price: $20

9 — Values UM $20 — NEW!
World's Greatest Student
#491586
Issued: 1999 • Open
Retail Price: $20

10 — Values UM $20 — NEW!
World's Greatest Student
#491616
Issued: 1999 • Open
Retail Price: $20

LITTLE MOMENTS – GENERAL FIGURINES

	Price Paid	Value Of My Collection
1.		
2.		
3.		
4.		
5.		
6.		
7.		

LITTLE MOMENTS – TROPHIES

8.		
9.		
10.		

PENCIL TOTALS

KEY: NM *Pre-1981* ▲ 1981 Ⅺ 1982 ◀ 1983 ✝ 1984 ✔ 1985 ⌀ 1986 ♣ 1987 ✿ 1988 ☼ 1989 ♣ 1990 ♦ 1991 ♪ 1992 ♈ 1993 ☲ 1994 △ 1995 ♡ 1996 ✝ 1997 ⌒ 1998 ★ 1999 UM *Unmarked*

① NEW!	Values UM $20	② NEW!	Values UM $20	③ NEW!	Values UM $20

World's Sweetest Girl
#491594
Issued: 1999 • Open
Retail Price: $20

You're No. 1
#491624
Issued: 1999 • Open
Retail Price: $20

You're No. 1
#491640
Issued: 1999 • Open
Retail Price: $20

LITTLE MOMENTS

LITTLE MOMENTS – TROPHIES

	Price Paid	Value Of My Collection
1.		
2.		
3.		

PENCIL TOTALS

KEY: NM *Pre-1981* ▲ 1981 ✗ 1982 ◀ 1983 ✝ 1984 ✪ 1985 ♪ 1986 ♣ 1987 ✿ 1988 ☦ 1989 ★ 1990 ♦ 1991 ✦ 1992 ⦾ 1993 ⬳ 1994 ⚠ 1995 ♡ 1996 ✝ 1997 ⚭ 1998 ★ 1999 UM *Unmarked*

145

ORNAMENT SERIES

Two new series, *Birthday Train* and *Twelve Days Of Christmas* made their debut in 1998, becoming the fifth and sixth ornament series in the PRECIOUS MOMENTS collection. While these series boast seven and eight pieces released respectively, one piece was added to the Annual Christmas Ornaments and one piece was added to the *Easter Seals Commemorative Ornaments* in 1999.

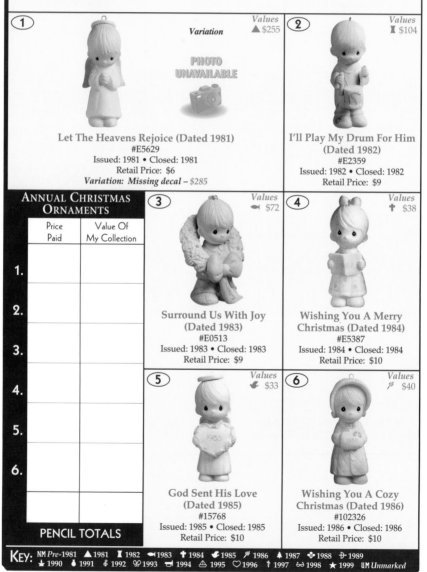

①

Variation

Values ▲ $255

Let The Heavens Rejoice (Dated 1981)
#E5629
Issued: 1981 • Closed: 1981
Retail Price: $6
Variation: Missing decal – $285

②

Values 𝕀 $104

I'll Play My Drum For Him (Dated 1982)
#E2359
Issued: 1982 • Closed: 1982
Retail Price: $9

③

Values ◄ $72

Surround Us With Joy (Dated 1983)
#E0513
Issued: 1983 • Closed: 1983
Retail Price: $9

④

Values ✝ $38

Wishing You A Merry Christmas (Dated 1984)
#E5387
Issued: 1984 • Closed: 1984
Retail Price: $10

⑤

Values 🐟 $33

God Sent His Love (Dated 1985)
#15768
Issued: 1985 • Closed: 1985
Retail Price: $10

⑥

Values ℱ $40

Wishing You A Cozy Christmas (Dated 1986)
#102326
Issued: 1986 • Closed: 1986
Retail Price: $10

ANNUAL CHRISTMAS ORNAMENTS

	Price Paid	Value Of My Collection
1.		
2.		
3.		
4.		
5.		
6.		
PENCIL TOTALS		

KEY: NM *Pre-1981* ▲ 1981 𝕀 1982 ◄ 1983 ✝ 1984 🐟 1985 ℱ 1986 ▲ 1987 ✿ 1988 ☐ 1989 ★ 1990 🌢 1991 ✦ 1992 ♀ 1993 ⊣ 1994 △ 1995 ♡ 1996 † 1997 ∞ 1998 ★ 1999 UM *Unmarked*

146

1 Values ♠ $47

**Love Is The Best Gift Of All
(Dated 1987)**
#109770
Issued: 1987 • Closed: 1987
Retail Price: $11

2 Values ✤ $52

**Time To Wish You A Merry
Christmas (Dated 1988)**
#115320
Issued: 1988 • Closed: 1988
Retail Price: $13

3 Values ᛞ $38

Oh Holy Night (Dated 1989)
#522848
Issued: 1989 • Closed: 1989
Retail Price: $13.50

4 Values ⚶ $30

**Once Upon A Holy Night
(Dated 1990)**
#523852
Issued: 1990 • Closed: 1990
Retail Price: $15

5 Values ⚬ $32

**May Your Christmas Be
Merry (Dated 1991)**
#524174
Issued: 1991 • Closed: 1991
Retail Price: $15

6 Values ℰ $46

**But The Greatest Of These
Is Love (Dated 1992)**
#527696
Issued: 1992 • Closed: 1992
Retail Price: $15

7 Values ℅ $42

**Wishing You The Sweetest
Christmas (Dated 1993)**
#530212
Issued: 1993 • Closed: 1993
Retail Price: $15

8 Values ⛵ $35

**You're As Pretty As A
Christmas Tree (Dated 1994)**
#530395
Issued: 1994 • Closed: 1994
Retail Price: $16

9 Values △ $33

**He Covers The Earth With
His Beauty (Dated 1995)**
#142662
Issued: 1995 • Closed: 1995
Retail Price: $17

10 Values ♡ $28

**Peace On Earth . . . Anyway
(Dated 1996)**
#183369
Issued: 1996 • Closed: 1996
Retail Price: $18.50

ANNUAL CHRISTMAS ORNAMENTS

	Price Paid	Value Of My Collection
1.		
2.		
3.		
4.		
5.		
6.		
7.		
8.		
9.		
10.		
	PENCIL TOTALS	

ORNAMENTS

KEY: NM *Pre-1981* ▲ 1981 ⚓ 1982 ◄1983 ✝ 1984 ✔ 1985 ⚘ 1986 ♠ 1987 ✤ 1988 ᛞ 1989
⚶ 1990 ⚬ 1991 ℰ 1992 ℅1993 ⛵ 1994 △ 1995 ♡1996 ✝ 1997 ᛦ 1998 ★ 1999 ∪M *Unmarked*

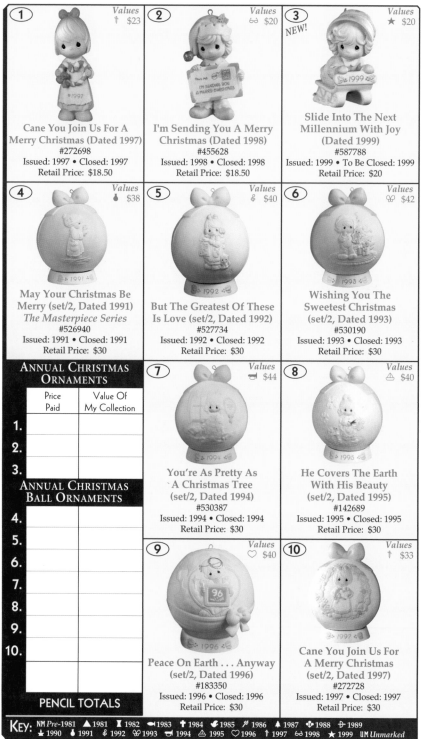

① *Values* † $23

Cane You Join Us For A Merry Christmas (Dated 1997)
#272698
Issued: 1997 • Closed: 1997
Retail Price: $18.50

② *Values* 👓 $20

I'm Sending You A Merry Christmas (Dated 1998)
#455628
Issued: 1998 • Closed: 1998
Retail Price: $18.50

③ *Values* ★ $20

NEW!

Slide Into The Next Millennium With Joy (Dated 1999)
#587788
Issued: 1999 • To Be Closed: 1999
Retail Price: $20

④ *Values* 🏺 $38

May Your Christmas Be Merry (set/2, Dated 1991)
The Masterpiece Series
#526940
Issued: 1991 • Closed: 1991
Retail Price: $30

⑤ *Values* 𝄞 $40

But The Greatest Of These Is Love (set/2, Dated 1992)
#527734
Issued: 1992 • Closed: 1992
Retail Price: $30

⑥ *Values* 🦋 $42

Wishing You The Sweetest Christmas (set/2, Dated 1993)
#530190
Issued: 1993 • Closed: 1993
Retail Price: $30

⑦ *Values* 🎺 $44

You're As Pretty As A Christmas Tree (set/2, Dated 1994)
#530387
Issued: 1994 • Closed: 1994
Retail Price: $30

⑧ *Values* ⛵ $40

He Covers The Earth With His Beauty (set/2, Dated 1995)
#142689
Issued: 1995 • Closed: 1995
Retail Price: $30

⑨ *Values* ♡ $40

Peace On Earth . . . Anyway (set/2, Dated 1996)
#183350
Issued: 1996 • Closed: 1996
Retail Price: $30

⑩ *Values* † $33

Cane You Join Us For A Merry Christmas (set/2, Dated 1997)
#272728
Issued: 1997 • Closed: 1997
Retail Price: $30

	Price Paid	Value Of My Collection
ANNUAL CHRISTMAS ORNAMENTS		
1.		
2.		
3.		
ANNUAL CHRISTMAS BALL ORNAMENTS		
4.		
5.		
6.		
7.		
8.		
9.		
10.		
PENCIL TOTALS		

KEY: NM *Pre-1981* ▲ 1981 ⧗ 1982 🐟 1983 ✝ 1984 🕊 1985 🌿 1986 🌲 1987 ✿ 1988 🏹 1989 🔥 1990 🏺 1991 𝄞 1992 🦋 1993 🎺 1994 ⛵ 1995 ♡ 1996 † 1997 👓 1998 ★ 1999 UM *Unmarked*

1 — *Values* $184

Reindeer (Dated 1986)
#102466
Issued: 1986 • Closed: 1986
Retail Price: $11

2 — *Values* $25

Bear The Good News Of
Christmas (Dated 1987)
#104515
Issued: 1987 • Closed: 1987
Retail Price: $12.50

3 — *Values* $33

Hang On For The Holly
Days (Dated 1988)
#520292
Issued: 1988 • Closed: 1988
Retail Price: $13

4 — *Values* $42

Christmas Is Ruff Without
You (Dated 1989)
#520462
Issued: 1989 • Closed: 1989
Retail Price: $13

5 — *Values* $39

Wishing You A Purr-fect
Holiday (Dated 1990)
#520497
Issued: 1990 • Closed: 1990
Retail Price: $15

6 — *Values* $35

Sno-Bunny Falls For You
Like I Do (Dated 1991)
#520438
Issued: 1991 • Closed: 1991
Retail Price: $15

7 — *Values* $27

I'm Nuts About You
(Dated 1992)
#520411
Issued: 1992 • Closed: 1992
Retail Price: $16

8 — *Values* $29

Slow Down And Enjoy The
Holidays (Dated 1993)
#520489
Issued: 1993 • Closed: 1993
Retail Price: $16

9 — *Values* $28

You Are Always In My
Heart (Dated 1994)
#530972
Issued: 1994 • Closed: 1994
Retail Price: $16

10 — *Values* $32

Hippo Holly Days
(Dated 1995)
#520403
Issued: 1995 • Closed: 1995
Retail Price: $17

BIRTHDAY SERIES ORNAMENTS

	Price Paid	Value Of My Collection
1.		
2.		
3.		
4.		
5.		
6.		
7.		
8.		
9.		
10.		
PENCIL TOTALS		

ORNAMENTS

KEY: NM *Pre-1981* ▲1981 ▮1982 ◀1983 ✝1984 ✦1985 ⅍1986 ♣1987 ♣1988 ♫1989 ⚓1990 ⚫1991 ♪1992 ♀1993 ⌁1994 △1995 ♡1996 ✝1997 ⚭1998 ★1999 UM *Unmarked*

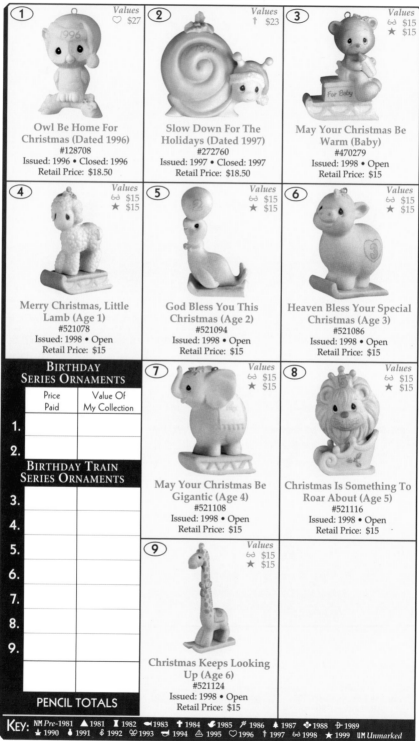

(1)
Values
♡ $27

Owl Be Home For Christmas (Dated 1996)
#128708
Issued: 1996 • Closed: 1996
Retail Price: $18.50

(2)
Values
† $23

Slow Down For The Holidays (Dated 1997)
#272760
Issued: 1997 • Closed: 1997
Retail Price: $18.50

(3)
Values
👓 $15
★ $15

May Your Christmas Be Warm (Baby)
#470279
Issued: 1998 • Open
Retail Price: $15

(4)
Values
👓 $15
★ $15

Merry Christmas, Little Lamb (Age 1)
#521078
Issued: 1998 • Open
Retail Price: $15

(5)
Values
👓 $15
★ $15

God Bless You This Christmas (Age 2)
#521094
Issued: 1998 • Open
Retail Price: $15

(6)
Values
👓 $15
★ $15

Heaven Bless Your Special Christmas (Age 3)
#521086
Issued: 1998 • Open
Retail Price: $15

(7)
Values
👓 $15
★ $15

May Your Christmas Be Gigantic (Age 4)
#521108
Issued: 1998 • Open
Retail Price: $15

(8)
Values
👓 $15
★ $15

Christmas Is Something To Roar About (Age 5)
#521116
Issued: 1998 • Open
Retail Price: $15

(9)
Values
👓 $15
★ $15

Christmas Keeps Looking Up (Age 6)
#521124
Issued: 1998 • Open
Retail Price: $15

BIRTHDAY SERIES ORNAMENTS

	Price Paid	Value Of My Collection
1.		
2.		
BIRTHDAY TRAIN SERIES ORNAMENTS		
3.		
4.		
5.		
6.		
7.		
8.		
9.		
PENCIL TOTALS		

KEY: NM Pre-1981 ▲ 1981 ⧗ 1982 🐟 1983 ✝ 1984 🕊 1985 🎺 1986 ⛪ 1987 ❀ 1988 ⚔ 1989 ★ 1990 🔥 1991 ♆ 1992 ∞ 1993 ⛵ 1994 △ 1995 ♡ 1996 † 1997 👓 1998 ★ 1999 UM Unmarked

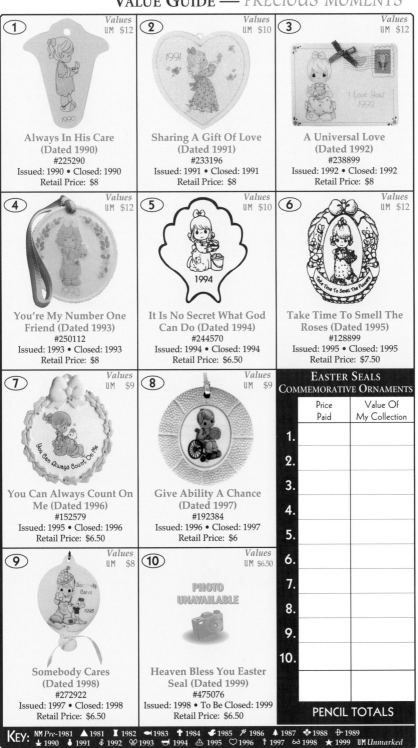

1 — Values UM $12

**Always In His Care
(Dated 1990)**
#225290
Issued: 1990 • Closed: 1990
Retail Price: $8

2 — Values UM $10

**Sharing A Gift Of Love
(Dated 1991)**
#233196
Issued: 1991 • Closed: 1991
Retail Price: $8

3 — Values UM $12

**A Universal Love
(Dated 1992)**
#238899
Issued: 1992 • Closed: 1992
Retail Price: $8

4 — Values UM $12

**You're My Number One
Friend (Dated 1993)**
#250112
Issued: 1993 • Closed: 1993
Retail Price: $8

5 — Values UM $10

**It Is No Secret What God
Can Do (Dated 1994)**
#244570
Issued: 1994 • Closed: 1994
Retail Price: $6.50

6 — Values UM $12

**Take Time To Smell The
Roses (Dated 1995)**
#128899
Issued: 1995 • Closed: 1995
Retail Price: $7.50

7 — Values UM $9

**You Can Always Count On
Me (Dated 1996)**
#152579
Issued: 1995 • Closed: 1996
Retail Price: $6.50

8 — Values UM $9

**Give Ability A Chance
(Dated 1997)**
#192384
Issued: 1996 • Closed: 1997
Retail Price: $6

9 — Values UM $8

**Somebody Cares
(Dated 1998)**
#272922
Issued: 1997 • Closed: 1998
Retail Price: $6.50

10 — Values UM $6.50

PHOTO UNAVAILABLE

**Heaven Bless You Easter
Seal (Dated 1999)**
#475076
Issued: 1998 • To Be Closed: 1999
Retail Price: $6.50

EASTER SEALS
COMMEMORATIVE ORNAMENTS

	Price Paid	Value Of My Collection
1.		
2.		
3.		
4.		
5.		
6.		
7.		
8.		
9.		
10.		
PENCIL TOTALS		

ORNAMENTS

KEY: NM *Pre-1981* ▲1981 Ⅱ1982 ◀1983 ✝1984 ✦1985 ✗1986 ▲1987 ✿1988 ⸉1989 ★1990 ♦1991 ⸋1992 ♈1993 ⊨1994 ⚠1995 ♡1996 ✝1997 ଶ1998 ★1999 UM *Unmarked*

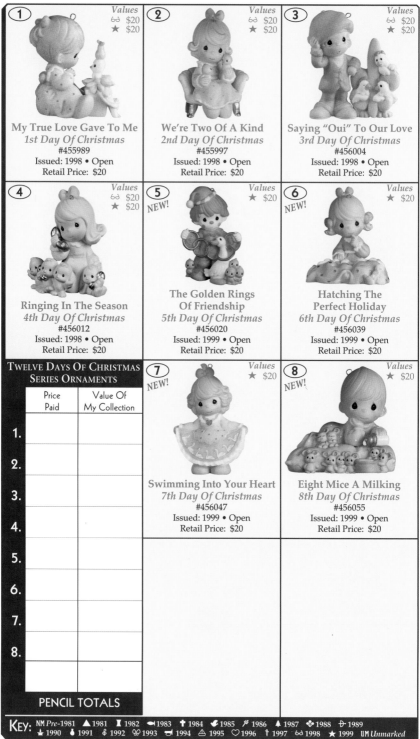

1 — Values 6ᵈ $20 ★ $20

My True Love Gave To Me
1st Day Of Christmas
#455989
Issued: 1998 • Open
Retail Price: $20

2 — Values 6ᵈ $20 ★ $20

We're Two Of A Kind
2nd Day Of Christmas
#455997
Issued: 1998 • Open
Retail Price: $20

3 — Values 6ᵈ $20 ★ $20

Saying "Oui" To Our Love
3rd Day Of Christmas
#456004
Issued: 1998 • Open
Retail Price: $20

4 — Values 6ᵈ $20 ★ $20

Ringing In The Season
4th Day Of Christmas
#456012
Issued: 1998 • Open
Retail Price: $20

5 NEW! — Values ★ $20

The Golden Rings Of Friendship
5th Day Of Christmas
#456020
Issued: 1999 • Open
Retail Price: $20

6 NEW! — Values ★ $20

Hatching The Perfect Holiday
6th Day Of Christmas
#456039
Issued: 1999 • Open
Retail Price: $20

TWELVE DAYS OF CHRISTMAS SERIES ORNAMENTS

	Price Paid	Value Of My Collection
1.		
2.		
3.		
4.		
5.		
6.		
7.		
8.		
PENCIL TOTALS		

7 NEW! — Values ★ $20

Swimming Into Your Heart
7th Day Of Christmas
#456047
Issued: 1999 • Open
Retail Price: $20

8 NEW! — Values ★ $20

Eight Mice A Milking
8th Day Of Christmas
#456055
Issued: 1999 • Open
Retail Price: $20

KEY: NM *Pre-1981* ▲ 1981 ▌ 1982 ◄ 1983 ✝ 1984 ✔ 1985 ʲ 1986 ▲ 1987 ✤ 1988 ⊕ 1989 ★ 1990 ♦ 1991 ♭ 1992 ⅋ 1993 ━ 1994 △ 1995 ♡ 1996 ✝ 1997 6ᵈ 1998 ★ 1999 UM *Unmarked*

GENERAL ORNAMENTS

Since their first appearance in 1981, there have been over 160 general ornaments produced, as well as many exclusive pieces available only at specific events, through the Care-A-Van or at select retailers. Less than 30 of these ornaments are still available. Fourteen ornaments were introduced in 1998, while nine were introduced in 1999. Eleven pieces have been closed or retired since 1998.

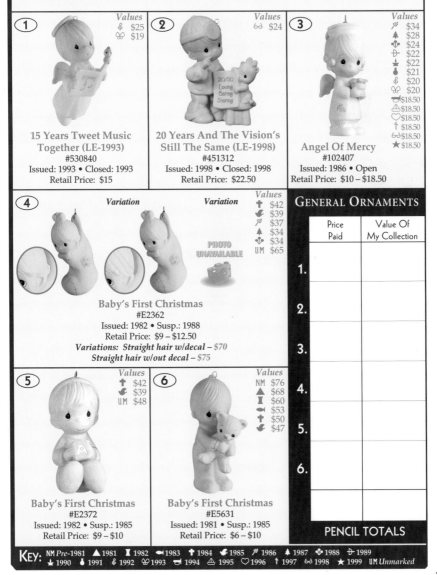

1 Values $25 / $19

15 Years Tweet Music Together (LE-1993)
#530840
Issued: 1993 • Closed: 1993
Retail Price: $15

2 Values 68 $24

20 Years And The Vision's Still The Same (LE-1998)
#451312
Issued: 1998 • Closed: 1998
Retail Price: $22.50

3 Values
$34 / $28 / $24 / $22 / $22 / $21 / $20 / $20 / $18.50 / $18.50 / $18.50 / $18.50 / $18.50 / $18.50

Angel Of Mercy
#102407
Issued: 1986 • Open
Retail Price: $10 – $18.50

4 *Variation* *Variation* PHOTO UNAVAILABLE

Values $42 / $39 / $37 / $34 / $34 / UM $65

Baby's First Christmas
#E2362
Issued: 1982 • Susp.: 1988
Retail Price: $9 – $12.50
Variations: Straight hair w/decal – $70
Straight hair w/out decal – $75

5 Values $42 / $39 / UM $48

Baby's First Christmas
#E2372
Issued: 1982 • Susp.: 1985
Retail Price: $9 – $10

6 Values NM $76 / $68 / $60 / $53 / $50 / $47

Baby's First Christmas
#E5631
Issued: 1981 • Susp.: 1985
Retail Price: $6 – $10

GENERAL ORNAMENTS

	Price Paid	Value Of My Collection
1.		
2.		
3.		
4.		
5.		
6.		
PENCIL TOTALS		

ORNAMENTS

KEY: NM Pre-1981 ▲1981 Ⅰ1982 ◄1983 ✝1984 ✿1985 ♫1986 ▲1987 ✤1988 ✲1989 ✦1990 ●1991 &1992 ♘1993 ◄1994 △1995 ♡1996 ✝1997 68 1998 ★1999 UM Unmarked

153

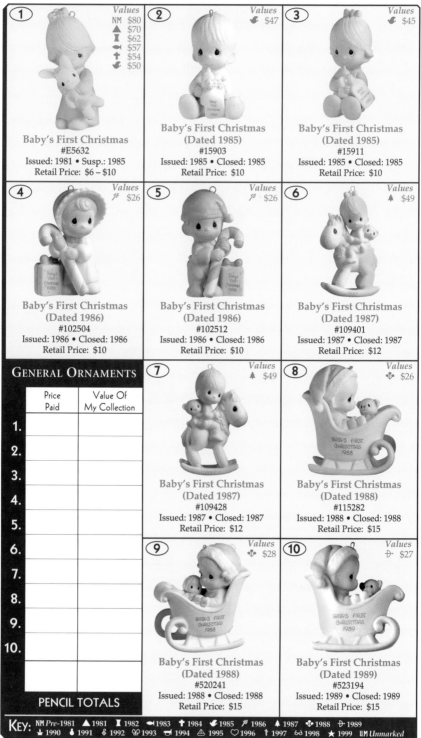

1

Values
NM $80
▲ $70
𝕀 $62
⬳ $57
✝ $54
⚓ $50

Baby's First Christmas
#E5632
Issued: 1981 • Susp.: 1985
Retail Price: $6 – $10

2

Values
🍂 $47

Baby's First Christmas
(Dated 1985)
#15903
Issued: 1985 • Closed: 1985
Retail Price: $10

3

Values
🍂 $45

Baby's First Christmas
(Dated 1985)
#15911
Issued: 1985 • Closed: 1985
Retail Price: $10

4

Values
ℱ $26

Baby's First Christmas
(Dated 1986)
#102504
Issued: 1986 • Closed: 1986
Retail Price: $10

5

Values
ℱ $26

Baby's First Christmas
(Dated 1986)
#102512
Issued: 1986 • Closed: 1986
Retail Price: $10

6

Values
▲ $49

Baby's First Christmas
(Dated 1987)
#109401
Issued: 1987 • Closed: 1987
Retail Price: $12

GENERAL ORNAMENTS

	Price Paid	Value Of My Collection
1.		
2.		
3.		
4.		
5.		
6.		
7.		
8.		
9.		
10.		

PENCIL TOTALS

7

Values
▲ $49

Baby's First Christmas
(Dated 1987)
#109428
Issued: 1987 • Closed: 1987
Retail Price: $12

8

Values
⚓ $26

Baby's First Christmas
(Dated 1988)
#115282
Issued: 1988 • Closed: 1988
Retail Price: $15

9

Values
⚓ $28

Baby's First Christmas
(Dated 1988)
#520241
Issued: 1988 • Closed: 1988
Retail Price: $15

10

Values
Ð $27

Baby's First Christmas
(Dated 1989)
#523194
Issued: 1989 • Closed: 1989
Retail Price: $15

KEY: NM *Pre*-1981 ▲ 1981 𝕀 1982 ⬳1983 ✝ 1984 🍂 1985 ℱ 1986 ▲ 1987 ⚓ 1988 Ð 1989 ⬧ 1990 ♦ 1991 ✦ 1992 ❀ 1993 ⬳ 1994 △ 1995 ♡ 1996 ✝ 1997 ᎶᎾ 1998 ★ 1999 **UM** *Unmarked*

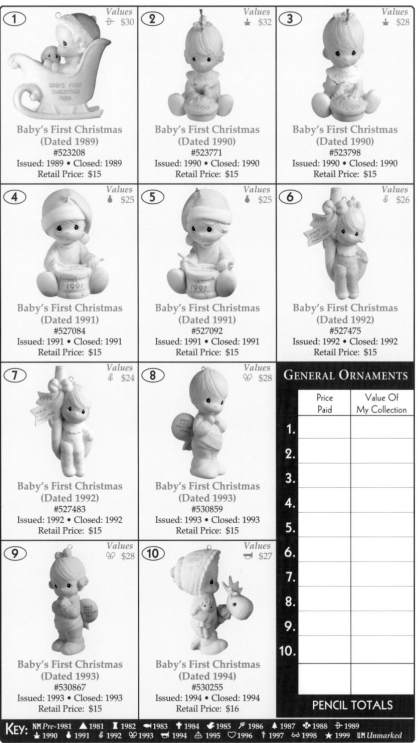

1 — *Values* ✝ $30
Baby's First Christmas
(Dated 1989)
#523208
Issued: 1989 • Closed: 1989
Retail Price: $15

2 — *Values* ⚓ $32
Baby's First Christmas
(Dated 1990)
#523771
Issued: 1990 • Closed: 1990
Retail Price: $15

3 — *Values* ⚓ $28
Baby's First Christmas
(Dated 1990)
#523798
Issued: 1990 • Closed: 1990
Retail Price: $15

4 — *Values* ♦ $25
Baby's First Christmas
(Dated 1991)
#527084
Issued: 1991 • Closed: 1991
Retail Price: $15

5 — *Values* ♦ $25
Baby's First Christmas
(Dated 1991)
#527092
Issued: 1991 • Closed: 1991
Retail Price: $15

6 — *Values* ♭ $26
Baby's First Christmas
(Dated 1992)
#527475
Issued: 1992 • Closed: 1992
Retail Price: $15

7 — *Values* ♭ $24
Baby's First Christmas
(Dated 1992)
#527483
Issued: 1992 • Closed: 1992
Retail Price: $15

8 — *Values* ✪ $28
Baby's First Christmas
(Dated 1993)
#530859
Issued: 1993 • Closed: 1993
Retail Price: $15

9 — *Values* ✪ $28
Baby's First Christmas
(Dated 1993)
#530867
Issued: 1993 • Closed: 1993
Retail Price: $15

10 — *Values* ⊣ $27
Baby's First Christmas
(Dated 1994)
#530255
Issued: 1994 • Closed: 1994
Retail Price: $16

GENERAL ORNAMENTS

	Price Paid	Value Of My Collection
1.		
2.		
3.		
4.		
5.		
6.		
7.		
8.		
9.		
10.		
PENCIL TOTALS		

ORNAMENTS

KEY: NM *Pre-1981* ▲ 1981 ✗ 1982 ◁ 1983 ✝ 1984 ✦ 1985 ✗ 1986 ▲ 1987 ✤ 1988 ✝ 1989
♠ 1990 ♦ 1991 ♭ 1992 ✪ 1993 ⊣ 1994 ⚠ 1995 ♡ 1996 ✝ 1997 ∞ 1998 ★ 1999 UM *Unmarked*

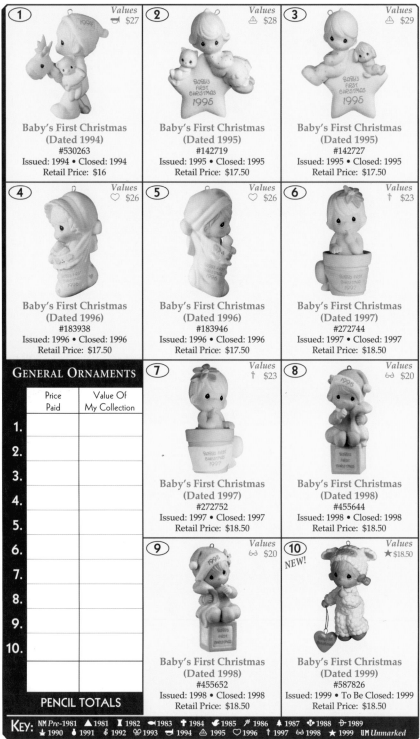

1 Values 🚼 $27

Baby's First Christmas (Dated 1994)
#530263
Issued: 1994 • Closed: 1994
Retail Price: $16

2 Values △ $28

Baby's First Christmas (Dated 1995)
#142719
Issued: 1995 • Closed: 1995
Retail Price: $17.50

3 Values △ $29

Baby's First Christmas (Dated 1995)
#142727
Issued: 1995 • Closed: 1995
Retail Price: $17.50

4 Values ♡ $26

Baby's First Christmas (Dated 1996)
#183938
Issued: 1996 • Closed: 1996
Retail Price: $17.50

5 Values ♡ $26

Baby's First Christmas (Dated 1996)
#183946
Issued: 1996 • Closed: 1996
Retail Price: $17.50

6 Values † $23

Baby's First Christmas (Dated 1997)
#272744
Issued: 1997 • Closed: 1997
Retail Price: $18.50

GENERAL ORNAMENTS

	Price Paid	Value Of My Collection
1.		
2.		
3.		
4.		
5.		
6.		
7.		
8.		
9.		
10.		
PENCIL TOTALS		

7 Values † $23

Baby's First Christmas (Dated 1997)
#272752
Issued: 1997 • Closed: 1997
Retail Price: $18.50

8 Values 6∂ $20

Baby's First Christmas (Dated 1998)
#455644
Issued: 1998 • Closed: 1998
Retail Price: $18.50

9 Values 6∂ $20

Baby's First Christmas (Dated 1998)
#455652
Issued: 1998 • Closed: 1998
Retail Price: $18.50

10 NEW! Values ★ $18.50

Baby's First Christmas (Dated 1999)
#587826
Issued: 1999 • To Be Closed: 1999
Retail Price: $18.50

KEY: NM *Pre-1981* ▲1981 Ⅱ1982 ◄1983 †1984 ✦1985 ✗1986 ▲1987 ✤1988 Ꝋ1989 ★1990 ♦1991 ✦1992 ⁹⁰1993 ◄1994 △1995 ♡1996 †1997 6∂1998 ★1999 UM *Unmarked*

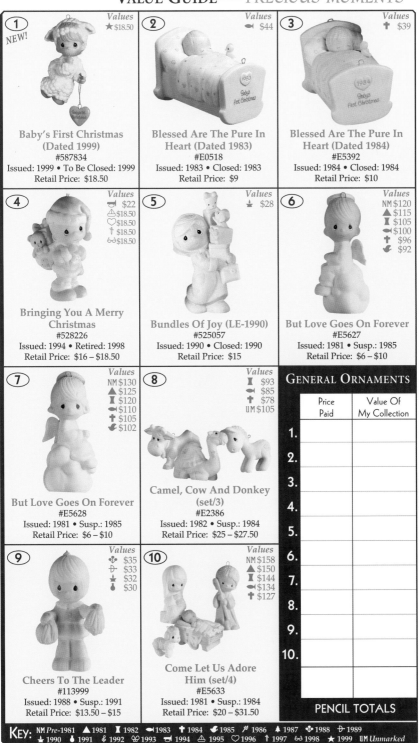

① NEW!
Values
★ $18.50

**Baby's First Christmas
(Dated 1999)**
#587834
Issued: 1999 • To Be Closed: 1999
Retail Price: $18.50

②
Values
🐟 $44

**Blessed Are The Pure In
Heart (Dated 1983)**
#E0518
Issued: 1983 • Closed: 1983
Retail Price: $9

③
Values
✝ $39

**Blessed Are The Pure In
Heart (Dated 1984)**
#E5392
Issued: 1984 • Closed: 1984
Retail Price: $10

④
Values
🔔 $22
⚠ $18.50
♡ $18.50
✝ $18.50
63 $18.50

**Bringing You A Merry
Christmas**
#528226
Issued: 1994 • Retired: 1998
Retail Price: $16 – $18.50

⑤
Values
⚖ $28

Bundles Of Joy (LE-1990)
#525057
Issued: 1990 • Closed: 1990
Retail Price: $15

⑥
Values
NM $120
▲ $115
Ⅱ $105
◀ $100
✝ $96
❧ $92

But Love Goes On Forever
#E5627
Issued: 1981 • Susp.: 1985
Retail Price: $6 – $10

⑦
Values
NM $130
▲ $125
Ⅱ $120
◀ $110
✝ $105
❧ $102

But Love Goes On Forever
#E5628
Issued: 1981 • Susp.: 1985
Retail Price: $6 – $10

⑧
Values
Ⅱ $93
◀ $85
✝ $78
UM $105

**Camel, Cow And Donkey
(set/3)**
#E2386
Issued: 1982 • Susp.: 1984
Retail Price: $25 – $27.50

⑨
Values
⚜ $35
Ð $33
⚖ $32
🔔 $30

Cheers To The Leader
#113999
Issued: 1988 • Susp.: 1991
Retail Price: $13.50 – $15

⑩
Values
NM $158
▲ $150
Ⅱ $144
◀ $134
✝ $127

**Come Let Us Adore
Him (set/4)**
#E5633
Issued: 1981 • Susp.: 1984
Retail Price: $20 – $31.50

GENERAL ORNAMENTS

	Price Paid	Value Of My Collection
1.		
2.		
3.		
4.		
5.		
6.		
7.		
8.		
9.		
10.		
PENCIL TOTALS		

ORNAMENTS

KEY: NM *Pre-1981* ▲1981 Ⅱ1982 ◀1983 ✝1984 ❧1985 ♪1986 ▲1987 ⚜1988 Ð1989
⚖1990 🔔1991 ♪1992 ♀1993 🔔1994 ⚠1995 ♡1996 ✝1997 63 1998 ★1999 UM *Unmarked*

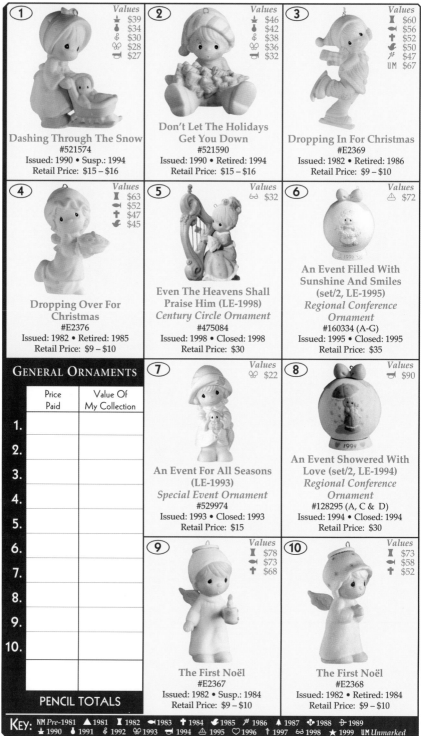

1

Values	
☀	$39
🕯	$34
⚶	$30
✿	$28
⌣	$27

Dashing Through The Snow
#521574
Issued: 1990 • Susp.: 1994
Retail Price: $15 – $16

2

Values	
🕯	$46
🕯	$42
⚶	$38
✿	$36
⌣	$32

**Don't Let The Holidays
Get You Down**
#521590
Issued: 1990 • Retired: 1994
Retail Price: $15 – $16

3

Values	
I	$60
⮞	$56
✝	$52
✦	$50
✗	$47
UM	$67

Dropping In For Christmas
#E2369
Issued: 1982 • Retired: 1986
Retail Price: $9 – $10

4

Values	
I	$63
⮞	$52
✝	$47
✦	$45

**Dropping Over For
Christmas**
#E2376
Issued: 1982 • Retired: 1985
Retail Price: $9 – $10

5

Values	
6∂	$32

**Even The Heavens Shall
Praise Him (LE-1998)**
Century Circle Ornament
#475084
Issued: 1998 • Closed: 1998
Retail Price: $30

6

Values	
△	$72

**An Event Filled With
Sunshine And Smiles**
(set/2, LE-1995)
*Regional Conference
Ornament*
#160334 (A-G)
Issued: 1995 • Closed: 1995
Retail Price: $35

GENERAL ORNAMENTS

	Price Paid	Value Of My Collection
1.		
2.		
3.		
4.		
5.		
6.		
7.		
8.		
9.		
10.		
PENCIL TOTALS		

7

Values	
✿	$22

An Event For All Seasons
(LE-1993)
Special Event Ornament
#529974
Issued: 1993 • Closed: 1993
Retail Price: $15

8

Values	
⌣	$90

**An Event Showered With
Love (set/2, LE-1994)**
*Regional Conference
Ornament*
#128295 (A, C & D)
Issued: 1994 • Closed: 1994
Retail Price: $30

9

Values	
I	$78
⮞	$73
✝	$68

The First Noël
#E2367
Issued: 1982 • Susp.: 1984
Retail Price: $9 – $10

10

Values	
I	$73
⮞	$58
✝	$52

The First Noël
#E2368
Issued: 1982 • Retired: 1984
Retail Price: $9 – $10

KEY: NM *Pre-1981* ▲ 1981 I 1982 ⮞1983 ✝ 1984 ✦ 1985 ✗ 1986 ▲ 1987 ✦ 1988 ✥ 1989 ☀ 1990 🕯 1991 ⚶ 1992 ✿ 1993 ⌣ 1994 △ 1995 ♡ 1996 ✝ 1997 6∂ 1998 ★ 1999 UM *Unmarked*

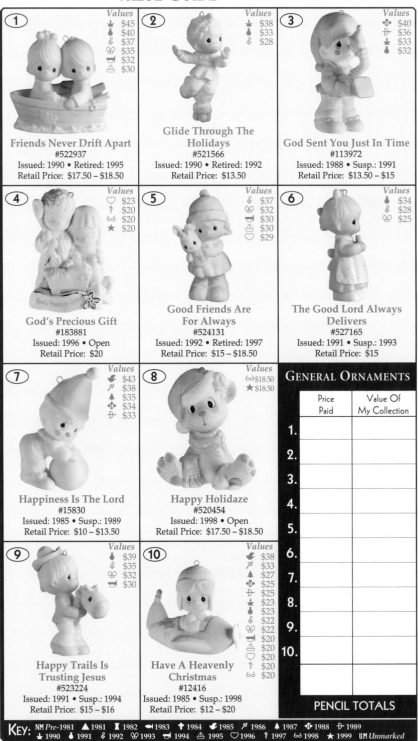

1 | Values
★ $45
🔔 $40
♬ $37
∞ $35
🗝 $32
⚠ $30

Friends Never Drift Apart
#522937
Issued: 1990 • Retired: 1995
Retail Price: $17.50 – $18.50

2 | Values
★ $38
🔔 $33
♬ $28

Glide Through The Holidays
#521566
Issued: 1990 • Retired: 1992
Retail Price: $13.50

3 | Values
♧ $40
Ð $36
★ $33
🔔 $32

God Sent You Just In Time
#113972
Issued: 1988 • Susp.: 1991
Retail Price: $13.50 – $15

4 | Values
♡ $23
† $20
6ð $20
★ $20

God's Precious Gift
#183881
Issued: 1996 • Open
Retail Price: $20

5 | Values
♬ $37
∞ $32
🗝 $30
⚠ $30
♡ $29

Good Friends Are For Always
#524131
Issued: 1992 • Retired: 1997
Retail Price: $15 – $18.50

6 | Values
🔔 $34
♬ $28
∞ $25

The Good Lord Always Delivers
#527165
Issued: 1991 • Susp.: 1993
Retail Price: $15

7 | Values
★ $43
♪ $38
▲ $35
♧ $34
Ð $33

Happiness Is The Lord
#15830
Issued: 1985 • Susp.: 1989
Retail Price: $10 – $13.50

8 | Values
6ð $18.50
★ $18.50

Happy Holidaze
#520454
Issued: 1998 • Open
Retail Price: $17.50 – $18.50

9 | Values
🔔 $39
♬ $35
∞ $32
🗝 $30

Happy Trails Is Trusting Jesus
#523224
Issued: 1991 • Susp.: 1994
Retail Price: $15 – $16

10 | Values
🍃 $38
♪ $33
▲ $27
♧ $25
Ð $25
🔔 $23
🔔 $23
♬ $22
♬ $22
🗝 $20
⚠ $20
♡ $20
† $20
6ð $20

Have A Heavenly Christmas
#12416
Issued: 1985 • Susp.: 1998
Retail Price: $12 – $20

GENERAL ORNAMENTS

	Price Paid	Value Of My Collection
1.		
2.		
3.		
4.		
5.		
6.		
7.		
8.		
9.		
10.		
PENCIL TOTALS		

ORNAMENTS

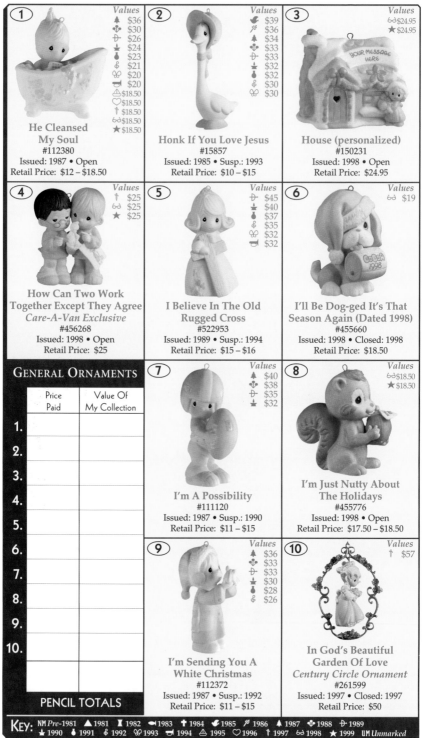

1

Values	
♠	$36
⬧	$30
⥁	$26
⌇	$24
◉	$23
✿	$21
♉	$20
⬤	$20
⟁	$18.50
♡	$18.50
†	$18.50
6∂	$18.50
★	$18.50

He Cleansed My Soul
#112380
Issued: 1987 • Open
Retail Price: $12 – $18.50

2

Values	
⬥	$39
⁒	$36
♠	$34
⬧	$33
⥁	$33
★	$32
◉	$32
✿	$30
♉	$30

Honk If You Love Jesus
#15857
Issued: 1985 • Susp.: 1993
Retail Price: $10 – $15

3

Values	
6∂	$24.95
★	$24.95

House (personalized)
#150231
Issued: 1998 • Open
Retail Price: $24.95

4

Values	
†	$25
6∂	$25
★	$25

How Can Two Work Together Except They Agree
Care-A-Van Exclusive
#456268
Issued: 1998 • Open
Retail Price: $25

5

Values	
⥁	$45
★	$40
◉	$37
✿	$35
♉	$32
⬤	$32

I Believe In The Old Rugged Cross
#522953
Issued: 1989 • Susp.: 1994
Retail Price: $15 – $16

6

Values	
6∂	$19

I'll Be Dog-ged It's That Season Again (Dated 1998)
#455660
Issued: 1998 • Closed: 1998
Retail Price: $18.50

General Ornaments

	Price Paid	Value Of My Collection
1.		
2.		
3.		
4.		
5.		
6.		
7.		
8.		
9.		
10.		

PENCIL TOTALS

7

Values	
♠	$40
⬧	$38
⥁	$35
★	$32

I'm A Possibility
#111120
Issued: 1987 • Susp.: 1990
Retail Price: $11 – $15

8

Values	
6∂	$18.50
★	$18.50

I'm Just Nutty About The Holidays
#455776
Issued: 1998 • Open
Retail Price: $17.50 – $18.50

9

Values	
♠	$36
⬧	$33
⥁	$33
★	$30
◉	$28
✿	$26

I'm Sending You A White Christmas
#112372
Issued: 1987 • Susp.: 1992
Retail Price: $11 – $15

10

Values	
†	$57

In God's Beautiful Garden Of Love
Century Circle Ornament
#261599
Issued: 1997 • Closed: 1997
Retail Price: $50

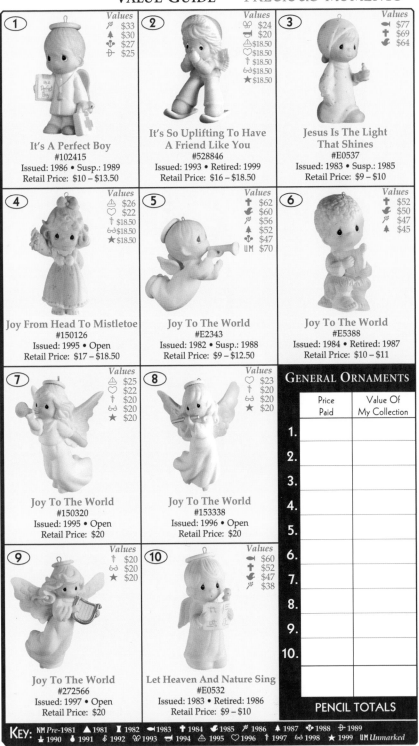

1 | Values
🎏 $33
🔺 $30
♦ $27
Đ $25

It's A Perfect Boy
#102415
Issued: 1986 • Susp.: 1989
Retail Price: $10 – $13.50

2 | Values
🎏 $24
🔺 $20
△ $18.50
♡ $18.50
† $18.50
68 $18.50
★ $18.50

It's So Uplifting To Have A Friend Like You
#528846
Issued: 1993 • Retired: 1999
Retail Price: $16 – $18.50

3 | Values
🐟 $77
✝ $69
🍃 $64

Jesus Is The Light That Shines
#E0537
Issued: 1983 • Susp.: 1985
Retail Price: $9 – $10

4 | Values
△ $26
♡ $22
† $18.50
68 $18.50
★ $18.50

Joy From Head To Mistletoe
#150126
Issued: 1995 • Open
Retail Price: $17 – $18.50

5 | Values
† $62
🍃 $60
🎏 $56
🔺 $52
♦ $47
UM $70

Joy To The World
#E2343
Issued: 1982 • Susp.: 1988
Retail Price: $9 – $12.50

6 | Values
† $52
🍃 $50
🎏 $47
🔺 $45

Joy To The World
#E5388
Issued: 1984 • Retired: 1987
Retail Price: $10 – $11

7 | Values
△ $25
♡ $22
† $20
68 $20
★ $20

Joy To The World
#150320
Issued: 1995 • Open
Retail Price: $20

8 | Values
♡ $23
† $20
68 $20
★ $20

Joy To The World
#153338
Issued: 1996 • Open
Retail Price: $20

9 | Values
† $20
68 $20
★ $20

Joy To The World
#272566
Issued: 1997 • Open
Retail Price: $20

10 | Values
🍃 $60
† $52
🍃 $47
🎏 $38

Let Heaven And Nature Sing
#E0532
Issued: 1983 • Retired: 1986
Retail Price: $9 – $10

GENERAL ORNAMENTS

	Price Paid	Value Of My Collection
1.		
2.		
3.		
4.		
5.		
6.		
7.		
8.		
9.		
10.		

PENCIL TOTALS

ORNAMENTS

KEY: NM *Pre-1981* ▲1981 ▯1982 ◄1983 †1984 🍃1985 🎏1986 ▲1987 ♦1988 Đ1989 ★1990 ♦1991 ♦1992 ♀1993 ◄1994 △1995 ♡1996 †1997 681998 ★1999 UM *Unmarked*

161

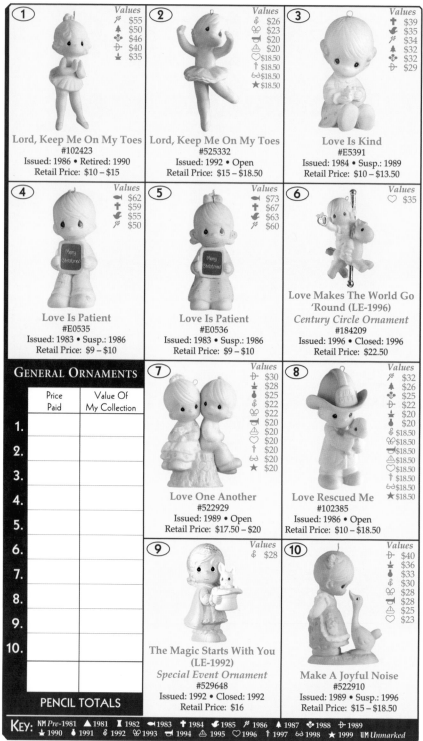

1 — Values
- ♫ $55
- ▲ $50
- ⚓ $46
- Đ $40
- ⚖ $35

Lord, Keep Me On My Toes
#102423
Issued: 1986 • Retired: 1990
Retail Price: $10 – $15

2 — Values
- ♣ $26
- ♀♀ $23
- ⬛ $20
- △ $20
- ♡ $18.50
- † $18.50
- ೮೩ $18.50
- ★ $18.50

Lord, Keep Me On My Toes
#525332
Issued: 1992 • Open
Retail Price: $15 – $18.50

3 — Values
- † $39
- ✺ $35
- ♫ $34
- ▲ $32
- ⚓ $32
- Đ $29

Love Is Kind
#E5391
Issued: 1984 • Susp.: 1989
Retail Price: $10 – $13.50

4 — Values
- ⚓ $62
- † $59
- ✺ $55
- ♫ $50

Love Is Patient
#E0535
Issued: 1983 • Susp.: 1986
Retail Price: $9 – $10

5 — Values
- ⚓ $73
- † $67
- ✺ $63
- ♫ $60

Love Is Patient
#E0536
Issued: 1983 • Susp.: 1986
Retail Price: $9 – $10

6 — Values
- ♡ $35

Love Makes The World Go 'Round (LE-1996)
Century Circle Ornament
#184209
Issued: 1996 • Closed: 1996
Retail Price: $22.50

GENERAL ORNAMENTS

	Price Paid	Value Of My Collection
1.		
2.		
3.		
4.		
5.		
6.		
7.		
8.		
9.		
10.		
PENCIL TOTALS		

7 — Values
- Đ $30
- ⚖ $28
- ♣ $25
- ♣ $22
- ♀♀ $22
- ⬛ $20
- △ $20
- ♡ $20
- † $20
- ೮೩ $20
- ★ $20

Love One Another
#522929
Issued: 1989 • Open
Retail Price: $17.50 – $20

8 — Values
- ♫ $32
- ▲ $26
- ⚓ $25
- ♣ $22
- ⚖ $20
- ♣ $20
- ♣ $18.50
- ♀♀ $18.50
- ⬛ $18.50
- △ $18.50
- ♡ $18.50
- † $18.50
- ೮೩ $18.50
- ★ $18.50

Love Rescued Me
#102385
Issued: 1986 • Open
Retail Price: $10 – $18.50

9 — Values
- ♣ $28

The Magic Starts With You (LE-1992)
Special Event Ornament
#529648
Issued: 1992 • Closed: 1992
Retail Price: $16

10 — Values
- Đ $40
- ⚖ $36
- ♣ $33
- ♣ $30
- ♀♀ $28
- ⬛ $28
- △ $25
- ♡ $23

Make A Joyful Noise
#522910
Issued: 1989 • Susp.: 1996
Retail Price: $15 – $18.50

KEY: NM *Pre-1981* ▲ 1981 ✗ 1982 ◀ 1983 † 1984 ✺ 1985 ♫ 1986 ▲ 1987 ⚓ 1988 Đ 1989 ⚖ 1990 ♣ 1991 ♣ 1992 ♀♀ 1993 ⬛ 1994 △ 1995 ♡ 1996 † 1997 ೮೩ 1998 ★ 1999 **UM** *Unmarked*

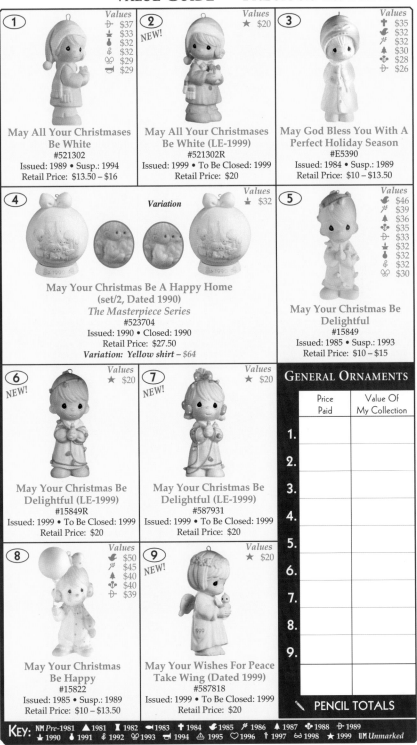

1

Values
- ♫ $37
- ♨ $33
- $32
- ⚖ $32
- ❀ $29
- ⊐ $29

May All Your Christmases Be White
#521302
Issued: 1989 • Susp.: 1994
Retail Price: $13.50 – $16

2 NEW!

Values
- ★ $20

May All Your Christmases Be White (LE-1999)
#521302R
Issued: 1999 • To Be Closed: 1999
Retail Price: $20

3

Values
- ✝ $35
- ✿ $32
- ⅉ $32
- ⚓ $30
- ⬥ $28
- Ð $26

May God Bless You With A Perfect Holiday Season
#E5390
Issued: 1984 • Susp.: 1989
Retail Price: $10 – $13.50

4

Variation

Values
- ★ $32

May Your Christmas Be A Happy Home
(set/2, Dated 1990)
The Masterpiece Series
#523704
Issued: 1990 • Closed: 1990
Retail Price: $27.50
Variation: Yellow shirt – $64

5

Values
- ✿ $46
- ⅉ $39
- ⚓ $36
- ⬥ $35
- Ð $33
- ★ $32
- ● $32
- ⚖ $32
- ❀ $30

May Your Christmas Be Delightful
#15849
Issued: 1985 • Susp.: 1993
Retail Price: $10 – $15

6 NEW!

Values
- ★ $20

May Your Christmas Be Delightful (LE-1999)
#15849R
Issued: 1999 • To Be Closed: 1999
Retail Price: $20

7 NEW!

Values
- ★ $20

May Your Christmas Be Delightful (LE-1999)
#587931
Issued: 1999 • To Be Closed: 1999
Retail Price: $20

8

Values
- ✿ $50
- ⅉ $45
- ⚓ $40
- ⬥ $40
- Ð $39

May Your Christmas Be Happy
#15822
Issued: 1985 • Susp.: 1989
Retail Price: $10 – $13.50

9 NEW!

Values
- ★ $20

May Your Wishes For Peace Take Wing (Dated 1999)
#587818
Issued: 1999 • To Be Closed: 1999
Retail Price: $20

GENERAL ORNAMENTS

	Price Paid	Value Of My Collection
1.		
2.		
3.		
4.		
5.		
6.		
7.		
8.		
9.		

PENCIL TOTALS

ORNAMENTS

KEY: NM *Pre-1981* ▲ 1981 Ⅰ 1982 ◀1983 ✝ 1984 ✿ 1985 ⅉ 1986 ⚓ 1987 ⬥ 1988 Ð 1989 ★ 1990 ● 1991 ⚖ 1992 ❀ 1993 ⊐ 1994 △ 1995 ♡ 1996 ✝ 1997 ⅋ 1998 ★ 1999 UM *Unmarked*

163

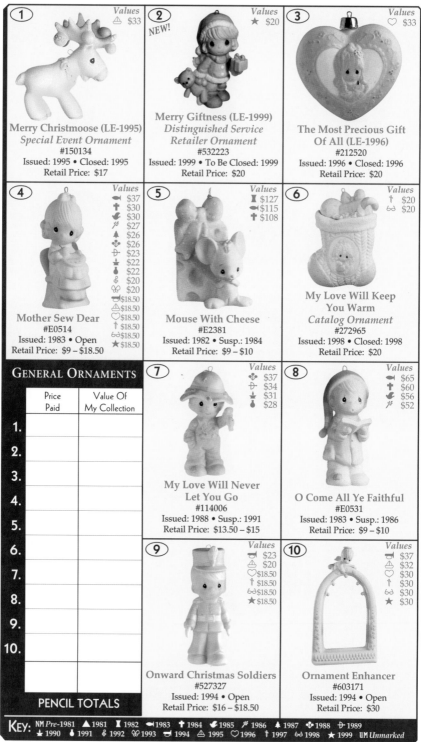

1
Values ⚠ $33

Merry Christmoose (LE-1995)
Special Event Ornament
#150134
Issued: 1995 • Closed: 1995
Retail Price: $17

2 NEW!
Values ★ $20

Merry Giftness (LE-1999)
*Distinguished Service
Retailer Ornament*
#532223
Issued: 1999 • To Be Closed: 1999
Retail Price: $20

3
Values ♡ $33

**The Most Precious Gift
Of All (LE-1996)**
#212520
Issued: 1996 • Closed: 1996
Retail Price: $20

4
Values
➳ $37
✝ $30
✿ $30
♪ $27
▲ $26
⚓ $26
Ð $23
★ $22
◊ $22
§ $20
♋ $20
🛷 $18.50
⚠ $18.50
♡ $18.50
✝ $18.50
6Ə $18.50
★ $18.50

Mother Sew Dear
#E0514
Issued: 1983 • Open
Retail Price: $9 – $18.50

5
Values
Ⅱ $127
➳ $115
✝ $108

Mouse With Cheese
#E2381
Issued: 1982 • Susp.: 1984
Retail Price: $9 – $10

6
Values
✝ $20
6Ə $20

**My Love Will Keep
You Warm**
Catalog Ornament
#272965
Issued: 1998 • Closed: 1998
Retail Price: $20

GENERAL ORNAMENTS

	Price Paid	Value Of My Collection
1.		
2.		
3.		
4.		
5.		
6.		
7.		
8.		
9.		
10.		
PENCIL TOTALS		

7
Values
🛷 $37
Ð $34
★ $31
◊ $28

**My Love Will Never
Let You Go**
#114006
Issued: 1988 • Susp.: 1991
Retail Price: $13.50 – $15

8
Values
✝ $65
✝ $60
✿ $56
♪ $52

O Come All Ye Faithful
#E0531
Issued: 1983 • Susp.: 1986
Retail Price: $9 – $10

9
Values
➳ $23
⚠ $20
♡ $18.50
✝ $18.50
6Ə $18.50
★ $18.50

Onward Christmas Soldiers
#527327
Issued: 1994 • Open
Retail Price: $16 – $18.50

10
Values
➳ $37
⚠ $32
♡ $30
✝ $30
6Ə $30
★ $30

Ornament Enhancer
#603171
Issued: 1994 • Open
Retail Price: $30

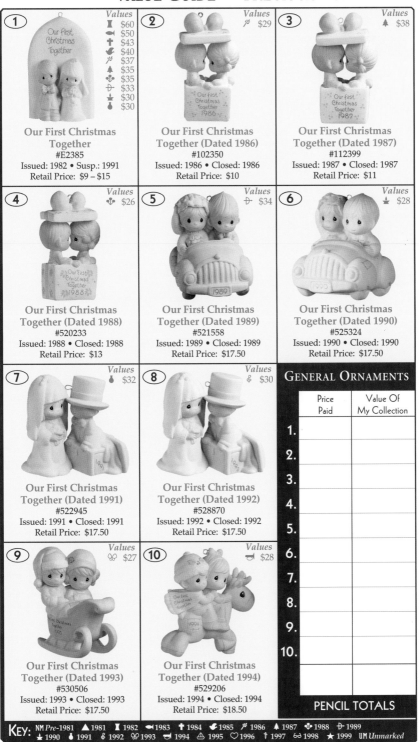

1

Values

⚷	$60
	$50
✝	$43
⚒	$40
♫	$37
▲	$35
⚓	$35
⊹	$33
✦	$30
⚮	$30

Our First Christmas Together
#E2385
Issued: 1982 • Susp.: 1991
Retail Price: $9 – $15

2

Values
♫ $29

Our First Christmas Together (Dated 1986)
#102350
Issued: 1986 • Closed: 1986
Retail Price: $10

3

Values
▲ $38

Our First Christmas Together (Dated 1987)
#112399
Issued: 1987 • Closed: 1987
Retail Price: $11

4

Values
⊹ $26

Our First Christmas Together (Dated 1988)
#520233
Issued: 1988 • Closed: 1988
Retail Price: $13

5

Values
⋺ $34

Our First Christmas Together (Dated 1989)
#521558
Issued: 1989 • Closed: 1989
Retail Price: $17.50

6

Values
✦ $28

Our First Christmas Together (Dated 1990)
#525324
Issued: 1990 • Closed: 1990
Retail Price: $17.50

7

Values
⚮ $32

Our First Christmas Together (Dated 1991)
#522945
Issued: 1991 • Closed: 1991
Retail Price: $17.50

8

Values
⚶ $30

Our First Christmas Together (Dated 1992)
#528870
Issued: 1992 • Closed: 1992
Retail Price: $17.50

9

Values
⚭ $27

Our First Christmas Together (Dated 1993)
#530506
Issued: 1993 • Closed: 1993
Retail Price: $17.50

10

Values
⊲ $28

Our First Christmas Together (Dated 1994)
#529206
Issued: 1994 • Closed: 1994
Retail Price: $18.50

GENERAL ORNAMENTS

	Price Paid	Value Of My Collection
1.		
2.		
3.		
4.		
5.		
6.		
7.		
8.		
9.		
10.		
PENCIL TOTALS		

ORNAMENTS

KEY: NM *Pre-1981* ▲ 1981 ⚷ 1982 ◄ 1983 ✝ 1984 ⚒ 1985 ♫ 1986 ▲ 1987 ⊹ 1988 ⋺ 1989 ✦ 1990 ⚮ 1991 ⚶ 1992 ⚭ 1993 ⊲ 1994 △ 1995 ♡ 1996 ✝ 1997 ☍ 1998 ★ 1999 UM *Unmarked*

165

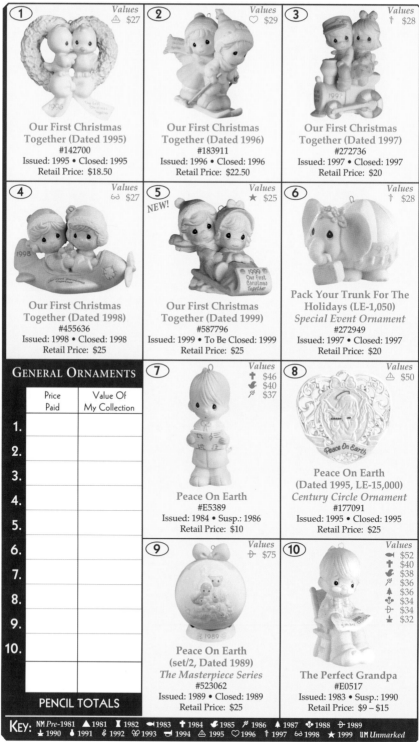

1 Values ⚠ $27

Our First Christmas
Together (Dated 1995)
#142700
Issued: 1995 • Closed: 1995
Retail Price: $18.50

2 Values ♡ $29

Our First Christmas
Together (Dated 1996)
#183911
Issued: 1996 • Closed: 1996
Retail Price: $22.50

3 Values ✝ $28

Our First Christmas
Together (Dated 1997)
#272736
Issued: 1997 • Closed: 1997
Retail Price: $20

4 Values 6ð $27

Our First Christmas
Together (Dated 1998)
#455636
Issued: 1998 • Closed: 1998
Retail Price: $25

5 NEW! Values ★ $25

Our First Christmas
Together (Dated 1999)
#587796
Issued: 1999 • To Be Closed: 1999
Retail Price: $25

6 Values ✝ $28

Pack Your Trunk For The
Holidays (LE-1,050)
Special Event Ornament
#272949
Issued: 1997 • Closed: 1997
Retail Price: $20

GENERAL ORNAMENTS

	Price Paid	Value Of My Collection
1.		
2.		
3.		
4.		
5.		
6.		
7.		
8.		
9.		
10.		
PENCIL TOTALS		

7 Values ✝ $46 🐦 $40 ≯ $37

Peace On Earth
#E5389
Issued: 1984 • Susp.: 1986
Retail Price: $10

8 Values ⚠ $50

Peace On Earth
(Dated 1995, LE-15,000)
Century Circle Ornament
#177091
Issued: 1995 • Closed: 1995
Retail Price: $25

9 Values Ð $75

Peace On Earth
(set/2, Dated 1989)
The Masterpiece Series
#523062
Issued: 1989 • Closed: 1989
Retail Price: $25

10 Values 🐟 $52 ✝ $40 🍃 $38 ≯ $36 ▲ $36 ⚓ $34 Ð $34 ★ $32

The Perfect Grandpa
#E0517
Issued: 1983 • Susp.: 1990
Retail Price: $9 – $15

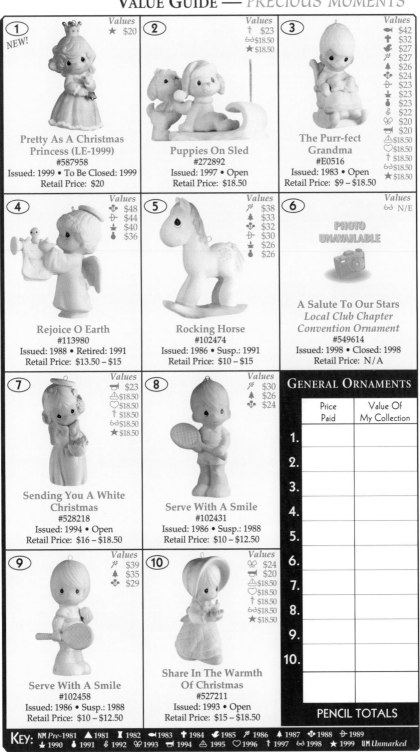

① NEW!

Pretty As A Christmas Princess (LE-1999)
#587958
Issued: 1999 • To Be Closed: 1999
Retail Price: $20

Values
★ $20

②

Puppies On Sled
#272892
Issued: 1997 • Open
Retail Price: $18.50

Values
✝ $23
👓 $18.50
★ $18.50

③

The Purr-fect Grandma
#E0516
Issued: 1983 • Open
Retail Price: $9 – $18.50

Values
🐟 $42
✝ $32
🦋 $27
♫ $27
▲ $26
✠ $24
⊕ $23
★ $23
⚬ $23
⚫ $22
♧ $20
🛒 $20
△ $18.50
♡ $18.50
✝ $18.50
👓 $18.50
★ $18.50

④

Rejoice O Earth
#113980
Issued: 1988 • Retired: 1991
Retail Price: $13.50 – $15

Values
✠ $48
⊕ $44
★ $40
⚬ $36

⑤

Rocking Horse
#102474
Issued: 1986 • Susp.: 1991
Retail Price: $10 – $15

Values
♫ $38
▲ $33
✠ $32
⊕ $30
★ $26
⚬ $26

⑥

PHOTO UNAVAILABLE

A Salute To Our Stars
Local Club Chapter Convention Ornament
#549614
Issued: 1998 • Closed: 1998
Retail Price: N/A

Values
👓 N/E

⑦

Sending You A White Christmas
#528218
Issued: 1994 • Open
Retail Price: $16 – $18.50

Values
🛒 $23
△ $18.50
♡ $18.50
✝ $18.50
👓 $18.50
★ $18.50

⑧

Serve With A Smile
#102431
Issued: 1986 • Susp.: 1988
Retail Price: $10 – $12.50

Values
♫ $30
▲ $26
✠ $24

GENERAL ORNAMENTS

	Price Paid	Value Of My Collection
1.		
2.		
3.		
4.		
5.		
6.		
7.		
8.		
9.		
10.		
PENCIL TOTALS		

⑨

Serve With A Smile
#102458
Issued: 1986 • Susp.: 1988
Retail Price: $10 – $12.50

Values
♫ $39
▲ $35
✠ $29

⑩

Share In The Warmth Of Christmas
#527211
Issued: 1993 • Open
Retail Price: $15 – $18.50

Values
♧ $24
🛒 $20
△ $18.50
♡ $18.50
✝ $18.50
👓 $18.50
★ $18.50

ORNAMENTS

KEY: NM *Pre-1981* ▲ 1981 Ⅰ 1982 ◄1983 ✝ 1984 ✦ 1985 ♫ 1986 ▲ 1987 ✠ 1988 ⊕ 1989 ★ 1990 ⚬ 1991 ♧ 1992 ♋ 1993 🛒 1994 △ 1995 ♡ 1996 ✝ 1997 👓 1998 ★ 1999 UM *Unmarked*

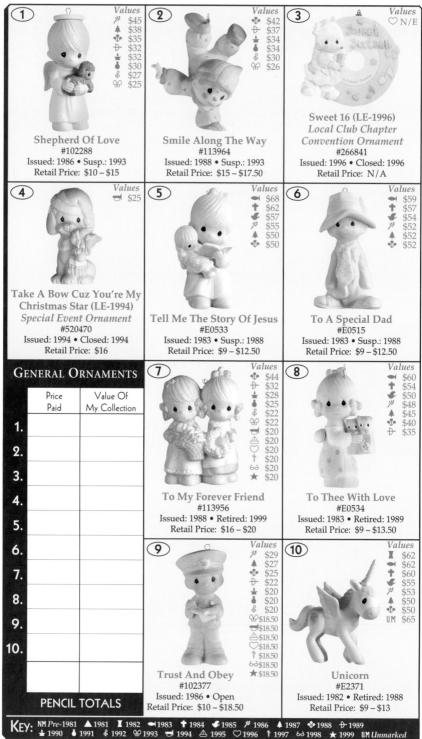

1 Values
- 🌿 $45
- ♣ $38
- ⚘ $35
- ⟊ $32
- ⚓ $32
- ✹ $32
- 🍍 $30
- 🔔 $27
- 🎀 $25

Shepherd Of Love
#102288
Issued: 1986 • Susp.: 1993
Retail Price: $10 – $15

2 Values
- ⚘ $42
- ⟊ $37
- ⚓ $34
- 🍍 $34
- 🔔 $30
- 🎀 $26

Smile Along The Way
#113964
Issued: 1988 • Susp.: 1993
Retail Price: $15 – $17.50

3 Values
- ♡ N/E

Sweet 16 (LE-1996)
Local Club Chapter Convention Ornament
#266841
Issued: 1996 • Closed: 1996
Retail Price: N/A

4 Values
- 🥣 $25

Take A Bow Cuz You're My Christmas Star (LE-1994)
Special Event Ornament
#520470
Issued: 1994 • Closed: 1994
Retail Price: $16

5 Values
- 🐚 $68
- ✝ $62
- ✦ $57
- 🌿 $55
- ♣ $50
- ⚓ $50

Tell Me The Story Of Jesus
#E0533
Issued: 1983 • Susp.: 1988
Retail Price: $9 – $12.50

6 Values
- 🐚 $59
- ✝ $57
- ✦ $54
- 🌿 $52
- ♣ $52
- ⚓ $52

To A Special Dad
#E0515
Issued: 1983 • Susp.: 1988
Retail Price: $9 – $12.50

General Ornaments

	Price Paid	Value Of My Collection
1.		
2.		
3.		
4.		
5.		
6.		
7.		
8.		
9.		
10.		
PENCIL TOTALS		

7 Values
- ⚘ $44
- ⟊ $32
- ⚓ $28
- 🍍 $25
- 🔔 $22
- 🎀 $22
- 🥣 $20
- △ $20
- ♡ $20
- ✝ $20
- 🔭 $20
- ★ $20

To My Forever Friend
#113956
Issued: 1988 • Retired: 1999
Retail Price: $16 – $20

8 Values
- 🐚 $60
- ✝ $54
- ✦ $50
- 🌿 $48
- ♣ $45
- ⚓ $40
- ⟊ $35

To Thee With Love
#E0534
Issued: 1983 • Retired: 1989
Retail Price: $9 – $13.50

9 Values
- 🌿 $29
- ♣ $27
- ⚘ $25
- ⟊ $22
- ⚓ $20
- 🍍 $20
- 🔔 $20
- 🎀 $18.50
- 🥣 $18.50
- △ $18.50
- ♡ $18.50
- ✝ $18.50
- 🔭 $18.50
- ★ $18.50

Trust And Obey
#102377
Issued: 1986 • Open
Retail Price: $10 – $18.50

10 Values
- I $62
- 🐚 $62
- ✦ $60
- ♣ $55
- 🌿 $53
- ♣ $50
- ⚓ $50
- UM $65

Unicorn
#E2371
Issued: 1982 • Retired: 1988
Retail Price: $9 – $13

Key: NM *Pre-1981* ▲1981 I 1982 🐚1983 ✝ 1984 ✦1985 🌿 1986 ♣ 1987 ⚘1988 ⟊1989
★ 1990 🍍 1991 🔔 1992 🎀1993 🥣 1994 △ 1995 ♡1996 ✝ 1997 🔭 1998 ★ 1999 UM *Unmarked*

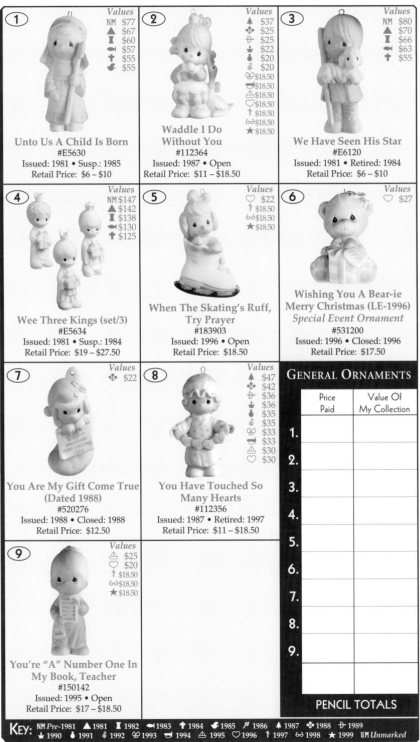

① Unto Us A Child Is Born
#E5630
Issued: 1981 • Susp.: 1985
Retail Price: $6 – $10

Values
NM $77
▲ $67
✕ $60
◄ $57
✝ $55
✦ $55

② Waddle I Do Without You
#112364
Issued: 1987 • Open
Retail Price: $11 – $18.50

Values
▲ $37
✦ $25
♭ $25
★ $22
🌡 $20
🔔 $20
❀ $18.50
🥨 $18.50
△ $18.50
♡ $18.50
✝ $18.50
🕶 $18.50
★ $18.50

③ We Have Seen His Star
#E6120
Issued: 1981 • Retired: 1984
Retail Price: $6 – $10

Values
NM $80
▲ $70
✕ $66
◄ $63
✝ $55

④ Wee Three Kings (set/3)
#E5634
Issued: 1981 • Susp.: 1984
Retail Price: $19 – $27.50

Values
NM $147
▲ $142
✕ $138
◄ $130
✝ $125

⑤ When The Skating's Ruff, Try Prayer
#183903
Issued: 1996 • Open
Retail Price: $18.50

Values
♡ $22
✝ $18.50
🕶 $18.50
★ $18.50

⑥ Wishing You A Bear-ie Merry Christmas (LE-1996)
Special Event Ornament
#531200
Issued: 1996 • Closed: 1996
Retail Price: $17.50

Values
♡ $27

⑦ You Are My Gift Come True (Dated 1988)
#520276
Issued: 1988 • Closed: 1988
Retail Price: $12.50

Values
✦ $22

⑧ You Have Touched So Many Hearts
#112356
Issued: 1987 • Retired: 1997
Retail Price: $11 – $18.50

Values
▲ $47
✦ $42
♭ $36
★ $36
🌡 $35
🔔 $35
❀ $33
🥨 $33
△ $30
♡ $30

⑨ You're "A" Number One In My Book, Teacher
#150142
Issued: 1995 • Open
Retail Price: $17 – $18.50

Values
△ $25
♡ $20
✝ $18.50
🕶 $18.50
★ $18.50

GENERAL ORNAMENTS

	Price Paid	Value Of My Collection
1.		
2.		
3.		
4.		
5.		
6.		
7.		
8.		
9.		
PENCIL TOTALS		

ORNAMENTS

OTHER PRECIOUS MOMENTS COLLECTIBLES

The PRECIOUS MOMENTS line includes a variety of products to complement the figurine and ornament collections, including plates, picture frames and musicals, plus candle climbers, medallions and jack-in-the-boxes. New categories for 1999 include die-cast metal (one truck was introduced in 1998) and hinged boxes (one as a club gift). This year, only one annual plate has been added to the collection. Of the over 200 accessories produced, only 22 are current.

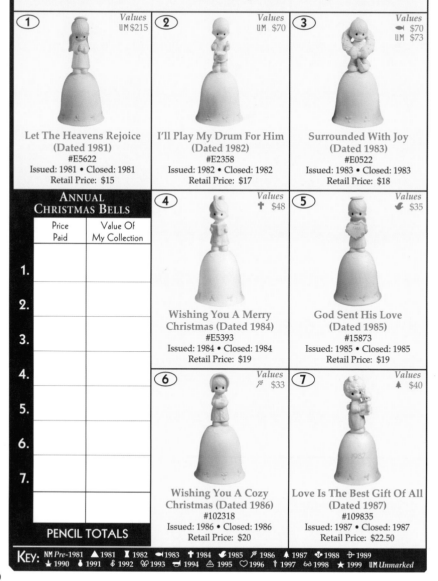

(1) Values UM $215

Let The Heavens Rejoice
(Dated 1981)
#E5622
Issued: 1981 • Closed: 1981
Retail Price: $15

(2) Values UM $70

I'll Play My Drum For Him
(Dated 1982)
#E2358
Issued: 1982 • Closed: 1982
Retail Price: $17

(3) Values ➤ $70 UM $73

Surrounded With Joy
(Dated 1983)
#E0522
Issued: 1983 • Closed: 1983
Retail Price: $18

ANNUAL CHRISTMAS BELLS

	Price Paid	Value Of My Collection
1.		
2.		
3.		
4.		
5.		
6.		
7.		
PENCIL TOTALS		

(4) Values † $48

Wishing You A Merry Christmas (Dated 1984)
#E5393
Issued: 1984 • Closed: 1984
Retail Price: $19

(5) Values 🍃 $35

God Sent His Love
(Dated 1985)
#15873
Issued: 1985 • Closed: 1985
Retail Price: $19

(6) Values ⌀ $33

Wishing You A Cozy Christmas (Dated 1986)
#102318
Issued: 1986 • Closed: 1986
Retail Price: $20

(7) Values ♠ $40

Love Is The Best Gift Of All
(Dated 1987)
#109835
Issued: 1987 • Closed: 1987
Retail Price: $22.50

KEY: NM *Pre-1981* ▲ 1981 ✗ 1982 ◄ 1983 † 1984 🍃 1985 ⌀ 1986 ♠ 1987 ✤ 1988 ⌀ 1989 ★ 1990 🍶 1991 ♪ 1992 ⚭ 1993 ⊟ 1994 △ 1995 ♡ 1996 † 1997 ᎲᎬ 1998 ★ 1999 UM *Unmarked*

170

1 *Values* ✣ $37

Time To Wish You A Merry Christmas (Dated 1988)
#115304
Issued: 1988 • Closed: 1988
Retail Price: $25

2 *Values* Ð $38

Oh Holy Night (Dated 1989)
#522821
Issued: 1989 • Closed: 1989
Retail Price: $25

3 *Values* ★ $38

Once Upon A Holy Night (Dated 1990)
#523828
Issued: 1990 • Closed: 1990
Retail Price: $25

4 *Values* ♦ $40

May Your Christmas Be Merry (Dated 1991)
#524182
Issued: 1991 • Closed: 1991
Retail Price: $25

5 *Values* ♪ $36

But The Greatest Of These Is Love (Dated 1992)
#527726
Issued: 1992 • Closed: 1992
Retail Price: $25

6 *Values* ♀ $35

Wishing You The Sweetest Christmas (Dated 1993)
#530174
Issued: 1993 • Closed: 1993
Retail Price: $25

7 *Values* ➹ $34

You're As Pretty As A Christmas Tree (Dated 1994)
#604216
Issued: 1994 • Closed: 1994
Retail Price: $27.50

8 *Values* † $47 UM $49

God Understands
#E5211
Issued: 1981 • Retired: 1984
Retail Price: $15 – $19

9 *Values* † $52 UM $65

Jesus Is Born
#E5623
Issued: 1981 • Susp.: 1984
Retail Price: $15 – $19

10 *Values* † $50 ✦ $47 UM $60

Jesus Loves Me
#E5208
Issued: 1981 • Susp.: 1985
Retail Price: $15 – $19

ANNUAL CHRISTMAS BELLS

	Price Paid	Value Of My Collection
1.		
2.		
3.		
4.		
5.		
6.		
7.		

GENERAL BELLS

8.		
9.		
10.		

PENCIL TOTALS

BELLS

KEY: NM *Pre-1981* ▲ 1981 ✕ 1982 ◀ 1983 † 1984 ✦ 1985 ♪ 1986 ♠ 1987 ✣ 1988 Ð 1989 ★ 1990 ♦ 1991 ♪ 1992 ♀ 1993 ➹ 1994 △ 1995 ♡ 1996 † 1997 ଌ 1998 ★ 1999 UM *Unmarked*

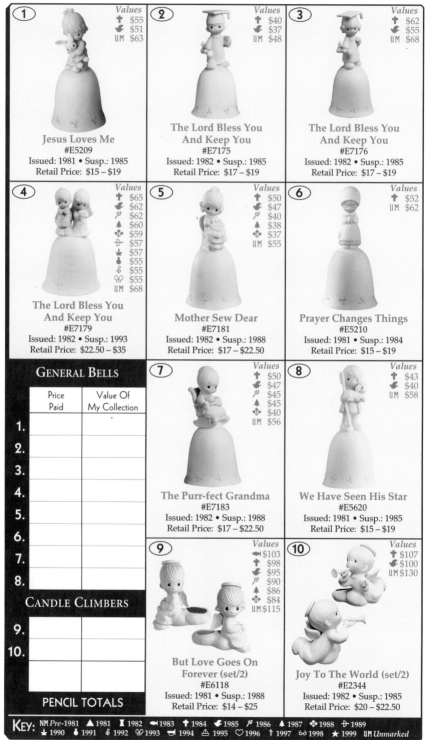

(1)
Values
✝ $55
🕊 $51
UM $63

Jesus Loves Me
#E5209
Issued: 1981 • Susp.: 1985
Retail Price: $15 – $19

(2)
Values
✝ $40
🕊 $37
UM $48

The Lord Bless You And Keep You
#E7175
Issued: 1982 • Susp.: 1985
Retail Price: $17 – $19

(3)
Values
✝ $62
🕊 $55
UM $68

The Lord Bless You And Keep You
#E7176
Issued: 1982 • Susp.: 1985
Retail Price: $17 – $19

(4)
Values
✝ $65
🕊 $62
𝄞 $62
▲ $60
⚓ $59
☸ $57
★ $57
🔔 $55
§ $55
∞ $55
UM $68

The Lord Bless You And Keep You
#E7179
Issued: 1982 • Susp.: 1993
Retail Price: $22.50 – $35

(5)
Values
✝ $50
🕊 $47
𝄞 $40
▲ $38
⚓ $37
UM $55

Mother Sew Dear
#E7181
Issued: 1982 • Susp.: 1988
Retail Price: $17 – $22.50

(6)
Values
✝ $52
UM $62

Prayer Changes Things
#E5210
Issued: 1981 • Susp.: 1984
Retail Price: $15 – $19

GENERAL BELLS

	Price Paid	Value Of My Collection
1.		
2.		
3.		
4.		
5.		
6.		
7.		
8.		

CANDLE CLIMBERS

9.		
10.		

PENCIL TOTALS

(7)
Values
✝ $50
🕊 $47
𝄞 $45
▲ $45
⚓ $40
UM $56

The Purr-fect Grandma
#E7183
Issued: 1982 • Susp.: 1988
Retail Price: $17 – $22.50

(8)
Values
✝ $43
🕊 $40
UM $58

We Have Seen His Star
#E5620
Issued: 1981 • Susp.: 1985
Retail Price: $15 – $19

(9)
Values
◀ $103
✝ $98
🕊 $95
𝄞 $90
▲ $86
⚓ $84
UM $115

But Love Goes On Forever (set/2)
#E6118
Issued: 1981 • Susp.: 1988
Retail Price: $14 – $25

(10)
Values
✝ $107
🕊 $100
UM $130

Joy To The World (set/2)
#E2344
Issued: 1982 • Susp.: 1985
Retail Price: $20 – $22.50

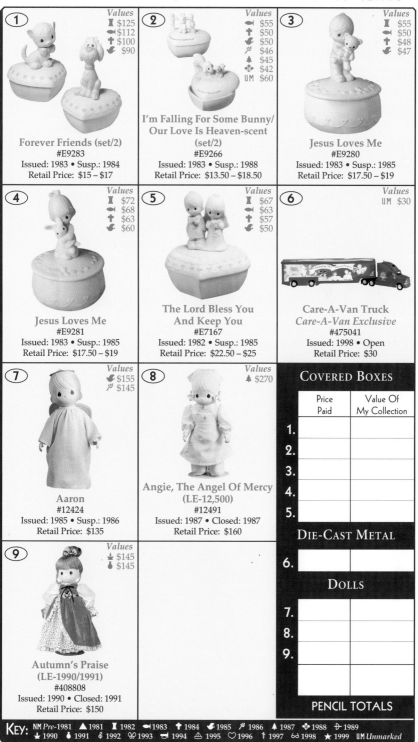

1 Values
- ⚷ $125
- ◀ $112
- ✝ $100
- 🐌 $90

Forever Friends (set/2)
#E9283
Issued: 1983 • Susp.: 1984
Retail Price: $15 – $17

2 Values
- 🐟 $55
- ✝ $50
- 🐌 $50
- ♫ $46
- ⚓ $45
- ⚓ $42
- UM $60

**I'm Falling For Some Bunny/
Our Love Is Heaven-scent
(set/2)**
#E9266
Issued: 1983 • Susp.: 1988
Retail Price: $13.50 – $18.50

3 Values
- ⚷ $55
- ◀ $50
- 🐌 $48
- 🐌 $47

Jesus Loves Me
#E9280
Issued: 1983 • Susp.: 1985
Retail Price: $17.50 – $19

4 Values
- ⚷ $72
- ◀ $68
- ✝ $63
- 🐌 $60

Jesus Loves Me
#E9281
Issued: 1983 • Susp.: 1985
Retail Price: $17.50 – $19

5 Values
- ⚷ $67
- ◀ $63
- ✝ $57
- 🐌 $50

**The Lord Bless You
And Keep You**
#E7167
Issued: 1982 • Susp.: 1985
Retail Price: $22.50 – $25

6 Values
- UM $30

Care-A-Van Truck
Care-A-Van Exclusive
#475041
Issued: 1998 • Open
Retail Price: $30

7 Values
- 🐌 $155
- ♫ $145

Aaron
#12424
Issued: 1985 • Susp.: 1986
Retail Price: $135

8 Values
- ⚓ $270

**Angie, The Angel Of Mercy
(LE-12,500)**
#12491
Issued: 1987 • Closed: 1987
Retail Price: $160

9 Values
- ⚓ $145
- 🕯 $145

**Autumn's Praise
(LE-1990/1991)**
#408808
Issued: 1990 • Closed: 1991
Retail Price: $150

COVERED BOXES

	Price Paid	Value Of My Collection
1.		
2.		
3.		
4.		
5.		

DIE-CAST METAL

6.		

DOLLS

7.		
8.		
9.		

PENCIL TOTALS

BELLS

KEY: NM *Pre-1981* ▲1981 ⚷ 1982 ◀1983 ✝ 1984 🐌1985 ♫ 1986 ⚓ 1987 🐌1988 🕀 1989 ★ 1990 🕯 1991 🔔 1992 ❀1993 🦃 1994 △ 1995 ♡1996 ✝ 1997 🔆1998 ★ 1999 UM *Unmarked*

1 Values
🐦 $155
♪ $145

Bethany
#12432
Issued: 1985 • Susp.: 1986
Retail Price: $135

2 Values
♪ $275

Bong Bong (LE-12,000)
#100455
Issued: 1986 • Closed: 1986
Retail Price: $150

3 Values
♪ $285

Candy (LE-12,000)
#100463
Issued: 1986 • Closed: 1986
Retail Price: $150

4 Values
♪ $250

Connie (LE-7,500)
#102253
Issued: 1986 • Closed: 1986
Retail Price: $160

5 Values
UM $480

Cubby (LE-5,000)
#E7267B
Issued: 1982 • Closed: 1982
Retail Price: $200

6 Values
🐦 $230
✝ $225
🐦 $220
UM $260

Debbie
#E6214G
Issued: 1981 • Susp.: 1985
Retail Price: $175 – $200

DOLLS

	Price Paid	Value Of My Collection
1.		
2.		
3.		
4.		
5.		
6.		
7.		
8.		
9.		
10.		

PENCIL TOTALS

7 Values
🕯 $75
🕯 $68
♧ $65
♀ $65
🍜 $65

The Eyes Of The Lord Are Upon You
♪ *"Brahms' Lullaby"*
#429570
Issued: 1991 • Susp.: 1994
Retail Price: $65

8 Values
🕯 $75
🕯 $68
♧ $65
♀ $65
🍜 $65

The Eyes Of The Lord Are Upon You
♪ *"Brahms' Lullaby"*
#429589
Issued: 1991 • Susp.: 1994
Retail Price: $65

9 Values
🐦 $185
✝ $180
🐦 $180
♪ $175
▲ $175
♧ $175
UM $195

Katie Lynne
#E0539
Issued: 1983 • Susp.: 1988
Retail Price: $150 – $175

10 Values
✝ $188
🐦 $180
♪ $175
▲ $175
♧ $170
🕭 $170

Kristy
#E2851
Issued: 1984 • Susp.: 1989
Retail Price: $150 – $170

1 Values
⚓ $155
🔥 $150
🕯 $150

**May You Have An Old
Fashioned Christmas
(LE-1991/1992)**
#417785
Issued: 1991 • Closed: 1992
Retail Price: $150

2 Values
◄ $235
✝ $230
⟋ $220
UM $255

Mikey
#E6214B
Issued: 1981 • Susp.: 1985
Retail Price: $175 – $200

3 Values
✝ $360
⟋ $355
UM $355

Mother Sew Dear
#E2850
Issued: 1984 • Retired: 1985
Retail Price: $350

4 Values
⟋ $80
ℐ $75
UM $85

P.D.
#12475
Issued: 1985 • Susp.: 1986
Retail Price: $50

5 Values
⚓ $140
🔥 $140

Summer's Joy (LE-1990/1991)
#408794
Issued: 1990 • Closed: 1991
Retail Price: $150

6 Values
UM $575

Tammy (LE-5,000)
#E7267G
Issued: 1982 • Closed: 1982
Retail Price: $300

7 Values
✝ $165
⟋ $158
ℐ $155
♠ $155
⚓ $150
Ð $150
⚓ $150
🔥 $150

Timmy
#E5397
Issued: 1984 • Susp.: 1991
Retail Price: $125 – $150

8 Values
◄ $90
ℐ $82
UM $95

Trish
#12483
Issued: 1985 • Susp.: 1986
Retail Price: $50

9 Values
⚓ $145
🔥 $145

**The Voice Of Spring
(LE-1990/1991)**
#408786
Issued: 1990 • Closed: 1991
Retail Price: $150

10 Values
⚓ $140
🔥 $140

Winter's Song (LE-1990/1991)
#408816
Issued: 1990 • Closed: 1991
Retail Price: $150

DOLLS

	Price Paid	Value Of My Collection
1.		
2.		
3.		
4.		
5.		
6.		
7.		
8.		
9.		
10.		
PENCIL TOTALS		

DOLLS

KEY: NM *Pre-1981* ▲1981 ✠1982 ◄1983 ✝1984 ⟋1985 ℐ1986 ♠1987 ⟍1988 Ð1989 ⚓1990 🔥1991 🕯1992 ❀1993 ⟍1994 △1995 ♡1996 ✝1997 ᴂ1998 ★1999 UM *Unmarked*

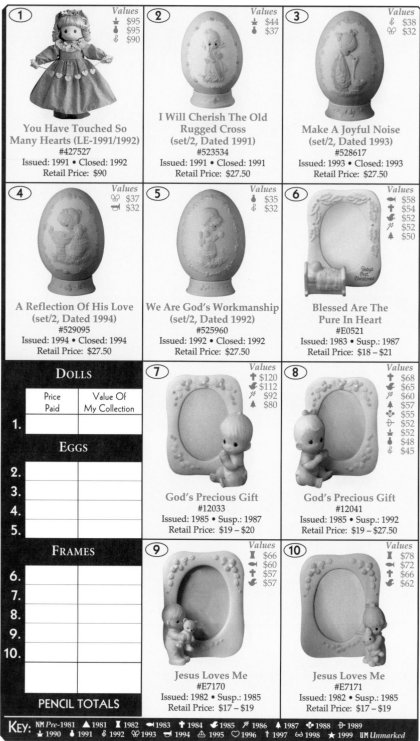

1

Values
★ $95
● $95
✆ $90

**You Have Touched So
Many Hearts (LE-1991/1992)**
#427527
Issued: 1991 • Closed: 1992
Retail Price: $90

2

Values
★ $44
● $37

**I Will Cherish The Old
Rugged Cross
(set/2, Dated 1991)**
#523534
Issued: 1991 • Closed: 1991
Retail Price: $27.50

3

Values
✆ $38
∾ $32

**Make A Joyful Noise
(set/2, Dated 1993)**
#528617
Issued: 1993 • Closed: 1993
Retail Price: $27.50

4

Values
∾ $37
⬅ $32

**A Reflection Of His Love
(set/2, Dated 1994)**
#529095
Issued: 1994 • Closed: 1994
Retail Price: $27.50

5

Values
● $35
✆ $32

**We Are God's Workmanship
(set/2, Dated 1992)**
#525960
Issued: 1992 • Closed: 1992
Retail Price: $27.50

6

Values
✝ $58
✦ $54
✿ $52
♪⁵ $52
▲ $50

**Blessed Are The
Pure In Heart**
#E0521
Issued: 1983 • Susp.: 1987
Retail Price: $18 – $21

DOLLS

	Price Paid	Value Of My Collection
1.		

EGGS

2.		
3.		
4.		
5.		

FRAMES

6.		
7.		
8.		
9.		
10.		

PENCIL TOTALS

7

Values
✝ $120
✦ $112
♪⁵ $92
▲ $80

God's Precious Gift
#12033
Issued: 1985 • Susp.: 1987
Retail Price: $19 – $20

8

Values
✝ $68
✦ $65
♪⁵ $60
▲ $57
✛ $55
Ð $52
● $52
● $48
✆ $45

God's Precious Gift
#12041
Issued: 1985 • Susp.: 1992
Retail Price: $19 – $27.50

9

Values
Ⅱ $66
← $60
✝ $57
✦ $57

Jesus Loves Me
#E7170
Issued: 1982 • Susp.: 1985
Retail Price: $17 – $19

10

Values
Ⅱ $78
← $72
✝ $66
✦ $62

Jesus Loves Me
#E7171
Issued: 1982 • Susp.: 1985
Retail Price: $17 – $19

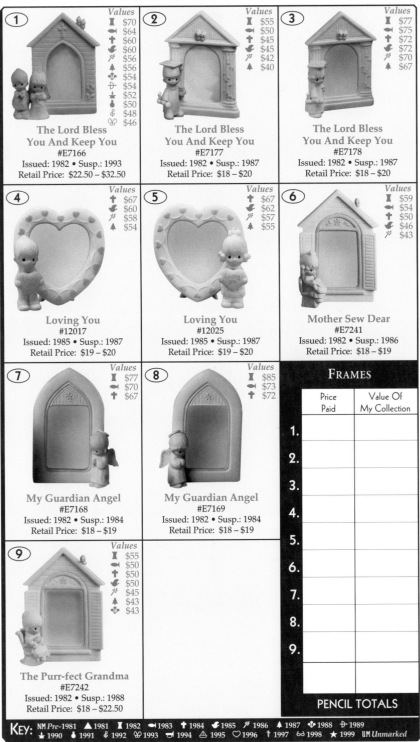

1 Values
- ♂ $70
- ◀ $64
- ✝ $60
- ✿ $60
- ♫ $56
- ♠ $56
- ⚓ $54
- ⅄ $54
- ★ $52
- ♨ $50
- ⚱ $48
- ∞ $46

The Lord Bless You And Keep You
#E7166
Issued: 1982 • Susp.: 1993
Retail Price: $22.50 – $32.50

2 Values
- ♂ $55
- ◀ $50
- ✝ $45
- ✿ $45
- ♫ $42
- ♠ $40

The Lord Bless You And Keep You
#E7177
Issued: 1982 • Susp.: 1987
Retail Price: $18 – $20

3 Values
- ♂ $77
- ◀ $75
- ✝ $72
- ✿ $72
- ♫ $70
- ♠ $67

The Lord Bless You And Keep You
#E7178
Issued: 1982 • Susp.: 1987
Retail Price: $18 – $20

4 Values
- ✝ $67
- ✿ $60
- ♫ $58
- ♠ $54

Loving You
#12017
Issued: 1985 • Susp.: 1987
Retail Price: $19 – $20

5 Values
- ✝ $67
- ✿ $62
- ♫ $57
- ♠ $55

Loving You
#12025
Issued: 1985 • Susp.: 1987
Retail Price: $19 – $20

6 Values
- ♂ $59
- ◀ $54
- ✝ $50
- ✿ $46
- ♫ $43

Mother Sew Dear
#E7241
Issued: 1982 • Susp.: 1986
Retail Price: $18 – $19

7 Values
- ♂ $77
- ◀ $70
- ✝ $67

My Guardian Angel
#E7168
Issued: 1982 • Susp.: 1984
Retail Price: $18 – $19

8 Values
- ♂ $85
- ◀ $73
- ✝ $72

My Guardian Angel
#E7169
Issued: 1982 • Susp.: 1984
Retail Price: $18 – $19

9 Values
- ♂ $55
- ◀ $50
- ✝ $50
- ✿ $50
- ♫ $45
- ♠ $43
- ⚓ $43

The Purr-fect Grandma
#E7242
Issued: 1982 • Susp.: 1988
Retail Price: $18 – $22.50

FRAMES

	Price Paid	Value Of My Collection
1.		
2.		
3.		
4.		
5.		
6.		
7.		
8.		
9.		
PENCIL TOTALS		

FRAMES

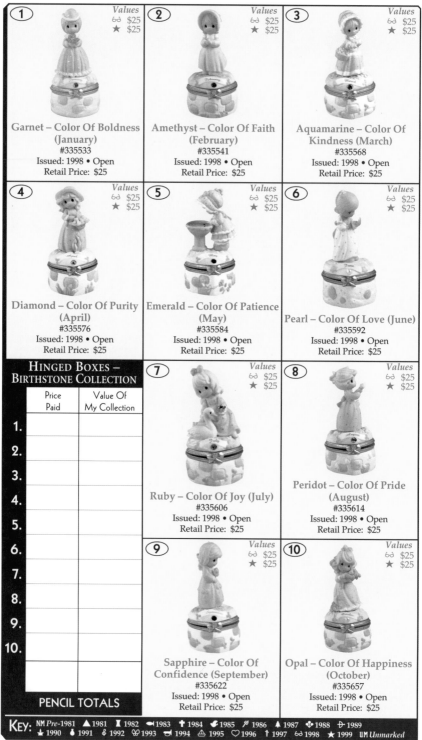

1 — *Values* 👓 $25 ★ $25
Garnet – Color Of Boldness (January)
#335533
Issued: 1998 • Open
Retail Price: $25

2 — *Values* 👓 $25 ★ $25
Amethyst – Color Of Faith (February)
#335541
Issued: 1998 • Open
Retail Price: $25

3 — *Values* 👓 $25 ★ $25
Aquamarine – Color Of Kindness (March)
#335568
Issued: 1998 • Open
Retail Price: $25

4 — *Values* 👓 $25 ★ $25
Diamond – Color Of Purity (April)
#335576
Issued: 1998 • Open
Retail Price: $25

5 — *Values* 👓 $25 ★ $25
Emerald – Color Of Patience (May)
#335584
Issued: 1998 • Open
Retail Price: $25

6 — *Values* 👓 $25 ★ $25
Pearl – Color Of Love (June)
#335592
Issued: 1998 • Open
Retail Price: $25

7 — *Values* 👓 $25 ★ $25
Ruby – Color Of Joy (July)
#335606
Issued: 1998 • Open
Retail Price: $25

8 — *Values* 👓 $25 ★ $25
Peridot – Color Of Pride (August)
#335614
Issued: 1998 • Open
Retail Price: $25

9 — *Values* 👓 $25 ★ $25
Sapphire – Color Of Confidence (September)
#335622
Issued: 1998 • Open
Retail Price: $25

10 — *Values* 👓 $25 ★ $25
Opal – Color Of Happiness (October)
#335657
Issued: 1998 • Open
Retail Price: $25

HINGED BOXES – BIRTHSTONE COLLECTION

	Price Paid	Value Of My Collection
1.		
2.		
3.		
4.		
5.		
6.		
7.		
8.		
9.		
10.		
PENCIL TOTALS		

KEY: NM *Pre-1981* ▲1981 ✗1982 ◄1983 ✝1984 ✦1985 ♪1986 ▲1987 ✿1988 ☊1989 ★1990 🕯1991 ♪1992 ♀1993 ⊟1994 ⚠1995 ♡1996 ✝1997 👓1998 ★1999 UM *Unmarked*

VALUE GUIDE — *PRECIOUS MOMENTS*®

(1)
Values
6ð $25
★ $25

Topaz – Color Of Truth (November)
#335665
Issued: 1998 • Open
Retail Price: $25

(2)
Values
6ð $25
★ $25

Turquoise – Color Of Loyalty (December)
#335673
Issued: 1998 • Open
Retail Price: $25

(3) NEW!
Values
6ð $25
★ $25

His Burden Is Light
#488429
Issued: 1999 • Open
Retail Price: $25

(4) NEW!
Values
6ð $25
★ $25

Jesus Is The Light
#488437
Issued: 1999 • Open
Retail Price: $25

(5) NEW!
Values
6ð $25
★ $25

Jesus Loves Me
#488380
Issued: 1999 • Open
Retail Price: $25

(6) NEW!
Values
6ð $25
★ $25

Jesus Loves Me
#488399
Issued: 1999 • Open
Retail Price: $25

(7) NEW!
Values
6ð $25
★ $25

Love One Another
#488410
Issued: 1999 • Open
Retail Price: $25

(8) NEW!
Values
6ð $25
★ $25

Make A Joyful Noise
#488402
Issued: 1999 • Open
Retail Price: $25

(9)
Values
⚓ $200
🕯 $200

Autumn's Praise (LE-1990/1991)
♪ *"Autumn Leaves"*
#408751
Issued: 1990 • Closed: 1991
Retail Price: $200

(10)
Values
🕯 $200
𝄢 $200

May You Have An Old Fashioned Christmas (LE-1991/1992)
♪ *"Have Yourself A Merry Little Christmas"*
#417777
Issued: 1991 • Closed: 1992
Retail Price: $200

HINGED BOXES – BIRTHSTONE COLLECTION

	Price Paid	Value Of My Collection
1.		
2.		

HINGED BOXES – "ORIGINAL 21" COLLECTION

3.		
4.		
5.		
6.		
7.		
8.		

JACK-IN-THE-BOXES

9.		
10.		

PENCIL TOTALS

KEY: NM *Pre-1981* ▲1981 Ⅱ1982 ◀1983 ✝1984 ✔1985 ♪♭1986 ♨1987 ✤1988 ♅1989 ⚓1990 🕯1991 𝄢1992 ♻1993 ⌇1994 △1995 ♡1996 ✝1997 6ð1998 ★1999 UM *Unmarked*

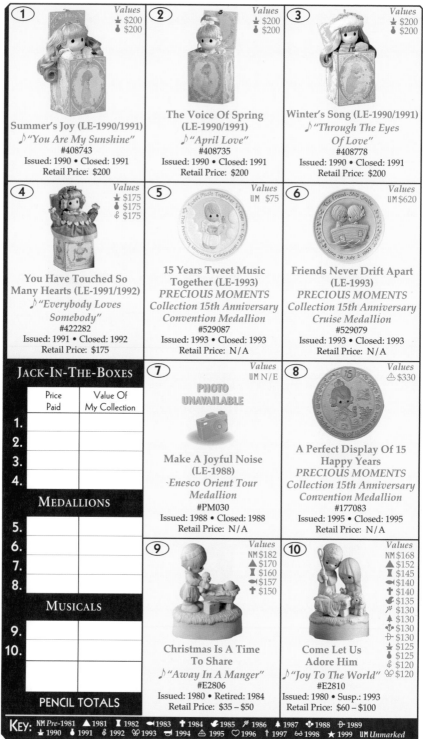

1

Values
★ $200
♦ $200

Summer's Joy (LE-1990/1991)
♪*"You Are My Sunshine"*
#408743
Issued: 1990 • Closed: 1991
Retail Price: $200

2

Values
★ $200
♦ $200

The Voice Of Spring
(LE-1990/1991)
♪*"April Love"*
#408735
Issued: 1990 • Closed: 1991
Retail Price: $200

3

Values
★ $200
♦ $200

Winter's Song (LE-1990/1991)
♪*"Through The Eyes*
Of Love"
#408778
Issued: 1990 • Closed: 1991
Retail Price: $200

4

Values
★ $175
♦ $175
♧ $175

You Have Touched So
Many Hearts (LE-1991/1992)
♪*"Everybody Loves*
Somebody"
#422282
Issued: 1991 • Closed: 1992
Retail Price: $175

5

Values
UM $75

15 Years Tweet Music
Together (LE-1993)
PRECIOUS MOMENTS
Collection 15th Anniversary
Convention Medallion
#529087
Issued: 1993 • Closed: 1993
Retail Price: N/A

6

Values
UM $620

Friends Never Drift Apart
(LE-1993)
PRECIOUS MOMENTS
Collection 15th Anniversary
Cruise Medallion
#529079
Issued: 1993 • Closed: 1993
Retail Price: N/A

JACK-IN-THE-BOXES

	Price Paid	Value Of My Collection
1.		
2.		
3.		
4.		

MEDALLIONS

5.		
6.		
7.		
8.		

MUSICALS

9.		
10.		

PENCIL TOTALS

7

Values
UM N/E

PHOTO
UNAVAILABLE

Make A Joyful Noise
(LE-1988)
Enesco Orient Tour
Medallion
#PM030
Issued: 1988 • Closed: 1988
Retail Price: N/A

8

Values
△ $330

A Perfect Display Of 15
Happy Years
PRECIOUS MOMENTS
Collection 15th Anniversary
Convention Medallion
#177083
Issued: 1995 • Closed: 1995
Retail Price: N/A

9

Values
NM $182
▲ $170
I $160
◄ $157
† $150

Christmas Is A Time
To Share
♪*"Away In A Manger"*
#E2806
Issued: 1980 • Retired: 1984
Retail Price: $35 – $50

10

Values
NM $168
▲ $152
I $145
◄ $140
† $140
◄ $135
♪ $130
♣ $130
♣ $130
♦ $130
★ $125
♦ $125
♧ $120
♥ $120

Come Let Us
Adore Him
♪*"Joy To The World"*
#E2810
Issued: 1980 • Susp.: 1993
Retail Price: $60 – $100

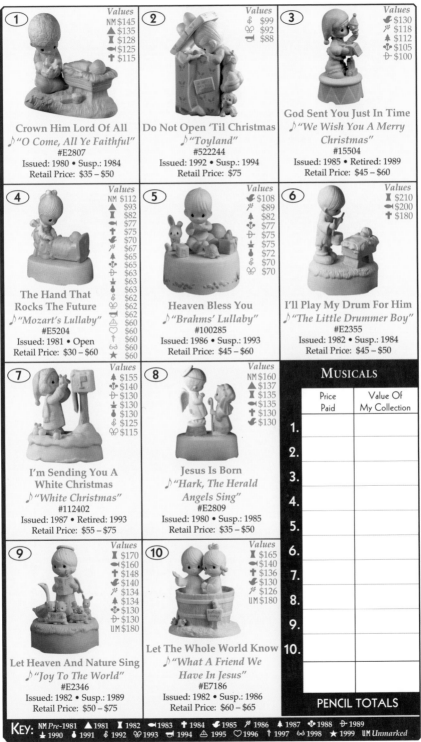

1 | Values
NM $145
▲ $135
Ⅰ $128
← $125
✝ $115

Crown Him Lord Of All
♪ *"O Come, All Ye Faithful"*
#E2807
Issued: 1980 • Susp.: 1984
Retail Price: $35 – $50

2 | Values
¢ $99
♋ $92
⌐ $88

Do Not Open 'Til Christmas
♪ *"Toyland"*
#522244
Issued: 1992 • Susp.: 1994
Retail Price: $75

3 | Values
✔ $130
▲ $118
♠ $112
✤ $105
Ð $100

God Sent You Just In Time
♪ *"We Wish You A Merry Christmas"*
#15504
Issued: 1985 • Retired: 1989
Retail Price: $45 – $60

4 | Values
NM $112
▲ $93
Ⅰ $82
← $77
✝ $75
♫ $70
♠ $67
♣ $65
✤ $65
Ð $63
♦ $63
♦ $63
¢ $62
♋ $62
△ $62
♡ $60
† $60
6ð $60
★ $60

The Hand That Rocks The Future
♪ *"Mozart's Lullaby"*
#E5204
Issued: 1981 • Open
Retail Price: $30 – $60

5 | Values
✔ $108
♫ $89
♠ $82
✤ $77
Ð $75
♦ $75
¢ $72
¢ $70
♋ $70

Heaven Bless You
♪ *"Brahms' Lullaby"*
#100285
Issued: 1986 • Susp.: 1993
Retail Price: $45 – $60

6 | Values
Ⅰ $210
← $200
✝ $180

I'll Play My Drum For Him
♪ *"The Little Drummer Boy"*
#E2355
Issued: 1982 • Susp.: 1984
Retail Price: $45 – $50

7 | Values
♠ $155
✤ $140
Ð $130
♦ $130
♦ $130
¢ $125
♋ $115

I'm Sending You A White Christmas
♪ *"White Christmas"*
#112402
Issued: 1987 • Retired: 1993
Retail Price: $55 – $75

8 | Values
NM $160
▲ $137
Ⅰ $135
← $135
✝ $130
✔ $130

Jesus Is Born
♪ *"Hark, The Herald Angels Sing"*
#E2809
Issued: 1980 • Susp.: 1985
Retail Price: $35 – $50

9 | Values
Ⅰ $170
← $160
✝ $148
✔ $140
♫ $134
♠ $134
✤ $130
Ð $130
UM $180

Let Heaven And Nature Sing
♪ *"Joy To The World"*
#E2346
Issued: 1982 • Susp.: 1989
Retail Price: $50 – $75

10 | Values
Ⅰ $165
← $140
✝ $136
✔ $130
♫ $126
UM $180

Let The Whole World Know
♪ *"What A Friend We Have In Jesus"*
#E7186
Issued: 1982 • Susp.: 1986
Retail Price: $60 – $65

MUSICALS

	Price Paid	Value Of My Collection
1.		
2.		
3.		
4.		
5.		
6.		
7.		
8.		
9.		
10.		
PENCIL TOTALS		

MUSICALS

KEY: NM *Pre-1981* ▲ 1981 Ⅰ 1982 ← 1983 ✝ 1984 ✔ 1985 ♫ 1986 ♠ 1987 ✤ 1988 Ð 1989 ♦ 1990 ♦ 1991 ¢ 1992 ♋ 1993 ⌐ 1994 △ 1995 ♡ 1996 † 1997 6ð 1998 ★ 1999 UM *Unmarked*

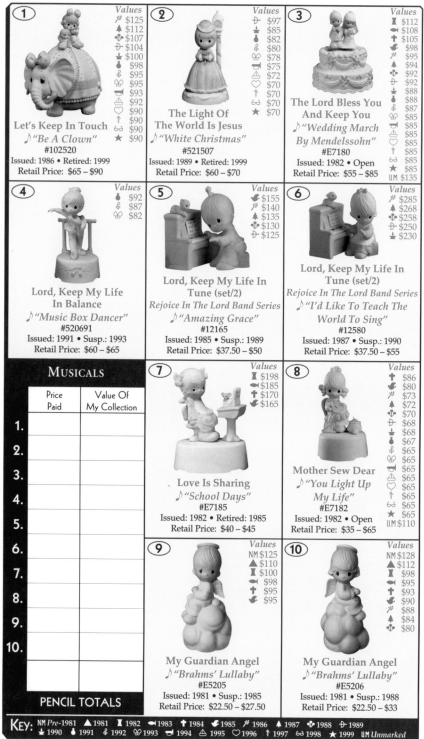

1 Let's Keep In Touch
♪ *"Be A Clown"*
#102520
Issued: 1986 • Retired: 1999
Retail Price: $65 – $90

Values
♫ $125
▲ $112
✤ $107
Ð $104
★ $100
⬠ $98
♣ $95
⬢ $95
◄ $93
△ $92
♡ $90
† $90
♀ $90
⌘ $90
★ $90

2 The Light Of
The World Is Jesus
♪ *"White Christmas"*
#521507
Issued: 1989 • Retired: 1999
Retail Price: $60 – $70

Values
Ð $97
★ $85
⬢ $82
♣ $80
◄ $78
⬠ $75
△ $72
♡ $70
♀ $70
⌘ $70
★ $70

3 The Lord Bless You
And Keep You
♪ *"Wedding March
By Mendelssohn"*
#E7180
Issued: 1982 • Open

Values
Ⅱ $112
▲ $108
† $105
⬠ $98
▲ $95
♣ $94
✤ $92
⬢ $92
◄ $88
★ $88
♀ $87
★ $85
△ $85
♡ $85
⌘ $85
★ $85
UM $135

4 Lord, Keep My Life
In Balance
♪ *"Music Box Dancer"*
#520691
Issued: 1991 • Susp.: 1993
Retail Price: $60 – $65

Values
⬢ $92
♣ $87
♀ $82

5 Lord, Keep My Life In
Tune (set/2)
Rejoice In The Lord Band Series
♪ *"Amazing Grace"*
#12165
Issued: 1985 • Susp.: 1989
Retail Price: $37.50 – $50

Values
✤ $155
♫ $140
▲ $135
✤ $130
Ð $125

6 Lord, Keep My Life In
Tune (set/2)
Rejoice In The Lord Band Series
♪ *"I'd Like To Teach The
World To Sing"*
#12580
Issued: 1987 • Susp.: 1990
Retail Price: $37.50 – $55

Values
♫ $285
▲ $268
✤ $258
Ð $250
★ $230

MUSICALS

	Price Paid	Value Of My Collection
1.		
2.		
3.		
4.		
5.		
6.		
7.		
8.		
9.		
10.		
PENCIL TOTALS		

7 Love Is Sharing
♪ *"School Days"*
#E7185
Issued: 1982 • Retired: 1985
Retail Price: $40 – $45

Values
Ⅱ $198
◄ $185
† $170
✦ $165

8 Mother Sew Dear
♪ *"You Light Up
My Life"*
#E7182
Issued: 1982 • Open

Values
† $86
✦ $80
♫ $73
▲ $72
✤ $70
Ð $68
★ $68
⬢ $67
♣ $65
♀ $65
◄ $65
△ $65
♡ $65
† $65
⌘ $65
★ $65
UM $110

9 My Guardian Angel
♪ *"Brahms' Lullaby"*
#E5205
Issued: 1981 • Susp.: 1985
Retail Price: $22.50 – $27.50

Values
NM $125
▲ $110
Ⅱ $100
◄ $98
† $95
✦ $95

10 My Guardian Angel
♪ *"Brahms' Lullaby"*
#E5206
Issued: 1981 • Susp.: 1988
Retail Price: $22.50 – $33

Values
NM $128
▲ $112
Ⅱ $98
◄ $95
† $93
✦ $90
♫ $88
▲ $84
✤ $80

KEY: NM *Pre-1981* ▲ 1981 Ⅱ 1982 ◄ 1983 † 1984 ✦ 1985 ♫ 1986 ▲ 1987 ✤ 1988 Ð 1989 ★ 1990 ⬢ 1991 ♣ 1992 ♀ 1993 ⌘ 1994 △ 1995 ♡ 1996 † 1997 ⌘ 1998 ★ 1999 UM *Unmarked*

1 — Values
- ⫞ $150
- ◄ $140
- † $137
- UM $176

O Come All Ye Faithful
♪ *"O Come, All Ye Faithful"*
#E2352
Issued: 1982 • Susp.: 1984
Retail Price: $45 – $50

2 — Values
- ♫ $128
- ▲ $120
- ✛ $115
- ⋺ $110
- ★ $108
- ● $100
- ⑧ $100

Our First Christmas Together
♪ *"We Wish You A Merry Christmas"*
#101702
Issued: 1986 • Retired: 1992
Retail Price: $50 – $70

3 — Values
- NM $158
- ▲ $140
- ⫞ $135
- ◄ $130
- † $125

Peace On Earth
♪ *"Jesus Loves Me"*
#E4726
Issued: 1981 • Susp.: 1984
Retail Price: $45 – $50

4 — Values
- ▲ $177
- ✛ $160
- ⋺ $160
- ★ $152
- ● $150
- ⑧ $150
- ⚭ $150

Peace On Earth
♪ *"Hark, The Herald Angels Sing"*
#109746
Issued: 1988 • Susp.: 1993
Retail Price: $100 – $130

5 — Values
- † $98
- ✛ $95
- ♫ $90
- ▲ $88
- ⚓ $82
- ⋺ $80
- ★ $76
- ● $73
- ⑧ $70
- ♡ $70
- UM $102

The Purr-fect Grandma
♪ *"Always In My Heart"*
#E7184
Issued: 1982 • Susp.: 1993
Retail Price: $35 – $60

6 — Values
- NM $145
- ▲ $135
- ⫞ $125
- ◄ $115
- † $110
- ✔ $98
- ♫ $95
- ▲ $88
- ✛ $85

Rejoice O Earth
♪ *"Joy To The World"*
#E5645
Issued: 1981 • Retired: 1988
Retail Price: $35 – $55

7 — Values
- ◄ $175
- † $160
- ✔ $152
- ♫ $140

Sharing Our Season Together
♪ *"Winter Wonderland"*
#E0519
Issued: 1983 • Retired: 1986
Retail Price: $70

8 — Values
- NM $400
- ▲ $390
- ⫞ $380
- ◄ $375
- † $370
- ✔ $350

Silent Knight
♪ *"Silent Night"*
#E5642
Issued: 1981 • Susp.: 1985
Retail Price: $45 – $60

9 — Values
- ✔ $112
- ♫ $105
- ▲ $97
- ✛ $94
- ⋺ $90
- ★ $88
- ● $88
- ⑧ $85

Silent Night
Family Christmas Series
♪ *"Silent Night"*
#15814
Issued: 1985 • Susp.: 1992
Retail Price: $37.50 – $55

10 — Values
- ● $83
- ⑧ $72
- ⚭ $68
- ⊸ $67
- △ $65
- ♡ $65
- † $65
- ᴥ $65
- ★ $65

This Day Has Been Made In Heaven
♪ *"Amazing Grace"*
#523682
Issued: 1992 • Open
Retail Price: $60 – $65

MUSICALS

	Price Paid	Value Of My Collection
1.		
2.		
3.		
4.		
5.		
6.		
7.		
8.		
9.		
10.		
	PENCIL TOTALS	

MUSICALS

KEY: NM *Pre-1981* ▲ 1981 ⫞ 1982 ◄ 1983 † 1984 ✔ 1985 ♫ 1986 ▲ 1987 ✛ 1988 ⋺ 1989 ★ 1990 ● 1991 ⑧ 1992 ⚭ 1993 ⊸ 1994 △ 1995 ♡ 1996 † 1997 ᴥ 1998 ★ 1999 UM *Unmarked*

183

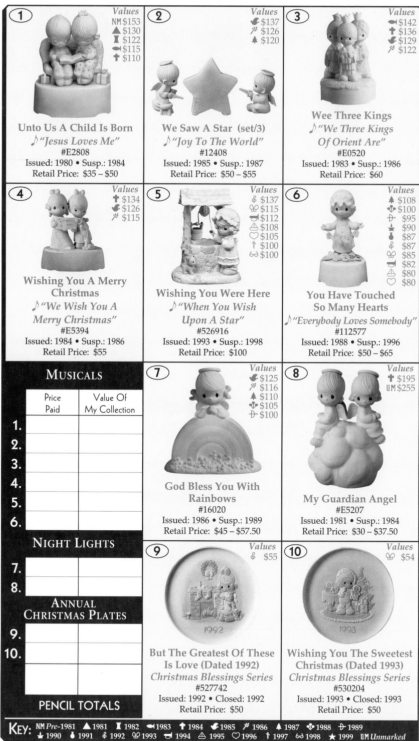

1 — Values
NM $153
▲ $130
✕ $122
◀ $115
✝ $110

Unto Us A Child Is Born
♪ *"Jesus Loves Me"*
#E2808
Issued: 1980 • Susp.: 1984
Retail Price: $35 – $50

2 — Values
✿ $137
♪ $126
▲ $120

We Saw A Star (set/3)
♪ *"Joy To The World"*
#12408
Issued: 1985 • Susp.: 1987
Retail Price: $50 – $55

3 — Values
✿ $142
✝ $136
◀ $129
♪ $122

Wee Three Kings
♪ *"We Three Kings
Of Orient Are"*
#E0520
Issued: 1983 • Susp.: 1986
Retail Price: $60

4 — Values
✝ $134
◀ $126
♪ $115

**Wishing You A Merry
Christmas**
♪ *"We Wish You A
Merry Christmas"*
#E5394
Issued: 1984 • Susp.: 1986
Retail Price: $55

5 — Values
✿ $137
✿ $115
◀ $112
△ $108
♡ $105
✝ $100
👓 $100

Wishing You Were Here
♪ *"When You Wish
Upon A Star"*
#526916
Issued: 1993 • Susp.: 1998
Retail Price: $100

6 — Values
▲ $108
✤ $100
Ð $95
★ $90
♦ $87
✿ $87
😊 $85
◀ $82
△ $80
♡ $80

**You Have Touched
So Many Hearts**
♪ *"Everybody Loves Somebody"*
#112577
Issued: 1988 • Susp.: 1996
Retail Price: $50 – $65

MUSICALS

	Price Paid	Value Of My Collection
1.		
2.		
3.		
4.		
5.		
6.		

NIGHT LIGHTS

7.		
8.		

ANNUAL CHRISTMAS PLATES

9.		
10.		

PENCIL TOTALS

7 — Values
◀ $125
♪ $116
▲ $110
✤ $105
Ð $100

**God Bless You With
Rainbows**
#16020
Issued: 1986 • Susp.: 1989
Retail Price: $45 – $57.50

8 — Values
✝ $195
UM $255

My Guardian Angel
#E5207
Issued: 1981 • Susp.: 1984
Retail Price: $30 – $37.50

9 — Values
✿ $55

**But The Greatest Of These
Is Love (Dated 1992)**
Christmas Blessings Series
#527742
Issued: 1992 • Closed: 1992
Retail Price: $50

10 — Values
❀ $54

**Wishing You The Sweetest
Christmas (Dated 1993)**
Christmas Blessings Series
#530204
Issued: 1993 • Closed: 1993
Retail Price: $50

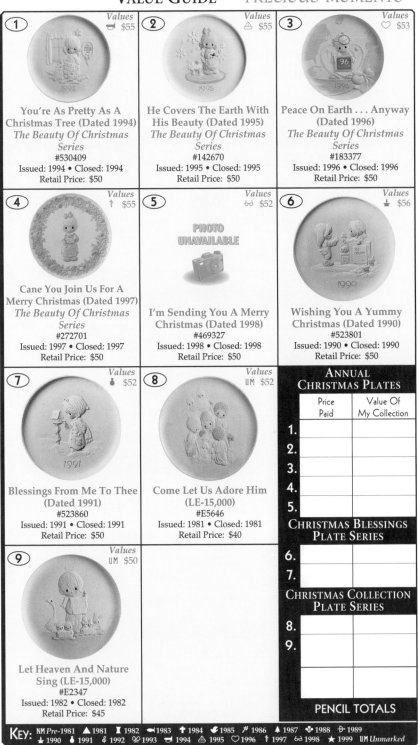

1 Values 🦢 $55

You're As Pretty As A
Christmas Tree (Dated 1994)
*The Beauty Of Christmas
Series*
#530409
Issued: 1994 • Closed: 1994
Retail Price: $50

2 Values 🔺 $55

He Covers The Earth With
His Beauty (Dated 1995)
*The Beauty Of Christmas
Series*
#142670
Issued: 1995 • Closed: 1995
Retail Price: $50

3 Values ♡ $53

Peace On Earth . . . Anyway
(Dated 1996)
*The Beauty Of Christmas
Series*
#183377
Issued: 1996 • Closed: 1996
Retail Price: $50

4 Values † $55

Cane You Join Us For A
Merry Christmas (Dated 1997)
*The Beauty Of Christmas
Series*
#272701
Issued: 1997 • Closed: 1997
Retail Price: $50

5 Values 6∂ $52

PHOTO
UNAVAILABLE

I'm Sending You A Merry
Christmas (Dated 1998)
#469327
Issued: 1998 • Closed: 1998
Retail Price: $50

6 Values ★ $56

Wishing You A Yummy
Christmas (Dated 1990)
#523801
Issued: 1990 • Closed: 1990
Retail Price: $50

7 Values 🦢 $52

Blessings From Me To Thee
(Dated 1991)
#523860
Issued: 1991 • Closed: 1991
Retail Price: $50

8 Values UM $52

Come Let Us Adore Him
(LE-15,000)
#E5646
Issued: 1981 • Closed: 1981
Retail Price: $40

9 Values UM $50

Let Heaven And Nature
Sing (LE-15,000)
#E2347
Issued: 1982 • Closed: 1982
Retail Price: $45

ANNUAL CHRISTMAS PLATES

	Price Paid	Value Of My Collection
1.		
2.		
3.		
4.		
5.		

CHRISTMAS BLESSINGS PLATE SERIES

6.		
7.		

CHRISTMAS COLLECTION PLATE SERIES

8.		
9.		

PENCIL TOTALS

PLATES

KEY: NM *Pre-1981* ▲1981 Ⅱ1982 ◄1983 †1984 🍃1985 ⅍1986 ▲1987 ⚜1988 ⸙1989
★1990 🦢1991 ℰ1992 ❀1993 🦢1994 🔺1995 ♡1996 †1997 6∂1998 ★1999 UM *Unmarked*

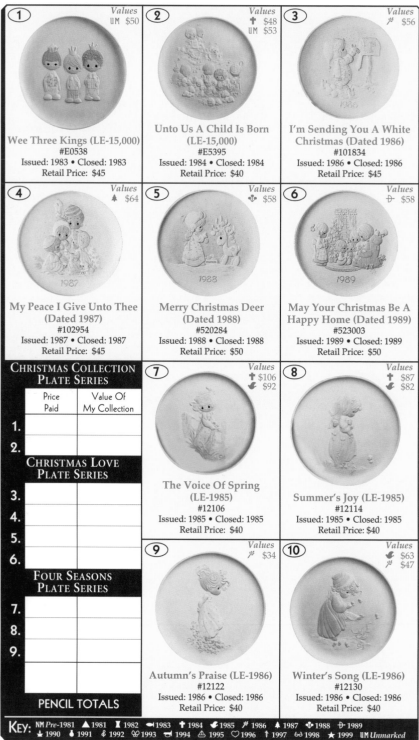

1 — Values UM $50
Wee Three Kings (LE-15,000)
#E0538
Issued: 1983 • Closed: 1983
Retail Price: $45

2 — Values † $48 / UM $53
Unto Us A Child Is Born (LE-15,000)
#E5395
Issued: 1984 • Closed: 1984
Retail Price: $40

3 — Values 𝄐 $56
I'm Sending You A White Christmas (Dated 1986)
#101834
Issued: 1986 • Closed: 1986
Retail Price: $45

4 — Values ♠ $64
My Peace I Give Unto Thee (Dated 1987)
#102954
Issued: 1987 • Closed: 1987
Retail Price: $45

5 — Values ✧ $58
Merry Christmas Deer (Dated 1988)
#520284
Issued: 1988 • Closed: 1988
Retail Price: $50

6 — Values Ð $58
May Your Christmas Be A Happy Home (Dated 1989)
#523003
Issued: 1989 • Closed: 1989
Retail Price: $50

CHRISTMAS COLLECTION PLATE SERIES

	Price Paid	Value Of My Collection
1.		
2.		

CHRISTMAS LOVE PLATE SERIES

3.		
4.		
5.		
6.		

FOUR SEASONS PLATE SERIES

7.		
8.		
9.		

PENCIL TOTALS

7 — Values † $106 / ❧ $92
The Voice Of Spring (LE-1985)
#12106
Issued: 1985 • Closed: 1985
Retail Price: $40

8 — Values † $87 / ❧ $82
Summer's Joy (LE-1985)
#12114
Issued: 1985 • Closed: 1985
Retail Price: $40

9 — Values 𝄐 $34
Autumn's Praise (LE-1986)
#12122
Issued: 1986 • Closed: 1986
Retail Price: $40

10 — Values ❧ $63 / 𝄐 $47
Winter's Song (LE-1986)
#12130
Issued: 1986 • Closed: 1986
Retail Price: $40

KEY: NM *Pre*-1981 ▲1981 ▮1982 ◄1983 †1984 ❧1985 𝄐1986 ♠1987 ✧1988 Ð1989 ★1990 ♦1991 ♪1992 ❀1993 ⛻1994 △1995 ♡1996 †1997 ͞1998 ★1999 UM *Unmarked*

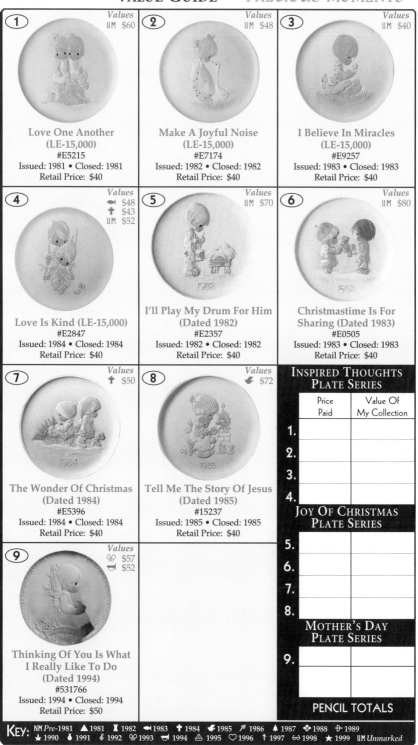

1 Values UM $60
Love One Another
(LE-15,000)
#E5215
Issued: 1981 • Closed: 1981
Retail Price: $40

2 Values UM $48
Make A Joyful Noise
(LE-15,000)
#E7174
Issued: 1982 • Closed: 1982
Retail Price: $40

3 Values UM $40
I Believe In Miracles
(LE-15,000)
#E9257
Issued: 1983 • Closed: 1983
Retail Price: $40

4 Values $48 / $43 / UM $52
Love Is Kind (LE-15,000)
#E2847
Issued: 1984 • Closed: 1984
Retail Price: $40

5 Values UM $70
I'll Play My Drum For Him
(Dated 1982)
#E2357
Issued: 1982 • Closed: 1982
Retail Price: $40

6 Values UM $80
Christmastime Is For Sharing (Dated 1983)
#E0505
Issued: 1983 • Closed: 1983
Retail Price: $40

7 Values $50
The Wonder Of Christmas
(Dated 1984)
#E5396
Issued: 1984 • Closed: 1984
Retail Price: $40

8 Values $72
Tell Me The Story Of Jesus
(Dated 1985)
#15237
Issued: 1985 • Closed: 1985
Retail Price: $40

9 Values $57 / $52
Thinking Of You Is What I Really Like To Do
(Dated 1994)
#531766
Issued: 1994 • Closed: 1994
Retail Price: $50

INSPIRED THOUGHTS PLATE SERIES

	Price Paid	Value Of My Collection
1.		
2.		
3.		
4.		

JOY OF CHRISTMAS PLATE SERIES

5.		
6.		
7.		
8.		

MOTHER'S DAY PLATE SERIES

9.		

PENCIL TOTALS

PLATES

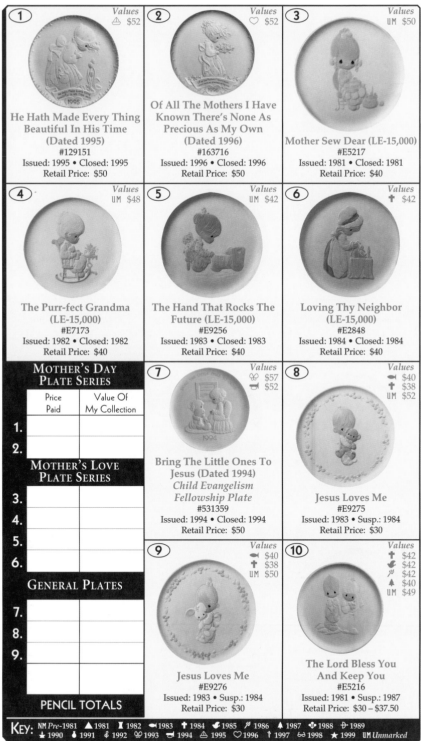

1 — *Values* ⚱ $52

He Hath Made Every Thing Beautiful In His Time
(Dated 1995)
#129151
Issued: 1995 • Closed: 1995
Retail Price: $50

2 — *Values* ♡ $52

Of All The Mothers I Have Known There's None As Precious As My Own
(Dated 1996)
#163716
Issued: 1996 • Closed: 1996
Retail Price: $50

3 — *Values* UM $50

Mother Sew Dear (LE-15,000)
#E5217
Issued: 1981 • Closed: 1981
Retail Price: $40

4 — *Values* UM $48

The Purr-fect Grandma
(LE-15,000)
#E7173
Issued: 1982 • Closed: 1982
Retail Price: $40

5 — *Values* UM $42

The Hand That Rocks The Future (LE-15,000)
#E9256
Issued: 1983 • Closed: 1983
Retail Price: $40

6 — *Values* ✝ $42

Loving Thy Neighbor
(LE-15,000)
#E2848
Issued: 1984 • Closed: 1984
Retail Price: $40

MOTHER'S DAY PLATE SERIES

	Price Paid	Value Of My Collection
1.		
2.		

MOTHER'S LOVE PLATE SERIES

3.		
4.		
5.		
6.		

GENERAL PLATES

7.		
8.		
9.		

PENCIL TOTALS

7 — *Values* 🐚 $57 / 🐌 $52

Bring The Little Ones To Jesus (Dated 1994)
Child Evangelism Fellowship Plate
#531359
Issued: 1994 • Closed: 1994
Retail Price: $50

8 — *Values* 🐚 $40 / ✝ $38 / UM $52

Jesus Loves Me
#E9275
Issued: 1983 • Susp.: 1984
Retail Price: $30

9 — *Values* 🐚 $40 / ✝ $38 / UM $50

Jesus Loves Me
#E9276
Issued: 1983 • Susp.: 1984
Retail Price: $30

10 — *Values* ✝ $42 / ⌇ $42 / ♪ $42 / ♠ $40 / UM $49

The Lord Bless You And Keep You
#E5216
Issued: 1981 • Susp.: 1987
Retail Price: $30 – $37.50

KEY: NM *Pre-1981* ▲ 1981 ✗ 1982 ◀ 1983 ✝ 1984 🍂 1985 ♪ 1986 ♠ 1987 ✿ 1988 ☗ 1989 ★ 1990 ◆ 1991 ⚜ 1992 🐚 1993 🐌 1994 ⚱ 1995 ♡ 1996 ✝ 1997 🐚 1998 ★ 1999 UM *Unmarked*

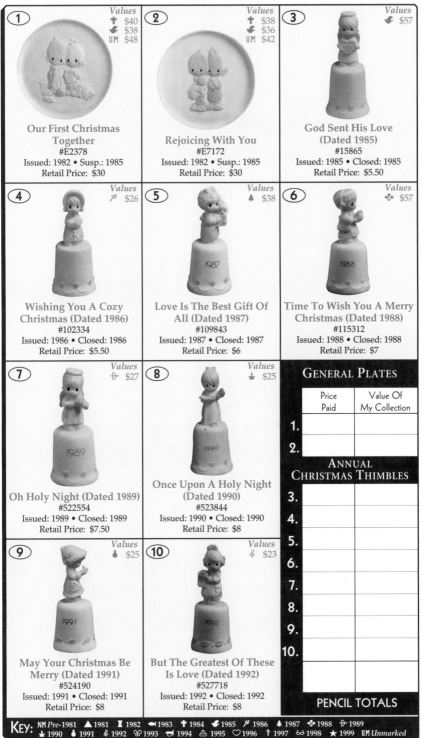

1 — *Values* ✝ $40 / ❦ $38 / UM $48

Our First Christmas Together
#E2378
Issued: 1982 • Susp.: 1985
Retail Price: $30

2 — *Values* ✝ $38 / ❦ $36 / UM $42

Rejoicing With You
#E7172
Issued: 1982 • Susp.: 1985
Retail Price: $30

3 — *Values* ❦ $57

God Sent His Love (Dated 1985)
#15865
Issued: 1985 • Closed: 1985
Retail Price: $5.50

4 — *Values* ⌗ $26

Wishing You A Cozy Christmas (Dated 1986)
#102334
Issued: 1986 • Closed: 1986
Retail Price: $5.50

5 — *Values* ▲ $38

Love Is The Best Gift Of All (Dated 1987)
#109843
Issued: 1987 • Closed: 1987
Retail Price: $6

6 — *Values* ✤ $57

Time To Wish You A Merry Christmas (Dated 1988)
#115312
Issued: 1988 • Closed: 1988
Retail Price: $7

7 — *Values* Ð $27

Oh Holy Night (Dated 1989)
#522554
Issued: 1989 • Closed: 1989
Retail Price: $7.50

8 — *Values* ⚓ $25

Once Upon A Holy Night (Dated 1990)
#523844
Issued: 1990 • Closed: 1990
Retail Price: $8

9 — *Values* ◐ $25

May Your Christmas Be Merry (Dated 1991)
#524190
Issued: 1991 • Closed: 1991
Retail Price: $8

10 — *Values* ⅋ $23

But The Greatest Of These Is Love (Dated 1992)
#527718
Issued: 1992 • Closed: 1992
Retail Price: $8

GENERAL PLATES

	Price Paid	Value Of My Collection
1.		
2.		

ANNUAL CHRISTMAS THIMBLES

3.		
4.		
5.		
6.		
7.		
8.		
9.		
10.		

PENCIL TOTALS

KEY: NM *Pre-1981* ▲ 1981 I 1982 ◀1983 ✝ 1984 ❦ 1985 ⌗ 1986 ▲ 1987 ✤ 1988 Ð 1989 ⚓ 1990 ◐ 1991 ⅋ 1992 ♉ 1993 ◀ 1994 △ 1995 ♡ 1996 ✝ 1997 ⚏ 1998 ★ 1999 UM *Unmarked*

Plates/Thimbles

1 — Values: 🏵 $15

Wishing You The Sweetest Christmas (Dated 1993)
#530182
Issued: 1993 • Closed: 1993
Retail Price: $8

2 — Values:
ℱ $47
▲ $43
⊹ $40

Clowns (set/2)
#100668
Issued: 1986 • Susp.: 1988
Retail Price: $11 – $14

3 — Values: ℱ $98

Four Seasons (set/4, LE-1986)
#100641
Issued: 1986 • Closed: 1986
Retail Price: $20

4 — Values:
🍂 $28
ℱ $23
▲ $20
⊹ $16
꠵ $16

God Is Love, Dear Valentine
#100625
Issued: 1986 • Susp.: 1989
Retail Price: $5.50 – $8

5 — Values:
🍂 $25
ℱ $22
▲ $22
⊹ $20
꠵ $20
✦ $18
🍥 $15

The Lord Bless You And Keep You
#100633
Issued: 1986 • Susp.: 1991
Retail Price: $5.50 – $8

6 — Values:
✝ $29
🍂 $24
ℱ $22
▲ $20
⊹ $17
꠵ $15
✦ $15
🍥 $14

Love Covers All
#12254
Issued: 1985 • Susp.: 1990
Retail Price: $5.50 – $8

ANNUAL CHRISTMAS THIMBLES

	Price Paid	Value Of My Collection
1.		

GENERAL THIMBLES

2.		
3.		
4.		
5.		
6.		
7.		
8.		

TREE TOPPERS

9.		
10.		

PENCIL TOTALS

7 — Values:
✝ $23
🍂 $21
ℱ $18
▲ $16
⊹ $15
꠵ $15
✦ $15
🍥 $14
🍧 $12
🏵 $12
🍜 $10
△ $10
♡ $10
✝ $8
👓 $8
★ $8

Mother Sew Dear
#13293
Issued: 1985 • Retired: 1999
Retail Price: $5.50 – $8

8 — Values:
✝ $23
🍂 $22
ℱ $20
▲ $18
⊹ $16
꠵ $15
✦ $14
🍥 $14
🍧 $13
🏵 $12
🍜 $10
△ $10
♡ $10
✝ $8
👓 $8
★ $8

The Purr-fect Grandma
#13307
Issued: 1985 • Retired: 1999
Retail Price: $5.50 – $8

9 — Values: ★ $130

Rejoice O Earth
♪ *"Hark, The Herald Angels Sing"*
#617334
Issued: 1990 • Retired: 1991
Retail Price: $125

10 — Values:
♡ $135
✝ $125
👓 $125
★ $125

Sing In Excelsis Deo
#183830
Issued: 1996 • Open
Retail Price: $125

KEY: NM *Pre-1981* ▲1981 ❚1982 ◀1983 ✝1984 🍂1985 ℱ1986 ▲1987 ⊹1988 ꠵1989 ★1990 🍥1991 🍧1992 🏵1993 🍜1994 △1995 ♡1996 ✝1997 👓1998 ★1999 **UM** *Unmarked*

TENDER TAILS

Since the line's introduction in 1997, TENDER TAILS has seen the addition of several new collections. Only limited edition pieces have year marks. The year mark for 1998 is a heart (♥) and the year mark for 1999 is a star (★).

① NEW!

Values
UM $7

Baby Bear
#610011
Issued: 1999 • Open
Retail Price: $7

② NEW!

Values
UM $7

Age 1
#600156
Issued: 1999 • Open
Retail Price: $7

③ NEW!

Values
UM $7

Age 2
#600164
Issued: 1999 • Open
Retail Price: $7

④ NEW!

Values
UM $7

Age 3
#600172
Issued: 1999 • Open
Retail Price: $7

⑤ NEW!

Values
UM $7

Age 4
#600180
Issued: 1999 • Open
Retail Price: $7

⑥ NEW!

Values
UM $7

Age 5
#600199
Issued: 1999 • Open
Retail Price: $7

⑦ NEW!

Values
UM $7

Age 6
#600210
Issued: 1999 • Open
Retail Price: $7

⑧ NEW!

Values
UM $10

Circus Clown
#648221
Issued: 1999 • Open
Retail Price: $10

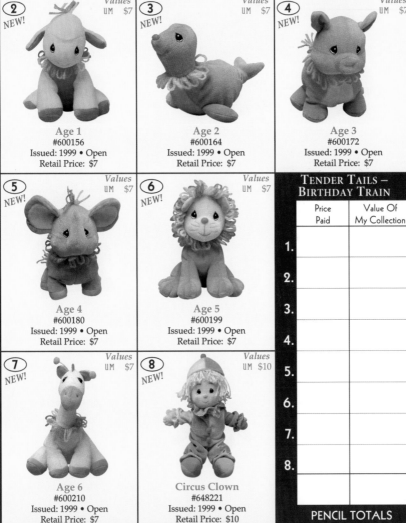

	TENDER TAILS – BIRTHDAY TRAIN	
	Price Paid	Value Of My Collection
1.		
2.		
3.		
4.		
5.		
6.		
7.		
8.		
	PENCIL TOTALS	

TENDER TAILS

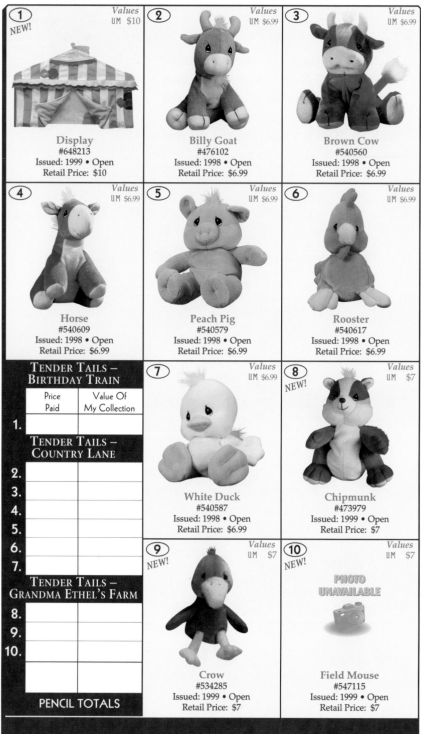

(1) NEW!
Values
UM $10

Display
#648213
Issued: 1999 • Open
Retail Price: $10

(2)
Values
UM $6.99

Billy Goat
#476102
Issued: 1998 • Open
Retail Price: $6.99

(3)
Values
UM $6.99

Brown Cow
#540560
Issued: 1998 • Open
Retail Price: $6.99

(4)
Values
UM $6.99

Horse
#540609
Issued: 1998 • Open
Retail Price: $6.99

(5)
Values
UM $6.99

Peach Pig
#540579
Issued: 1998 • Open
Retail Price: $6.99

(6)
Values
UM $6.99

Rooster
#540617
Issued: 1998 • Open
Retail Price: $6.99

(7)
Values
UM $6.99

White Duck
#540587
Issued: 1998 • Open
Retail Price: $6.99

(8) NEW!
Values
UM $7

Chipmunk
#473979
Issued: 1999 • Open
Retail Price: $7

(9) NEW!
Values
UM $7

Crow
#534285
Issued: 1999 • Open
Retail Price: $7

(10) NEW!
Values
UM $7

PHOTO UNAVAILABLE

Field Mouse
#547115
Issued: 1999 • Open
Retail Price: $7

TENDER TAILS – BIRTHDAY TRAIN		
	Price Paid	Value Of My Collection
1.		
TENDER TAILS – COUNTRY LANE		
2.		
3.		
4.		
5.		
6.		
7.		
TENDER TAILS – GRANDMA ETHEL'S FARM		
8.		
9.		
10.		
PENCIL TOTALS		

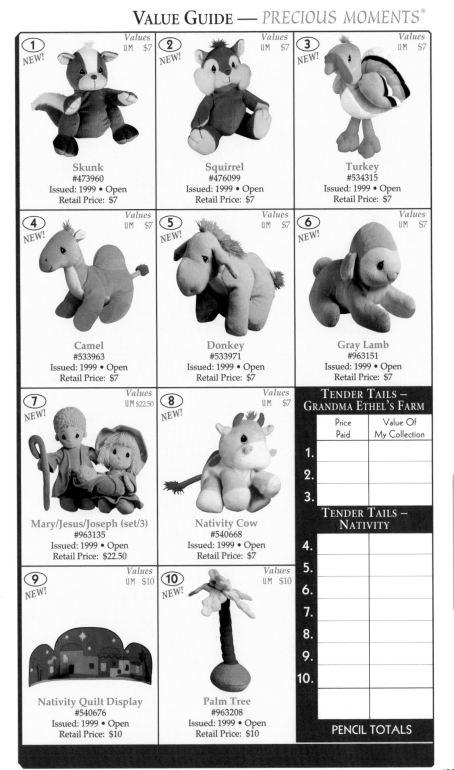

1 NEW!
Values
UM $7

Skunk
#473960
Issued: 1999 • Open
Retail Price: $7

2 NEW!
Values
UM $7

Squirrel
#476099
Issued: 1999 • Open
Retail Price: $7

3 NEW!
Values
UM $7

Turkey
#534315
Issued: 1999 • Open
Retail Price: $7

4 NEW!
Values
UM $7

Camel
#533963
Issued: 1999 • Open
Retail Price: $7

5 NEW!
Values
UM $7

Donkey
#533971
Issued: 1999 • Open
Retail Price: $7

6 NEW!
Values
UM $7

Gray Lamb
#963151
Issued: 1999 • Open
Retail Price: $7

7 NEW!
Values
UM $22.50

Mary/Jesus/Joseph (set/3)
#963135
Issued: 1999 • Open
Retail Price: $22.50

8 NEW!
Values
UM $7

Nativity Cow
#540668
Issued: 1999 • Open
Retail Price: $7

9 NEW!
Values
UM $10

Nativity Quilt Display
#540676
Issued: 1999 • Open
Retail Price: $10

10 NEW!
Values
UM $10

Palm Tree
#963208
Issued: 1999 • Open
Retail Price: $10

TENDER TAILS — GRANDMA ETHEL'S FARM

	Price Paid	Value Of My Collection
1.		
2.		
3.		

TENDER TAILS — NATIVITY

4.		
5.		
6.		
7.		
8.		
9.		
10.		
PENCIL TOTALS		

TENDER TAILS

1 — *Values* ♥ $6.99 UM $6.99

20th Anniversary Bear (LE-1998)
Care-A-Van Exclusive
#462829
Issued: 1998 • Closed: 1998
Retail Price: $6.99

2 — *Values* UM $11

Bear
#358274
Issued: 1997 • Retired: 1998
Retail Price: $6.99

3 — *Values* UM $20

Bear Couple (w/ornament, "Our First Christmas Together")
#966771
Issued: 1998 • Open
Retail Price: $20

4 NEW! — *Values* UM $7

Bee
#464295
Issued: 1999 • Open
Retail Price: $7

5 — *Values* UM $12

Blue Bird
#382531
Issued: 1998 • Retired: 1998
Retail Price: $6.99

6 — *Values* UM $15

Boy Bear (w/ornament, "Baby's First Christmas")
#966755
Issued: 1998 • Open
Retail Price: $15

TENDER TAILS – GENERAL PLUSH

	Price Paid	Value Of My Collection
1.		
2.		
3.		
4.		
5.		
6.		
7.		
8.		
9.		
PENCIL TOTALS		

7 — *Values* UM $14

Brown Bunny
#464422
Issued: 1998 • Retired: 1999
Retail Price: $6.99

8 NEW! — *Values* UM $7

Butterfly
#482234
Issued: 1999 • Open
Retail Price: $7

9 — *Values* UM $9

Cardinal
#471909
Issued: 1998 • Retired: 1999
Retail Price: $6.99

1 *Values* UM $$11

Cat
#382256
Issued: 1998 • Retired: 1999
Retail Price: $6.99

2 *Values* UM $$10

Cow
#475890
Issued: 1998 • Retired: 1999
Retail Price: $6.99

3 *Values* UM $9

Duck
#382515
Issued: 1998 • Retired: 1998
Retail Price: $6.99

4 *Values* UM $13

Elephant
#358320
Issued: 1997 • Retired: 1998
Retail Price: $6.99

5 NEW! *Values* ★ $7

Elephant
Special Event Plush
#609692
Issued: 1999 • To Be Closed: 1999
Retail Price: $7

6 *Values* UM $15

**Girl Bear (w/ornament,
"Baby's First Christmas")**
#966763
Issued: 1998 • Open
Retail Price: $15

7 NEW! *Values* UM $7

Goose
#473952
Issued: 1999 • Open
Retail Price: $7

8 *Values* UM N/E

Gorilla
*Local Club Chapter
Convention Plush*
#480355
Issued: 1998 • Closed: 1998
Retail Price: N/A

9 *Values* UM $9

Harp Seal
#382086
Issued: 1998 • Retired: 1999
Retail Price: $6.99

TENDER TAILS – GENERAL PLUSH

	Price Paid	Value Of My Collection
1.		
2.		
3.		
4.		
5.		
6.		
7.		
8.		
9.		
PENCIL TOTALS		

TENDER TAILS

1 Values UM $6.99

Hippo
#475912
Issued: 1998 • Open
Retail Price: $6.99

2 Values UM $12

Horse
#358290
Issued: 1997 • Retired: 1998
Retail Price: $6.99

3 NEW! Values ★ $7

Koala (LE-1999)
Catalog Plush
#535141
Issued: 1999 • To Be Closed: 1999
Retail Price: $7

4 NEW! Values UM $9

Ladybug
#476080
Issued: 1999 • Retired: 1999
Retail Price: $7

5 Values UM $9

Lamb
#463299
Issued: 1998 • Retired: 1999
Retail Price: $6.99

6 NEW! Values UM $12.99

Lamb (12")
#477192
Issued: 1999 • Open
Retail Price: $12.99

TENDER TAILS –
GENERAL PLUSH

	Price Paid	Value Of My Collection
1.		
2.		
3.		
4.		
5.		
6.		
7.		
8.		
9.		
10.		

PENCIL TOTALS

7 NEW! Values UM $20

Lamb (16")
#544094
Issued: 1999 • Open
Retail Price: $20

8 NEW! Values UM $7

Lavender Bunny
#516597
Issued: 1999 • Open
Retail Price: $7

9 Values UM $13

Lion
#358266
Issued: 1997 • Retired: 1998
Retail Price: $6.99

10 NEW! Values UM $10 (Can.)

Loon
Exclusive To Canada
#535354
Issued: 1999 • Open
Retail Price: $10 (Canadian)

1 *Values* UM $6.99

Monkey
#475939
Issued: 1998 • Open
Retail Price: $6.99

2 *Values* ♥ $42

Monkey Triplets
(set/3, LE-1998)
Special Event Plush
#537977
Issued: 1998 • Closed: 1998
Retail Price: $14.99

3 NEW! *Values* UM $10 (Can.)

Moose
Exclusive To Canada
#549509
Issued: 1999 • Open
Retail Price: $10 (Canadian)

4 *Values* UM $6.99

Owl
#475882
Issued: 1998 • Open
Retail Price: $6.99

5 NEW! *Values* ♥ $7 ★ $7

Panda Bear (LE-1999)
Care-A-Van Exclusive
#600873
Issued: 1999 • To Be Closed: 1999
Retail Price: $7

6 NEW! *Values* ★ $7

Parrot (LE-1999)
#480371
Issued: 1999 • To Be Closed: 1999
Retail Price: $7

7 *Values* UM $6.99

Penguin
#471917
Issued: 1998 • Open
Retail Price: $6.99

8 *Values* UM $14

Pink Bunny
#464414
Issued: 1998 • Retired: 1999
Retail Price: $6.99

9 *Values* ♥ $15

Pink Flamingo (LE-1998)
#482889
Issued: 1998 • Closed: 1998
Retail Price: $6.99

10 NEW! *Values* UM $12.99

Pink Flamingo (12")
N/A
Issued: 1999 • Open
Retail Price: $12.99

TENDER TAILS – GENERAL PLUSH

	Price Paid	Value Of My Collection
1.		
2.		
3.		
4.		
5.		
6.		
7.		
8.		
9.		
10.		
PENCIL TOTALS		

TENDER TAILS

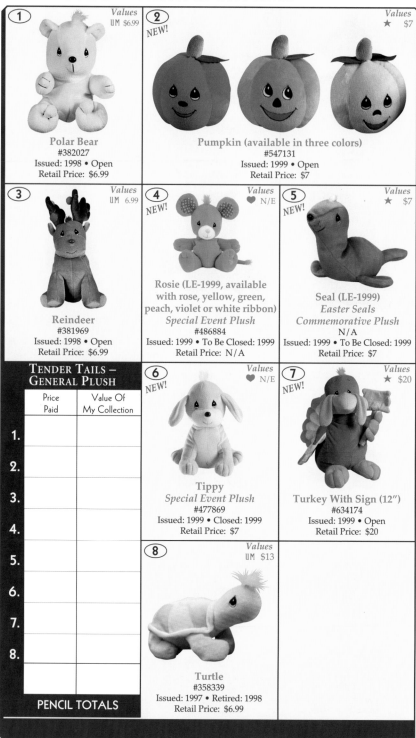

1 Values UM $6.99

Polar Bear
#382027
Issued: 1998 • Open
Retail Price: $6.99

2 NEW! Values ★ $7

Pumpkin (available in three colors)
#547131
Issued: 1999 • Open
Retail Price: $7

3 Values UM 6.99

Reindeer
#381969
Issued: 1998 • Open
Retail Price: $6.99

4 NEW! Values ♥ N/E

**Rosie (LE-1999, available
with rose, yellow, green,
peach, violet or white ribbon)**
Special Event Plush
#486884
Issued: 1999 • To Be Closed: 1999
Retail Price: N/A

5 NEW! Values ★ $7

Seal (LE-1999)
*Easter Seals
Commemorative Plush*
N/A
Issued: 1999 • To Be Closed: 1999
Retail Price: $7

TENDER TAILS – GENERAL PLUSH

	Price Paid	Value Of My Collection
1.		
2.		
3.		
4.		
5.		
6.		
7.		
8.		
PENCIL TOTALS		

6 NEW! Values ♥ N/E

Tippy
Special Event Plush
#477869
Issued: 1999 • Closed: 1999
Retail Price: $7

7 NEW! Values ★ $20

Turkey With Sign (12")
#634174
Issued: 1999 • Open
Retail Price: $20

8 Values UM $13

Turtle
#358339
Issued: 1997 • Retired: 1998
Retail Price: $6.99

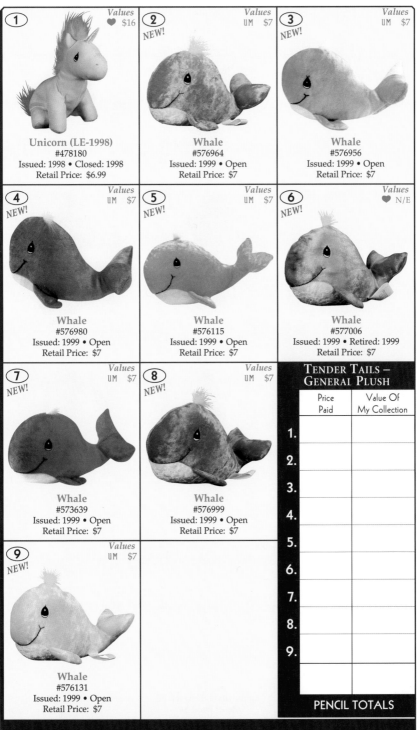

1 — Values ♥ $16

Unicorn (LE-1998)
#478180
Issued: 1998 • Closed: 1998
Retail Price: $6.99

2 NEW! — Values UM $7

Whale
#576964
Issued: 1999 • Open
Retail Price: $7

3 NEW! — Values UM $7

Whale
#576956
Issued: 1999 • Open
Retail Price: $7

4 NEW! — Values UM $7

Whale
#576980
Issued: 1999 • Open
Retail Price: $7

5 NEW! — Values UM $7

Whale
#576115
Issued: 1999 • Open
Retail Price: $7

6 NEW! — Values ♥ N/E

Whale
#577006
Issued: 1999 • Retired: 1999
Retail Price: $7

7 NEW! — Values UM $7

Whale
#573639
Issued: 1999 • Open
Retail Price: $7

8 NEW! — Values UM $7

Whale
#576999
Issued: 1999 • Open
Retail Price: $7

9 NEW! — Values UM $7

Whale
#576131
Issued: 1999 • Open
Retail Price: $7

TENDER TAILS – GENERAL PLUSH

	Price Paid	Value Of My Collection
1.		
2.		
3.		
4.		
5.		
6.		
7.		
8.		
9.		
PENCIL TOTALS		

TENDER TAILS

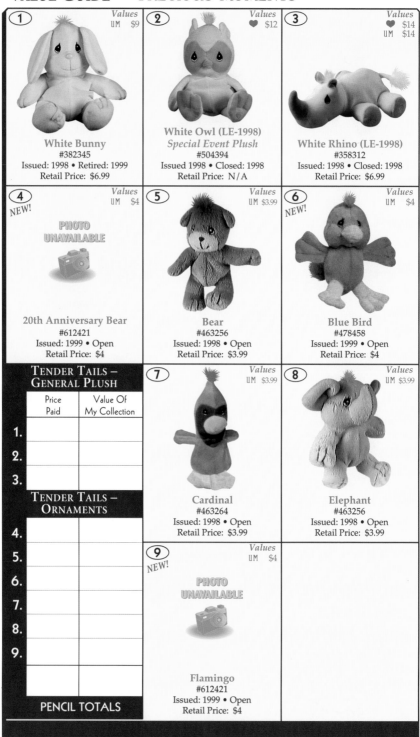

1
Values
UM $9

White Bunny
#382345
Issued: 1998 • Retired: 1999
Retail Price: $6.99

2
Values
♥ $12

White Owl (LE-1998)
Special Event Plush
#504394
Issued 1998 • Closed: 1998
Retail Price: N/A

3
Values
♥ $14
UM $14

White Rhino (LE-1998)
#358312
Issued: 1998 • Closed: 1998
Retail Price: $6.99

4
NEW!
Values
UM $4

PHOTO UNAVAILABLE

20th Anniversary Bear
#612421
Issued: 1999 • Open
Retail Price: $4

5
Values
UM $3.99

Bear
#463256
Issued: 1998 • Open
Retail Price: $3.99

6
NEW!
Values
UM $4

Blue Bird
#478458
Issued: 1999 • Open
Retail Price: $4

TENDER TAILS – GENERAL PLUSH		
	Price Paid	Value Of My Collection
1.		
2.		
3.		
TENDER TAILS – ORNAMENTS		
4.		
5.		
6.		
7.		
8.		
9.		
PENCIL TOTALS		

7
Values
UM $3.99

Cardinal
#463264
Issued: 1998 • Open
Retail Price: $3.99

8
Values
UM $3.99

Elephant
#463256
Issued: 1998 • Open
Retail Price: $3.99

9
NEW!
Values
UM $4

PHOTO UNAVAILABLE

Flamingo
#612421
Issued: 1999 • Open
Retail Price: $4

1 — *Values* UM $3.99

Harp Seal
#463264
Issued: 1998 • Open
Retail Price: $3.99

2 — *Values* UM $3.99

Horse
#463256
Issued: 1998 • Open
Retail Price: $3.99

3 NEW! — *Values* UM $4

PHOTO UNAVAILABLE

Lamb
#478458
Issued: 1999 • Open
Retail Price: $4

4 — *Values* UM $3.99

Lion
#463256
Issued: 1998 • Open
Retail Price: $3.99

5 NEW! — *Values* UM $4

Monkey
#612421
Issued: 1999 • Open
Retail Price: $4

6 NEW! — *Values* UM $4

Monkey
#612421
Issued: 1999 • Open
Retail Price: $4

7 NEW! — *Values* UM $4

Monkey
#612421
Issued: 1999 • Open
Retail Price: $4

8 NEW! — *Values* UM $4

PHOTO UNAVAILABLE

Owl
#612421
Issued: 1999 • Open
Retail Price: $4

9 — *Values* UM $3.99

Pig
#463256
Issued: 1998 • Open
Retail Price: $3.99

TENDER TAILS – ORNAMENTS

	Price Paid	Value Of My Collection
1.		
2.		
3.		
4.		
5.		
6.		
7.		
8.		
9.		
PENCIL TOTALS		

TENDER TAILS

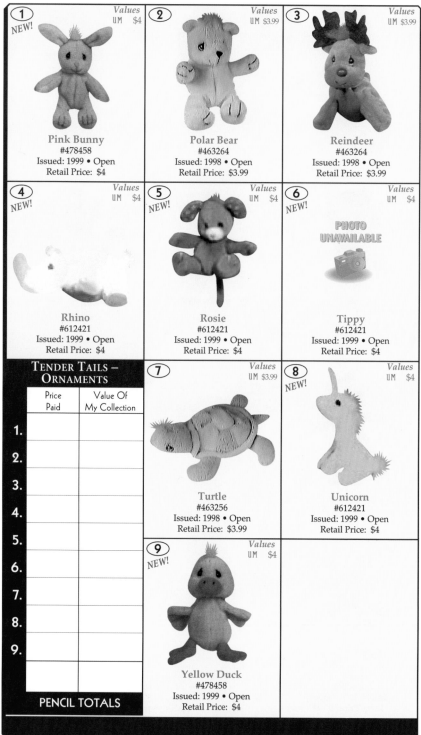

1 NEW! — Values UM $4
Pink Bunny
#478458
Issued: 1999 • Open
Retail Price: $4

2 — Values UM $3.99
Polar Bear
#463264
Issued: 1998 • Open
Retail Price: $3.99

3 — Values UM $3.99
Reindeer
#463264
Issued: 1998 • Open
Retail Price: $3.99

4 NEW! — Values UM $4
Rhino
#612421
Issued: 1999 • Open
Retail Price: $4

5 NEW! — Values UM $4
Rosie
#612421
Issued: 1999 • Open
Retail Price: $4

6 NEW! — Values UM $4
PHOTO UNAVAILABLE
Tippy
#612421
Issued: 1999 • Open
Retail Price: $4

TENDER TAILS – ORNAMENTS

	Price Paid	Value Of My Collection
1.		
2.		
3.		
4.		
5.		
6.		
7.		
8.		
9.		
PENCIL TOTALS		

7 — Values UM $3.99
Turtle
#463256
Issued: 1998 • Open
Retail Price: $3.99

8 NEW! — Values UM $4
Unicorn
#612421
Issued: 1999 • Open
Retail Price: $4

9 NEW! — Values UM $4
Yellow Duck
#478458
Issued: 1999 • Open
Retail Price: $4

VALUE GUIDE — *PRECIOUS MOMENTS*®

1 NEW!
Values
UM $5

Cat
#661546
Issued 1999 • Open
Retail Price: $5

2 NEW!
Values
UM $5

Elephant
#661546
Issued 1999 • Open
Retail Price: $5

3 NEW!
Values
UM $5

Hippo
#661546
Issued 1999 • Open
Retail Price: $5

4 NEW!
Values
UM $5

Monkey
#661546
Issued 1999 • Open
Retail Price: $5

5 NEW!
Values
UM $5

Panda
#661546
Issued 1999 • Open
Retail Price: $5

6 NEW!
Values
UM $5

Unicorn
#661546
Issued 1999 • Open
Retail Price: $5

TENDER TAILS – ATTACHABLES

	Price Paid	Value Of My Collection
1.		
2.		
3.		
4.		
5.		
6.		
PENCIL TOTALS		

CHAPEL EXCLUSIVES

This section features figurines, ornaments and accessories that are only available through the **PRECIOUS MOMENTS** Chapel in Carthage, Missouri or the **PRECIOUS MOMENTS** Chapel catalog. Ten new figurines and one ornament were added in 1998, while six figurines and two ornaments have been introduced so far for 1999. This brings the total number of pieces to 51, with only 33 currently available.

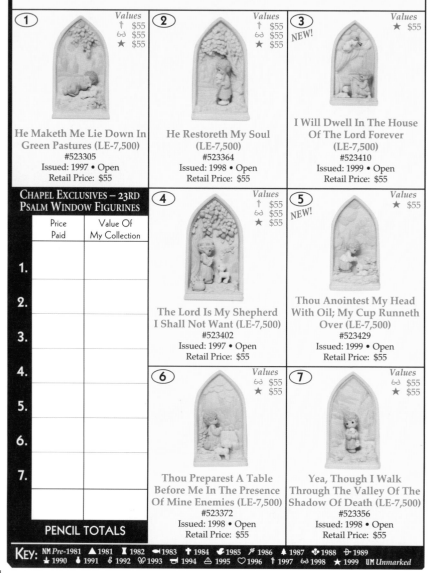

① Values
† $55
6ᴅ $55
★ $55

He Maketh Me Lie Down In Green Pastures (LE-7,500)
#523305
Issued: 1997 • Open
Retail Price: $55

② Values
† $55
6ᴅ $55
★ $55

He Restoreth My Soul (LE-7,500)
#523364
Issued: 1998 • Open
Retail Price: $55

③ NEW! Values
★ $55

I Will Dwell In The House Of The Lord Forever (LE-7,500)
#523410
Issued: 1999 • Open
Retail Price: $55

④ Values
† $55
6ᴅ $55
★ $55

The Lord Is My Shepherd I Shall Not Want (LE-7,500)
#523402
Issued: 1997 • Open
Retail Price: $55

⑤ NEW! Values
★ $55

Thou Anointest My Head With Oil; My Cup Runneth Over (LE-7,500)
#523429
Issued: 1999 • Open
Retail Price: $55

⑥ Values
6ᴅ $55
★ $55

Thou Preparest A Table Before Me In The Presence Of Mine Enemies (LE-7,500)
#523372
Issued: 1998 • Open
Retail Price: $55

⑦ Values
6ᴅ $55
★ $55

Yea, Though I Walk Through The Valley Of The Shadow Of Death (LE-7,500)
#523356
Issued: 1998 • Open
Retail Price: $55

CHAPEL EXCLUSIVES – 23RD PSALM WINDOW FIGURINES

	Price Paid	Value Of My Collection
1.		
2.		
3.		
4.		
5.		
6.		
7.		
PENCIL TOTALS		

KEY: NM *Pre-1981* ▲ 1981 ✗ 1982 ◀ 1983 † 1984 ✦ 1985 ⌘ 1986 ▲ 1987 ❄ 1988 ᵭ 1989 ⚓ 1990 ♦ 1991 ∮ 1992 ♀ 1993 ⬸ 1994 △ 1995 ♡ 1996 † 1997 6ᴅ 1998 ★ 1999 UM *Unmarked*

1 — Values ♔ $63

Blessed Are The Meek, For They Shall Inherit The Earth (LE-1993/1994)
#523313
Issued: 1993 • Closed: 1994
Retail Price: $55

2 — Values ⌐ $65

Blessed Are The Merciful, For They Shall Obtain Mercy (LE-1994)
#523291
Issued: 1994 • Closed: 1994
Retail Price: $55

3 — Values ⌐ $62

Blessed Are The Peacemakers, For They Shall Be Called The Children Of God (LE-1995)
#523348
Issued: 1995 • Closed: 1995
Retail Price: $55

4 — Values ∮ $73

Blessed Are The Poor In Spirit, For Theirs Is The Kingdom Of Heaven (LE-1992)
#523437
Issued: 1992 • Closed: 1992
Retail Price: $55

5 — Values ⌐ $63

Blessed Are The Pure In Heart, For They Shall See God (LE-1994/1995)
#523399
Issued: 1994 • Closed: 1995
Retail Price: $55

6 — Values ♔ $65

Blessed Are They That Hunger And Thirst After Righteousness, For They Shall Be Filled (LE-1993)
#523321
Issued: 1993 • Closed: 1993
Retail Price: $55

7 — Values ∮ $73

Blessed Are They That Mourn, For They Shall Be Comforted (LE-1992)
#523380
Issued: 1992 • Closed: 1992
Retail Price: $55

8 — Values
† $32.50
6ð $32.50
★ $32.50
UM $32.50

Coleenia
#204889
Issued: 1996 • Open
Retail Price: $32.50

9 — Values
† $35
6ð $35
★ $35
UM $42

Crown Him Lord Of All
#261602
Issued: 1997 • Open
Retail Price: $35

10 — Values
⌐ $34
△ $32
♡ $30
† $30
6ð $30
★ $30
UM $45

Death Can't Keep Him In The Ground
#531928
Issued: 1994 • Open
Retail Price: $30

CHAPEL EXCLUSIVES – BEATITUDES WINDOW FIGURINES

	Price Paid	Value Of My Collection
1.		
2.		
3.		
4.		
5.		
6.		
7.		

CHAPEL EXCLUSIVES – GENERAL FIGURINES

8.		
9.		
10.		
PENCIL TOTALS		

CHAPEL EXCLUSIVES

KEY: NM *Pre-1981* ▲ 1981 ✗ 1982 ◄ 1983 † 1984 ✔ 1985 ✗ 1986 ▲ 1987 ✤ 1988 ♭ 1989 ★ 1990 ♦ 1991 ∮ 1992 ♔ 1993 ⌐ 1994 △ 1995 ♡ 1996 † 1997 6ð 1998 ★ 1999 UM *Unmarked*

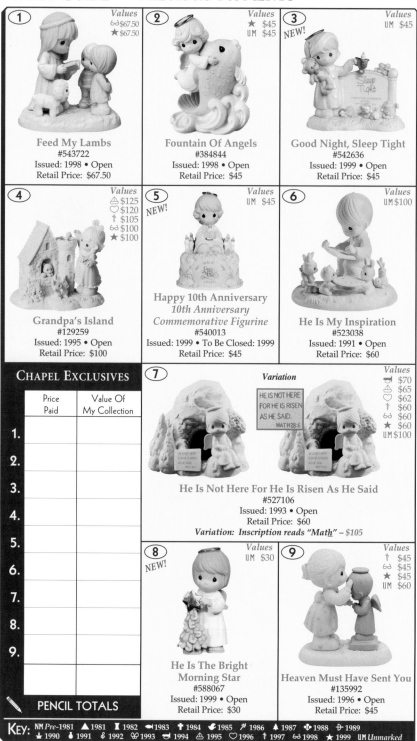

(1) *Values*
6∂ $67.50
★ $67.50

Feed My Lambs
#543722
Issued: 1998 • Open
Retail Price: $67.50

(2) *Values*
★ $45
UM $45

Fountain Of Angels
#384844
Issued: 1998 • Open
Retail Price: $45

(3) NEW! *Values*
UM $45

Good Night, Sleep Tight
#542636
Issued: 1999 • Open
Retail Price: $45

(4) *Values*
△ $125
♡ $120
✝ $105
6∂ $100
★ $100

Grandpa's Island
#129259
Issued: 1995 • Open
Retail Price: $100

(5) NEW! *Values*
UM $45

Happy 10th Anniversary
10th Anniversary
Commemorative Figurine
#540013
Issued: 1999 • To Be Closed: 1999
Retail Price: $45

(6) *Values*
UM $100

He Is My Inspiration
#523038
Issued: 1991 • Open
Retail Price: $60

CHAPEL EXCLUSIVES

	Price Paid	Value Of My Collection
1.		
2.		
3.		
4.		
5.		
6.		
7.		
8.		
9.		
✎ **PENCIL TOTALS**		

(7) *Variation*

Values
🛡 $70
△ $65
♡ $62
✝ $60
6∂ $60
★ $60
UM $100

> HE IS NOT HERE
> FOR HE IS RISEN
> AS HE SAID.
> MATH 28:6

He Is Not Here For He Is Risen As He Said
#527106
Issued: 1993 • Open
Retail Price: $60
Variation: Inscription reads "Math" – $105

(8) NEW! *Values*
UM $30

He Is The Bright Morning Star
#588067
Issued: 1999 • Open
Retail Price: $30

(9) *Values*
✝ $45
6∂ $45
★ $45
UM $60

Heaven Must Have Sent You
#135992
Issued: 1996 • Open
Retail Price: $45

KEY: NM *Pre-1981* ▲ 1981 Ⅱ 1982 ◀1983 ✝ 1984 🍂1985 ♪ 1986 ♣ 1987 ❄ 1988 ⊕ 1989 ★ 1990 ♂ 1991 🎵 1992 ❀1993 ⌐ 1994 △ 1995 ♡1996 ✝ 1997 6∂ 1998 ★ 1999 UM *Unmarked*

206

1

Values
♡ $28
† $25
👓 $25

His Presence Is Felt In The Chapel
#163872
Issued: 1996 • Retired: 1998
Retail Price: $25

2 NEW!

Values
UM $50

I'm Gonna Let It Shine
#349852
Issued: 1999 • Open
Retail Price: $50

3

Values
UM $47

A King Is Born
#604151
Issued: 1994 • Retired: 1995
Retail Price: $25

4

Values
△ $45
♡ $38
† $30
👓 $30

Lighting The Way To A Happy Holiday
#129267
Issued: 1995 • Retired: 1998
Retail Price: $30

5

Values
UM $45

The Lord Is Our Chief Inspiration
#204862
Issued: 1996 • Open
Retail Price: $45

6

Values
UM $282

The Lord Is Our Chief Inspiration (9", LE-1996/1997)
#204870
Issued: 1996 • Closed: 1997
Retail Price: $250

7

Values
♡ $50
† $45
👓 $45
UM $85

On The Hill Overlooking The Quiet Blue Stream
#603503
Issued: 1994 • Retired: 1998
Retail Price: $45

8 NEW!

Values
UM $90

Our Love Will Flow Eternal
#588059
Issued: 1999 • Open
Retail Price: $90

9

Values
★ $45
UM $45

A Prayer Warrior's Faith Can Move Mountains
#354406
Issued: 1998 • Open
Retail Price: $45

10

Values
👓 $250
★ $250

A Prayer Warrior's Faith Can Move Mountains (9", LE-1998)
#354414
Issued: 1998 • Closed: 1998
Retail Price: $250

CHAPEL EXCLUSIVES

	Price Paid	Value Of My Collection
1.		
2.		
3.		
4.		
5.		
6.		
7.		
8.		
9.		
10.		
PENCIL TOTALS		

CHAPEL EXCLUSIVES

KEY: NM *Pre-1981* ▲ 1981 Ⅰ 1982 ◀1983 † 1984 ◢1985 ⌗ 1986 ♠ 1987 ❀1988 ☼ 1989 ★ 1990 ♦ 1991 ✦ 1992 ❀1993 ⬤ 1994 △ 1995 ♡ 1996 † 1997 👓 1998 ★ 1999 UM *Unmarked*

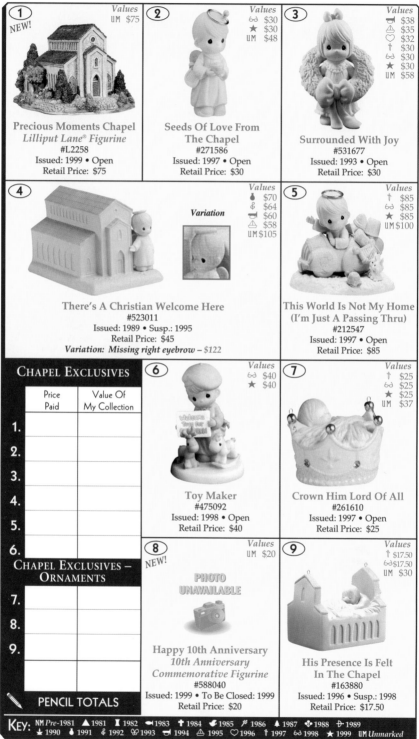

1 NEW!

Values
UM $75

Precious Moments Chapel
Lilliput Lane® Figurine
#L2258
Issued: 1999 • Open
Retail Price: $75

2

Values
6ə $30
★ $30
UM $48

Seeds Of Love From The Chapel
#271586
Issued: 1997 • Open
Retail Price: $30

3

Values
⊸ $38
△ $35
♡ $32
† $30
6ə $30
★ $30
UM $58

Surrounded With Joy
#531677
Issued: 1993 • Open
Retail Price: $30

4

Values
♦ $70
₰ $64
⊸ $60
△ $58
UM $105

Variation

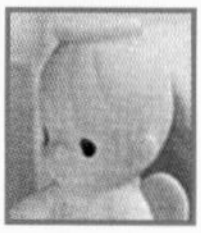

There's A Christian Welcome Here
#523011
Issued: 1989 • Susp.: 1995
Retail Price: $45
Variation: Missing right eyebrow – $122

5

Values
† $85
6ə $85
★ $85
UM $100

This World Is Not My Home (I'm Just A Passing Thru)
#212547
Issued: 1997 • Open
Retail Price: $85

CHAPEL EXCLUSIVES

	Price Paid	Value Of My Collection
1.		
2.		
3.		
4.		
5.		
6.		

CHAPEL EXCLUSIVES – ORNAMENTS

	Price Paid	Value Of My Collection
7.		
8.		
9.		
PENCIL TOTALS		

6

Values
6ə $40
★ $40

Toy Maker
#475092
Issued: 1998 • Open
Retail Price: $40

7

Values
† $25
6ə $25
★ $25
UM $37

Crown Him Lord Of All
#261610
Issued: 1997 • Open
Retail Price: $25

8 NEW!

Values
UM $20

PHOTO
UNAVAILABLE

Happy 10th Anniversary
10th Anniversary Commemorative Figurine
#588040
Issued: 1999 • To Be Closed: 1999
Retail Price: $20

9

Values
† $17.50
6ə $17.50
UM $30

His Presence Is Felt In The Chapel
#163880
Issued: 1996 • Susp.: 1998
Retail Price: $17.50

KEY: NM *Pre*-1981 ▲ 1981 Ⅰ 1982 ◄ 1983 ✝ 1984 ❦ 1985 ⚘ 1986 ♠ 1987 ✤ 1988 ⊕ 1989 ⚓ 1990 ♦ 1991 ₰ 1992 ⚘ 1993 ⊸ 1994 △ 1995 ♡ 1996 † 1997 6ə 1998 ★ 1999 UM *Unmarked*

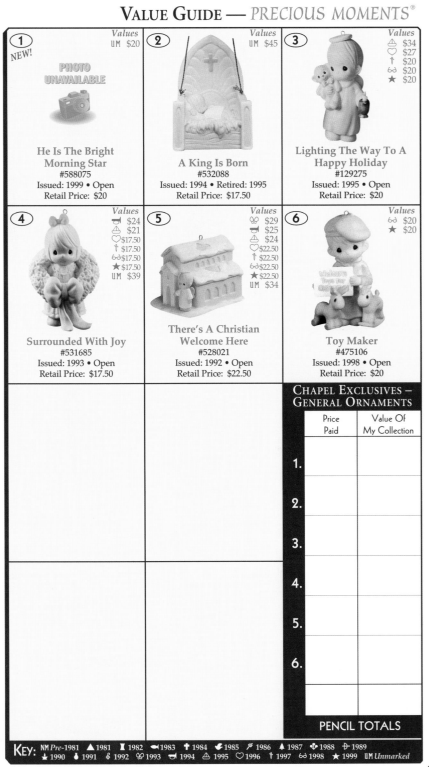

1 NEW!

Values
UM $20

PHOTO UNAVAILABLE

He Is The Bright Morning Star
#588075
Issued: 1999 • Open
Retail Price: $20

2

Values
UM $45

A King Is Born
#532088
Issued: 1994 • Retired: 1995
Retail Price: $17.50

3

Values
△ $34
♡ $27
† $20
ᵔ $20
★ $20

Lighting The Way To A Happy Holiday
#129275
Issued: 1995 • Open
Retail Price: $20

4

Values
◁ $24
△ $21
♡ $17.50
† $17.50
ᵔ $17.50
★ $17.50
UM $39

Surrounded With Joy
#531685
Issued: 1993 • Open
Retail Price: $17.50

5

Values
ᏇᏇ $29
◁ $25
△ $24
♡ $22.50
† $22.50
ᵔ $22.50
★ $22.50
UM $34

There's A Christian Welcome Here
#528021
Issued: 1992 • Open
Retail Price: $22.50

6

Values
ᵔ $20
★ $20

Toy Maker
#475106
Issued: 1998 • Open
Retail Price: $20

CHAPEL EXCLUSIVES – GENERAL ORNAMENTS

	Price Paid	Value Of My Collection
1.		
2.		
3.		
4.		
5.		
6.		

PENCIL TOTALS

CHAPEL EXCLUSIVES

KEY: NM *Pre*-1981 ▲1981 Ⅱ1982 ◄1983 †1984 ◄1985 ∦1986 ▲1987 ✤1988 ꝯ1989 ✦1990 ♦1991 ₰1992 ᏇᏇ1993 ◁1994 △1995 ♡1996 †1997 ᵔ1998 ★1999 UM *Unmarked*

COLLECTORS' CLUB

This section features pieces that are only available to club members and is divided into three sections: *Collectors' Club* pieces, *Birthday Club* pieces and *Fun Club* pieces. So far for 1999, there are 12 pieces for members to collect.

①

Values
NM $195
▲ $158
✗ $155

But Love Goes On Forever
(charter member figurine)
#E0001
Issued: 1981 • Closed: 1981
Retail Price: N/A

②

Values
▲ $92
✗ $78
UM $120

But Love Goes On Forever
(charter member plaque)
#E0102
Issued: 1982 • Closed: 1982
Retail Price: N/A

③

Variation

PHOTO
UNAVAILABLE

Values
▲ $82
✗ $70
UM $115

But Love Goes On Forever
#E0202
Issued: 1982 • Closed: 1982
Retail Price: N/A
Variation: 🍃 *(mistakenly produced and shipped to Canada)* – $122

COLLECTORS' CLUB – SYMBOL OF MEMBERSHIP FIGURINES

	Price Paid	Value Of My Collection
1.		
2.		
3.		
4.		
5.		
6.		
7.		
PENCIL TOTALS		

④

Values
✗ $72
🍃 $62

Let Us Call The Club To Order
(charter member figurine)
#E0103
Issued: 1983 • Closed: 1983
Retail Price: N/A

⑤

Values
✗ $68
🍃 $60
† $58

Let Us Call The Club To Order
#E0303
Issued: 1983 • Closed: 1983
Retail Price: N/A

⑥

Values
🍃 $66
† $54

Join In On The Blessings
(charter member figurine)
#E0104
Issued: 1984 • Closed: 1984
Retail Price: N/A

⑦

Values
🍃 $58
† $46

Join In On The Blessings
#E0404
Issued: 1984 • Closed: 1984
Retail Price: N/A

KEY: NM *Pre-1981* ▲ 1981 ✗ 1982 🍃 1983 † 1984 🍃 1985 ⌇ 1986 ▲ 1987 ✦ 1988 ⊕ 1989
★ 1990 ● 1991 ✦ 1992 ♈ 1993 ⌇ 1994 △ 1995 ♡ 1996 † 1997 ᵔ 1998 ★ 1999 UM *Unmarked*

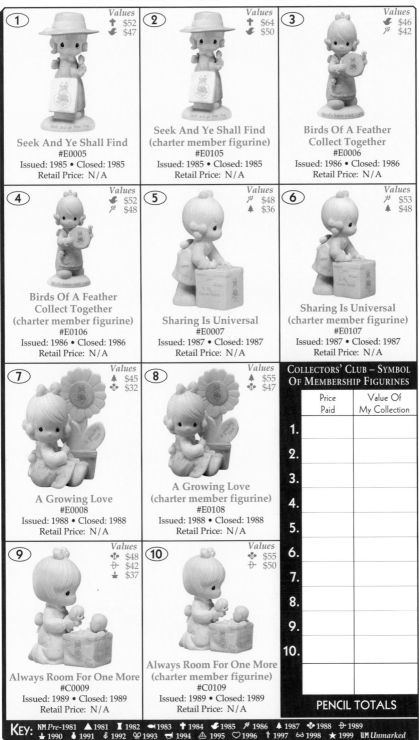

1 Values
† $52
🦋 $47

Seek And Ye Shall Find
#E0005
Issued: 1985 • Closed: 1985
Retail Price: N/A

2 Values
† $64
🦋 $50

Seek And Ye Shall Find
(charter member figurine)
#E0105
Issued: 1985 • Closed: 1985
Retail Price: N/A

3 Values
🦋 $46
♫ $42

Birds Of A Feather
Collect Together
#E0006
Issued: 1986 • Closed: 1986
Retail Price: N/A

4 Values
🦋 $52
♫ $48

Birds Of A Feather
Collect Together
(charter member figurine)
#E0106
Issued: 1986 • Closed: 1986
Retail Price: N/A

5 Values
♫ $48
♠ $36

Sharing Is Universal
#E0007
Issued: 1987 • Closed: 1987
Retail Price: N/A

6 Values
♫ $53
♠ $48

Sharing Is Universal
(charter member figurine)
#E0107
Issued: 1987 • Closed: 1987
Retail Price: N/A

7 Values
♠ $45
⚓ $32

A Growing Love
#E0008
Issued: 1988 • Closed: 1988
Retail Price: N/A

8 Values
♠ $55
⚓ $47

A Growing Love
(charter member figurine)
#E0108
Issued: 1988 • Closed: 1988
Retail Price: N/A

9 Values
⚓ $48
🕊 $42
⚘ $37

Always Room For One More
#C0009
Issued: 1989 • Closed: 1989
Retail Price: N/A

10 Values
⚓ $55
🕊 $50

Always Room For One More
(charter member figurine)
#C0109
Issued: 1989 • Closed: 1989
Retail Price: N/A

COLLECTORS' CLUB – SYMBOL OF MEMBERSHIP FIGURINES

	Price Paid	Value Of My Collection
1.		
2.		
3.		
4.		
5.		
6.		
7.		
8.		
9.		
10.		
PENCIL TOTALS		

KEY: NM *Pre-1981* ▲ 1981 ▐ 1982 ◄ 1983 † 1984 🦋 1985 ♫ 1986 ♠ 1987 ⚓ 1988 🕊 1989 ⚘ 1990 🔔 1991 🔥 1992 ✿ 1993 🍴 1994 △ 1995 ♡ 1996 † 1997 🔗 1998 ★ 1999 UM *Unmarked*

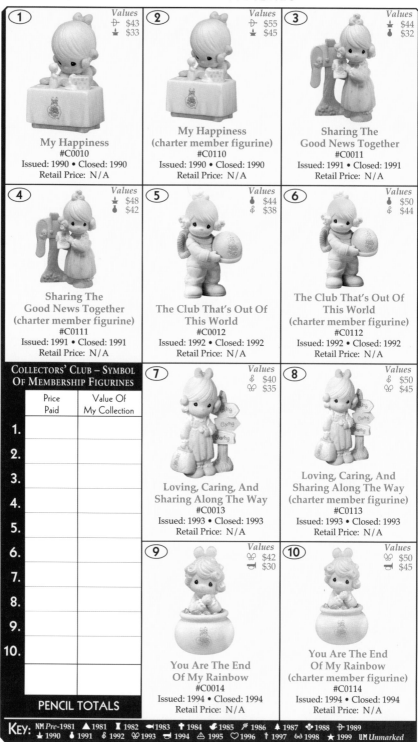

1

Values
🕭 $43
★ $33

My Happiness
#C0010
Issued: 1990 • Closed: 1990
Retail Price: N/A

2

Values
🕭 $55
★ $45

My Happiness
(charter member figurine)
#C0110
Issued: 1990 • Closed: 1990
Retail Price: N/A

3

Values
★ $44
🌡 $32

Sharing The
Good News Together
#C0011
Issued: 1991 • Closed: 1991
Retail Price: N/A

4

Values
★ $48
🌡 $42

Sharing The
Good News Together
(charter member figurine)
#C0111
Issued: 1991 • Closed: 1991
Retail Price: N/A

5

Values
🌡 $44
🎗 $38

The Club That's Out Of
This World
#C0012
Issued: 1992 • Closed: 1992
Retail Price: N/A

6

Values
🌡 $50
🎗 $44

The Club That's Out Of
This World
(charter member figurine)
#C0112
Issued: 1992 • Closed: 1992
Retail Price: N/A

COLLECTORS' CLUB – SYMBOL
OF MEMBERSHIP FIGURINES

	Price Paid	Value Of My Collection
1.		
2.		
3.		
4.		
5.		
6.		
7.		
8.		
9.		
10.		

PENCIL TOTALS

7

Values
🎗 $40
🎗🎗 $35

Loving, Caring, And
Sharing Along The Way
#C0013
Issued: 1993 • Closed: 1993
Retail Price: N/A

8

Values
🎗 $50
🎗🎗 $45

Loving, Caring, And
Sharing Along The Way
(charter member figurine)
#C0113
Issued: 1993 • Closed: 1993
Retail Price: N/A

9

Values
🎗🎗 $42
🥄 $30

You Are The End
Of My Rainbow
#C0014
Issued: 1994 • Closed: 1994
Retail Price: N/A

10

Values
🎗🎗 $50
🥄 $45

You Are The End
Of My Rainbow
(charter member figurine)
#C0114
Issued: 1994 • Closed: 1994
Retail Price: N/A

KEY: NM *Pre-1981* ▲1981 Ⅱ1982 ◄1983 ✝1984 ✦1985 ♪1986 ▲1987 ❖1988 🕭1989 ★1990 🌡1991 🎗1992 🎗🎗1993 🥄1994 ⚠1995 ♡1996 ✝1997 ∾1998 ★1999 UM *Unmarked*

212

VALUE GUIDE — *PRECIOUS MOMENTS*®

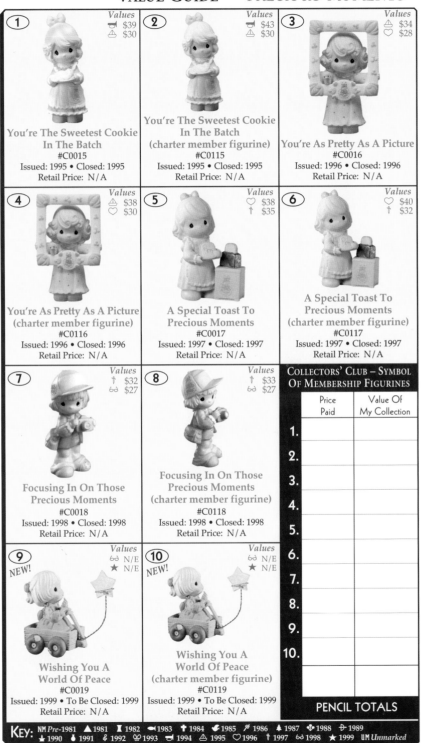

1 Values
🏺 $39
⬜ $30

You're The Sweetest Cookie
In The Batch
#C0015
Issued: 1995 • Closed: 1995
Retail Price: N/A

2 Values
🏺 $43
⬜ $30

You're The Sweetest Cookie
In The Batch
(charter member figurine)
#C0115
Issued: 1995 • Closed: 1995
Retail Price: N/A

3 Values
⬜ $34
♡ $28

You're As Pretty As A Picture
#C0016
Issued: 1996 • Closed: 1996
Retail Price: N/A

4 Values
⬜ $38
♡ $30

You're As Pretty As A Picture
(charter member figurine)
#C0116
Issued: 1996 • Closed: 1996
Retail Price: N/A

5 Values
♡ $38
† $35

A Special Toast To
Precious Moments
#C0017
Issued: 1997 • Closed: 1997
Retail Price: N/A

6 Values
♡ $40
† $32

A Special Toast To
Precious Moments
(charter member figurine)
#C0117
Issued: 1997 • Closed: 1997
Retail Price: N/A

7 Values
† $32
6ð $27

Focusing In On Those
Precious Moments
#C0018
Issued: 1998 • Closed: 1998
Retail Price: N/A

8 Values
† $33
6ð $27

Focusing In On Those
Precious Moments
(charter member figurine)
#C0118
Issued: 1998 • Closed: 1998
Retail Price: N/A

9 NEW! Values
6ð N/E
★ N/E

Wishing You A
World Of Peace
#C0019
Issued: 1999 • To Be Closed: 1999
Retail Price: N/A

10 NEW! Values
6ð N/E
★ N/E

Wishing You A
World Of Peace
(charter member figurine)
#C0119
Issued: 1999 • To Be Closed: 1999
Retail Price: N/A

COLLECTORS' CLUB – SYMBOL OF MEMBERSHIP FIGURINES

	Price Paid	Value Of My Collection
1.		
2.		
3.		
4.		
5.		
6.		
7.		
8.		
9.		
10.		
PENCIL TOTALS		

KEY: NM *Pre-1981* ▲1981 Ⅱ1982 ◀1983 †1984 ◢1985 ♪1986 ♣1987 ♣1988 ♫1989 ★1990 ♦1991 ♬1992 ♀1993 🏺1994 ⬜1995 ♡1996 †1997 6ð1998 ★1999 UM *Unmarked*

COLLECTORS' CLUB

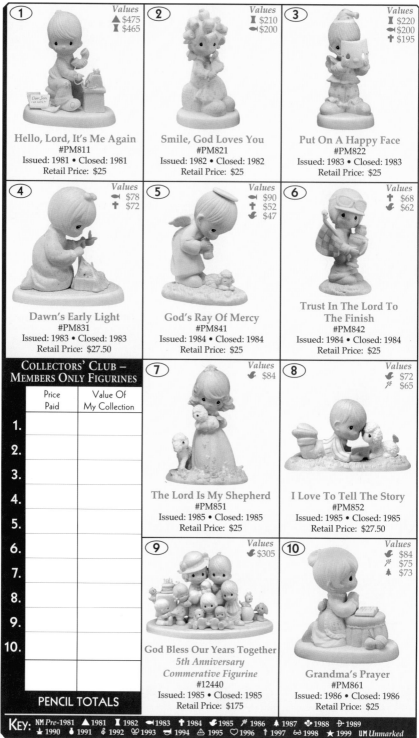

① *Values* ▲ $475 ⧗ $465

Hello, Lord, It's Me Again
#PM811
Issued: 1981 • Closed: 1981
Retail Price: $25

② *Values* ⧗ $210 🐟 $200

Smile, God Loves You
#PM821
Issued: 1982 • Closed: 1982
Retail Price: $25

③ *Values* ⧗ $220 🐟 $200 ✝ $195

Put On A Happy Face
#PM822
Issued: 1983 • Closed: 1983
Retail Price: $25

④ *Values* 🐟 $78 ✝ $72

Dawn's Early Light
#PM831
Issued: 1983 • Closed: 1983
Retail Price: $27.50

⑤ *Values* 🐟 $90 ✝ $52 🕊 $47

God's Ray Of Mercy
#PM841
Issued: 1984 • Closed: 1984
Retail Price: $25

⑥ *Values* ✝ $68 🕊 $62

Trust In The Lord To The Finish
#PM842
Issued: 1984 • Closed: 1984
Retail Price: $25

COLLECTORS' CLUB – MEMBERS ONLY FIGURINES

	Price Paid	Value Of My Collection
1.		
2.		
3.		
4.		
5.		
6.		
7.		
8.		
9.		
10.		
PENCIL TOTALS		

⑦ *Values* 🕊 $84

The Lord Is My Shepherd
#PM851
Issued: 1985 • Closed: 1985
Retail Price: $25

⑧ *Values* 🕊 $72 🌿 $65

I Love To Tell The Story
#PM852
Issued: 1985 • Closed: 1985
Retail Price: $27.50

⑨ *Values* 🕊 $305

God Bless Our Years Together
5th Anniversary Commerative Figurine
#12440
Issued: 1985 • Closed: 1985
Retail Price: $175

⑩ *Values* 🕊 $84 🌿 $75 🌲 $73

Grandma's Prayer
#PM861
Issued: 1986 • Closed: 1986
Retail Price: $25

KEY: NM *Pre*-1981 ▲ 1981 ⧗ 1982 🐟 1983 ✝ 1984 🕊 1985 🌿 1986 🌲 1987 ✿ 1988 ➹ 1989 🔥 1990 ⚱ 1991 𝄞 1992 🦋 1993 🎺 1994 ⛵ 1995 ♡ 1996 🗡 1997 👓 1998 ★ 1999 UM *Unmarked*

(1) Values
🎨 $88

I'm Following Jesus
#PM862
Issued: 1986 • Closed: 1986
Retail Price: $25

(2) Values
🎨 $92
▲ $65
⚓ $58

Feed My Sheep
#PM871
Issued: 1987 • Closed: 1987
Retail Price: $25

(3) Values
🎨 $64
▲ $55
⚓ $50

In His Time
#PM872
Issued: 1987 • Closed: 1987
Retail Price: $25

(4) Values
🎨 $47
▲ $40
⚓ $37

Loving You Dear Valentine
#PM873
Issued: 1987 • Closed: 1987
Retail Price: $25

(5) Values
🎨 $49
▲ $44
⚓ $40

Loving You Dear Valentine
#PM874
Issued: 1987 • Closed: 1987
Retail Price: $25

(6) Values
▲ $68
⚓ $57
🕯 $50

God Bless You For Touching My Life
#PM881
Issued: 1988 • Closed: 1988
Retail Price: $27.50

(7) Values
⚓ $55
🕯 $49

You Just Cannot Chuck A Good Friendship
#PM882
Issued: 1988 • Closed: 1988
Retail Price: $27.50

(8) Values
🕯 $49
🌟 $43

You Will Always Be My Choice
#PM891
Issued: 1989 • Closed: 1989
Retail Price: $27.50

(9) Values
🕯 $64
🌟 $56

Mow Power To Ya!
#PM892
Issued: 1989 • Closed: 1989
Retail Price: $27.50

(10) Values
🌟 $52
🌡 $50

Ten Years And Still Going Strong
#PM901
Issued: 1990 • Closed: 1990
Retail Price: $30

COLLECTORS' CLUB – MEMBERS ONLY FIGURINES

	Price Paid	Value Of My Collection
1.		
2.		
3.		
4.		
5.		
6.		
7.		
8.		
9.		
10.		
PENCIL TOTALS		

KEY: NM *Pre-1981* ▲ 1981 ✠ 1982 ◄ 1983 ✝ 1984 ✦ 1985 🎨 1986 ▲ 1987 ⚓ 1988 🕯 1989 🌟 1990 🌡 1991 ✎ 1992 ✿ 1993 ✦ 1994 ⚠ 1995 ♡ 1996 ✝ 1997 👓 1998 ★ 1999 UM *Unmarked*

① You Are A Blessing To Me
Values
★ $63
🌡 $55
#PM902
Issued: 1990 • Closed: 1990
Retail Price: $27.50

② One Step At A Time
Values
🌡 $60
✿ $52
#PM911
Issued: 1991 • Closed: 1991
Retail Price: $33

③ Lord, Keep Me In Teepee Top Shape
Values
🌡 $64
✿ $57
#PM912
Issued: 1991 • Closed: 1991
Retail Price: $27.50

④ Only Love Can Make A Home
Values
✿ $70
❀ $63
#PM921
Issued: 1992 • Closed: 1992
Retail Price: $30

⑤ Sowing The Seeds Of Love
Values
✿ $45
❀ $41
#PM922
Issued: 1992 • Closed: 1992
Retail Price: $30

⑥ This Land Is Our Land (LE-1992)
Values
✿ $390
#527386
Issued: 1992 • Closed: 1992
Retail Price: $350

**COLLECTORS' CLUB –
MEMBERS ONLY FIGURINES**

	Price Paid	Value Of My Collection
1.		
2.		
3.		
4.		
5.		
6.		
7.		
8.		
9.		
10.		
PENCIL TOTALS		

⑦ His Little Treasure
Values
❀ $50
◁ $46
#PM931
Issued: 1993 • Closed: 1993
Retail Price: $30

⑧ Loving
Values
❀ $78
◁ $70
#PM932
Issued: 1993 • Closed: 1993
Retail Price: $30

⑨ Caring
Values
◁ $63
△ $60
#PM941
Issued: 1994 • Closed: 1994
Retail Price: $35

⑩ Sharing
Values
◁ $63
△ $60
#PM942
Issued: 1994 • Closed: 1994
Retail Price: $35

KEY: NM *Pre-1981* ▲1981 ✗1982 ◀1983 ✝1984 ✦1985 ♯1986 ♣1987 ❧1988 ♉1989
★1990 🌡1991 ✿1992 ❀1993 ◁1994 △1995 ♡1996 ✝1997 ໖1998 ★1999 **UM** *Unmarked*

1 *Values* ⚰ $82

You Fill The Pages Of My Life (w/book, stock number for figurine is #530980)
#PMB034
Issued: 1994 • Closed: 1995
Retail Price: $67.50

2 *Values* △ $45

You're One In A Million To Me
#PM951
Issued: 1995 • Closed: 1995
Retail Price: $35

3 *Values* △ $48

Always Take Time To Pray
#PM952
Issued: 1995 • Closed: 1995
Retail Price: $35

4 *Values* △ $125

A Perfect Display Of Fifteen Happy Years
15th Anniversary Commemorative Figurine
#127817
Issued: 1995 • Closed: 1995
Retail Price: $100

5 *Values* △ $56 ♡ $50

Teach Us To Love One Another
#PM961
Issued: 1996 • Closed: 1996
Retail Price: $40

6 *Values* ♡ $62

Our Club Is Soda-licious
#PM962
Issued: 1996 • Closed: 1996
Retail Price: $35

7 *Values* ✝ $55

You Will Always Be A Treasure To Me
#PM971
Issued: 1997 • Closed: 1997
Retail Price: $50

8 *Values* ✝ $48

Blessed Are The Merciful
#PM972
Issued: 1997 • Closed: 1997
Retail Price: $40

9 *Values* 6ð $52

Happy Trails
#PM981
Issued: 1998 • Closed: 1998
Retail Price: $50

10 *Values* 6ð $47

Lord, Please Don't Put Me On Hold
#PM982
Issued: 1998 • Closed: 1998
Retail Price: $40

COLLECTORS' CLUB – MEMBERS ONLY FIGURINES

	Price Paid	Value Of My Collection
1.		
2.		
3.		
4.		
5.		
6.		
7.		
8.		
9.		
10.		
·		
PENCIL TOTALS		

COLLECTORS' CLUB

KEY: NM *Pre-1981* ▲ 1981 ❚ 1982 ◀1983 ✝ 1984 ✔ 1985 ♯ 1986 ▲ 1987 ✤ 1988 ♉ 1989 ☘ 1990 ▲ 1991 ✤ 1992 ❀ 1993 ◁ 1994 △ 1995 ♡ 1996 ✝ 1997 6ð 1998 ★ 1999 UM *Unmarked*

1 *Values* 6ð N/E

How Can Two Work Together Except They Agree
20th Anniversary Commemorative Figurine
#PM983
Issued: 1998 • Closed: 1998
Retail Price: $125

2 NEW! *Values* ★ $30

Jumping For Joy
#PM991
Issued: 1999 • To Be Closed: 1999
Retail Price: $30

3 NEW! *Values* ★ $30

God Speed
#PM992
Issued: 1999 • To Be Closed: 1999
Retail Price: $30

4 NEW! *Values* ★ $225

He Watches Over Us All
Millennium Figurine
#PM993
Issued: 1999 • To Be Closed: 1999
Retail Price: $225

5 *Values* UM $22

Blessed Are The Meek, For They Shall Inherit The Earth
#PM390
Issued: 1990 • Closed: 1990
Retail Price: $15

6 *Values* UM $22

Blessed Are The Merciful, For They Shall Obtain Mercy
#PM590
Issued: 1990 • Closed: 1990
Retail Price: $15

COLLECTORS' CLUB – MEMBERS ONLY FIGURINES

	Price Paid	Value Of My Collection
1.		
2.		
3.		
4.		

COLLECTORS' CLUB – MEMBERS ONLY ORNAMENTS

5.		
6.		
7.		
8.		
9.		
10.		

PENCIL TOTALS

7 *Values* UM $22

Blessed Are The Peacemakers, For They Shall Be Called Sons Of God
#PM790
Issued: 1990 • Closed: 1990
Retail Price: $15

8 *Values* UM $22

Blessed Are The Poor In Spirit, For Theirs Is The Kingdom Of Heaven
#PM190
Issued: 1990 • Closed: 1990
Retail Price: $15

9 *Values* UM $22

Blessed Are The Pure In Heart, For They Shall See God
#PM690
Issued: 1990 • Closed: 1990
Retail Price: $15

10 *Values* UM $22

Blessed Are They That Hunger And Thirst, For They Shall Be Filled
#PM490
Issued: 1990 • Closed: 1990
Retail Price: $15

KEY: NM *Pre-1981* ▲ 1981 ✗ 1982 ◄1983 ✝ 1984 ✦ 1985 ♪ 1986 ▲ 1987 ✿ 1988 Ꝺ 1989 ★ 1990 ● 1991 ℰ 1992 ❀1993 ➡ 1994 △ 1995 ♡1996 ✝ 1997 6ð 1998 ★ 1999 UM *Unmarked*

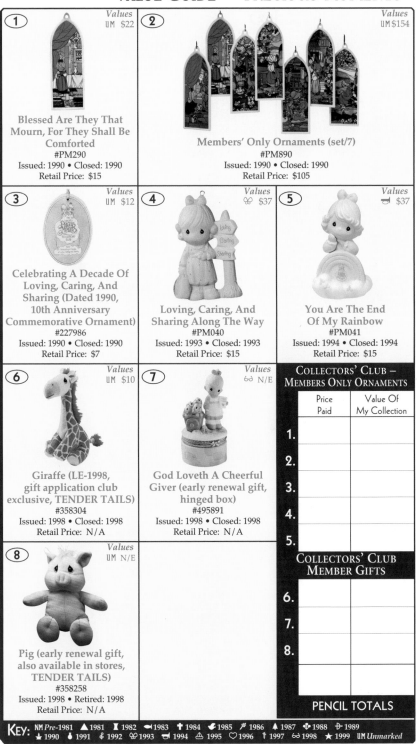

1 — *Values* UM $22

Blessed Are They That Mourn, For They Shall Be Comforted
#PM290
Issued: 1990 • Closed: 1990
Retail Price: $15

2 — *Values* UM $154

Members' Only Ornaments (set/7)
#PM890
Issued: 1990 • Closed: 1990
Retail Price: $105

3 — *Values* UM $12

Celebrating A Decade Of Loving, Caring, And Sharing (Dated 1990, 10th Anniversary Commemorative Ornament)
#227986
Issued: 1990 • Closed: 1990
Retail Price: $7

4 — *Values* ♉ $37

Loving, Caring, And Sharing Along The Way
#PM040
Issued: 1993 • Closed: 1993
Retail Price: $15

5 — *Values* ⊐ $37

You Are The End Of My Rainbow
#PM041
Issued: 1994 • Closed: 1994
Retail Price: $15

6 — *Values* UM $10

Giraffe (LE-1998, gift application club exclusive, TENDER TAILS)
#358304
Issued: 1998 • Closed: 1998
Retail Price: N/A

7 — *Values* �6Ꮷ N/E

God Loveth A Cheerful Giver (early renewal gift, hinged box)
#495891
Issued: 1998 • Closed: 1998
Retail Price: N/A

8 — *Values* UM N/E

Pig (early renewal gift, also available in stores, TENDER TAILS)
#358258
Issued: 1998 • Retired: 1998
Retail Price: N/A

COLLECTORS' CLUB – MEMBERS ONLY ORNAMENTS

	Price Paid	Value Of My Collection
1.		
2.		
3.		
4.		
5.		

COLLECTORS' CLUB MEMBER GIFTS

6.		
7.		
8.		
PENCIL TOTALS		

COLLECTORS' CLUB

1
Values
† $85
6ð $85

Faith Is The Victory
#283592
Issued: 1997 • Closed: 1998
Retail Price: N/A

2
Values
† $68
6ð $68

God Bless You With Bouquets Of Victory
#283584
Issued: 1997 • Closed: 1998
Retail Price: N/A

3
Values
UM N/E

PHOTO UNAVAILABLE

Lord, It's Hard To Be Humble
N/A
Issued: 1998 • Closed: 1998
Retail Price: N/A

4
Values
† $45
6ð $45

Rejoice In The Victory
#283541
Issued: 1997 • Closed: 1998
Retail Price: N/A

5
Values
† $115

PRECIOUS MOMENTS LAST FOREVER

Precious Moments Last Forever (medallion)
#12246
Issued: 1984 • Closed: 1984
Retail Price: N/A

6
Values
✝ $175

Birds Of A Feather Collect Together (ornament)
#PM864
Issued: 1986 • Closed: 1986
Retail Price: N/A

COLLECTORS' CLUB – PRECIOUS REWARDS FIGURINES

	Price Paid	Value Of My Collection
1.		
2.		
3.		
4.		

COLLECTORS' CLUB SHARING SEASON GIFTS

5.		
6.		
7.		
8.		
9.		
10.		

PENCIL TOTALS

7
Values
❖ $70

A Growing Love (ornament)
#520349
Issued: 1988 • Closed: 1988
Retail Price: N/A

8
Values
Ð $98

Always Room For One More (ornament)
#522961
Issued: 1989 • Closed: 1989
Retail Price: N/A

9
Values
★ $88

My Happiness (ornament)
#PM904
Issued: 1990 • Closed: 1990
Retail Price: N/A

10
Values
🌢 $83

Sharing The Good News Together (ornament)
#PM037
Issued: 1991 • Closed: 1991
Retail Price: N/A

KEY: NM *Pre-1981* ▲1981 ✗1982 ◄1983 † 1984 ✦1985 ℣ 1986 ▲ 1987 ❖ 1988 Ð 1989 ★ 1990 🌢 1991 ℰ 1992 ♋1993 ⊟ 1994 △ 1995 ♡1996 † 1997 6ð 1998 ★ 1999 UM *Unmarked*

220

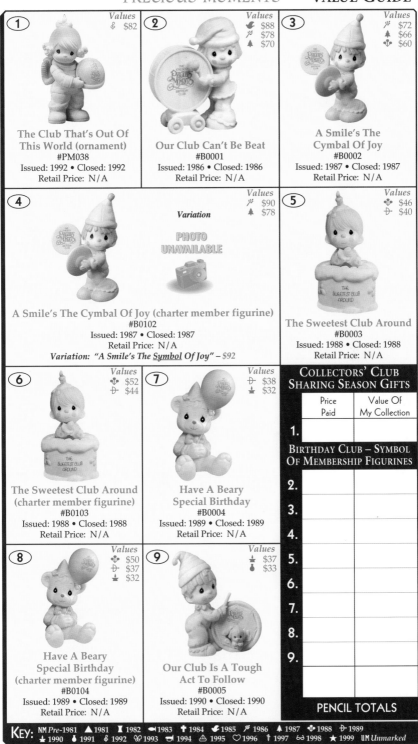

(1)
Values
& $82

The Club That's Out Of This World (ornament)
#PM038
Issued: 1992 • Closed: 1992
Retail Price: N/A

(2)
Values
✔ $88
♠ $78
♣ $70

Our Club Can't Be Beat
#B0001
Issued: 1986 • Closed: 1986
Retail Price: N/A

(3)
Values
♪ $72
♠ $66
⚓ $60

A Smile's The Cymbal Of Joy
#B0002
Issued: 1987 • Closed: 1987
Retail Price: N/A

(4)
Values
♪ $90
♠ $78

Variation

PHOTO UNAVAILABLE

A Smile's The Cymbal Of Joy (charter member figurine)
#B0102
Issued: 1987 • Closed: 1987
Retail Price: N/A
Variation: "A Smile's The Symbol Of Joy" – $92

(5)
Values
⬥ $46
ᵭ $40

The Sweetest Club Around
#B0003
Issued: 1988 • Closed: 1988
Retail Price: N/A

(6)
Values
⬥ $52
ᵭ $44

The Sweetest Club Around (charter member figurine)
#B0103
Issued: 1988 • Closed: 1988
Retail Price: N/A

(7)
Values
ᵭ $38
★ $32

Have A Beary Special Birthday
#B0004
Issued: 1989 • Closed: 1989
Retail Price: N/A

(8)
Values
⬥ $50
ᵭ $37
★ $32

Have A Beary Special Birthday (charter member figurine)
#B0104
Issued: 1989 • Closed: 1989
Retail Price: N/A

(9)
Values
★ $37
♦ $33

Our Club Is A Tough Act To Follow
#B0005
Issued: 1990 • Closed: 1990
Retail Price: N/A

COLLECTORS' CLUB SHARING SEASON GIFTS

	Price Paid	Value Of My Collection
1.		

BIRTHDAY CLUB – SYMBOL OF MEMBERSHIP FIGURINES

2.		
3.		
4.		
5.		
6.		
7.		
8.		
9.		
PENCIL TOTALS		

COLLECTORS'/BIRTHDAY

1

Values
⭐ $34
🕯 $30

**Our Club Is A Tough
Act To Follow**
(charter member figurine)
#B0105
Issued: 1990 • Closed: 1990
Retail Price: N/A

2

Values
🕯 $36
🔔 $32

**Jest To Let You Know
You're Tops**
#B0006
Issued: 1991 • Closed: 1991
Retail Price: N/A

3

Values
🕯 $37
🔔 $30

**Jest To Let You Know
You're Tops**
(charter member figurine)
#B0106
Issued: 1991 • Closed: 1991
Retail Price: N/A

4

Values
🔔 $39
🌼 $33

**All Aboard For
Birthday Club Fun**
#B0007
Issued: 1992 • Closed: 1992
Retail Price: N/A

5

Values
🔔 $42
🌼 $35

**All Aboard For
Birthday Club Fun**
(charter member figurine)
#B0107
Issued: 1992 • Closed: 1992
Retail Price: N/A

6

Values
🌼 $30
🛋 $25

Happiness Is Belonging
#B0008
Issued: 1993 • Closed: 1993
Retail Price: N/A

BIRTHDAY CLUB – SYMBOL OF MEMBERSHIP FIGURINES

	Price Paid	Value Of My Collection
1.		
2.		
3.		
4.		
5.		
6.		
7.		
8.		
9.		
10.		
PENCIL TOTALS		

7

Values
🌼 $37
🛋 $32

Happiness Is Belonging
(charter member figurine)
#B0108
Issued: 1993 • Closed: 1993
Retail Price: N/A

8

Values
🛋 $33
△ $29

**Can't Get Enough
Of Our Club**
#B0009
Issued: 1994 • Closed: 1995
Retail Price: N/A

9

Values
🛋 $38
△ $32

**Can't Get Enough
Of Our Club**
(charter member figurine)
#B0109
Issued: 1994 • Closed: 1995
Retail Price: N/A

10

Values
△ $34
♡ $29

Hoppy Birthday
#B0010
Issued: 1995 • Closed: 1996
Retail Price: N/A

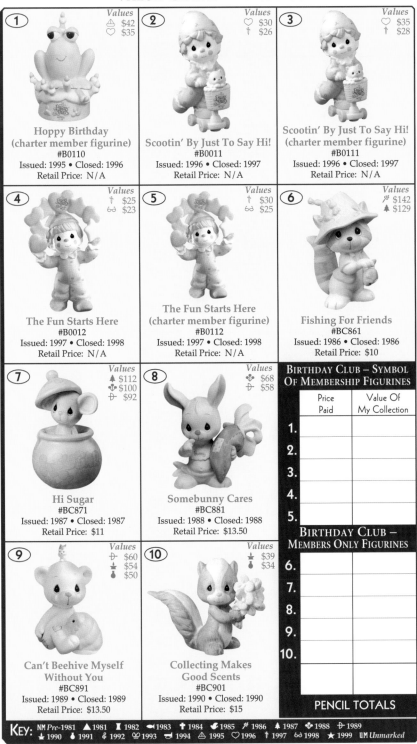

1 Values
△ $42
♡ $35

Hoppy Birthday
(charter member figurine)
#B0110
Issued: 1995 • Closed: 1996
Retail Price: N/A

2 Values
♡ $30
† $26

Scootin' By Just To Say Hi!
#B0011
Issued: 1996 • Closed: 1997
Retail Price: N/A

3 Values
♡ $35
† $28

Scootin' By Just To Say Hi!
(charter member figurine)
#B0111
Issued: 1996 • Closed: 1997
Retail Price: N/A

4 Values
† $25
👓 $23

The Fun Starts Here
#B0012
Issued: 1997 • Closed: 1998
Retail Price: N/A

5 Values
† $30
👓 $25

The Fun Starts Here
(charter member figurine)
#B0112
Issued: 1997 • Closed: 1998
Retail Price: N/A

6 Values
𝄞 $142
♠ $129

Fishing For Friends
#BC861
Issued: 1986 • Closed: 1986
Retail Price: $10

7 Values
♠ $112
✤ $100
Đ $92

Hi Sugar
#BC871
Issued: 1987 • Closed: 1987
Retail Price: $11

8 Values
✤ $68
Đ $58

Somebunny Cares
#BC881
Issued: 1988 • Closed: 1988
Retail Price: $13.50

9 Values
Đ $60
★ $54
🌡 $50

Can't Beehive Myself
Without You
#BC891
Issued: 1989 • Closed: 1989
Retail Price: $13.50

10 Values
★ $39
🌡 $34

Collecting Makes
Good Scents
#BC901
Issued: 1990 • Closed: 1990
Retail Price: $15

BIRTHDAY CLUB – SYMBOL OF MEMBERSHIP FIGURINES

	Price Paid	Value Of My Collection
1.		
2.		
3.		
4.		
5.		

BIRTHDAY CLUB – MEMBERS ONLY FIGURINES

6.		
7.		
8.		
9.		
10.		

PENCIL TOTALS

BIRTHDAY CLUB

KEY: NM *Pre-1981* ▲1981 ✕1982 ◄1983 †1984 ✔1985 𝄞1986 ♠1987 ✤1988 Đ1989 ★1990 🌡1991 ♪1992 ❀1993 ⊷1994 △1995 ♡1996 †1997 👓1998 ★1999 **UM** *Unmarked*

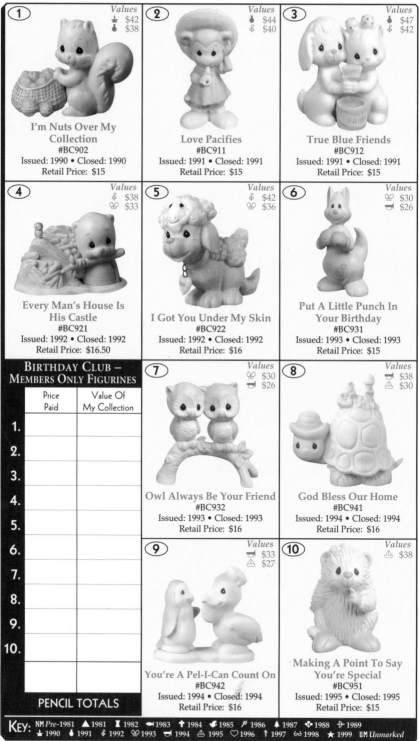

1 Values
♣ $42
🌢 $38

I'm Nuts Over My Collection
#BC902
Issued: 1990 • Closed: 1990
Retail Price: $15

2 Values
🌢 $44
🔹 $40

Love Pacifies
#BC911
Issued: 1991 • Closed: 1991
Retail Price: $15

3 Values
🌢 $47
🔹 $42

True Blue Friends
#BC912
Issued: 1991 • Closed: 1991
Retail Price: $15

4 Values
🔹 $38
♈ $33

Every Man's House Is His Castle
#BC921
Issued: 1992 • Closed: 1992
Retail Price: $16.50

5 Values
🔹 $42
♈ $36

I Got You Under My Skin
#BC922
Issued: 1992 • Closed: 1992
Retail Price: $16

6 Values
♈ $30
🛏 $26

Put A Little Punch In Your Birthday
#BC931
Issued: 1993 • Closed: 1993
Retail Price: $15

BIRTHDAY CLUB – MEMBERS ONLY FIGURINES

	Price Paid	Value Of My Collection
1.		
2.		
3.		
4.		
5.		
6.		
7.		
8.		
9.		
10.		
PENCIL TOTALS		

7 Values
♈ $30
🛏 $26

Owl Always Be Your Friend
#BC932
Issued: 1993 • Closed: 1993
Retail Price: $16

8 Values
🛏 $38
⚠ $30

God Bless Our Home
#BC941
Issued: 1994 • Closed: 1994
Retail Price: $16

9 Values
🛏 $33
⚠ $27

You're A Pel-I-Can Count On
#BC942
Issued: 1994 • Closed: 1994
Retail Price: $16

10 Values
⚠ $38

Making A Point To Say You're Special
#BC951
Issued: 1995 • Closed: 1995
Retail Price: $15

1 — Values ⚠ $65

10 Wonderful Years Of Wishes
#BC952
Issued: 1995 • Closed: 1995
Retail Price: $50

2 — Values ♡ $25

There's A Spot In My Heart For You
#BC961
Issued: 1996 • Closed: 1996
Retail Price: $15

3 — Values ♡ $30 † $25

You're First In My Heart
#BC962
Issued: 1996 • Closed: 1996
Retail Price: $15

4 — Values † $24

Hare's To The Birthday Club
#BC971
Issued: 1997 • Closed: 1997
Retail Price: $16

5 — Values † $25

Holy Tweet
#BC972
Issued: 1997 • Closed: 1997
Retail Price: $18.50

6 — Values 6ꝺ $15 ★ $15

Slide Into The Celebration (LE-1999)
#BC981
Issued: 1998 • To Be Closed: 1999
Retail Price: $15

7 NEW! — Values 6ꝺ N/E ★ N/E

You Are My Mane Inspiration (charter member figurine)
#B0014
Issued: 1999 • To Be Closed: 1999
Retail Price: N/A

8 NEW! — Values 6ꝺ N/E ★ N/E

You Are My Mane Inspiration (double charter member figurine)
#B0114
Issued: 1999 • To Be Closed: 1999
Retail Price: N/A

9 NEW! — Values UM $7

Chester (TENDER TAILS)
#BC992
Issued: 1999 • To Be Closed: 1999
Retail Price: $7

10 NEW! — Values ★ $15

Ewe Are So Special To Me
#BC991
Issued: 1999 • To Be Closed: 1999
Retail Price: $15

BIRTHDAY CLUB – MEMBERS ONLY FIGURINES

	Price Paid	Value Of My Collection
1.		
2.		
3.		
4.		
5.		
6.		

FUN CLUB – SYMBOL OF MEMBERSHIP FIGURINES

7.		
8.		

FUN CLUB – MEMBERS ONLY PIECES

9.		
10.		

PENCIL TOTALS

KEY: NM *Pre-1981* ▲ 1981 ✠ 1982 ◄1983 † 1984 ✦ 1985 ✗ 1986 ▲ 1987 ✿ 1988 ꝺ 1989 ★ 1990 ♦ 1991 ✦ 1992 ✾1993 ◄ 1994 ⚠ 1995 ♡ 1996 † 1997 6ꝺ 1998 ★ 1999 UM *Unmarked*

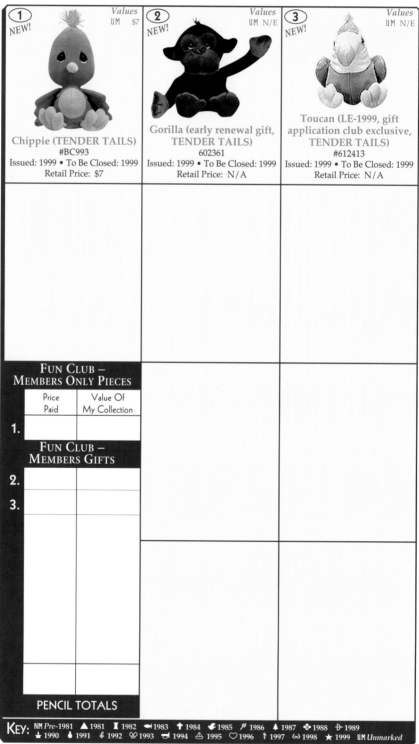

① NEW! *Values* UM $7

Chippie (TENDER TAILS)
#BC993
Issued: 1999 • To Be Closed: 1999
Retail Price: $7

② NEW! *Values* UM N/E

Gorilla (early renewal gift, TENDER TAILS)
602361
Issued: 1999 • To Be Closed: 1999
Retail Price: N/A

③ NEW! *Values* UM N/E

Toucan (LE-1999, gift application club exclusive, TENDER TAILS)
#612413
Issued: 1999 • To Be Closed: 1999
Retail Price: N/A

FUN CLUB – MEMBERS ONLY PIECES	
Price Paid	Value Of My Collection
1.	

FUN CLUB – MEMBERS GIFTS	
2.	
3.	
PENCIL TOTALS	

KEY: NM *Pre-1981* ▲1981 Ⅰ1982 ◄1983 ✝1984 ✦1985 ✳1986 ♣1987 ✿1988 ✢1989 ✦1990 ✦1991 ✦1992 ✿1993 ✦1994 ⬠1995 ♡1996 ✝1997 ∞1998 ★1999 UM *Unmarked*

226

Use these pages to record future PRECIOUS MOMENTS releases.

FIGURINES	Item Number	Status	Production Mark	Market Value	Price Paid	Value of My Collection
PENCIL TOTALS					Price Paid	Market Value

VALUE GUIDE — FUTURE RELEASES

Use these pages to record future PRECIOUS MOMENTS releases.

ORNAMENTS	Item Number	Status	Production Mark	Market Value	Price Paid	Value of My Collection

OTHER PIECES						
PENCIL TOTALS						
					Price Paid	Market Value

TOTAL VALUE OF MY COLLECTION

Record the value of your collection here by adding the pencil totals from the bottom of each Value Guide page.

PRECIOUS MOMENTS

Page Number	Price Paid	Market Value
Page 39		
Page 40		
Page 41		
Page 42		
Page 43		
Page 44		
Page 45		
Page 46		
Page 47		
Page 48		
Page 49		
Page 50		
Page 51		
Page 52		
Page 53		
Page 54		
Page 55		
Page 56		
Page 57		
Page 58		
Page 59		
Page 60		
Page 61		
TOTAL		

PRECIOUS MOMENTS

Page Number	Price Paid	Market Value
Page 62		
Page 63		
Page 64		
Page 65		
Page 66		
Page 67		
Page 68		
Page 69		
Page 70		
Page 71		
Page 72		
Page 73		
Page 74		
Page 75		
Page 76		
Page 77		
Page 78		
Page 79		
Page 80		
Page 81		
Page 82		
Page 83		
Page 84		
TOTAL		

PAGE TOTALS

PRICE PAID   MARKET VALUE

TOTAL VALUE OF MY COLLECTION

Record the value of your collection here by adding the pencil totals from the bottom of each Value Guide page.

PRECIOUS MOMENTS

Page Number	Price Paid	Market Value
Page 85		
Page 86		
Page 87		
Page 88		
Page 89		
Page 90		
Page 91		
Page 92		
Page 93		
Page 94		
Page 95		
Page 96		
Page 97		
Page 98		
Page 99		
Page 100		
Page 101		
Page 102		
Page 103		
Page 104		
Page 105		
Page 106		
Page 107		
Page 108		
TOTAL		

PRECIOUS MOMENTS

Page Number	Price Paid	Market Value
Page 109		
Page 110		
Page 111		
Page 112		
Page 113		
Page 114		
Page 115		
Page 116		
Page 117		
Page 118		
Page 119		
Page 120		
Page 121		
Page 122		
Page 123		
Page 124		
Page 125		
Page 126		
Page 127		
Page 128		
Page 129		
Page 130		
Page 131		
Page 132		
TOTAL		

PAGE TOTALS

PRICE PAID   MARKET VALUE

TOTAL VALUE OF MY COLLECTION

*Record the value of your collection here by adding the pencil totals
from the bottom of each Value Guide page.*

PRECIOUS MOMENTS

Page Number	Price Paid	Market Value
Page 133		
Page 134		
Page 135		
Page 136		
Page 137		
Page 138		
Page 139		
Page 140		
Page 141		
Page 142		
Page 143		
Page 144		
Page 145		
Page 146		
Page 147		
Page 148		
Page 149		
Page 150		
Page 151		
Page 152		
Page 153		
Page 154		
Page 155		
Page 156		
TOTAL		

PRECIOUS MOMENTS

Page Number	Price Paid	Market Value
Page 157		
Page 158		
Page 159		
Page 160		
Page 161		
Page 162		
Page 163		
Page 164		
Page 165		
Page 166		
Page 167		
Page 168		
Page 169		
Page 170		
Page 171		
Page 172		
Page 173		
Page 174		
Page 175		
Page 176		
Page 177		
Page 178		
Page 179		
Page 180		
TOTAL		

PAGE TOTALS

Price Paid	Market Value

TOTAL VALUE OF MY COLLECTION

Record the value of your collection here by adding the pencil totals
from the bottom of each Value Guide page.

PRECIOUS MOMENTS

Page Number	Price Paid	Market Value
Page 181		
Page 182		
Page 183		
Page 184		
Page 185		
Page 186		
Page 187		
Page 188		
Page 189		
Page 190		
Page 191		
Page 192		
Page 193		
Page 194		
Page 195		
Page 196		
Page 197		
Page 198		
Page 199		
Page 200		
Page 201		
Page 202		
Page 203		
Page 204		
TOTAL		

PRECIOUS MOMENTS

Page Number	Price Paid	Market Value
Page 205		
Page 206		
Page 207		
Page 208		
Page 209		
Page 210		
Page 211		
Page 212		
Page 213		
Page 214		
Page 215		
Page 216		
Page 217		
Page 218		
Page 219		
Page 220		
Page 221		
Page 222		
Page 223		
Page 224		
Page 225		
Page 226		
Page 227		
Page 228		
TOTAL		

PAGE TOTALS

Price Paid	Market Value

$\mathcal{P}$ RECIOUS MOMENTS figurines are now in their 21st year of production and with more than 1,600 pieces released since the debut in 1978, it's likely that a few are missing from your collection. And perhaps you've gone to your local retailer and found that the pieces you're looking for have already been retired, closed or suspended. If this is the case, you won't be able to get these pieces at a retail store; however, all hope is not lost. There is a way to get those pieces – the secondary market. The secondary market is a place where collectors can turn for the opportunity to purchase hard-to-find, or "gotta have," pieces they can't get anywhere else.

What Is The Secondary Market?

The secondary market allows collectors to "shop" for pieces that are no longer for sale in retail stores. Logically, if the "primary market" (retailers) is drained, there is no way to obtain the piece you're looking for. However, these pieces can still be found on the secondary market, sold by collectors and/or secondary market dealers.

As a piece is retired, the mold is destroyed to prevent a re-introduction of the piece. Once the piece is out of stock in retail stores, the secondary market begins to form. Perhaps a collector has the piece and is willing to part with it for just the right price. Maybe a dealer may have it in inventory and will sell it for a marked increase over the retail value. For example, "God Loveth A Cheerful Giver" was one of the first pieces to debut in the PRECIOUS MOMENTS line. Since it retired in 1981, collectors only had two years to purchase it and while that was 18 years ago, people are still trying to get their hands on this piece. It now goes for around $1,000 on the secondary market.

When Enesco suspends a piece, the piece "goes away" with the understanding that it could one day be re-introduced, leaving the door open for another production run. Just last year, two of the "Original 21" pieces that had been suspended in 1984 were re-introduced. "Love Is Kind" and "He Leadeth Me" were brought back with slight design changes for the "Turn Back The Clock" event celebrating the 20th anniversary of the PRECIOUS MOMENTS line.

Other PRECIOUS MOMENTS pieces that collectors may have to turn to the secondary market for are ones that are "closed." This status generally affects pieces that are dated and therefore only available for that year, like the *Annual Christmas Figurines*. In addition to the dated pieces, there are also PRECIOUS MOMENTS limited editions that are limited to the number of pieces produced. For example, the COUNTRY LANE musical "Bringing In The Sheaves" was limited to a production run of 12,000 pieces. When that number was reached, production was ceased. So while 12,000 may sound like a large amount, it's not when you think of the numerous PRE-CIOUS MOMENTS collectors who could be searching for this piece. Pieces can also be limited to production during a specific year. "An Event For All Seasons" was limited to 1993 and at the end of that year, it was closed and no more were made.

Pieces that tend to be high in demand, but low in production, also include those available only at PRECIOUS MOMENTS events or through selected retailers such as Century Circle pieces. PRECIOUS MOMENTS *Chapel Exclusives* and *Club* pieces are also elusive and consequently vulnerable to higher prices on the secondary market.

WHERE TO LOOK FOR
THE SECONDARY MARKET

When looking for a piece on the secondary market, start with your local PRECIOUS MOMENTS retailer. While most retailers are not actively involved in the secondary market, they can often provide you with information on where to turn to find your piece, including who to contact (such as local collectors and secondary market dealers) and where and when collecting events may be held.

There are many publications that list collectibles for sale. Services, called secondary market exchanges, list pieces for sale or trade. The exchanges are a good way to do business, but note that they are considered a service and do charge a fee. Another place to check for a piece you just have to have is the classifieds section of your newspaper, usually listed under "antiques and collectibles." There may also be information in this section about local shows featuring PRECIOUS MOMENTS pieces, or locations and times for "Swap and Sells." These shows are often listed in the back of collector magazines, as well.

One of the best ways to search for any pieces you want is through the Internet. Searching the World Wide Web gives collectors the freedom to check out prices in different areas of the country and work with a variety of stores, not to mention thousands of collectors, without ever leaving the comfort of their own homes. In addition to the plethora of PRECIOUS MOMENTS information and pieces for sale on web sites, is the plethora of resources in chat rooms and on bulletin boards. It's also become popular for collectors to bid on desired pieces at on-line auctions. So not only is the Internet a good tool in searching for pieces, but also for obtaining information about the ever popular line.

Here it is very important to remember that old saying "if it sounds too good to be true, it probably is." With this wealth of information comes a wealth of options and the key to being a savvy collector is to examine all of them.

Factors That Affect Secondary Market Value

Whether or not a piece will do well on the secondary market depends in part on its condition. On the secondary market, a damaged piece is going to be less valuable than a piece in perfect, or "mint," condition. "Damaged" can mean anything from a crack to a stray paint wisp to a faded area. If you are buying on the secondary market, always inspect the piece before completing the transaction. You also need to protect yourself if you are selling. Always be honest about your collection, letting potential buyers know of adverse conditions that may be present. Expect to pay less, or receive less, for pieces that have problems, including those that have been restored.

It is also good to note how the product that you're buying on the secondary market is packaged. It is important to remember to keep the original box. A lot of buyers and sellers today don't consider a piece to be complete unless its box is included. Boxes also provide protection for the piece during shipping, as well as during storage.

As far as the secondary market is concerned, here are some terms that are often used in the "for sale" listings that you may want to familiarize yourself with before you begin your search: "MIB" (mint in box), "NB" (no box), "DB" (damaged box) or "NT" (no original price tag). "Mint In Box" pieces are those that are in perfect condition – some have never even been taken out of their boxes.

At first, the secondary market can sound a bit overwhelming. But with just the right combination of patience and common sense, you should be able to build your collection with few problems. So just relax and have some fun in your adventure. After all, isn't the fun of it why you started your collection anyway?

RUB-A-DUB-DUB, NO PRECIOUS MOMENTS PIECES IN A TUB

One of the biggest factors in secondary market value is condition. Naturally, pieces in poor condition, whether it be due to chips, scratches or fractures are going to be worth less if you try to sell them. To keep your collectibles in top condition, try the following tips:

FIGURINES

For cleaning porcelain bisque pieces, Enesco recommends a gentle wash with a damp cloth, using warm water and a mild soap. Be sure to place a towel down where you will be working in case the piece slips from your grasp. Once the piece is clean, let it air dry.

TENDER TAILS

Enesco does not recommend machine washing your TENDER TAILS. To remove dirt, surface wash with a damp cloth.

In the plush market, hang tags are very important to a piece's value. TENDER TAILS come with tags that you send in to name your animal and receive its "Certificate Of Adoption" (a "Love And Care Guide" accompanies this as well). If you would rather not remove the tag, you can send in the following information:

1. Your name and address.
2. The name you have chosen.
3. Animal type or stock number.

Paperwork and certificates, as well as boxes, can be replaced depending on availability. For more information, contact Enesco at 1-800-4-ENESCO.

VARIATIONS

Variations

*S*ometimes that piece on your shelf doesn't exactly look like the one your neighbor has. When two pieces of the same design differ, the one that varies from the standard is considered to be a variation. This may occur intentionally, as is the case when a piece is reintroduced after a period of suspension with slight modifications. For the most part however, variations occur as the result of human error. Since each PRECIOUS MOMENTS figurine is worked on by over 100 people, there is always the possibility that a mistake could be made. Therefore, while Enesco maintains stringent quality control standards, the law of averages allows for occasions where errors will make it through production.

One common type of variation occurs with the decal or inspiration on a figurine. In some instances, it is an error in spelling or phrasing. For example, the figurine "Be Not Weary In Well Doing" has been seen with an inspiration that reads "Be Not Weary **And** Well Doing." Also, the *Chapel Exclusive* piece "He Is Not Here For He Is Risen As He Said" was to have "Matt 28:6" following the Biblical passage on the sign, but was incorrectly produced with "Math" instead.

HE IS NOT HERE
FOR HE IS RISEN
AS HE SAID.
MATH28:6

Another common mistake seen with PRECIOUS MOMENTS pieces is a "bare" area where the paint was inadvertently left off. When this occurs, it does not often affect the value of the piece, unless a large portion (or the entire figurine) is left unpainted. Variations associated with the painting process also include a change in the color of paint used. Most of the time this is due to the way the pigment is mixed and merely causes a subtle difference. On some occasions however, an entirely different color is used on a piece, as was the case in "May Your Christmas Be A Happy Home," where the boy sports a yellow shirt in some versions and a blue one in others.

Another variation that may not affect a piece's value is an upside down or sideways decal. Also, missing decals have been spotted from time to time, as was the case with the ornament "Let The Heavens Rejoice," whose angel is missing the patch on her gown.

A variation can occur when an intentional change is made to a current piece. These changes usually take place when there is a structural problem with the piece that may cause it to crack or break, or if Enesco is unhappy with the final product and wishes to improve upon the design. This was the case when the mouth was changed from a smile to a frown on the piece "Faith Takes The Plunge" in order to give the girl a more serious appearance. These types of changes are not announced by Enesco and often happen when a piece is still new, allowing for only a limited number of the first design to be produced.

PRECIOUS MOMENTS VARIATIONS

The following is a list of well-known variations that have yet to achieve significant secondary market value. Variations that have value have been placed in the Value Guide section to help you total the value of your collection.

Baby's First Christmas (#E2372): Just prior to this ornament's suspension, an inscription was added. The piece without the caption, "Baby's First Christmas," was available for a shorter period of time and is considered the variation.

Dropping In For The Holidays (#531952): The cup featured in this ornament has been seen either pink or blue.

He Careth For You (#E1377B) and ***He Leadeth Me (#E1377A):*** In a case of switched identities, these pieces have been found with their inspirations reversed.

VARIATIONS

I'm Falling For Somebunny/Our Love Is Heaven-scent (#E9266): Sold as a set, these pieces were often mislabeled with the inscription "Somebunny Cares."

Isn't He Precious (#E5379): Considered very rare, the variation of this piece is completely unpainted.

O Worship The Lord (#102229): The correct title of this piece is a source of confusion, since many can be found without the "O."

Praise The Lord Anyhow (#E1374B): While the dog on this figurine should have a black nose, some noses were mistakenly painted brown.

Rejoicing With You (#E4724): Some of the figurines have the little girl's hand covering the "e" in the word "Bible" while a change exposed the entire word, allowing it to be read completely.

Sending My Love Your Way (#528609): This figurine has shown up with and without the kitten and with and without the painted stripes on the kite.

Smile, God Loves You (#E1373B): For a short time in the 1980s, the little boy's black eye appeared a shade of brown.

Twenty Years And The Vision's Still The Same (LE-1998, #306843): Your eyes aren't deceiving you, both the "sword" and the "eyeglass" year marks have appeared stamped to the bottom of this piece at the same time.

Wishing You A Season Filled With Joy (#E2805): The dog featured in this piece should have only one eye painted. In the variation, both eyes are painted and the variation has only been found on pieces with the "dove" production mark.

INSURING

*W*hen insuring your collection, there are three major points to consider:

1. Know your coverage. Collectibles are typically included in homeowner's or renter's insurance policies. Ask your agent if your policy covers fire, theft, floods, hurricanes, earthquakes and damage or breakage through routine handling. Also, ask if your policy covers claims at "current replacement value" – the amount it would cost to replace items if they were damaged, lost or stolen. This is extremely important since the secondary market value of a piece may well exceed its original retail price.

> Many companies will accept a reputable secondary market price guide – such as the Collector's Value Guide™ – as a valid source for determining your collection's value.

2. Document your collection. In the event of a loss, your insurance company will need proof of your collection and its value. Ask your insurance agent what information is acceptable. Keep receipts and an inventory of your collection in a different location, such as a safe deposit box, to protect them in case of emergency. Include the purchase date, price paid, size, issue year, edition limit, special markings and secondary market value for each piece.

3. Weigh the risk. To determine the coverage you need, calculate how much it would cost to replace your collection and compare it to the total amount your current policy would pay. If the amount of insurance does not cover your collection, ask your agent about adding a Personal Articles Floater or a Fine Arts Floater or "rider" to your policy, or insuring your collection under a separate policy. As with all insurance, you must weigh the risk of loss against the cost of additional coverage.

THE PRECIOUS MOMENTS® PRODUCTION PROCESS

*E*ach piece in the PRECIOUS MOMENTS collection begins as a drawing by artist Sam Butcher. Once Butcher is done, the illustration is photographed and sent to a design studio in Nagoya, Japan. There, Master Sculptor Yasuhei Fujioka oversees the production of the prototype.

With wet clay, the artisan begins shaping the model. Once this is complete and it meets Enesco's high standards, it will continue on in the production process; first, it is disassembled into a variety of parts. This is so that smaller molds can be made, which are easier to manipulate.

When the molds are complete, wet clay – commonly known as "slip" – is poured in and briefly allowed to air dry. The piece is allowed to stand until it forms a solid piece of porcelain called "greenware."

After all the pieces that will make up the figurine are complete, they are assembled with slip, the seams then are removed and the piece is allowed again to thoroughly air dry. When the piece is dry, it is deposited in the kiln, where it will be fired for 14 hours at 2,300° F.

Next, PRECIOUS MOMENTS pieces are bathed in a solution of pumice and water, which creates their smooth feel. Once the piece has been polished, it is ready to be painted. The PRECIOUS MOMENTS "tear-drop eyes" are the hardest parts to paint, and it usually takes about three years for an artisan to master this process.

Finally, the piece is fired for four hours, resulting in the paint adhering to the porcelain. As soon as it's removed from the kiln, the figurine undergoes a final inspection (each piece is inspected at least six times throughout the production process) to ensure that it meets Enesco's high standards of excellence.

THE PRECIOUS MOMENTS® CHAPEL

*I*n 1984, Sam Butcher set out to find a new home for his family, with nothing but his faith in God to guide him. Butcher was beginning to lose hope when, after days of driving, he came across 17 acres of land in the Ozark Mountains that would become not just his family's home, but his personal tribute to all the Lord had given him. And after five years of arduous work, The PRECIOUS MOMENTS Chapel opened in 1989 in Carthage, Missouri. Now, a decade later, this place of inspiration to over one million visitors a year is celebrating its 10th anniversary.

A visit to the Chapel is one that guests won't soon forget. Upon arrival, you begin by walking down the "Avenue Of Angels", where you're led to the front gate of The Chapel. Just in front of the elaborately designed iron gates is a fountain with angels who welcome you in to their home. A poem written by Butcher in 1993 stands nearby, etched in marble. Beyond the gates is a walkway that ends at The Chapel's front doors.

Upon entering The Chapel, visitors can't help but be overwhelmed by its beauty, often enhanced by the sunlight shinning through the many stained glass windows The Chapel contains. Hand-painted murals by Butcher line the walls, the largest of which is high above the heads of visitors. Inspired by a trip to the Sistine Chapel in Rome, Butcher wanted to create a similar "tribute to the Lord." The result is a breathtaking 1,408-square-foot painting to complete, which Butcher spent several hundred hours painting laying upside down on scaffolding 35 feet above the ground.

> **Did You Know?**
>
> When construction on The Chapel began in 1984, the site contained 17½ acres. Now, by 1999, expansion has added almost 3,000 acres.

There are two rooms in The Chapel that are especially close to Sam Butcher's heart. The Philip D. Butcher

Memorial Room is in memory of his son, Philip, who lost his life in 1990 in a tragic car accident. The second room is dedicated to Tim Ryan, a close friend of Butcher's who died of cancer. Throughout The Chapel, there are remembrance books filled with stories of lost loved ones, as well as pictures of the people depicted in "Hallelujah Square," a mural that depicts friends as they meet in Heaven.

The Chapel itself is surrounded by many attractions. A museum containing PRECIOUS MOMENTS memorabilia, as well as many of Sam Butcher's collected works, can be found in The Chapel Gallery. On display is original artwork, greeting cards and posters from the early days of "Jonathan And David," and just about every PRECIOUS MOMENTS figurine ever produced. The Gallery is also home to numerous awards Butcher has acquired throughout his many years as an artist.

Memorial gardens lay scattered throughout The Chapel Complex and each is named for one of Butcher's granddaughters. Last year, one million dollars was donated by Enesco to fund the addition of many flowers, plants and trees, further enhancing the beauty of the grounds.

The Chapel grounds are also home to a 40-acre man-made lake. Seven islands inhabit the lake and, similar to the gardens, each bears the name of one of Butcher's grandsons. Another island, Grandpa's Island, was made for Butcher's grandchildren to play on and comes complete with it's own castle. Dusty's Honeymoon Island is the largest of the islands and is home to both a Victorian mansion, transported from a nearby town, and a Wedding Chapel, a gift from a small congregation in nearby Stotts City, Missouri. The Wedding

Chapel has become a popular spot for couples to exchange and renew vows while the mansion underwent two years of restoration and is now home to an elegant ballroom and two honeymoon suites.

No visit to The Chapel would be complete without seeing the Fountain of Angels™. Opened in 1997, the Fountain of Angels is the largest show fountain in the world. Music by members of the London Philharmonic Symphony Orchestra blasts from 42 speakers as the fountains pump water over 75 feet into the air. Colorful lights from an accompanying laser-light show dance over the 120 bronze angel sculptures that adorn the fountain. As part of the 10th Anniversary Celebration, the fountain is being enclosed by a nine-story structure, allowing the magnificent display of art and entertainment to be enjoyed in any kind of weather.

Another renewal project that is underway as The Chapel reaches its tenth year includes the expansion of the popular Royal Delights Deli in the Visitor's Center. The Chapel Gift Shop is also being enlarged to offer more PRECIOUS MOMENTS products. The newly updated Visitor's Center is reminiscent of a European village, with lights glistening from the ceiling, and walkways winding around an enclosed castle and moat. And for children (both big and small), many of the familiar PRECIOUS MOMENTS characters can be spotted walking the grounds.

THE PRECIOUS MOMENTS® CHAPEL

Visitors traveling a distance to The Chapel can get a good night's rest at several hotels nearby. Just minutes from the Chapel is the 121-room Best Western PRECIOUS MOMENTS® Hotel. Designed by Sam Butcher, the hotel displays exclusive Sam Butcher paintings throughout. Cubby Bear's® RV Park, a 70-unit recreational vehicle facility, is complete with shower and laundry facilities, as well as an outdoor heated swimming pool.

For more information on planning a trip or on special events at The Chapel, call 1-800-543-7975.

Keep In Touch!

Unless you're lucky enough to live in the Missouri area, you probably can't visit The Chapel as often as you like. To avoid missing out on the latest Chapel happenings, you can keep in touch with a subscription to Chapel Bells Magazine. Filled with fun and informative sections, this quarterly magazine will let you know of upcoming events, new PRECIOUS MOMENTS products and will inspire you with stories from collectors. For more information please contact:

Chapel Bells Magazine
P.O. Box 802
Carthage, MO 64836
or call
(800) 543-7975 ext. 3000

Behind Those PRECIOUS MOMENTS®

*A*ccording to PRECIOUS MOMENTS artist Sam Butcher, new ideas for the line come to him on a daily basis. In fact, sometimes 15 to 20 ideas may appear during the course of his workday. Butcher often turns to the Bible or to memories of his childhood to help him create new pieces; while many ideas come from his constant interaction with fans and friends that have their own unique stories to share.

The following are a variety of PRECIOUS MOMENTS figurines, along with the sometimes funny, sometimes sad, stories of how they came to be:

"Bringing In The Sheaves" (#307084): When Sam Butcher met Jason Eric Wilson's aunt at a signing event, he was deeply saddened to hear her story. By the age of 21, Jason had followed his heart and become a farmer. But the dream tragically ended one night when Jason was killed by several men who had crossed onto his land and killed one of his calves. Butcher designed "Bringing In The Sheaves" for Jason's family and dedicated the entire COUNTRY LANE collection to his memory.

"Coleenia" (#204889): This figurine was inspired by a beautiful young girl who was a fan of the PRECIOUS MOMENTS collection. In fact, Coleenia's most prized possession was her PRECIOUS MOMENTS clown doll. Although Coleenia was terminally ill, she was able to visit the Chapel with her mother and stepfather, and meet Sam Butcher before she passed away. Following the little girl's death, the artist created a figurine of her holding her clown doll, and later added her to "Hallelujah Square."

> ## What's In A Yearmark?
>
> Through the years, there have been a variety of marks used by Enesco to note the year of production of a piece from the PRECIOUS MOMENTS collection.
>
> While the yearmarks have varied, they are all chosen by Sam Butcher to symbolize an inspirational Christian message.

"Enter Into His Courts With Thanksgiving" (#521221):
When John and Sharon Shively lost their son, Bradley, in an automobile accident, friends insisted that they visit The PRECIOUS MOMENTS Chapel, hoping that a visit to the grounds would help ease their pain. While there, they contacted Sam Butcher about his experience coping with the loss of a child. Upon speaking to them about their son, who was a star basketball player, Butcher was struck with the idea to create a figurine in his likeness. A picture of Bradley is also in "Hallelujah Square."

"God Blessed The Day We Found You" (#100145):
Butcher designed this piece in honor of his daughter, Heather, who was four years old and living with foster parents when the Butchers adopted her. Although it took her some time to adjust, Heather was quickly accepted into her new, loving family.

"Going Home" (#525979): A piece close to the artist's heart, this figurine was designed in memory of his son Philip. Philip died in a car accident in 1990 and this figurine shows him on his way to heaven, "hitching a ride" with a passing angel.

"The Hand That Rocks The Future" (#E3108): The inspiration for this piece was actually the result of an argument between Butcher and his wife, Katie. Even though the fight left Katie in tears, the artist was surprised at how she seemed so happy as she fed their baby, Jon. Upon being questioned, Katie said her smile calmed the child and that this was the only way to get him to eat.

"I Believe In Miracles" (#E7156): Bill Biel was told by doctors that his eyesight was diminishing to the point of no return. Through constant prayer, Biel's eyesight did indeed return, leading Butcher to create the figurine "I Believe In Miracles" for his friend and former business partner.

"I'm Sending You A White Christmas" (#E2829): One of Sam Butcher's favorite stories is about his mother as a little girl, shortly after she had moved to Michigan from Florida. The morning after a night of snow, her grandmother noticed her outside packing snowballs in a box. When asked what she was doing, Sam's mother said she was sending the package to relatives in Florida who had never seen snow.

"The Lord Giveth And The Lord Taketh Away" (#100226): While this piece is light in tone, the events that inspired it were anything but humorous at the time. Butcher created "The Lord Giveth And The Lord Taketh Away" after losing his family's pet canary to their cat. Apparantly when he came home from a business trip, he found his wife standing over a bird cage and a mass of feathers, with no bird (or cat for that matter) in sight. The evidence alone told the story.

"Make A Joyful Noise" (#E1374G): While traveling together on a business trip, Sam Butcher and Bill Biel spotted a bumper sticker on the car ahead of them that read "Honk If You Love Jesus." Feeling friendly, they did honk and were surprised by the unfriendly response they received from the woman in the vehicle bearing the sticker. Hoping she would catch on, they tried again, but to no avail. Quickly realizing that she was in no mood to be honked at, they drove off with the artist already toying with the idea for this piece.

"A Prayer Warrior's Faith Can Move Mountains" (#354406): Sam Butcher was recently awarded a Honorary Doctorate Degree in Humane Letters from Oral Roberts University in Tulsa, Oklahoma. It was there that Butcher met Oral Roberts. Butcher read the preacher's autobiography and shortly afterward completed this piece, inspired the story of Robert's Native American mother, Claudia Priscilla Irwin Roberts, who made it her mission to never miss her daily prayer for her son.

*F*or many collectors, the love of PRECIOUS MOMENTS designs goes far beyond collecting the figurines. These inspirational figurines capture the hearts of young and old alike, spreading love and joy to all.

Since 1982, more than 455 local clubs have been established across the United States and Canada, allowing members another way to share their love of collecting with others. Members don't just talk about their favorite pieces, they gather to learn more about PRECIOUS MOMENTS collectibles. Groups like the "Blossomland Collector's Club" in Benton Harbor, Michigan, invite guest speakers in to teach their members about various aspects of collecting.

Local clubs take the PRECIOUS MOMENTS "loving, caring and sharing" philosophy to heart by volunteering their time to others. Members of the "Dreams Really Do Come True" club in Topsham, Maine, visit children and adults in hospitals, while "Savannah's Soda-licious PMCC" club in Georgia collects clothing and other items for the "Living Vine," a local home for unwed mothers. Fundraisers such as bake sales, raffles and canned goods drives are additional ways that chapters support their communities.

The local clubs do not go unnoticed by Enesco. In October 1998, the company held its 10th Annual PRECIOUS MOMENTS Local Club Chapter Convention in Rosemont, Illinois. Collectors were treated to two full days of shows, contests, parties . . . even a tour of the Enesco showroom. The Local Club Chapter Conventions always offer a "theme" party for collectors, and at this year's event, collectors received a special ornament titled "A Salute To Our Stars," as well as several other goodies to take home.

In "sailabration" of PRECIOUS MOMENTS and their collectors, Enesco offers club members a week of fun in the sun on a Royal Caribbean cruise. This cruising tradition began in 1993 in honor of PRECIOUS MOMENTS' 15th anniversary. So far, there have been three cruises. The most recent voyage made its way to the Caribbean in April 1998 with nearly 1,200 collectors on board. Plans are already in the works for the fourth exciting trip! This one promises to be a fun one, as the ship sets sail in June 2000 and heads for Alaska. A club member from Miami said the last week-long cruise was " . . . quite an experience. The once-in-a-lifetime journey reunited old friends, and brought together new ones."

To further honor the clubs, each year The Chapel is turned into a display of lights at the annual Collector's Christmas Weekend. A variety of festive events occur in the beautiful confines of The Chapel for the three days celebrating the season. The weekend includes a candlelight service, seminars, tours, music shows and more!

If you're interested in joining a local club, but don't know if there's one in your area, contact Enesco's Local Club Chapter Coordinator for a listing.

*F*or 20 years, PRECIOUS MOMENTS designs have touched people's lives in amazing ways. The inspirational figurines, or "little messengers" of joy and hope, have brought years of happiness, love and memories to collectors everywhere.

So when the 20th Anniversary of PRECIOUS MOMENTS arrived, Enesco added some very special events to their calender. As a "thank you" for making the line of of the most popular in the industry, a year full of events, special

figurines and appearances was planned in celebration. Now that the year has come to a close, collectors will agree it was truly a memorable time.

Perhaps one of the biggest events in celebration of this milestone was the launch of the 20th Anniversary PRECIOUS MOMENTS Care-A-Van. The 53-foot-long traveling museum set out in April 1998 for a journey across the United States and Canada, making over 300 stops. The trip kept up the PRECIOUS MOMENTS spirit, raising more than $75,000 and 56,000 pounds of food for Second Harvest, the largest charitable hunger relief organization in the nation. The success was so enormous that the Care-A-Van will travel through 1999 as well!

Along the Care-A-Van's route, Enesco held 20 events called "Hometown Celebrations." At these events, collectors had the chance to bid on an extremely limited piece, "How Can Three Work Together Except They Agree," honoring Sam

Butcher, Eugene Freedman and Yasuhei Fujioka. Only 20 figurines were made, and with three of them given to those in the piece, there were only 17 available for auction.

In July, the Care-A-Van made a stop at The Chapel in Carthage, Missouri for "PRECIOUS MOMENTS Week." More than 7,000 people toured the truck. During the weeklong celebration, Butcher and Freedman took part in a ribbon cutting ceremony dedicating the new gardens on the Chapel grounds. The beautiful new scenery features 40,000 bushes, flowers and trees.

Along with new figurines and ornaments, 1998 also brought new series, a line of plush bean-filled animals and many special events. The COUNTRY LANE collection made its debut, inspired from childhood memories of Sam Butcher's grandmother's farm. There are now 11 figurines and one musical, all with familiar scenes from life on the farm. These pieces are slightly different, with a more vibrant look, than their fellow PRECIOUS MOMENTS figurines.

A new line of bean-bag animals called TENDER TAILS was also introduced. The variety of animals, from cows to unicorns, quickly made their way into the hearts of collectors. They're also available in ornaments, about half the size.

Did You Know?
1998 Care-A-Van Facts & Figures!

- Enesco nearly tripled its goal of raising 20,000 pounds of food for the food bank, Second Harvest!

- Between April and November, the Care-A-Van logged over 20,000 miles!

- The Care-A-Van is 53-feet long and is accompanied on its trip across country by a custom RV designed to inform fans about The PRECIOUS MOMENTS Chapel!

- The Care-A-Van is driven by Nick Dokianos, whose travels are documented on the Enesco website *(www.enesco.com)* in "Postcards From Nick;" while the Chapel RV is driven by John and Sharon Shively!

- By the end of the year, the Care-A-Van visited more than 90,000 people!

- A Hometown Celebration in Pittsburgh, Pennsylvania, gave collectors the rare opportunity to see Sam Butcher, Eugene Freedman and Yasuhei Fujioka together!

A Sweet Farewell!

Those who got their hands on the final vignette of Sugar Town got a surprise sign of thanks from Enesco . . . literally. The 1998, limited edition "Sugar Town Post Office Collector's Set" which was previously announced as a seven piece set, arrived in stores with a last minute addition. (So last minute that while the box says it is an eight piece set, the pictures on the box and in the 1998 catalog reflect only seven pieces). In a gesture of gratitude to all of the Sugar Town fans, a final sign was added which proclaims, "Thank You For Visiting Sugar Town" and is complete with Sam Butcher's famous "Sam B" signature.

Two figurines, "Love Is Kind" and "He Leadeth Me" were *re*-introduced from suspension in a special promotional event called "Turn Back The Clock." The two pieces were part of the "Original 21" introduced in 1978, returned 20 years later with only a slight color change. And for the PRECIOUS MOMENTS Fall event, the "Jungle Jamboree," collectors were given the opportunity to get *two* PRECIOUS MOMENTS exclusives: the new figurine "Life Can Be A Jungle" and the special edition TENDER TAILS "Monkey Triplets."

In further celebration of the 20th Anniversary, Enesco sponsored a "Loving, Caring And Sharing" contest. Twenty winners received nine-inch versions of "God Loveth A Cheerful Giver," commonly known as the "Girl With Puppies," based on the "Original 21" figurine that remains one of the most sought after pieces in the line. Contestants had to nominate someone who demonstrates the "loving, caring and sharing" philosophy.

The 1998 year was a special one for PRECIOUS MOMENTS and their collectors. For 20 years, the line has brought people happiness, comfort and love, among other things. So there was no better way to celebrate than with a year filled with special surprises and events that served to unite collectors together for the next 20 years!

*S*ince 1981, Enesco has been bringing collectors together from all over to share their love for the PRECIOUS MOMENTS collection. With the introduction of the Enesco PRECIOUS MOMENTS *Collectors' Club®* in 1981, fans of the inspirational figurines were given a way of learning more about the line they love so much.

Becoming a member of this award-winning club is a sure way to be kept up-to-date on the events surrounding the PRECIOUS MOMENTS collection. Four times a year, Enesco publishes the "GOODNEWSLETTER," filled with articles about the line, the company and collectors. Members will also find out about introductions, retirements, closings and suspensions. The "GOODNEWSLETTER" is a wonderful way to stay in touch with all the latest PRECIOUS MOMENTS collectible news and events, and even other collectors.

When you become a club member, you'll receive a *Symbol Of Membership Figurine* as a gift. For 1999, the piece is "Wishing You A World Of Peace." This adorable figurine has a little girl sitting in a wagon, gazing up at her very own lucky star. As a member, you also have the chance to purchase three exclusive *Members Only Figurines:* "He Watches Over Us All," the members only millennium piece "Jumping For Joy," and "God Speed."

A one-year membership begins January 1 and runs until December 31, and costs only $28. Members also get a national membership card and special mailings throughout the yea to keep them up to date, plus a gift registry listing all the PRECIOUS MOMENTS figurines.

New Club Web Site Hits The Net!

On October 1, 1998, a web site just for members of Enesco's clubs debuted. Located separately from the regular Enesco web site, this new site has lots of fun and informative sections. For the Collectors' Club and the Fun Club there are sections with the latest information on events, new releases and retirements, copies of club newsletters, a photo museum of the collection and also a section where collectors can voice their opinions. Enesco is also planning on games and raffles and the capabilities so that collectors can join or renew on-line.

To locate the site go to www.enescoclubs.com and enter the main site by using your club membership number.

The new PRECIOUS MOMENTS *Fun Club*ᔆᴹ by Enesco is in its charter year, replacing The Enesco PRECIOUS MOMENTS *Birthday Club*®. The *Fun Club* is geared toward families with younger children . . . getting everyone involved with the "loving, caring and sharing" philosophy through contests, family activities and special offerings! Since this is the first year of the club, all members joining in 1999 will be "Charter Members."

Like the Enesco PRECIOUS MOMENTS Collectors' *Club*, the PRECIOUS MOMENTS *Fun Club* membership begins January 1 and ends December 31. The cost is $24. As a member, you'll receive a membership kit containing the membership figurine "You Are My Mane Inspiration;" "Boots," the huggable stuffed kitten; and a membership card holder that can be attached to your youngsters' backpack!

As if those benefits weren't enough, members also receive the quarterly *Fun Club* newsletter and the opportunity to order "Ewe Are So Special To Me," the 1999 *Members Only Figurine,* and "Chester," the *Members Only* TENDER TAILS plush pig. You can also log on to the club's web site full of games and family activities.

So, if you want to join in the fun, contact your local retailer for information on how to join The Enesco PRECIOUS MOMENTS *Collectors' Club* or *The* PRECIOUS MOMENTS *Fun Club,* or visit the Enesco web site at www.enescoclubs.com.

The Enesco PRECIOUS MOMENTS
Collectors' Clubs
P.O. Box 219
Itasca, IL 60143-0219
(630) 875-5722

D isplays are the perfect way to showcase your treasured collection and with a wide variety of themes and sentiments, the PRECIOUS MOMENTS line can inspire even the "creatively challenged" to display with style! Whether you opt for a traditional display in your curio cabinet, or to create a world of wonder for your favorite pieces; always keep in mind that there is no right or wrong way to display. All you need to do is adapt different ideas to suit your personality and your decor. With that in mind, the following tips are sure to help you get a jump-start on the process of building displays with a uniqueness that is sure to impress!

TIP: PRECIOUS MOMENTS are loved for their inspirational themes and, therefore, some of the simplest displays can be the most poignant. Try placing your PRECIOUS MOMENTS pieces throughout the house, wherever they can easily be seen and admired. Try grouping pieces with a "friendship" theme together, interspersed with pictures of you and your loved ones. To brighten up any room in the house, take some of your favorite pieces that remind you of your own children and group them with frames containing pictures that your own young "Picassos" drew for you. Try

placing your LITTLE MOMENTS *International Collection* around a globe, offset by postcards from your favorite locations. To bring a little beauty to your bath, try placing one or two pieces on a shelf surrounded by decorative soaps and accessories. Or perhaps you can install a high, stable shelf over your kitchen sink and place favorite pieces on top like "Be Not Weary In Well Doing" and "This Is Your Day To Shine." What better way to take your mind off that sink full of dirty dishes and put things into perspective?

TIP: Think themes! PRECIOUS MOMENTS are suitable for all seasons and, therefore, there are hundreds of pieces that can be grouped together to create interesting displays. Try grouping all your pieces with a "loving" sentiment together on bright red fabric, littered with foil hearts and silk roses for a Valentine's Day display. Place all your harvest-themed pieces together and add a cornucopia, some small pumpkins and (clean) dried leaves to one shelf of your curio cabinet to celebrate the beauty of fall all year through!

TIP: Accessorizing isn't just fashionable; it's a necessity. Take a trip to your local hobby or craft store and walk through, aisle by aisle, and see what attracts you. There is a variety of inexpensive accessories such as fake trees, snow, fences and brightly-colored baskets that you can add to your display, as well as a variety of fabric to create the perfect backdrop. Try the miniatures section, where you're sure to find tons of accent pieces that you can use! (Try placing your PRECIOUS MOMENTS pieces in front of a painting of the interior of a house and mixing in the miniatures.)

TIP: Create a pond to the let your favorite PRECIOUS MOMENTS men (and women) have fun in the great outdoors. Many of the new PRECIOUS MOMENTS pieces carry a fishing theme and these are perfect to use alongside some of the other outdoor or sports-themed figurines. Use a shallow baking pan and fill it with aquarium gravel, fake trees and grass. (Try the pet supply department of your favorite store for plastic signs that are used in aquariums. They will surely add a touch of humor to your display!) Add a piece of glass painted blue to complete the scene, just be sure not to use real water as it will ruin the porcelain.

TIP: Plan a PRECIOUS MOMENTS party! Whether it's Thanksgiving dinner or a backyard barbeque, your favorite PRECIOUS MOMENTS figurines can add a lovely touch to any event. You can create a wonderful centerpiece by grouping PRECIOUS MOMENTS pieces together with the proper accessories. Delight your guests by using your figurines as place cards and having them guess which seat is theirs. PRECIOUS MOMENTS ornaments can be used to add flair to chandeliers, candlesticks or napkin rings. Plus, Enesco makes a wide variety of cake-toppers that can add a sentimental touch to wedding and anniversary cakes; especially when some favorite pieces surround the base of the cake. (Use care to create a safe distance from the frosting.)

TIP: Children love PRECIOUS MOMENTS figurines and there's no end to the options when you decorate a nursery or

child's room with a PRECIOUS MOMENTS theme. There are a variety a PRECIOUS MOMENTS licensees that make everything from comforters to furniture, but it is your own touches that will truly make this room special. You can start by painting pieces of wood in colors that offset those in the room. Once they are dry, nail them together and then screw in small brass hooks on the opposite side. Next hang your favorite PRECIOUS MOMENTS ornaments threaded through brightly colored ribbons for your own unique mobile.

TIP: Use your pieces to create a PRECIOUS MOMENTS-style Christmas. Decorate your tree with all PRECIOUS MOMENTS ornaments, or hang them from a banister or fireplace with layers of garland, beads and tulle. Perhaps you can move your *Sugar Town* village from the mantel to beneath the tree, framed by the "Sugar Town Express (set/3)," and use the mantel to create a "winter wonderland" for your figurines.

TIP: Remember, no matter what it is you decide to do, be sure to have fun with it!

bottomstamp—any identifying marks on the underside of a figurine such as the title, registration number or copyright year.

catalog pieces—PRECIOUS MOMENTS pieces offered exclusively through retailers participating in different catalog programs. Catalog "early release" pieces typically become available through all retailers the following year, often with small design modifications.

closed—a piece whose production is limited by either time or quantity which is no longer available from the manufacturer.

Century Circle—a select group of retailers (40 nationwide) who receive early shipments of new pieces and exclusive products. This is the highest PRECIOUS MOMENTS dealer level.

Chapel Exclusives—special pieces only available from the The PRECIOUS MOMENTS Chapel Complex in Carthage, Missouri or through their catalog.

collectibles—anything and everything that is "able to be collected," whether it's figurines, dolls . . . or even *autographs* can be considered a "collectible," but it is generally recognized that a true collectible should be something that increases in value over time.

damaged box (DB)—a secondary market term used when a collectible's original box is in poor condition, often times diminishing the value of the item.

Distinguished Service Retailers (DSR)—the second highest dealer level designation, these retailers also receive early shipments of new pieces and exclusive products.

exchange—a secondary market service which lists pieces that collectors wish to buy, sell or trade. The exchange works as a middleman and usually requires a commission.

International Collectible Exposition (I.C.E.)—national collectible show held in Rosemont, Illinois each June or July, and in April alternating between Long Beach, California (1999) and Edison, New Jersey (2000).

limited edition (LE)—a piece scheduled for a predetermined production quantity or time. Some pieces have been limited to a specific number (ex. "Jesus Loves Me" is limited to 1,500 pieces) or limited by year of production (ex. "Sharing Our Winter Wonderland" is limited to 1999 production).

markings—any of the various identifying features found on a collectible. It can be information found on bottomstamps or backstamps, an artist's signature or production mark.

Members Only piece—special pieces only available for purchase by members of The Enesco PRECIOUS MOMENTS *Collectors' Club* or The PRECIOUS MOMENTS *Fun Club* By Enesco.

mint in box (MIB)—a secondary market term used when a collectible's original box is in "good as new" condition, which usually adds to the value of the item.

no box (NB)—a secondary market term used when a collectible's original box is missing. For most collectibles, having the original box is a factor in the value.

no mark (NM)—since 1981, PRECIOUS MOMENTS pieces have had a production mark incised on the back or bottom of the piece, which indicates the year it was produced. Pieces produced *prior to 1981* are classified as having "no mark" (see also *unmarked*).

open—a PRECIOUS MOMENTS piece which is currently in production and available in retail stores.

porcelain bisque—the hard and nonabsorbent material used to make PRECIOUS MOMENTS figurines; ceramic made primarily with kaolin (a pure form of clay) that is fired at temperatures approaching 2300° F.

primary market—the conventional collectibles purchasing process in which collectors buy directly from dealers for retail price.

production mark—also called a "year mark." Each PRECIOUS MOMENTS piece has a production mark incised on the bottom or back which indicates the year the piece was produced. These marks have been used since 1981 and change every year (see page 38).

retired—a piece which is taken out of production, never to be made again, usually followed by a scarcity of the piece and a rise in value on the secondary market.

secondary market—the source for buying, selling and trading collectibles according to basic supply-and-demand principles ("pay what the market will bear"). Popular pieces which have retired or pieces with low edition numbers can appreciate in value far above the original issue price.

special event piece—a piece made available only at Enesco sponsored PRECIOUS MOMENTS events.

suspended—a piece that has been removed from production by Enesco but may return in the future, possibly with slight design modifications.

Symbol Of Membership piece—special pieces offered as a gift to collectors joining or renewing their membership to The Enesco PRECIOUS MOMENTS *Collectors' Club* or The PRECIOUS MOMENTS *Fun Club* By Enesco.

unmarked (UM)—term for PRECIOUS MOMENTS pieces produced *after 1981,* which are either missing the annual production mark or were produced intentionally without the mark (see also *no mark*).

variations—pieces that have color, design or printed text changes from the "original" piece. Some of these changes are minor, while some are important enough to affect the value of a piece on the secondary market.

– Key –

All PRECIOUS MOMENTS pieces are listed below in alphabetical order. Following each piece in parentheses is an abbreviation for the type of item (see key) and the stock number. The first number in the page and picture column refers to the piece's location within the Value Guide section and the second to the box in which it is pictured on that page.

ABBREVIATION KEY

A	Accessories
B	Bells
CB	Covered Boxes
CC	Candle Climbers
DI	Displays
DM . . .	Die-Cast Metal
DO	Dolls
E	Eggs
F	Figurines
FR	Frames
HB	Hinged Boxes
J	Jack-In-The-Boxes
LM	LITTLE MOMENTS
ME	Medallions
MU	Musicals
N	Night Lights
O	Ornaments
P	Plates
TH	Thimbles
TR	Tree Toppers
TA	TENDER TAILS Attachables
TO	TENDER TAILS Ornaments
TT	TENDER TAILS

Alphabetical Index

ALPHABETICAL INDEX

ALPHABETICAL INDEX

ALPHABETICAL INDEX

ALPHABETICAL INDEX

ALPHABETICAL INDEX

ALPHABETICAL INDEX

	Page #	Pict #
You Are Always There For Me (F, 163600)	132	9
You Are Always There For Me (F, 163619)	132	10
You Are Always There For Me (F, 163627)	133	1
You Are Always There For Me (F, 163635)	133	2
You Are My Amour (LM, 456918)	142	5
You Are My Favorite Star (F, 527378)	133	3
You Are My Gift Come True (O, 520276)	169	7
You Are My Happiness (F, 526185)	133	4
You Are My Main Event (F, 115231)	133	5
You Are My Mane Inspiration (F, B0014)	225	7
You Are My Mane Inspiration (F, B0114)	225	8
You Are My Number One (F, 520829)	133	6
You Are My Once In A Lifetime (F, 531030)	133	7
You Are Such A Purr-fect Friend (F, 526010)	47	2
You Are Such A Purr-fect Friend (F, 524395)	133	8
You Are The End Of My Rainbow (F, C0014)	212	9
You Are The End Of My Rainbow (F, C0114)	212	10
You Are The End Of My Rainbow (O, PM041)	219	5
You Are The Rose Of His Creation (F, 531243)	47	4
You Are The Type I Love (F, 523542)	133	9
You Brighten My Field Of Dreams (F, 587850)	138	4
You Can Always Bring A Friend (F, 527122)	134	1
You Can Always Count On Me (F, 526827)	46	3
You Can Always Count On Me (F, 487953)	134	2
You Can Always Count On Me (O, 152579)	151	7
You Can Always Fudge A Little During The Season (F, 455792)	134	3
You Can Fly (F, 12335)	134	4
You Can't Beat The Red, White And Blue (LM, 456411)	142	6
You Can't Run Away From God (F, E0525)	134	5
You Can't Take It With You (F, 488321)	134	6
You Color Our World With Loving, Caring And Sharing (F, 644463)	134	7
You Count (F, 488372)	134	8
You Deserve A Halo - Thank You (F, 531693)	134	9
You Deserve An Ovation (F, 520578)	134	10
You Fill The Pages Of My Life (F, PMB034)	217	1
You Fill The Pages Of My Life (F, 530980)	217	1
You Have Mastered The Art Of Caring (F, 456276)	135	1
You Have Such A Special Way Of Caring Each And Every Day (LM, 320706)	143	9
You Have Touched So Many Hearts (F, 272485)	42	1
You Have Touched So Many Hearts (F, 523283)	46	10
You Have Touched So Many Hearts (F, E2821)	135	2
You Have Touched So Many Hearts (F, 261084)	135	3
You Have Touched So Many Hearts (F, 527661)	135	4
You Have Touched So Many Hearts (O, 112356)	169	8
You Have Touched So Many Hearts (DO, 427527)	176	1
You Have Touched So Many Hearts (J, 422282)	180	4
You Have Touched So Many Hearts (MU, 112577)	184	6
You Just Can't Replace A Good Friendship (F, 488054)	135	5
You Just Cannot Chuck A Good Friendship (F, PM882)	215	7
You Make My Spirit Soar (LM, 139564)	143	10
You Make The World A Sweeter Place (LM, 139521)	144	1
You Make Such A Lovely Pair (F, 531588)	135	6
You Oughta Be In Pictures (F, 490327)	135	7
You Set My Heart Ablaze (LM, 320625)	144	2
You Suit Me To A Tee (F, 526193)	135	8
You Will Always Be A Treasure To Me (F, PM971)	217	7
You Will Always Be A Winner To Me (LM, 272612)	144	3
You Will Always Be A Winner To Me (LM, 283460)	144	4
You Will Always Be My Choice (F, PM891)	215	8
You Will Always Be Our Hero (F, 136271)	135	9
You're A Life Saver To Me (F, 204854)	135	10
You're "A" Number One In My Book, Teacher (O, 150142)	169	9
You're A Pel-I-Can Count On (F, BC942)	224	9
You're As Pretty As A Christmas Tree (F, 530425)	40	4
You're As Pretty As A Christmas Tree (O, 530395)	147	8
You're As Pretty As A Christmas Tree (O, 530387)	148	7
You're As Pretty As A Christmas Tree (B, 604216)	171	7
You're As Pretty As A Christmas Tree (P, 530409)	185	1
You're As Pretty As A Picture (F, C0016)	213	3
You're As Pretty As A Picture (F, C0116)	213	4
You're First In My Heart (F, BC962)	225	3
You're Forever In My Heart (LM, 139548)	144	5
You're Just As Sweet As Pie (F, 307017)	138	5
You're Just Perfect In My Book (LM, 320560)	144	6
You're Just Too Sweet To Be Scary (F, 183849)	136	1
You're My Honey Bee (F, 487929)	136	2
You're My Number One Friend (F, 530026)	45	10
You're My Number One Friend (O, 250112)	151	4
You're No. 1 (LM, 491640)	145	3
You're No. 1 (LM, 491624)	145	2
You're One In A Million To Me (F, PM951)	217	2
You're The Berry Best (LM, 139513)	144	7
You're The Sweetest Cookie In The Batch (F, C0015)	213	1
You're The Sweetest Cookie In The Batch (F, C0115)	213	2
You're Worth Your Weight In Gold (F, E9282B)	136	3
Your Love Is So Uplifting (F, 520675)	136	4
Your Precious Spirit Comes Shining Through (F, 212563)	136	5

279

– Key –

All PRECIOUS MOMENTS pieces are listed below in numerical order by stock number. The first number refers to the piece's location within the Value Guide section and the second to the box in which it is pictured on that page.

Page #	Pict #	Page #	Pict #	Page #	Pict #	Page #	Pict #
E2846 78	7	E5215 187	1	E7155 123	10	E9267E 73	4
E2847 187	4	E5216 188	10	E7156 94	6	E9267F 73	5
E2848 188	6	E5217 188	3	E7156R 94	7	E9268 111	5
E2850 175	3	E5376 107	9	E7157 124	4	E9273 100	4
E2851 174	10	E5377 104	7	E7158 103	9	E9274 123	2
E2852A ... 74	5	E5378 56	4	E7159 101	8	E9275 188	8
E2852B ... 74	8	E5379 55	5	E7160 114	3	E9276 188	9
E2852C ... 74	4	E5380 56	8	E7161 55	1	E9278 99	3
E2852D ... 74	6	E5381 54	10	E7161 203	6	E9279 99	4
E2852E ... 74	3	E5382 54	2	E7162 104	9	E9280 173	3
E2852F ... 74	7	E5383 39	1	E7163 87	5	E9281 173	4
E2853 86	2	E5384 50	7	E7164 76	8	E9282A ... 127	2
E2854 86	1	E5385 51	4	E7165 100	6	E9282B ... 136	3
E2855 86	3	E5386 51	5	E7166 177	1	E9282C 82	4
E2856 86	4	E5387 146	4	E7167 173	5	E9283 173	1
E2857 86	5	E5388 161	6	E7168 177	7	E9285 97	5
E2859 86	6	E5389 166	7	E7169 177	8	E9287 113	9
E2860 86	7	E5390 163	3	E7170 176	9	E9287R 72	5
E3104 77	9	E5391 162	3	E7171 176	10	E9288 118	1
E3105 92	7	E5392 157	3	E7172 189	2	E9289 127	6
E3106 110	3	E5393 170	4	E7173 188	4		
E3107 77	8	E5394 184	4	E7174 187	2	L2258 208	1
E3108 90	3	E5395 186	2	E7175 172	2		
E3109 116	5	E5396 187	7	E7176 172	3	PM030 ... 180	7
E3110B ... 106	1	E5397 175	7	E7177 177	2	PM037 ... 220	10
E3110G ... 106	2	E5619 53	2	E7178 177	3	PM038 ... 221	1
E3111 75	9	E5620 172	8	E7179 172	4	PM040 ... 219	4
E3112 88	3	E5621 53	7	E7180 182	3	PM041 ... 219	5
E3113 125	6	E5622 170	1	E7181 172	5	PM190 ... 218	8
E3114 101	1	E5623 171	9	E7182 182	8	PM290 ... 219	1
E3115 79	4	E5624 57	9	E7183 172	7	PM390 ... 218	5
E3116 124	2	E5627 157	6	E7184 183	5	PM490 ... 218	10
E3117 128	7	E5628 157	7	E7185 182	7	PM590 ... 218	6
E3118 81	10	E5629 146	1	E7186 181	10	PM690 ... 218	9
E3119 98	2	E5630 169	1	E7241 177	6	PM790 ... 218	7
E3120 127	5	E5631 153	6	E7242 177	9	PM811 ... 214	1
E4720 101	2	E5632 154	1	E7267B ... 174	5	PM821 ... 214	2
E4721 101	3	E5633 157	10	E7267G ... 175	6	PM822 ... 214	3
E4722 104	1	E5634 169	4	E7350 79	4	PM831 ... 214	4
E4723 113	6	E5635 58	4	E9251 104	8	PM841 ... 214	5
E4724 116	7	E5636 57	4	E9252 83	8	PM842 ... 214	6
E4725 113	8	E5637 54	9	E9253 82	2	PM851 ... 214	7
E4726 183	3	E5638 53	5	E9254 115	2	PM852 ... 214	8
E5200 76	1	E5639 55	6	E9255 77	6	PM861 ... 214	10
E5201 105	4	E5640 55	7	E9256 188	5	PM862 ... 215	1
E5202 123	7	E5641 57	10	E9257 187	3	PM864 ... 220	6
E5203 100	5	E5642 183	8	E9258 129	2	PM871 ... 215	2
E5204 181	4	E5644 57	1	E9259 129	7	PM872 ... 215	3
E5205 182	9	E5645 183	6	E9260 88	2	PM873 ... 215	4
E5206 182	10	E5646 185	9	E9261 117	7	PM874 ... 215	5
E5207 184	8	E6118 172	9	E9262 117	8	PM881 ... 215	6
E5208 171	10	E6120 169	3	E9263 94	4	PM882 ... 215	7
E5209 172	1	E6214B ... 175	2	E9265 115	8	PM890 ... 219	2
E5210 172	6	E6214G ... 174	6	E9266 173	2	PM891 ... 215	8
E5211 171	8	E6613 87	8	E9267A 73	6	PM892 ... 215	9
E5212 126	2	E6901 80	6	E9267B 73	2	PM901 ... 215	10
E5213 87	1	E7153 87	2	E9267C 73	1	PM902 ... 216	1
E5214 115	4	E7154 87	3	E9267D 73	3	PM904 ... 220	9

No.	Page #	Pict #	No.	Page #	Pict #	No.	Page #	Pict #	No.	Page #	Pict #
463256	200	5	488259	93	9	520683	118	4	521817	88	6
463256	200	8	488283	139	2	520691	182	4	521825	45	2
463256	201	3	488291	139	1	520705	75	4	521833	45	1
463256	201	5	488305	139	3	520721	100	1	521841	104	4
463256	201	10	488321	134	6	520748	84	5	521868	89	4
463256	202	7	488356	72	3	520756	98	10	521884	114	5
463264	200	7	488364	116	4	520764	116	2	521892	81	9
463264	201	2	488372	134	8	520772	106	8	521906	94	2
463264	202	2	488380	179	5	520780	132	1	521914	114	4
463264	202	4	488399	179	6	520799	121	3	521922	117	2
463299	196	5	488402	179	8	520802	110	4	521949	131	1
464295	194	4	488410	179	7	520810	129	5	521957	93	3
464414	197	8	488429	179	3	520829	133	6	521965	126	3
464422	194	7	488437	179	4	520837	102	8	521973	79	5
469327	185	5				520845	131	4	521981	107	1
			490245	46	7	520853	94	9	522015	127	4
470279	150	3	490327	135	7	520861	119	1	522023	108	6
471909	194	9	490342	143	5	520934	92	9	522031	123	8
471917	197	7	491586	144	9	521000	124	5	522058	111	8
473952	195	7	491594	145	1	521043	43	8	522082	108	8
473960	193	1	491608	144	8	521078	150	4	522090	124	6
473979	192	8	491616	144	10	521086	150	6	522104	97	10
475041	173	6	491624	145	2	521094	150	5	522112	81	3
475068	47	9	491640	145	3	521108	150	7	522120	131	6
475076	151	10	492140	132	6	521116	150	8	522201	78	5
475084	158	5	495891	219	7	521124	150	9	522244	181	2
475092	208	6				521175	42	7	522252	92	4
475106	209	6	504394	200	2	521183	124	1	522260	43	7
475882	197	4				521191	103	2	522279	116	6
475890	195	2	516597	196	8	521205	94	1	522287	124	9
475912	196	1				521213	84	6	522317	109	1
475939	197	1	520233	165	4	521221	82	3	522325	46	5
476080	196	4	520241	154	9	521272	122	9	522333	122	8
476099	193	2	520268	51	6	521280	91	2	522376	45	6
476102	192	2	520276	169	7	521299	94	5	522546	39	6
477869	198	6	520284	186	5	521302	163	1	522554	189	7
478180	199	2	520292	149	3	521302R	163	2	522821	171	2
478458	200	6	520322	46	9	521310	132	5	522848	147	3
478458	201	4	520349	220	7	521329	91	6	522856	91	3
478458	202	1	520357	56	3	521388	93	1	522864	99	10
478458	202	9	520403	149	10	521396	82	8	522872	112	6
			520411	149	7	521418	96	8	522910	162	10
480355	195	8	520438	149	6	521434	126	5	522929	162	7
482234	194	8	520454	159	8	521450	102	1	522937	159	1
482242	105	1	520462	149	4	521477	123	3	522945	165	7
482889	197	9	520470	168	4	521485	124	7	522953	160	5
486884	198	4	520489	149	8	521493	121	10	522961	220	8
487902	111	2	520497	149	5	521507	182	2	522988	50	8
487910	76	3	520535	103	6	521515	128	9	522996	51	9
487929	136	2	520543	97	7	521558	165	5	523003	186	6
487945	98	5	520551	103	5	521566	159	2	523011	208	4
487953	134	2	520578	134	10	521574	158	1	523038	206	6
487988	130	3	520624	110	5	521590	158	2	523062	166	9
488003	45	3	520632	83	9	521671	42	8	523097	56	2
488046	109	6	520640	97	4	521698	125	7	523178	99	6
488054	135	5	520659	43	9	521701	120	3	523194	154	10
488178	80	9	520667	77	7	521728	110	7	523208	155	1
488240	128	3	520675	136	4	521779	122	7	523224	159	9

Acnkowledgements

CheckerBee Publishing would like to extend a special thanks to David and Susan Adams, Mary Bowen, Annie Jo Cuervo, Helen Davis, Jia Miller, Ovada Ousley, Kristi Shult, Peggy Smith, Sheryl Williams and Don Yoshida. Many thanks to the great people at Enesco Corporation, The PRECIOUS MOMENTS Chapel and PRECIOUS MOMENTS Inc.